OBLIGED TO ASK FOR RELIEF

The Journal
of
Cheshire County
New Hampshire

Pauper Records
from
1885-1900

Milli S. Knudsen

HERITAGE BOOKS
2009

HERITAGE BOOKS
AN IMPRINT OF HERITAGE BOOKS, INC.

Books, CDs, and more—Worldwide

For our listing of thousands of titles see our website
at
www.HeritageBooks.com

Published 2009 by
HERITAGE BOOKS, INC.
Publishing Division
100 Railroad Ave. #104
Westminster, Maryland 21157

Copyright © 2009 Milli S. Knudsen

Other books by the author:

Hard Time in Concord, New Hampshire: The Crimes, the Victims, and the Lives of the State Prison Inmates, 1812-1883 (Book & CD)

Manchester in the Mirror: Abstracts from The Mirror & Farmer Newspaper, *Manchester, New Hampshire, 1865-1866*

The Knowledge of Mankind: The Vermont Journal *and the* Universal Advertiser, *1783-1786*

'Til Divorce Do Us Part: Marriages and Divorces from Cheshire County, New Hampshire from 1776-1899

What's News in Coos County? Volume 2

All rights reserved. No part of this book may be reproduced or transmitted in any form or by any means, electronic or mechanical, including photocopying, recording or by any information storage and retrieval system without written permission from the author, except for the inclusion of brief quotations in a review.

International Standard Book Numbers
Paperbound: 978-0-7884-5001-3
Clothbound: 978-0-7884-8190-1

Introduction to
Obliged to Ask for Relief

Obliged to Ask for Relief is basically a transcription of a clerk's notebook from Keene, NH, which kept a record of the interviews held for those who came seeking assistance from Cheshire County between 1885 and 1900. While a group of us were transferring court records from the county to our state archives, another volunteer handed me a volume of records she had stumbled across called *Cheshire County Paupers*. Between the sometimes illegible handwriting and the sketchy note-taking of this journal, it was at first hard to figure out exactly what I was holding. Over time as I transcribed the entire book, it began to unfold as an account book of the people who came in to plead their cases of poverty to the county clerks. Patterns of answers suggested what questions must have been asked each person in an interview format. As the journal progressed, it was obvious that additional questions were being added, such as whether the applicant had a bank account, or how long they had lived in a town, whether they owned any real estate, and if they had received aid in any other towns. I assumed these additional questions must have followed some kind of rule change or the enactment of legislation which required the new information. There were changes in law concerning paupers throughout the 15 years covered by this journal; however, any legislative committee notes, which might have explained the intent behind the amendments, no longer exist.

The Poor are Always with Us

Josiah Benton did a great job explaining the system of removing unwanted visitors from the towns of New Hampshire in his book *Warning Out in New England* (1911, W. B. Clarke Company). According to Benton's research, by 1718 it had been decided that strangers in town had to prove their industry and ability to provide for their own needs within a year of residence or else the selectmen could "warn out" the individual or family and thus dissolve their responsibility for providing support. Unwed mothers needed to swear a bastard child on the offending father of the child prior to birth if they hoped to receive any financial help from the town. The father, plus other male members of his family, often had to guarantee payment to the pregnant woman or face imprisonment.

On the other hand, from its beginning as a state, New Hampshire provided for the poor and unfortunate who resided in NH towns. In 1787 steps were taken in the legislature to accept the judgment of three justices of the peace in matters concerning the poor. This suggests that before this time petitions were reviewed by the entire Assembly. That same year an act was passed for the maintenance of paupers by the town they were born in. Major towns and cities had an official Overseer of the Poor who either resided at the poor farm or who arranged for the lodging and care of the town paupers. In 1787 Benjamin Dearborn of Portsmouth petitioned the General Assembly for twelve shillings and four pence for the care of a stranger named George Drake, and received the money from the state treasury.

By 1791, the state legislature outlined the duties and the powers granted to the overseers of the poor, and had assigned punishment to "idle and disorderly persons." State law read in 1797 that anyone "having no visible means of support" could be physically removed from town after 14 days of being warned out. If they returned voluntarily and stayed for the span of seven days they could be publicly whipped "not exceeding ten stripes."

With a state population declining in the early 1800's, it was deemed necessary to deal with town paupers who lived in towns that no longer existed, or as it was called, an "unorganized" town. Where there was no longer a slate of town officers who were legally qualified to conduct business, any paupers who had relied on that town's support were to be supported by the county. In 1820, the General Court demanded an accounting of all expenses dating from 1799 that had been made for the support of the poor from each town, including the price of any lawsuits that arose from such support.

Caring for some town paupers could be a trying and even dangerous occupation. Mrs. Hannah Leighton and her husband in New Durham cared for a number of the town poor. On July 8th, 1841, she fed her charges as usual, including 76-year-old Chandler Peavy, who came to the table intoxicated. He demanded to be fed something better, but Hannah, probably used to his abusive tone, went about her business and paid him no mind. Chandler left, returning with an axe, which he used to cleave through Hannah's shoulder bone. He died in prison at the age of 81. Hannah survived.

It is evident that over time, some towns felt they were becoming victims of double-dippers or opportunistic families who were attempting to use the system for their own greedy purposes. The selectmen of Whitefield took to advertising in the local paper in 1859 when they suspected local paupers of taking advantage of their good faith efforts to help at least one family:

> "We hereby forbid all persons trusting or harboring John Wear or his family, Town Paupers, as we have made suitable provisions for their support. (signed by] Joseph Colby, Charles Libby and Samuel L. Bray." [from the *Coos Republican* of Lancaster, NH, March 24, 1859]

County and city poor farms had been established throughout the state by the mid-1800's. An account written in 1865 of a visit to Mr. Simpson's "Poor-Farm and House of Correction" in Manchester declared

> "...how well the farm has yielded this year under his supervision. To outward appearance it is all that could be desired; an inward inspection strengthens that opinion, except one particular---the manner in which the criminals and paupers are obliged to associate on account of the insufficiency of accommodations...The criminals and paupers now confined there number twenty-two...The stock upon the farm is admirable, a pair of six-years-old

oxen being particularly noticeable. They weigh upwards of thirty-seven hundred pounds, and were exhibited at the N. E. Fair at Concord, where they took the first prize." [from *The Mirror and Farmer* of Manchester, NH, October 7, 1865]

The Hillsborough County Farm in Goffstown also made the papers that year because of a destructive fire that destroyed all the buildings except the barn and granary in the early morning hours. All 120 residents were saved from a fiery death by Superintendent Bumpus, who did so "without creating a panic." The steamer Fire King arrived by rail from Manchester to douse the last of the flames, and the inhabitants were taken by railroad to the corporate hospital near the jail which became their temporary abode.

In 1874, a gang of delinquent girls from Wilton tried to burn down the Hillsborough County House of Corrections while they were incarcerated there. Besides the jail, the building also housed elderly and infirm paupers of the county, so what was clearly seen as an arson case turned to attempted murder.

Problems arose as a result of Vermont paupers moving into the state and being charged to NH towns prior to 1883, when the legislature passed a bill fining anyone who aided and abetted poor and indigent citizens from Vermont coming here to live. Vermont wasn't the only place from where out-of-towners appeared:

> "Sunday last, a woman called at the house of a Frenchman in the northern part of the city and got lodging for herself and four children for the night, and the next day she ran away, supposing they would be supported by the county, and thus leave herself to go where she pleased...but wits set to work to discover the mother, the search last evening proving successful, and now she goes to keep company with her children." [from *The Mirror and Farmer*, Manchester, NH, October 28, 1865]

In this same year it was decided that a NH town was not liable to support anyone who had not achieved a "settlement" from that town since January 1870.

By amendment to Chapter 83, the pauper law, the state began to require a standard affidavit in 1883, which covered the person's age, place of birth, the times and places of residence, plus times and places where support had been previously received. It appears that the journal I had been handed called *Cheshire County Paupers* had been instituted to record these affidavits.

A further chapter written into NH law in 1895 provided support for people who became paupers while residing at one of the many institutions of the state, including orphan's homes, hospitals, homes for the aged and other charitable organizations. Their support was derived from the county they resided in prior to the stay at the institution.

Open Wide Your Hand to Your Brother

As is also the case today, some people in the 19th century questioned the need for public support. But illness and death of family members often led to poverty for those left behind. Women abandoned by their husbands account for many appeals for assistance, though elderly applicants and those who had immigrated and hadn't found work far outnumber them.

The stories of aging Civil War veterans, accidents in the factories and on the railroad, plus the ravages of disease cried out for the medical discoveries and health care improvements that rapidly modernized the medical world in the years 1883-1905. The pension systems which operated for soldiers after the Revolutionary War and Civil War eventually were seen to benefit all workers. It was this understanding of the broader benefit of public assistance which led to Social Security being established in the 1930's.

Notes on the Process of Transcription

At first I was determined to transcribe the journal exactly as written with very little editing, but it became apparent with each successive clerk who wrote the affidavits that the individual styles of wording and spelling were going to confuse the reader and make it necessary to use repeated ellipses, parentheses, and editorial explanations.

Occasionally the clerks would refer to earlier pages in their notes, so I needed to preserve the page numbers enabling readers to look back and find the right entries. Also, it was impossible to type the journal in a font that would preserve the original page numbers, so at the beginning of each page from the original journal I have that page number in a square bracket, followed by the entry number assigned by the clerk. See example below.

I adopted a pattern found in most of the entries that listed the applicant's name, present residence, age, place of birth, places lived, and sometimes the circumstances that led to the need to ask for help. The last notation in most entries was the date of the application and when the case was adjudged, which I placed in square brackets [ ]. Occasionally I abbreviated place names to save space or cut down on unnecessary wordiness. If the clerk added a note after the initial interview, I kept those remarks inside curly parentheses { }. For example

> [7] 19. Cyrina M. Doolittle, Hinsdale, American, born 7 Apr 1845 in Hinsdale. My father Titus Doolittle died 16 Feb 1871. He left a small estate. Have 3 brothers and 3 sisters. I rec'd as my share from my father's estate $85.00. Am an invalid have not worked any since I was eight years old. Have no relatives able to aid me. Have been assisted by the town of Hinsdale since 10 Nov 1874. Becomes a county charge under the law of 11 Sep 1883. {13 Nov '86: Ordered to the Almshouse on or before 21 Nov. Application to house order rescinded. Miss D has always resided in H and has 2 brothers there. All the rest of the family are dead.} [Affidavit 23 Apr 1885; adjudged 5 Jun 1885]

This was on page 7 of the original journal. Entry #19 is Cyrina Doolittle's story from Hinsdale, the interview completed in

April of 1885. A note was added in 1886 about her transfer to the County Almshouse.

After the last page of the text, there are 3 indices. The first is a subject index for frequently mentioned topics. The second is a place name index for all towns and cities mentioned, except Keene, NH, which was mentioned on nearly every page so I deemed it unnecessary to list it in the index. The last index is an all name index. There are two listings found for women if both a maiden and married name is recorded. A woman's maiden name is enclosed in parentheses (Armstrong) and a former married name is inside square brackets [Bates].

Occasionally, the handwriting was so poor it was impossible to figure out the spelling of a last name, so I typed that name in square brackets. For example, see Mary [Boestr] on page 218. In a few circumstances, no first name is given, so the individual was listed by surname only. See Burchstead on page 165. Some surnames were spelled many different ways, and I have cross-referenced them, such as the many spellings of Champaigne. If you are looking for a particular surname, be sure to check all possible spellings before deciding that your target name is not included. In rare cases where only a first name is recorded, it has been alphabetized by first name. See "Pattie" on page 109.

I want to thank Verne Greene again for her patient assistance with proofreading, fact-checking and continuing to ask "How's that book coming?" Also, my thanks go to BJ Shoja of the NH Archives for proofreading this introduction. Of course, I couldn't do any of these projects of mine without the loving support of my husband Paul. I admire how his eyes no longer glaze over when I babble endlessly about my latest find in archival rubble. How do you do that? Most certainly, I would have dedicated this book to my grandson Liam Asher Knudsen, except who wants to have a book about poverty dedicated to them? The sound of his chuckling, shrieking, and attempts to swallow the phone in far away California are music to my ears. They remind me of the importance of salvaging the paper records so that his generation and beyond will have those tangible links to the past.

Milli S. Knudsen
Milford, NH
February 28, 2009

Cheshire County Paupers
1885-1900

[1] 1. Joseph Benjamin, in Westmoreland. Application for aid made by H. M. Fletcher in July 1884, notice given by C. M. Scovell, Selectman, to Comr. Abbott, at the time. Benjamin was passing through Westmoreland & stopped at Fletchers over night and in the morning when leaving was thrown from his wagon and quite severely injured. Was attended by Dr. Twitchell. Resides in Vermont, where he returned as soon as he was able to travel. About 50 yrs of age. Had a young lad with him. Paid Dr. T's bill & a small sum on account of board while at Fletchers. [Adjudged Apr T 1885]

2. Alanson Bingham, American, Keene, born in Alstead, 72 years of age. Has several children all of age, names: Mrs. Albert Wright, Osmon A. Bingham, both of Keene and Laura Ann Wiloby of Fitchburg. Has been well off. Claims to be the rightful owner of several of the best patents for sealing & backing chairs with cane, etc. Is an inveterate taker of opium or morphine, which injures his brain & makes him irritable & unpleasant to live with. He is now residing with his daughter Mrs. Wright. {note, dated 29 Oct 1884: Ordered Overseer of the Poor to allow him mean to go to Fitchburg where one of his children lives & with whom he proposes to live & without further relief from the County.} [May 1885]

3. Lenora Birch, Harrisville, American, born in Jericho,[1] VT, 25 yrs of age. Married Nelson Birch 1878 at Westville, NY. Husband deserted her in July last. Applied soon after for aid. Children furnished some clothing & all were sent to Shirley, MA, where she claimed to have friends who would assist her. Names of children: Josephine, aged 4 and Charles, 1 ½ yrs. Mrs. B's parents both dead. Husband always lived in Westville, NY until we were married. {note: Mrs. B & her boy were

---

[1] The original looks like "Pcoroce", but the author is suggesting "Jericho" is the town intended. See also entry #97, page 33.

Cheshire County Paupers
1885-1900

ordered to the Co. Almshouse 14 Apr 1885. Mrs. C. Mudgett of Harrisville takes the little girl and papers were executed binding her to Mrs. B & her husband until her 18th birthday} [Adjudged Oct Term 1884; applied again in Harrisville Mar 1885; admitted 20 Apr 1885]

[2] 4. Mary Bosley, Jaffrey, born in St. George, Canada, French. Husband's name Raymond Bosley. I am 40 yrs old. Have 4 children: Fred, born 3 Dec 1869; Emma, born 15 Dec 1873; Angeline, born 23 Mar 1876; and Exennce, born 4 Oct 1879. We have lived in various places in NY, VT & NH. Am sick and my husband is unable to render me the medical aid I need. Relief suspended after April Term 1885. [Date of affidavit 24 Mar 1885]

5. William H. Bosworth, in Troy, American, resided in MA from 1870 to 1884. Am married & neither my parents or the parents of my wife ever resided in NH. Am 26 yrs of age, one child, an infant. Out of work and destitute. [Date of affidavit 23 Feb 1885]

6. Bradley Briggs, Westmoreland, American, born in VT, 63 yrs old, never owned any real or personal estate except an undivided sixth part of the real estate his mother had at her decease, worth some $200. Is an imbecile, resides with his sister on home place. Never married. Has relatives in the state of NY in good circumstances, but not able & liable to support him. [Date of affidavit 10 Jan 1885]

[3] 7. Donald Cameron, in Keene, French, born in Canada East. 38 yrs old, resided in Keene 9 yrs. Married, wife 40 yrs old, native of Canada. 9 children: Elizabeth, 17 yrs; Minnie, 14 yrs; Alexander, 13 yrs; Carrie, 11 yrs; Donald, 9 yrs; Annie M., 6 yrs; Gertie, 3 yrs; Edith, 2 yrs; and Frank, 3 mos old. Out of

Cheshire County Paupers
1885-1900

work, wants a little assistance until he can get work. [Date of affidavit 13 Dec 1884]

8. Benj. F. Capron, in Troy, American, 37 yrs old. Married Ellen M. Wheeler in 1870, age 34 yrs. Since 1870 have lived in Troy 2 yrs; in Alstead 1 yr; in Troy again 3 yrs; in Jaffrey 2 yrs; in Kccnc 5 yrs; and in Troy since 1883. Two children: Emma J., age 13 yrs and Mary E., age 9 yrs. Am in need of relief by reason that I am out of work. Has been assisted in Keene & Troy. {note: Jan 1886. Sawed his left hand badly at a mill in Fitzwilliam where his family now resides. Applies to overseers of T for relief.} [Date of affidavit 21 Feb 1885; adjudged Apr T 1885]

9. Robert Cope, Winchester, Irish, born in Belfast, Ireland. Have resided in America only about two weeks. Parents both dead, died in Ireland. No work, no means. Therefore ask for relief, age 23 yrs, single. [Affidavit 6 Apr 1885]

[4] 10. George W. Cragin, American, Rindge, born in Mason, NH, 23 Sep 1836, 47 yrs old, last Sep. Am married; wife, Lucy J., aged 48 yrs. Resided in Rindge since 1865. Was in the army. Have one child, Fred O., age 10 yrs last Jul. In Dec, 1875, cut off all my fingers on my right hand in a planing machine. By reason of being out of work I am obliged to ask for some relief. Was aided by the town of Rindge in 1876. [Affidavit 2 Jan 1884; adjudged Apr T 1885]

11. Timothy Donovan, Irish, Keene, born in Ireland. Age 44 yrs, widower, wife died in May 1884. Five children: James, aged 17 yrs, sick with consumption; Dennis, 14 yrs; Margaret 12 yrs; Michael & Timothy twins 8 yrs. Resided in Keene 1871 to 1876; Swanzey, 8 yrs, 1876 to 1884; in Keene since. {Son James since died} [Affidavit 25 Feb 1885.]

Cheshire County Paupers
1885-1900

12. Philana D. Doolittle, American, Westmoreland, born in W in 1823. Lived in W for 30 yrs, except about 7 yrs, previous to 1867. Married Titus Doolittle in 1862 or 3. In 1867 I left him and came to W. My husband afterwards got a divorce, have heard that he is dead. Am a sister[2] of Bradley Briggs (See entry #6) Own an undivided sixth part in my mother's place. Able to earn her own support, but for her brother, an imbecile whom she cares for. [Affidavit 7 Jun 1885]

[5] 13. George Dorr (Laporte), French, Nelson, born in Canada, 39 yrs old. Came to the U. S. 20 yrs ago. Lived in various places, in no place over 5 yrs. Wife and six small children, the oldest 12 yrs. Have been sick, have the need of the relief asked for. Came to VT in Oct last. Has a brother residing in Fitzwilliam. His wife at Co. Almshouse. [Affidavit 16 Mar 1885; admitted Apr T 1885]

14. Joseph Duprei, French in Westmoreland, born in Canada, married. Four children: Eva, aged 10; Dolly, 8 yrs; Robert, 2 yrs; and an infant. Am 44 yrs of age. Resided in Gilsum from 1873 to 1878, and in several other towns in the county a short time in each. Mother's name Laura, 43 years old in Feb 1889. {note, dated 11 Nov 1889: He was 50 years old in Nov 1889. Present children: Eva, 14 yrs; Carrie, 13 yrs in April; Reuben, 6 yrs in Aug; Joseph, 5 in Dec (died Nov 10, 1889); Effie, 2 last Feb; and Marion, 1 yr this Nov 1889. Robert died Nov 16, 1889.} [Affidavit taken 15 Apr 1885; admitted Apr T 1885]

15. Mrs. G. I. Scripture, American, Keene, born in Brattleboro, VT. 30 yrs of age, am a widow. Always lived in Brattleboro. Have been over to see friends in NH and am without means to get home. All the aid I want is means to get home. (Overseer

---

[2] Original said "brother", but according to entry #6, this is the sister Bradley lives with.

of the Poor directed to furnish her a ticket to Brattleboro, see p. 12.) [Affidavit 25 Mar 1885]

[6] 16. George D. Squire, Chesterfield, American, born in Stafford, Tolland Co., CT. Resided in Chesterfield since 1873. Previously in the state of NY. Do not, nor have I possessed any real or personal state to be taxed for in NH. Am a single man, sick and unable to take care of myself being sixty nine years old. [Affidavit 16 Apr 1885; adjudged 5 Jun 1885]

17. Clarrisa Glidden, Winchester, American, born in Alton, NH, 71 yrs old 27 Apr '84. Resided in New Durham, NH from 1870 to 1878, then came to Winchester & have lived here since. My husband died in the Almshouse in Laconia in March 1877. Has had no property of any kind since 1870. Has lived with Maria B. Glidden and her husband for 14 yrs. Draws pension of $96 per year and has since 1870. Directed F. H. Eames, Overseer of the Poor not to render any aid at the expense of the county. [Affidavit 22 Apr 1885; adjudged 1 Jul 1885]

18. Louis Gongan, Keene, in French, born in Canada, 38 yrs of age, married. Wife Rose, 32 yrs of age. 3 children: Luke E., 4 yrs; Joseph, 3 yrs; and Archer, 10 mos. Always lived in Canada until we came to Keene, four months ago. My parents & my wife's parents never lived in NH. Are very destitute. [Affidavit 22 Apr 1885; adjudged 20 May 1885]

18 ½. Franklin G. Nevers,[3] American, 43 yrs of age. Married Mary L. Bates in Jun 1868. Wife died in 1879. Two children: Chas. Albert, 18 yrs, and Lizzie Ellen, 15 yrs. She was married Aug't last to Geo. L. Nash, who has abandoned her. Mrs. B claims to be with child by one Whitcomb of Troy, NH. Is

---

[3] Original handwriting appears to say "Nevens", but according to the *History of Gilsum* his name was "Nevers."

Cheshire County Paupers
1885-1900

residing with Geo. Davis of Gilsum. [Gilsum, 6 Nov 1885. Application rejected; application renewed 3 Mar 1887 and accepted]

[7] 19. Cyrina M. Doolittle, Hinsdale, American, born 7 Apr 1845 in Hinsdale. My father Titus Doolittle died 16 Feb 1871. He left a small estate. Have 3 brothers and 3 sisters. I rec'd as my share from my father's estate $85.00 Am an invalid have not worked any since I was eight years old. Have no relatives able to aid me. Have been assisted by the town of Hinsdale since 10 Nov 1874. Becomes a county charge under the law of 11 Sep 1883. {13 Nov '86: Ordered to the Almshouse on or before 21 Nov. Application to house order rescinded. Miss D has always resided in H and has 2 brothers there. All the rest of the family are dead.} [Affidavit 23 Apr 1885; adjudged 5 Jun 1885]

20. Cora A. Grout, Marlborough, American, age 18 yrs. My father Milan Grout was born in Acworth, NH, in 1833; lived there until 1854 when he was married to Emily Putnam of Springfield, VT, where he lived 'til 1856; moved to Dabuke (*sic*) Iowa & lived until 1867; resided in Keene 'til 1872; back to Springfield. Father died in Springfield, VT 10 Jul 1879. Since father's death we have lived in Keene, Harrisville & Marlborough. Have one brother John, about 14 yrs old. Mother being very sick we are obliged to call for relief. Mrs. E. Grout, mother of the above applicant died in May. Report says that Cora & John, her children, treated their mother very unkindly, giving her very little care during her sickness. [Affidavit 2 May 1885; adjudged 5 Jun 1885]

21. Frank Duplex, Rindge, French, born in Vergennes, VT, 33 yrs old. Wife Mary, 28 yrs of age. One child Emma 4 yrs old. My wife's parents never lived in NH. We have always been poor, but never have been obliged to call for aid before. My

Cheshire County Paupers
1885-1900

child is sick with typhoid fever, and hence I am obliged to ask for relief. [Affidavit 2 May 1885; adjudged 7 May 1885]

[8] 22. John Burnell, Rindge, French, born in Burlington, VT, age 28. Married; wife age 20 yrs; name Angeline. Two children, names: John Henry, age 2 yrs, last January; an infant (not named), 4 months old. My parents and my wife's parents never lived in any town in this state over two years in succession. Are very destitute. [Affidavit 16 May 1885; adjudged 20 May 1885]

23. Frank Hawley, Keene, American, born in Suncook, NH, age 36. Married, wife's name, ____ age ___ . Am destitute and out of work. [Affidavit 16 May 1885; adjudged 20 May 1885]

23 1/3. Frank Warren, Keene, American, born in Ashby, MA, 40 yrs old. Married. Resided in Stoddard three years, in Keene five years. [Affidavit 28 Feb 1885; adjudged Apr T 1885]

24. Frank Urbane, Troy, French, born in Canada, 35 yrs old. Never lived in NH but one year & three months. Married Maria Long of Winchendon, MA in 1881. Her age 26 yrs. Her parents never resided in NH. One child 3 yrs old. Destitute and in need of relief. [No date of affidavit or adjudgment given]

[9] 25. Clarissa A. Treax, Keene, American, born in Montpelier, VT. Age 68 yrs. Widow. Husband died in 1872. Has resided in several of the western states, went to Sullivan, NH in 1878, resided there & in Gilsum nearly 3 yrs. Came to Keene to live in 1884, lives with her daughter, who is poor and unable to take care of her mother, who is sick and at times delirious. Removed to Co. Almshouse, 20 Jan 1885. Died 3 Feb '85 of consumption. [Affidavit 14 Jan 1885; adjudged Apr T 1885. Dead]

Cheshire County Paupers
1885-1900

26. George Shedd, American, Stoddard, born in Stoddard. Age 63 yrs, never was married. Has no house. For 5 yrs last past has wandered about town, working for his board and begging. Has no relatives able to aid him. [Affidavit 24 Feb 1885; adjudged 7 Mar 1885]

26 ½. John Sullivan, Gilsum, Irish, born in Enfield, MA. 24 yrs old. Out of funds and looking for a job. [Affidavit 14 Jan 1885; not adjudged]

27. Mary A. Spooner, Winchester, American, born in Granville, VT, age 17 years, last March. Father Alonzo A. Spooner now resides in Granville. My mother was divorced from father about 3 yrs ago. She married Zenas Lewis in Oct 1883. She came to live with her mother in February 1883. Her father is about 40 yrs of age and has always lived in G. since he was a small boy. Mary A. is sick with a female disease and is very nervous & unable to do any work & very troublesome to take care of. Her mother is not able to support & give her medical care. [Affidavit 13 Dec 1884; adjudged 7 Mar 1885]

[10] 28. John Stevens, Winchester, Irish, born in Ireland, 48 years old, came to America in 1850. Resided in Randolph from 1850 to 1878; then to So. Brookline where he lived 3 years; lived in Fitchburg, Clinton & Erving, MA for 4 years. Is not married. Out of employment, in search of work. [Affidavit 28 Mar 1885; not adjudged]

28 ½. James O'Brien, Winchester, Irish. Transient in search of work. [Affidavit 24 Mar 1885; not adjudged]

29. Arebella Robinson, Keene, American, born in Montegue, MA, age 55 yrs. Resided in Keene since 1871. Husband left her about twenty years ago. One son & one daughter, both of age and both reside in Keene, but they are unable to support her

Cheshire County Paupers
1885-1900

without assistance. Names: Aaron L. & Louisa B. [Affidavit 10 Oct 1884; adjudged Apr T 1885]

30. Charles Rives,[4] Marlborough, French, born in St. David, Canada, 5 Sep 1837 and lived there until 1853. Then came to Sheldon, VT and remained until Dec 1880; came to M, where he has since lived. My father and mother live in Sheldon, VT. Was married 8 Nov 1860; name, Mary. Have five children, oldest 14 years and the youngest less than 1 year. Mrs. Rives was born in St. David Nov 1843. Have no relatives able to render us any relief. Very needy. [Marlboro, 21 May 1885; admitted Apr T 1885]

[11] 31. Julia A. Orne, Alstead, American, born in Alstead. Age 22 years. Married Frank Orne about six years ago. Have resided in Alstead since our marriage. Age of husband 34 yrs. He had a residence in Marlow at the time of his marriage to Julia A. which he held until the new law went into effect 11 Sep 1883. Were helped in Marlow several years. His parents died previous to 1871. Her parents Kendall Austin reside in Alstead, are poor. Husband confined in jail for six months, tried and sentenced to State Prison for 2 or 3 years. Committed suicide by hanging. Widow since married. She has two children. [Affidavit 22 Jan 1885; adjudged Apr T 1885]

32. Parker Larkins,[5] Swanzey, American, born in Groton, MA, 76 years old. Widower, wife died about 1870. Has lived a wandering life, since the death of his wife. Drinks badly. Mrs. David Wilson, Swanzey is a niece of the said Parker Larkin. Ordered to Co. Almshouse, 20 Jun 1880. Escaped once and

---

[4] Original handwritten record appears to say "Rines," but according to the 1880 census for Sheldon, VT, his name is "Rives."
[5] Original had written "Lakins;" however the index indicates his name to be "Larkins."

Cheshire County Paupers
1885-1900

retaken. Died at Almshouse 8 Feb 1886. [Date of Aff, 19 Jan 1885; adjudged Apr T 1885]

33. Chas. Moultroup, Alstead, American, born in Sutton, VT 20 Sep 1844. Lived in VT until the fall of 1861 when he went into the Army & served until July 1863. Lived in Walpole from 1863 to the fall of 1864. Then re-enlisted in the 18th NH Vols. Came back to Walpole in 1865 & lived there nearly seven years; lived in several places in VT since 1870; 8 years in Whitefield, NH; then came to Alstead, NH where he has since resided. Married, 4 children: Myrtie A., age 13; Harley E., age 11; Addie May, age 4; and Elisha C., age 2. Confined in House of Correction, sentenced for one year, shooting one Smith. Wife & children need relief and it is asked in their behalf. On petition of the citizens of Alstead, he has been released. Pension granted in May 1887. [Alstead, 13 Nov 1884; adjudged Apr T 1885]

[12] Martin Mclister, Hinsdale, Irish, born in Ireland. Came to this country in 1864. Resided in various places in MA. Has not resided in NH over seven weeks. Poor and obliged to call for relief. Has no relatives liable & able to assist him. Martin McCallester is probably the true name. [Hinsdale, 1 Jan 1885; adjudged 2 Jun 1885]

35. Mrs. G. I. Scripture, Keene, American, born in Brattleboro, VT. 30 yrs old. Widow, claims her home to be in Brattleboro, VT. Has been at work in Concord, NH. Started home. Purchasing her ticket at Concord to Keene. Between Concord and Keene lost her money amounting to $17.00 and is without means to get from Keene to B. Was referred to J. A. Wright, Keene, who is acquainted with her. Mr. W states that she is "an honest woman." She is ill and anxious to get home. Overseer Davis of Keene was directed to aid her to her house in

Cheshire County Paupers
1885-1900

Brattleboro at the expense of the county. [Keene, 25 Mar 1885; adjudged Apr T 1885]

36. Mrs. Fanny Emery, Marlborough, American, born in Hebron, NH 1 Oct 1857. Father James Percival died at Milford, NH 16 Nov 1873 to which place he moved about the year 1864. In December 1877 moved to Greenfield, NH with my mother, Josephine Percival. In Jan 1878 removed with her mother to Nelson, NH. In March following they moved to Harrisville; in April moved to New Ipswich, NH; in Nov following returned to Nelson; in Febry 1879 returned to New Ipswich; in Oct went to Nashua, NH; in April following returned to New Ipswich; in June 1880 went to Roxbury, NH; in Aug to Keene; in Dec to Harrisville; then to Langdon; then Harrisville; in July (17) came to Marlborough. Married 9 Jun 1881 to Eugene R. Emery, who was born in Hopkinton, MA in Nov 1857. Has one son Chas W. Richards, born in Milford, 21 Jul 1877. Husband left her in June 1883, since which time he has not contributed to her support nor has she known where he is. She was divorced from her husband Chas. E. Richards in April 1879. Allowed $1.00 per week aid. [Marlborough, 31 Oct 1884; adjudged Apr T 1885]

37. [6]

[13] 38. Frank Gibson, Keene, French, born in Canada, 42 years old, married. Lived in the state of NY from 1 Jan 1870 to Augt 1873; Westmoreland to the spring of 1880; in Chesterfield; and in the fall of 1880 came to Keene where he has resided since. [Keene, 9 Feb 1885; adjudged Apr T 1885]

38 ½. John Hubert, Keene, French, born in Canada, 25 years old, married. Always resided in Canada until 1879. Has lived

---

[6] Entry left blank.

Cheshire County Paupers
1885-1900

in NH about six months. [Keene, 19 Jan 1885; adjudged Apr T 1885]

39. Peter McNamara, Keene, Irish, born in Ireland, 50 years old. Married; wife's name Ann; has eight children: Thomas, 16 yrs; Margaret, 15 yrs; Patrick, 13 yrs; Bridget ,12 yrs; Mary, 8 yrs; Michael, 7 yrs; Ann, 4 yrs; and Hanora, 2 yrs. Always resided in Ireland until 1881. Has lived in Keene since. [Keene, 14 Jan 1885; adjudged Apr T 1885]

[14] 40. Larry Mansfield, Walpole, Irish descent, born in Worcester, about 35 years old. Has lived a roving life. Has for three years last past lived in Rockingham, VT and the House of Corrections at Rutland; about one year in the latter place. Was sentenced for a term of three years. {note, dated 7 Apr 1885: was pardoned by the Governor of the state the 16th Mar 1885.} Since has been at his brother's in North Walpole. "My father," he says "is dead." His mother resides with her son at North Walpole. Has been very intemperate. Is badly afflicted with sores that do not heal. {Died 12 Mar 1886. Body removed to B. Falls for burial.} [Walpole, 31 Mar 1885; adjudged Apr T 1885]

41. Hartley D. Mason, Keene, American, born in Dublin, NH. 37 years of age. Married; wife's name Eliza, age 35 yrs. One child Willie H., 12 years of age. Resided in Marlborough from 1870 to 1875; Peterborough to 1880; Marlborough again to 1882 and since in Keene. Painter by trade. Wife very sick with consumption. Wife has since died, and he is now taking care of himself & child. [Keene, 31 Jan 1885; adjudged Apr T 1885]

42. LuPrelett Wilber, Jaffrey, American, 81 years old, 2 Aug 1884. Married Hannah Heath in 1829. Has resided in Jaffrey 38 years. Has never possessed property to the amount of $250. Never received any relief from any town until now, but he is

Cheshire County Paupers
1885-1900

now sick and unable to work and is obliged to call for some relief. [Jaffrey, 3 Jan 1885; adjudged after Apr T 1885]

[15] 43. Willard Martin, Swanzey, American, born in Richmond. Age 66 years. Parents both dead. Has one sister living in North Richmond, Mrs. Roxana Swan. Has one brother residing somewhere in MA. Resided in Fitchburg, MA from 1870 to 1875, and in Swanzey for the last ten years, with Mrs. Nahum Perry, a sister. Is feeble and unable to earn his board. Was worth a thousand dollars or more at one time. Has been married, wife dead. One child living, Mrs. Chamberlain of Keene. [Swanzey, 1 Apr 1885; adjudged Apr T 1885]

44. Heber Riel, Winchester, French, born in Canada, age 67 years. Has resided in Winchester for five years last past, and for 32 years before in the state of NY. Married and has children. One child has been assisted. Sick and unable to work. [Winchester, 9 Jun 1885; adjudged Oct T 1882. New application filed Apr T 1885]

45. Nathaniel Heath, Marlow, American, born in Stoddard, age 70 years. Married, name of wife: Amanda. Date of marriage 1851. Four children, only one a minor. Has resided with his family in Marlow since 1865. {Is in poor health and unable to labor very much. Reported dead by S. L. Kingsbury, died} [Marlow, 3 Jul 1885; adjudged 22 Aug 1885]

[16] 46. Edward W. Eastman, American, Keene, born in _____. Age ____ years. Father's name Hiram W., age 44. Mother's name Elizabeth, age 42; maiden name Belknap. Parents have lived in Keene since 1869, most of the time. Has four brothers and sisters. Oldest 17 years. Sentenced to State

Cheshire County Paupers
1885-1900

Industrial School. See P. C. Docket.[7] [Keene, 21 Oct 1884; adjudged 1 Oct 1884]

47. Thomas Mulvie, Keene, Irish, born in Keene. Age ___ years. Father born in Ireland, 42 years of age. Mother's maiden name Elizabeth Fitzgerald, age ___ years. They have six children; oldest 18 yrs, youngest 1 year. Thomas, on complaint of his father was brought before the Police Court, and sentenced to the State Industrial School on the charge of willful disobedience etc. for a term of ___. [Keene, 25 Oct 1885; adjudged Oct T 1885]

48. Harriet Columbia,[8] Gilsum, born in Lyme, NH. Age 28 years, 11 Mar 1885. Parents always resided in Lyme. Father enlisted and died in the army. Does not know whether mother is living or not. Never was married, but has two children: Irving, 3 years old, 13 Dec 1883 and Vangybelle, born the 27 Nov 1883. Has resided in various places in this state and VT. Has lived in Gilsum since 1880. Has kept house for a man who recently died very suddenly. {note: July 29, Mother Sophia Columbia married Geo. Dunbar in 1868 or 1869 and since last Nov has been living in Lyme. (See Letter on file)} [Gilsum, 2 Jul 1885; adjudged 7 Aug 1885]

[17] 49. Josiah T. Swinington, Nelson, American, born in _____, age 64 years. Has been married twice; name of present wife Georgianna. Has ten children, six of whom are minors. Names: Charles, age 20; Mary Etta, age 16; Emily L., age 13; Walter P., age 10; Leroy L. Burter, age 6, next August; and Etta May, age 3. From 1869 to 1874 resided in VT; from Sept 1874 to Nov 14, 1879 in Greenfield, NH; since 14 Nov 1879 in Nelson. No settlement. Wants aid in supporting and taking

---

[7] Docket of Keene's police court.
[8] See entry #119.

Cheshire County Paupers
1885-1900

care of daughter Emily L. who is pregnant with child. [Nelson, 31 Jul 1885; adjudged 4 Sep 1885. See complaint A. H. White]

50. Rufus E. Guillow,[9] Gilsum, American, born in ____, age 35 years. Single. Has resided in Gilsum since 1 Jan 1870. Claims to be in poor health and unable to earn his own support. Ordered to Co. Almshouse. Has relatives residing in G. but none are able to support him. {Discharged and readmitted 5 Feb 1891} [Gilsum, 15 Aug 1885; adjudged 22 Aug 1885]

51. Charles F. Hill, Jaffrey, American, born in Winchester, NH, 7 Jun 1856. Father died 12 Jan 1883; mother Mary A. married Dexter B. Knowlton of Jaffrey in 1884. Parents resided in Richmond, NH six years or more. He married Nellie Webster of Sturbridge, MA in 1875. Has three children. Wife & children reside with her parents in Sturbridge, MA. He lives with his mother in Jaffrey, is sick, insane and his mother is unable to take care of him. Ordered to the NH Asylum for the Insane. [Jaffrey, 30 Jul 1885; adjudged 9 Sep 1885]

[18] 52. Mary A. Lewis, Keene, French, born in Canada, 25 years old. Married; husband an intemperate man, abandoned his wife in April last. They were living in Minnesota at the time. Has three children dependent upon her for support, viz: Minnie, aged 8 yrs; Harrison, 6; and Rosa, 4. Lived in Roxbury about two years before we went to Minnesota. Mrs. L. returned to Keene about four months ago. Her father went to Roxbury, NH to live in 1879, resided there 5 years. His parents never lived in NH. [Keene, 2 Sep 1885; adjudged 4 Sep 1885]

53. Mary Livingston, Walpole, American, 94 years old. Admitted to Almshouse 15 Dec 1882. Has one daughter, Mrs.

---

[9] According to the *History of Gilsum*, his name is "Guillow," though the handwriting seems to be "Guellow."

Cheshire County Paupers
1885-1900

John Swartelle, 13 Cherry St., West Summerville (sic), MA. Has friends in Walpole, Mrs. John Farnsworth. She receives a pension of $96 per year which is surrendered to the County on account of her support. Had some few effects at Mr. Punts in Walpole. Were given to Mrs. J. Farnsworth of Walpole by Mr. Burt, they being of no use to the County. Died at County Almshouse Sunday, 4 Oct 1885. Body sent to Walpole for burial. [Walpole; adjudged Oct T 1882]

54. D. W. Sawyer, committed to the NH Asylum from Keene. Has been supported at the NH Asylum by relatives to 1 Jul 1885, since which time support has been withdrawn and the County became liable for his maintenance under Chapter10, Sec. 20, Gen. Laws. Received official notice of the withdrawal of support from Dr. C. P. Bancroft, Supt. NH Asylum, as required by law, 13 Jun 1885. (See file of affidavits #54) [Keene; at the NH Asylum]

[19] 55. Sally Seward, Marlow, American, 85 years old. Husband Thomas Seward died in Stoddard, Sept 1867. The farm on which they lived was willed to Thomas by his father Josiah Seward of Sullivan. For the last ten years Sally has resided with her daughter Mrs. Sarah V. Towne of Marlow. She had not possessed a sufficient amount of property since 1870 (Janry 1) to give her a settlement in Marlow or any other town. Has no relatives who are liable and able to support her. David Seward of Keene is her husband's nephew. She is fearfully afflicted with scrofula disease. {Date of death 25 Jul 1885} [Marlow; adjudged Oct T 1882]

56. Geo. W. Young, Walpole, American, born in Petersham, MA. 41 years old. Always resided in MA. Until 1882, except 1 ½ years that he served in the US Army. In March 1882 came to Keene, later went to Brandon & Bellows Falls, VT; came to Walpole in Nov 1883. Has been married twice; first wife died

Cheshire County Paupers
1885-1900

14 or 15 years ago. Second wife's maiden name Lucy A. Blood, born in Goshen, VT is 28 years of age. Was a widow when Y. married her five years ago. She had one child by her first husband and four by Y; one dead. Her child resides with Y & is 5 yrs old. My oldest is 4 yrs. The other two are twins, 1 ½ mos. old. My wife is now insane. Sent to County Farm 19 Jun 1884. {Recovered & discharged 4 Sep 1884 & go to Saxton's River, VT to reside} [Walpole; adjudged 4 Jul 1884]

57. Rosa Wood, Winchester, French, born in Canada. 45 years old. Married; has six children, 4 live with her, two are away from home. Husband took what money she had and left some six months ago, about the 1st of Jan 1884. Names of boys at home: Leander, age 16 years; Henry, age 15 years; and a girl, Julia, age 13 yrs. Have worked in the mills at Ashuelot. But Mrs. W is now sick with a fever and therefore is compelled to ask for relief. Aided temporarily. [Winchester; adjudged Aug 1884]

[20] 58. William H. West, Stoddard, American, born in Bradford, NH, age 40 years. Has been assisted in Stoddard. Left Stoddard in the fall of 1883 and went to Bradford, NH, where he has been assisted and the town has applied to be reimbursed for the amt of relief furnished. Resided in S. from May 1878 to the fall of 1883. Has six minor children, viz: Willie F., age 12; Mable, age 4; Leonard, age 10 years; Freddie F., age 8; Scott, age 6; and Angie, age 1 year. Served in the army from 1861 to 1865 & was honorably discharged. [Stoddard, 17 Apr 1879; adjudged Oct T 1879 & again in 1884]

59. Lucia A. White, Marlborough, American, born in Westminster, VT, age ___. Married Wm. R. White of Marlborough, 1847. Taken insane about 1873; removed to the County Almshouse; supported there from 15 Aug 1873 to 11 Sep 1877, when she was removed to the NH Asylum for the

Cheshire County Paupers
1885-1900

Insane where she remained until she died. {25 Jun 1885} She was supported at the expense of the town of Marlborough until 11 Sep 1883 when she became a county charge under the new law. Her husband resides in Marlborough and is unable to support her. [Marlborough; adjudged Oct T 1883]

60. Charles Vigneau, Winchester, French, born in Canada, came to the United States to live about 1881. Has a wife and 5 children. His wife, alone can speak English. His oldest child is 14 years and the youngest 5 years old. He applies for help by reason of sickness and his inability to work, he being destitute of means. [Winchester; adjudged Oct T 1884]

[21] 61. Caroline H. Turner, Fitzwilliam, French, born in Lower Canada. 32 years of age, single. Deformed and insane at times. Has two brothers residing in Fitzwilliam, one sick with consumption, is supported by his brother who has a wife and three children. Her parents never lived in the United States. Admitted to the Almshouse 13 May 1884. [Fitzwilliam; adjudged after Apr T 1884]

62. Solomon F. Towne, Rindge, American, 72 years of age, 28 Mar 1883. Married; wife Mary A., age 45, 29 Mar 1883. Son, Francis L., 14 years old, 26 Jan 1884. Have resided in Rindge only since May 1879. That is since 1 Jun 1870. [Rindge; adjudged Oct T 1884]

63. Bridget Ryan, Keene, Irish, born in Ireland, 74 years of age. Married, husband dead, died in Ireland. Came to Keene about 17 years ago. Have 2 children: John Ryan and Mrs. Thomas Fitzgerald. [Keene; adjudged Oct T 1884]

[22] 64. Nancy Rines, Jaffrey, age 73, in May 1883. Came from Peterborough to Jaffrey to live with her daughter, Mrs. Lizzie A. Towne in June 1882. Husband died in Peterborough

in 1876. She is sick and her daughter is poor as well as herself and therefore they are obliged to apply for relief. [Jaffrey; adjudged after Apr T 1884]

65. Hannah Barry, Hinsdale, Irish, born in Syracuse, NY, 37 years old, widow. Husband Jas. Barry was born in Pittsfield, MA, and was thirty five years old when he died. He was killed in G & GA Robertson's paper mill the 6 Feb 1882 by explosion of boiler. Has three children: Wm J., 3 mos old; John, 4 years old; and Nellie, 5 years old, at the time their father was killed. Mr. B. was honorably discharged from US Army. Mrs. Barry is an invalid and unable to work very much. {Mrs. Barry died 13 Nov 1885} Children placed in care of their mother's sister, Mrs. Sullivan of Hinsdale. [Hinsdale; adjudged Oct T 1884. Rec'd notice Apr T 1884.]

66. Julia Pickett, Walpole, Irish, born in Ireland. 39 years old, widow. Husband died in Jan 1884. Came to VT when 14 years old. Resided in Ely, VT until 1883. Has nine children living, viz: Catharine, 21 yrs; Stephen, 19 yrs; Mary, 16 yrs; Alice, 12 yrs; James & John, twins 9 yrs; Anna, 7 in July 1884; and Thomas, 5 yrs old. Has been married twice. Came to Walpole to live in Feb 1884. Rec'd from Mr. Eddy, overseer of the poor of Rockingham, VT some aid after my husband died. [Walpole; adjudged Oct T 1884. Rec'd notice in April 1884]

[23] 67. Amanda Peterson, Hinsdale, born in Troy, NY, 67 years old, widow. Husband died some 14 years ago. Has two children, neither able to assist her. [Hinsdale; adjudged Oct T 1884]

68. Ella A. Putney, Richmond, American, born in Brandon, NY, 29 years old. Married to Geo. A. Putney 10 Dec 1876. He neglects to support and has abandoned her and the children. Has 3 children: Emma M., 7 yrs; Henry E., 4 yrs; and Etta M.,

Cheshire County Paupers
1885-1900

1 year. She is now pregnant with child, which if born alive will be an illegitimate child. Her husband was born in Richmond and his mother still resides there. Her parents reside in Rindge. Father's name Allen W. Davis. He was adjudged a county charge April term 1876 and was assisted in the town of Fitzwilliam. {Committed to Almshouse with her children 15 Sept 1885 from Rindge.} [Richmond; adjudged Oct T 1884]

69. William Nailer, Jaffrey, Irish (?), born in Plattsburg, NY in 1837. Married Julia Joiyle of Plattsburg in 1867. Has eight children: Felix, born 13 Jul 1868; Mary F., 18 Apr 1869: Chas., 4 Mar 1870; Maggie, 7 Mar 1871; Jessie M., 1 May 1873; Jennie, 25 Nov 1877; William, 7 Aug 1879; and Carrie, 15 Dec 1883. Has resided in Jaffrey only 10 or 11 months. [Jaffrey; adjudged after Apr T 1884]

[24] 70. Peter Meyett, Jaffrey, French (?), born in Plattsburg, NY, 47 years old. Resided in P until 1881; in Keene 2 years; went to Jaffrey. Married Mary Sharkee in 1881 at Keene. 2 children, viz: Emily, born in Keene in Oct 1882 and Peter, born in Jaffrey in Dec 1884. Mrs. M's parents reside in Jaffrey. [Jaffrey; adjudged Apr T 1871. Re-examined Apr T 1885]

71. Joseph Montegney, Jaffrey, French, born in St. Amey, Canada. 26 years old. Married Louisa Shaker in Canada in Nov 1879. She is 18 years old. Her parents live in Jaffrey. Has one child, viz: Mary Montegney, born in Keene Jan. 2, 1883. Was assisted in Keene in 1883, at which time the family were proven to be entitled to relief from the county. Mr. M is sick & unable to work at this time, 20 Feb 1885. [Jaffrey; adjudged Oct T 1882 at Keene]

72. James Mann, Nelson, Irish, born in Ireland, 52 years old. Came to America in 1864; have resided in Keene and Nelson most of the time. Has been married; wife died ten years ago.

Cheshire County Paupers
1885-1900

One child. Unable to work by reason of a severe cut with an axe in one foot. Admitted to County Almshouse 25 Jun 1884. Discharged 2 May 1885. Readmitted 21 Oct 1890 and discharged. [Nelson, 17 Jun 1884; adjudged after Apr T 1884]

[25] 73. David Marsh,[10] Keene, American, born in Keene, 68 years old. Has always resided in Keene. In 1840, married Frances Marsh; she died in Feb 1883, age 69. Has had 9 children, 3 living, all poor. In April 1883 married Catharine Allridge. She left him in Oct 1883. Has been assisted by the town of Keene several times since 1869. Feeble and unable to do much work. {Admitted to County Almshouse 17 Jun 1884. Mrs. Catharine Marsh died 2 Dec 1886. David committed suicide by hanging himself to the steam radiator in his room, 13 Aug 1891, buried at farm} [Keene, 16 Jun 1884; adjudged after Apr T 1884]

74. Joseph Leon, Marlborough, French, born in Terrebonne,[11] Canada, 31 years old, the 25 of Jun 1883. Married, wife and 3 children living. Was never assisted before. Has resided in NH only about one year. [Marlborough, 24 Apr 1884; adjudged after Apr T 1884]

75. Fred LeClair, Winchester, French, born in Montreal, Canada, 19 years of age, single. Parents never resided in NH. Sick and calls for temporary relief. [Winchester, 6 Apr 1885; adjudged Apr T 1885]

[26] 76. Eugene LeClaire, Rindge, French, born in Canada, age 41 years, married Louisa Morsett in 1857. Has 9 children at this time. Has resided in various places in VT and NH. Has

---

[10] Original gives his name as James; however the index refers to him as Davis, as does the note later in the entry.
[11] Text says "Teebon," but the placename should read "Terrebonne."

Cheshire County Paupers
1885-1900

resided in Rindge since 1866 most of the time. Was aided at one time by the town of Stoddard. [Rindge, 5 Apr 1875; adjudged Apr T 1875. Re-examined & allowed Apr T 1884]

77. Richard Kelley, Irish, about 62 years of age, came to Marlborough to work on the Keene & Manchester Railroad from Royalston, MA. Family resides in Royalston, MA. Has wife Ellen Kelley, and several children. Was taken sick soon after he came to Marlborough and having no means had to be assisted. {Admitted to Co. Almshouse 7 Jul 1884 and discharged 20 Aug 1884} [Marlborough, 7 Jul 1884. Adjudged after Apr T 1884]

78. Daniel Keizer, French, 39 years of age. Resided in Chesterfield with John Buel from 1860 or 1861 until 1879 when he went to his father's in Westmoreland, Chas. Keizer. He has never been able to earn more than his board being a non compos. His father is poor and unable to support him, and therefore applies for help. Admitted to the Co. Almshouse 12 May 1883 as a town pauper, but at the Oct T 1884, he was adjudged a county pauper upon the evidence furnished this office. From Jun 1883 to 19 Sep 1885 he resided with a Mr. Hubbard of Westmoreland, the county paying 50 cents per week. {He died 19 Sep 1885.} [Westmoreland, notice rec'd in May 1883; adjudged Oct T 1884]

[27] 79. Gertie Mable Hale, American, born in Richmond, NH, 16 years old. Father's name is Jonis S. Hale, 51 yrs old; mother's maiden name is Asenath Swan, daughter of Ebenezer Swan, and is about 40 years old. Upon complaint Gertie was sentenced to the State Industrial School for being a stubborn child, etc. by the Police Court, Keene. [Keene, 29 Jul 1884; adjudged Oct T 1884]

Cheshire County Paupers
1885-1900

80. Francilla Holbrook, American, daughter of Erastus Holbrook, formerly of Westmoreland, is about 39 years old. She claims to have been married once to a man by the name of Holbrook, but he never resided in Chesterfield. Has one child, Fred, about 20 yrs old. The said Francilla Holbrook died 20 Mar 1884 and was buried at the expense of the town, and claim is made against the county to recover cost of burial. [Chesterfield, notice rec'd in Mar 1884; allowed Oct T 1884]

81. James Hale, Marlborough, born in the north of England, 27 years old. Came to America in 1881. Parents never resided in this state. [Marlborough, 22 Oct 1884; adjudged Oct T 1884]

[28] 82. Reuben Gassett, Marlborough, American, born in Townshend, MA, 56 years old. Has resided in Acworth for 6 months last past, and was on my way to Worcester, MA when he was taken sick at Marlborough. Has two minor children 13 and 15 years of age. Applies for such relief as he may need during his sickness. Has a wife but does not live with her. {Died Dec 1890.} [Marlborough,18 Oct 1884; adjudged Oct T 1884]

83. William G. Evans, Walpole, American, born in Springfield, VT, 75 years old in Aug 1884. Never married. "Have resided in Rockingham, VT since I was a boy. Have resided in NH only since the fall of 1882." He does not consider that he has any residence in NH. Has always paid taxes in Rockingham until within a few years. Assisted temporarily and then delivered up to the overseer of the poor of Rockingham, VT. [Walpole, 3 Aug 1884; adjudged Oct T 1884]

84. Phoeba Dodge, Walpole, American, born in Stoddard 18 Apr 1798, and is now 86 years old. Resided in Stoddard nearly all of the time until 28 Oct 1837. Has resided and made it her home since with Richard Knapp. She is now extremely weak,

Cheshire County Paupers
1885-1900

nearly blind and unable to walk across the room without aid. [Walpole, Sep 1884; adjudged Oct T 1884]

[29] 85. George Doucette, Marlborough, French, father b. at Three Rivers, Canada; George b. 24 Jul 1873 at Ashuelot, son of John whose age is 33 yrs. Resided 11 yrs in Ashuelot and 5 in Marlborough. Committed to State Industrial School for some offense. Has two brothers and one sister. Parents unable to support him at the S. I. School. County pay costs at State Industrial School and recover sums paid of the town of Winchester. [Marlborough, 12 Jun 1884; not adjudged, his father having paid a settlement in Winchester.]

86. Thomas Curtin, Marlborough, Irish, born in Ireland, city of Cork, 26 May 1838, where he resided until 1862, when he came to Manchester, NH. Came to Marlborough in Jul 1883. Was married at Manchester in 1867, she was born in 1838. Her parents died in Ireland. They have three children, the oldest 11 years and the youngest 7 years old. His wife has not resided with him since he came to Marlborough to live or in the State of NH since they were married. Claims to be out of work and unable to get any employment, and hence, calls for relief. [Marlborough, 24 Jan 1884; adjudged Oct T 1884]

87. Miss Mercy Crain, Alstead, American, born in Alstead, 74 years old, never married. Resided in Alstead until 1852; in Walpole until 1862; in Nunda, NY until 15 Dec 1883; resided with my brother in Nunda. He died and his children did not feel able to support me. Mr. Mitchell of Alstead is a relative of Miss Crain. She has but one foot and is obliged to walk with a cane. Admitted to the County Almshouse, Westmoreland 24 Mar 1884. [Alstead, 24 Mar 1884; adjudged Apr T 1884]

[30] 88. John Costello, Marlborough, Italian, born in CT, 29 years old, married. Never had to ask for relief before. Out of

Cheshire County Paupers
1885-1900

work and only want temporary aid. [Marlborough, 7 Mar 1884; adjudged Oct T 1884]

89. Sarah O. Bartlett, Hinsdale, American, born in Marlborough, VT, 30 years old. Married, does not live with him. Have resided in Guilford, VT and been assisted by said town of Guilford for the last six or eight years. Have lived in Hinsdale for two years last past. The town of Guilford, VT has assisted her to the amount of nearly one hundred dollars since she came to H to live. Has one child, Clarance C., 6 years old. Gave her temporary assistance and notified the selectmen of Guilford that the county would return her to Guilford if more help should be required. [Hinsdale, rec'd notice in Jan 1885; adjudged Apr T 1885]

90. Ezekiel B. Collins, Fitzwilliam, American, born in Fitzwilliam 23 Sep 1816 and is 68 years old. Was never married. Is not of sound mind and for several years has not been capable of taking care of himself. Has several brothers and sisters. One brother and sister reside in Winchendon, MA, and one brother in Wardsboro, VT. Admitted to the County Almshouse 5 Dec 1884. {Discharged to live with his brother in VT 2 Jul 1885.} [Fitzwilliam, rec'd notice Dec 1884; adjudged after Oct T 1884]

[31] 91. Lewis Champney, Fitzwilliam, French. Has resided in Fitzwilliam about a year. Is about 70 years of age. Wants temporary aid. [Fitzwilliam, 8 Apr 1885; adjudged Apr T 1885]

92. Cyprian Carran, Keene, French, born in Canada, 37 years old. Married, wife 35 years old. She came from Canada. Have 7 children. Have call for relief by reason of an accident. Can support myself and family as soon as I get able to work. [Keene, 26 Jun 1884; adjudged after Apr T 1884]

Cheshire County Paupers
1885-1900

93. James Corey, Keene, French, born in Canada, 37 years old. Married, age of wife 30. Have eight children: Herman, aged 12 yrs; Delor, aged 10; Ellen, 9; Nestor, 7; Medon, 6; Herbert, 4; Henry, 2; and Mary Jane, 8 months. Resided in Canada until 1879. [Keene, 20 May 1885; adjudged after Apr T 1885]

[32] 94. Louis Chabut, Keene, French, born in France, 28 years of age. Has a wife, 26 years of age and one child 4 mos. Wife was born in Canada. She is now sick and hence, the cause of my calling for help. Have no relatives in this country. [Keene, 18 Apr 1884; adjudged after Apr T 1884]

95. Elbridge H. Black, Keene, age 12 years old. Father Orrin Black was born in Swanzey, age 49 yrs. Mother was born in Canada, age 44 yrs. They have but two children: Winfield M., 8 yrs old, the youngest. Elbridge has been sentenced to the Reform or Industrial School, Manchester for stubbornness and his father claims that he is not able to support him there. [Keene, 18 Oct 1884; adjudged Oct T 1884]

96. Honora Leakey, Winchester, Irish, born in Ireland, 65 years old. Married, husband died in Ireland in 1873. I came to this country in 1883. Came to Keene in Sep 1883 to live with my son John. He died three days after I came, leaving me destitute & without a house. James Cadigan out of charity gave me a house with him in Winchester. I have one son and three daughters living. The son is insane and an inmate of an asylum in NY. Two daughters married and live in NY. One daughter, a widower, traveling with a NY family, in Europe, as nurse. She has one son, who is living with Mrs. Leakey, 6 yrs old, named Scott. Mrs. L. & the boy came to Keene to live after Apr term of Court, 1885. [Winchester, 12 Mar 1884; adjudged Apr T 1884; Keene, Oct T 1885]

Cheshire County Paupers
1885-1900

[33] 97. Lenora Birch, Marlborough, American, born in Jericho, VT, 26 Feb 1860. Married Nelson Birch at Westville, NY on 17 Jan 1879. First came to NH in Jul 1883. On the 4th Jul 1884 Mr. Birch deserted his wife, and she has not since heard from him. He was born at Westville, NY 17 Sep 1846. Mrs. B. has two children, aged 4 years and less than one year. {By request she was assisted to Shirley, MA where she claimed she had friends. Later she returned to Harrisville and from then sent to the C. F. 30 Apr 1885 and discharged 30 Aug 1885. Report is that she married a man by the name of King in Jaffrey} [Marlborough, 28 Aug 1884; adjudged Oct T 1884. Harrisville.]

98. Harry Knowlton, Hinsdale, American, born in Hinsdale, 4 years old in Jul 1884. His father was a native of Gill, MA and is 27 years old. Don't know where he is, last heard from in Northampton, MA. Given name is Howard. The boy is living with Chas. Frary who is poor and unable to take care of him. Ordered to C. F. [Hinsdale, 25 Apr 1885; adjudged Oct T 1885]

99. Daniel Blanchard, Stoddard, American, 37 years old. Came to Stoddard in 1876 from Bennington, NH. Married wife over 30 years of age. Have five children, viz: Willie, 14 yrs; Frances, 12 yrs; Mary, 10 yrs; Fred, 16 yrs; and Bertha, 10 months old. He and some of the children are sick, hence are obliged to call for aid; were never aided by the public before. [Stoddard, 10 Apr 1885; adjudged Oct T 1885]

[34] 100. Harry Adams, Nelson, French, born in Canada, 44 years old. Came to the United States 13 yrs ago. Have been living in Brattleboro, VT, am on my way to Manchester to get work, and being out of money asked for food and lodging. [Nelson, 8 Dec 1884; transient not adjudged.]

Cheshire County Paupers
1885-1900

101. Joseph Pallidee, Troy, French, born in Canada, 60 years of age. Married; wife Mary 58 yrs old. Never resided in NH until 1880. Was adjudged in Marlborough Oct T 1883. Assisted by the town of Troy to go to Southbridge, MA, claiming to have friends there who would aid him. Later returned to NH and asks admission to the C. Almshouse, admitted. Wife supports herself. [Troy, 23 Oct 1885; adjudged Oct T 1883 from Marlborough]

102. Stephen E. Jodrey, Keene, born in Nova Scotia, 23 years old. Not married, never resided in NH before Nov 1884, when I came to Keene. Neither of my parents ever resided in NH. Has been very sick with typhoid fever, hence the call for assistance. [Keene, 6 Nov 1885; notice 15 Jun; adjudged Oct T 1885]

[35] 103. Bridget Batty, Hinsdale, Irish, born in Ireland, 58 years old. Came to America 28 years ago; 26 years ago married Lewis Waskins with whom I lived about 4 yrs. At that time I resided in Winchester. He left little or no property. I married Joseph Batty 18 or 19 years ago and lived with him 3 or 4 years, when I left him by reason that he abused me and had very intemperate habits. The last I heard of him was in Lowell, MA. Have no children. Resided a greater part of the time since I came to this country in Winchester. [Hinsdale, 19 Nov 1884; adjudged after Oct T 1884]

104. Henry Bevens, Swanzey, English, born in England, 39 years of age. Married. Parents reside in Lowell, MA where he has resided most of the time. Came to Swanzey in March 1884. For 3 years previous lived in Virginia. Out of work and in need of temporary relief. [Swanzey, 18 Oct 1884; adjudged Oct T 1884]

105. Joseph Beaufor, Winchester, French, born in Canada and always resided there until last December, when he came to

Cheshire County Paupers
1885-1900

Winchester, 25 or 26 years old. Call for aid by reason of having cut his leg badly and being without money. Have no relatives in this state; a single man. Rosa Beaufor, his sister resided in W for a while, and had to ask for relief when they mills where she worked shut down, & the selectmen aided her to go back to Canada. [Winchester, 16 Sep 1884; adjudged Oct T 1884]

[36] 106. Rosetta W. Green, daughter of Thankful P. who married Edward Bixby of Walpole in 1872 with whom she lived until 1881 when she deserted said Bixby and run away with another man. At the Apr term of the Supreme Court 1883, the said Bixby obtained a divorce from her. Rosetta was just 2 years old when I married her mother, whose maiden name was Felch.[12] Rosetta was sentenced to the State Industrial School in 1884. [Walpole; adjudged Oct T 1884]

107. Edward Bixby, Walpole, American, married does not live with his wife, age 41 years. Her age is 31 years. Was married in 1872 & divorced from his wife Thankful P. in 1883. Her maiden name was Felch. She had one child, Rosetta W. Green, who is in the State Industrial School. [Walpole; adjudged Oct T 1885]

108. Elizabeth Nash, Stoddard, American, 38 years old, wife of Stillman D. Nash, about age 45. Mother of Jennie Bates, wife of Francis Bates. Jennie is 17 years old, Francis Bates is about 37 years old. Jennie married said Francis Bates in Aug 1883. Mrs. N was born in Readfield, NY, was married to S. D. N. at Camden, NY 16 Oct 1862. Four children: Geo. L., 19 years; Eliza Jane, 14 years; William H., 12 years; and Alexander, 2 years. [Stoddard, 5 Sep 1885; adjudged Apr T 1883[13]]

---

[12] No record of who gave this deposition.
[13] Date transcribed as written in original. It should probably read "1886." For more on George L. Nash, see entry #18 ½, page 6.

Cheshire County Paupers
1885-1900

[37] 109. Jennie Bates, Stoddard, American, 17 years old, wife of Francis Bates of Gilsum, whose age is about 37 years. The said Jennie is sick at this time (5 Sep 1885) and hence applies for relief. [Stoddard, 5 Sep 1885; adjudged after Apr T 1885]

110. Balinda Priest, Keene, American, born in VT, 84 years old, widow. Husband d. in VT in 1866. Have several children, one son in Keene and a daughter, Mrs. Fairbanks in Hancock. Gone to reside with her daughter in Hancock. [Keene; adjudged Oct T 1885]

111. Phillip Levine, Hinsdale, French, born in Canada, parents both dead, age about 12 years. Has an uncle by the name of Joseph Levine residing in Hinsdale at this time, who complained that said Phillip Levine is a stubborn, willful & disobedient child. Sent to State Industrial School. [Hinsdale; adjudged Oct T 1885]

[38] 112. Timothy Ryan, Keene, Irish, born in Ireland, 30 years of age. Married; wife's name Catherine, age 28 years, b. in Ireland. [Keene; transient; not adjudged]

113. Lester L. Hubbard, Keene, born in VT, 25 years of age, married Carrie G. Gilmore of Swanzey, age 24 years. Have one child, Alice, 2 ½ years old. Her parents Chas. G. and Fannie M. Gilmore resided in Swanzey from 1870 to 1881 and since that time in Keene. He resided in VT until 1879, then in Swanzey, Royalston, MA, and then in Keene. Applies for aid for himself only. Wife and child having gained a settlement in Swanzey under her father, and therefore are not adjudged. [Keene, 3 Nov 1885; adjudged Oct T 1885]

114. Albert H. Waldron, Gilsum, born in Taunton, MA, 43 years old, married and has nine children, eight under 15 years of

age. His wife's maiden name was Fanny Howard, age 44 years. Has resided in several towns in Cheshire County since 1870. Is intemperate, and hence the secret of his indigence. Children: Alice M., 14 years, the 14 Oct 1884; (twins) Homer J. & Harry J., age 12, the 30 Oct 1885; Susan R., age 9, the 14 Nov 1884; Berton, age 7, the 7 last Aug; Lena L., age 6, the 29th last Mar; Otis H., age 4, the 30th of last Jan; and baby, 2 years, the 19th of Sep 1885. [Gilsum, 4 May 1885; adjudged after Apr T 1885]

[39] 115. Olive Surprenout, Keene, French, born in Canada, age 33 years, married and has three children. Husband Joseph S., age 34 years. He was born in Canada. Names of children: Mary, 15; Albert, 4; and George, 2 years of age. Resided in MA from 1870 to 1882; since that time in Swanzey and Keene. Husband deserted her the last of Sep 1885. {note: dated 8 Oct. Sent to friends in New Britain, CT.} [Keene, 7 Oct 1885; adjudged Oct T 1885]

116. Catharine Tufts, Swanzey, American, born in Albany, NY, 84 years old. Married James Tufts when about 21 years old at Chester, VT. Soon after removed to Keene, NH and has resided there most of the time since. Her husband died in Keene 26 years ago. Has five children, four now living, all live in Keene except Jane, the wife of Geo. W. Eastman of Swanzey. Names: Abby, William, George and Jane. Sarah died 14 years ago. Abby married Samuel Richardson. Mrs. T is quite feeble and none of her children feel able to support her. [Swanzey, 11 Mar 1884; continued and adjudged Oct T 1885]

117. Ellsworth E. Preston, Swanzey, American, born in Searsburg, VT, 23 years old, last May. Married in May 1881 to Lula Cooper of Hinsdale. One child: Esther, 2 years old. Wife and child reside with her parents in Hinsdale, she having a settlement under her father. Has not lived with his wife for more than 2 years; is living with his parents. They have been in

Cheshire County Paupers
1885-1900

Swanzey about 3 weeks; came there from Marlborough. Sick with disease of the kidneys. Ordered to the County Almshouse; refuses to go; moves to Keene and decides to take care of himself. [Swanzey, 17 Oct 1885; adjudged Oct T 1885]

[40] 118. James C. Chapman, Gilsum, American. This man was found dead not far from his house Wednesday morning, 17 Jun 1885. He had left home to go to a neighbor to assist him in butchering. He has resided with a woman by the name of Hattie McColumbia by whom it is reported, to have had two children whose ages are 3 years and 18 months. He has lived in Gilsum more than 15 years. The records show that he was taxed from 1871 to 1879, and that $1.00 was abated in 1872 which was on acct of a dog, hence he gains a settlement in Gilsum. [Gilsum; rejected Oct T 1885]

119. Hattie McColumbia, Gilsum. This is the correct name of the person entered on page 16, #48.

120. Alice Pratt, Swanzey, American, came to Swanzey from Montague, MA. Married, husband's name Horace Pratt. Has a father living in New Salem, MA; name: Lyman Lanfair. Has been in Swanzey at the house of Luther B. Sparke about six weeks and where she died 17 Jul 1885. Body sent to Montague, MA. It is supposed that she has led a rather disreputable life. [Swanzey, Jul 1885; allowed Oct T 1885]

[41] 121. Joseph Champaigne, Hinsdale, French, born in Canada, 40 years old. Married, wife came from Canada, is 43 years old. Five children: Myrta, 13; Charles, 12; Franklin, 10; David, 7; and "Baby," 8 days old. Applies for temporary aid during the sickness of his wife. [Hinsdale, 16 Oct 1885; adjudged Oct T 1885]

Cheshire County Paupers
1885-1900

122. Lucy Pratt, Richmond, American, 66 years old, married Calvin S. Pratt, 40 years ago. For the last 15 to 20 years have resided in Salem, Northfield and Royalston, MA, came to Richmond last spring. Husband is aid by the town of Naticke, MA. Said town refuses to aid his wife by reason as they claim that she was married to another man and was not divorced at the time of her marriage to Pratt. She fell and broke her wrist some few weeks ago, and hence the application for relief. [Richmond, 23 Jan 1885; adjudged Apr T 1885]

123. Jane A. Page, Fitzwilliam, American, born in Jaffrey. Parents still reside there. Single, thirty-seven years old. Has been aided by said town of Jaffrey some nine or ten years, prior to the passage of the new law relating to settlement, 11 Sep 1883, under which she was adjudged a county subject. She is badly diseased, and her face and body is covered with sores and badly eaten. Her reputation is bad. Ordered to the ____ [14]in June 1884. Rc'd no help until 19 Nov 1884 when she was taken sick and was unable to be removed. Was taken to the Alms House 3 Mar 1885 and discharged 14 Apr 1885. [Fitzwilliam, Oct T 1883; adjudged Oct T 1883]

[42.] 124. Jesse P. Wellman, Dublin, American, born in Lyndeborough, NH, Jul 1821 and is 64 years old. Was married to Achsah J. 4 Jul 1848. Eight children, two minors, viz: Carrie E., 13 years old and Mary E., ten years old. Went to Dublin to reside 1866. Family still resides there. Mrs. W. has gained a settlement in Dublin by owning $150 worth of real estate, and paying all taxes assessed thereon. Her husband has no settlement, is now insane and an inmate of the NH Asylum. Has no means and no one liable for his support. [Dublin, 2 Dec 1885; adjudged after Oct T 1885]

---

[14] Transcribed as written in the original.

Cheshire County Paupers
1885-1900

125. Geo. W. Seward, Keene, American, born in Sullivan, NH, 64 years old. Wife Ruth C., 66 years old. Has resided in various places in NH since 1870, but in only one place over three years. Resided in Marlow seven years. [Keene, 20 Apr 1885; adjudged Apr T 1885]

126. William N. Arling, Hinsdale, American, born in Northfield, MA, 31 years old last August. Always resided in Northfield until within 5 years. Married; wife born in Chesterfield. Father's name Luther Streeter. Three children, oldest ten years old. Never paid but one tax in NH. Evidence of the liability of the county insufficient. Paid expenses to return to his home in MA. [Hinsdale, 31 Jan 1885; Apr T 1885, not adjudged]

[43] 127. James M. Bates,[15] Keene, American, born in Lundsgan,[16] VT, 1824 and is now 63 years old. Married in 1864, Lucy Whittimore of Swanzey, NH who is 38 years of age. Six children, viz: Edward H., 20 years; Mary L., 16 years; Minnie F., 14 years; Rosa, 9 years; Lillie, 4 years; and Daisy M., 1 year old. Have lived in Keene and Winchester nearly all my life. {Lucy W. Bates died 1 Jun 1891 & James M. Bates died 1892.} [Keene, Apr 1883; adjudged Apr T 1884]

128. Mary Barnard, Swanzey, French, born in Canada, 40 years old. Married; husband, 52 years old, born in Canada. Always lived in Canada until three years ago. Five children: Emma, 14 years; Henrietta, 13 years; Clara, 11 years; Henry, 7 years; and Alvin, 5 years of age. All born in Canada; Mr. B is a tanner, but is now out of employment and therefore obliged to ask for relief. [Swanzey, 29 Dec 1883; adjudged after Oct T 1883]

---

[15] See # 863 and 865. See also #1011.
[16] Possibly Landsgrove, VT.

Cheshire County Paupers
1885-1900

129. Clara A. Beal, Harrisville, American, formerly of Marlborough. Father's name, Jones. Married Lyman Beal. He died 13 Mar 1874. Has resided in Harrisville ever since her marriage until committed to the NH Asylum some few years since. She is about 34 years of age and has been supported at the Asylum for three years last past. Transferred from the NH Asylum to Westmorland 3 Dcc 1890. Is a hard case, required to be kept in a room by herself. [Harrisville, 19 Oct 1883; adjudged after Oct T 1883]

[44] 130. Keziah E. Billings, Keene, American, born in Keene, 76 years old. Has always resided in Keene, single, never married. Died Sunday, 27 Mar 1887, pneumonia. [Keene, Apr 1884; adjudged Apr T 1884]

131. Andrew Weber, Walpole, German, native of Germany, age 64 years. Has resided in Walpole for about twenty-five years. Applies for aid on account of his daughter Carrie L., who is twenty-one years old, the 12th of Mar 1884. She is idiotic and helpless. It was found upon examination that the said Andrew Weber had gained a settlement in Walpole. [Walpole, 29 Mar 1884; rejected Apr T 1884]

132. Edward Weston, Surry, Englishman, born in London; came to America about four months ago, 64 years old. Applies for only so much aid as will enable him to reach Chelsea, MA, where he claims to have friends. Furnished him with the necessary transportation. [Surry, 24 Dec 1883; adjudged after Oct T 1883]

[45] 133. Arthur E. Buzzell, Alstead, American, born in Chelsea, VT, 27 years old. Married Nellie M., age 22 years. Two children, viz: Ellen Mabel, five years old and Olive V. M., 3 years old. Has cut his foot badly recently and hence his

Cheshire County Paupers
1885-1900

application for relief. [Alstead, 11 Feb 1884; adjudged after Oct T 1883]

134. Chas. Burns, Keene, Irish, born in Ireland, 62 years old. Came to US 38 years ago. Has been married twice; 12 children, all dead but three: One minor Timothy C., about 9 years old. Last wife, Mary Hickey is about 40 years old. She asks for no relief for herself. Wants her husband taken care of, as he does nothing toward supporting himself, and drinks badly when he can get money to buy liquor. Sent to County Almshouse 26 Nov 1884. [Keene, 4 Apr 1884; adjudged Apr T 1884]

135. Asaph E. Burpee, Dublin, American, born in Dublin, 2 Feb 1836. Always resided in Dublin, never married. Was taken partially insane in 1870 or 1871 and has since been supported by the town, until the passage of the law relating to the settlement of person which went into effect 11 Sep 1883, under which he became a county charge. Was admitted to the County Almshouse as a town pauper 13 Dec 1875. {Oct T 1885} Still at the Almshouse. Total amt. rec'd from the town of Dublin for his board exceeds $1000. [Dublin, 25 Jan 1884; adjudged 1 Feb 1884]

[46] 136. Jasher R. Cummings, Keene, American, 42 years old 25 Dec 1883. Married, name: Mary Jane, age 36 years. Five children, viz: George Frank J., 18 years; Isabelle Jane, 17 years; Adelene N., 7 years; Mamie, age 6; and Russell W., 1 month old. Resided in Keene for six years last past. Hardly knew his children's names, is evidently very shiftless. [Keene, 22 Dec 1883; adjudged after Oct T 1883]

137. Ann Cumings, Keene, American, 63 years old in May 1883. Widow; husband died in 1865. Has been assisted by the city of Keene for three or four years last past. Became a county charge under the law of 1883 relating to time of settlement.

Cheshire County Paupers
1885-1900

Resides above at the corner of Gilsum Road & Howard Street. {Died Friday, 15 Apr 1887.} [Keene, 15 Dec 1883; adjudged after Oct T 1883]

138. John Daginon, Keene, Irish, about 22 years of age, single. Has resided in Keene about 3 years. Parents both dead. They resided in Lebanon for 12 or 14 years prior to their deaths. The said Daginon is boarding at the house of John Murphy, is sick with consumption. [Keene, 17 Nov 1883; not adjudged. Has settlement in the town of Lebanon]

[47] 139. Joseph Door, Fitzwilliam, French, born in Montreal, Canada, 39 years of age. Has been married twice, two children by first wife, viz: Jennie S., age 11, and Joseph Chester, age 10. My present wife was born in VT and is an American; her name is Jane, age 41 years. Have resided most of the time since 1870 in Fitzwilliam and Jaffrey. Was married to his present wife in 1880. {noted later: She and the two children were admitted to the Almshouse as follows: the children 3 Mar 1884, and Mrs. D 17 Jun 1884. Mrs. D was discharged 20 Jun 1885. Admitted to the Almshouse under the name of Laporte. Jane Dore died at the residence of B.B. Abbott 10 Mar 1891 of pneumonia.} [Fitzwilliam, 24 Nov 1883; adjudged after Oct T 1883. Jos. Door was sent to H. C. for cruelty to his children for 3 months]

140. Landers B. Doolittle, Hinsdale, American, born in Hinsdale 20 Apr 1802. Has made it his home in H for the last 40 years. Never own any real estate, no wife or children. Have relatives in Hinsdale and Winchester. {note: Admitted to the Almshouse 30 Mar 1885. Died 2 Apr 1885.} [Hinsdale, 7 Apr 1884; adjudged Apr T 1884]

141. Sylvester Doyle, Jr., Dublin, born in Lowell, MA on 20 May 1849, and is now 34 years old. His father moved to Dublin in 1854; he and his father have resided there since. Was

married in Feb 1876. Suppose his wife to be living, but her whereabouts are unknown. One child Fred, born in the autumn of 1876. Sylvester Doyle, Jr. was taken insane some time in 1876 and is now an inmate of the NH Asylum for the insane. He has no means of support and his father is poor. [Dubli, 25 Jan 1884; adjudged after Oct T 1883]

[48] 142. John Driscoll, Keene, Irish, eight years of age, resides with Patrick Quinlan. Mother died about two years ago; father living but his whereabouts are unknown. He left John with Mr. Quinlan in Apr 1883, promising to pay his board and cloth him, but he has not been heard from since. Admitted to the Home at Westmoreland 3 May 1884 and discharged 30 Dec 1884, and now resides with his uncle Mr. Quinlan without expense to the county, except occasionally a suit of clothes. [Keene, 7 Jan 1884; adjudged after Oct T 1883]

143. Louis Duprey, Gilsum, French, 41 years old. Married in 1865, wife is 42 years old. Three minor children. Names and ages as follows: Julia Ann, 10 years; Fredie, 7 years; and Joseph Elder, 3 mos. old. Resided in Nashua from 1870-1881. No property of any amount either real or personal. [Gilsum, 29 Jun 1884; examined Apr T 1884 and continued]

144. John Durant, Keene, French, born in Canada, 56 years of age. Married Sophia Arington. 8 children, viz: James, Eddie, Mary, John, Moses, Ella, Willie and Frank. Have resided in Keene eleven years. Resides in Ward 4 on Castle St. [Keene, 21 Jan 1884; adjudged Apt T 1884]

[49] 145. Henry Ellis, Roxbury, American, 39 years old. Married, wife: Louisa E., 30 years old last Jun. Have six children, viz: Birdie C., 11 years; Rosa E., 10 years; Louisa A., 7 years; Eunice A., 5 years; John H. M., 2 years; and Edwin W., 1 year old. Have resided in Keene and Roxbury since 1870.

Cheshire County Paupers
1885-1900

Three of his children have been sick with typhoid fever; he is sick with the same disease. [Roxbury, 3 Jan 1884; adjudged after Oct T 1883]

146. John Ellis, Keene, American, born in Keene, 76 years old and 9 months. Widower; wife died eleven years ago. Has nine children living, all poor and all emancipated. {Died in Fitchburg Feb 1891.} [Keene, 8 Dec 1883; adjudged after Oct T 1883]

147. Lydia L. Eddy, Winchester, American, born in Pine Grove, PA, 32 years old. Married 24 Dec 1868. Husband's name is Sidney H. Eddy, an adopted son of David Eddy of Stratton, VT, is 35 years old. His own father's name was James A. Packard who resided at the time of Sidney's birth at Stratton, VT and at this time in Newfane, VT. "Have resided most of the time since my marriage at South Londonderry, VT" until about 3 years ago, when "I left him by reason that he did not provide for myself and children, and since which time I have made it my home at my father's in Somerset, VT, and worked out when I could do so." Five children, viz: Flora L., 14 years; Willie H., 11 years; Alvaretta M., 9 years; Idella M., 7 years; and Louisa L., aged 4 years. Wants homes for Alvaretta and Idella. Consents to have them placed in the Baldwin Place House, Boston, where they were taken by J. B. Abbott 26 Feb 1884. These two girls are quite bright, pretty girls and no doubt can be placed in good homes. [Keene, Winchester 6 Feb 1884; adjudged 6 Mar 1884]

[50] 148. James Foley, Keene, Irish, 68 years old. Married; wife Ellen is about 45 years old. Two children: William, age 18, and Mary, age 5. Resided in Keene for 26 years. Ordered removed to Co. Almshouse. They refuse to go; relief stopped except at the expense of the city of Keene. [Keene, 24 Nov 1883; adjudged Nov 1883]

Cheshire County Paupers
1885-1900

149. John Daigle, Keene, French, born in Canada, 45 years old. Married, Nathlie D., age 36 years. Two children, viz: Angelena, 4 years old, and John W., age six months. Was honorably discharged from the US Army 4 Jul 1865. Belonged to Co. C, 1 Prol. Regt. NY Mounted Vols. Resided in Canada from 1870 to Jun 1884 when he came to Keene where he has since resided. Is nearly blind. Furnished him with an order for some clothing, and he removed to Hudson, MA where he claims to have a friend who has secured him work of some kind. [Keene; admitted 9 Jan 1886]

[51] 150. Nora Frame, Keene, Irish, born in Ireland, 30 years of age. Married, four children, viz: Mora Ain, age 9; Chavin, 6 years; Jane, 5 years; and Millor. Husband John Frame is now in Boston, came from Ireland in 1877. Resided in Manchester four years and then came to Keene where I have since resided. Husband's parents never resided in America. Asks aid to go to her husband with her children. [Keene, 3 Nov 1885; adjudged 9 Jan 1886]

151. Calista R. Carey, Keene, born in Ashburnham, MA, 27 years of age. Married, but does not live with her husband, claims that he abuses her. Have always lived in MA. Two children, wants aid to get back to MA. Neither her parents or his parents ever resided in NH. [Keene, 3 Nov 1885; adjudged 9 Jan 1886]

152. Joseph E. Riley, Keene, Irish, born in Ireland, 56 years old. Not married, has not resided in any city or town in NH for a period of one year. [Keene, 9 Dec 1885; admitted 9 Jan 1886]

153. H. D. Fletcher, Roxbury, American, 54 years old. Married; three children, names and ages: wife Jannette, age 27 years; children: Effie Rose, age 7; Earnest Mann, age 5; and

Cheshire County Paupers
1885-1900

May Bell, age 3. Have resided in various places in Cheshire County. This man is evidently shiftless and lazy. His wife it is claimed is not what she ought to be. {1 Jan 1886} Mrs. F and children are at this time residing with Mr. Baldwin, her son at So. Keene. [Roxbury, 19 Dec 1883; adjudged 18 Jan 1884.]

154. Gco. Gillett, Chesterfield, came from the northern part of VT, is about 50 years old. Is a sawyer by trade. Has resided in Chesterfield more or less of the time since 1874. He died very suddenly on 26 Jul 1883 at Geo. L. Fullam's house; cause: some kind of fit. [Chesterfield, 29 Mar 1884; adjudged Apr T 1884]

155. E. S. Greenwood, Keene, American, born in the state of NY. Came to Keene about thirty-five years ago, and married Mary Laws of Peterborough. Has resided here most of the time since; age 64 years. Has four children, all residing in Keene, none able to assist me. [Keene, 20 Mar 1884; admitted Apr T 1884]

[53] 156. Eunice Hall, Keene, American. Has lived nearly all her life in Keene, is 84 years old. Has been supported by charity for many years. Is at present an inmate of the Invalid's Home. {Died at the Invalid's Home.} [Keene, 6 Jan 1884; adjudged 18 Jan 1884]

156. Sarah M. Hale, Rindge, American. Always resided with parents in Rindge. 38 years old, 28 Jul 1883. [Rindge, 23 Nov 1883; admitted 7 Dec 1883]

157. Lizzie S. Hall,[17] Chesterfield, American. Has always resided in Chesterfield, age 26 years. Married Henry Hall, 20 Mar 1874. 3 children: Eva B., 8 years; Hermon H., 6 years;

---

[17] See #856, page 288.

Cheshire County Paupers
1885-1900

and Gracie M., 4 years. Husband, 30 years old. Has resided in various places since 1874. Her husband left her in Sep 1881. He is a son of Jonathan Hall of Keene. He is a miserable shiftless man. {1885} She has gone to Wardsboro, VT to keep house for a man by the name of DeBell with whom she has lived for a year or more in C. Her husband is in state prison for stealing, sentence from Sullivan Co. [Chesterfield, 12 Dec 1883; adjudged 4 Jan 1884]

[54] 158. Fred E. Hill, Westmoreland, American, 26 years old, was born in Westmoreland, not married. Has to cull for relief by reason of chronic inflammatory rheumatism, which has drawn his limbs considerably out of shape. He has the reputation of being an honest upright boy. Admitted to the Almshouse 7 Jul 1884. {1 Jan 1886} Still at the Almshouse, condition no better. {1 May 1891} Still remains at Almshouse, condition no better. [Westmoreland, 16 Apr 1884; adjudged Apr T 1884]

159. Catherine Hustis, Keene, born in Halifax, NS in 1802, age 82 years. Widow, husband died about 20 years ago. Had one son who was killed in the army. Rec'd a pension of $96 per year. Has been aided by charity persons considerably. Resides alone in Ward 3. [Keene, 7 Apr 1884; adjudged Apr T 1884]

160. Christine Julian , Keene, French, born in Canada, 32 years old, married. Husband Jule Julian was born in Canada, never resided in NH. Have two children: Freddie, age 7 years and Lavinia, age 2 years. [Keene, 30 Oct 1883; adjudged Apr T 1884]

[55] 161. Ella A. Jillson, Richmond, American, born in Richmond, about 32 years old, is deformed, head greatly enlarged, mind impaired. Has been in the same condition most of the time from birth. Her father died in 1865. Her mother

Cheshire County Paupers
1885-1900

still resides in Richmond. Has several brothers and sisters, none able to provide her support. {1885} Died at her mother's in Richmond. [Richmond, 27 Oct 1883; adjudged Oct T 1883]

162. Florence D. King, Jaffrey, born in Champlain, NY, 20 Dec 1854, age 28 years. Married, husband Philip King, born in Canada, 41 years old. I married in 1871. Has six children, viz: Rosa C., born 9 Mar 1871; Mary A., born 10 Oct 1873; Josephine C., born 18 Jan 1875; Hattie E., born 16 May 1877; Henry P., born 19 Feb 1879; and Emma E., born 20 Mar 1882. Has resided less than a year in Jaffrey. Her husband is a very intemperate man, and cruelly beats his wife and children when intoxicated. Does not properly provide for his family. Mrs. King is sick with consumption, cannot live long. {1885} Mrs. King died. Husband arrested and put in jail for cruel treatment of children, no indictment found. Children at the Almshouse from 19 Mar to 3 Jul 1885. [Jaffrey, 15 Oct 1883; adjudged Oct T 1883]

163. Rose Kelley, Keene, Irish, born in Ireland, 30 years old. Came to Keene in Sep 1883. Parents never lived in this country. Sick at Moses Ellis;' applies for relief until she can get so as to work. [Keene, 1 Apr 1884; adjudged Apr T 1884]

[56] 164. Nora LaMore, Jaffrey, American, born in Ashburnham, MA, 22 years old, the 5th day of Aug 1884. Married Joseph Shullon in 1879. He died in 1881 in Jaffrey, age 20 years. Her father died in the Army during the war of 1861. Her husband's parents came from Canada. Gave birth to an illegitimate male child 14 Feb 1884, and she declares that Thomas Needham of New Ipswich is the father of her child. Made complaints about Needham but without suit on his payment of $25. {Again in 1885 she finds herself in trouble again and she is taken to the Almshouse at Westmoreland,

Cheshire County Paupers
1885-1900

where she is 30 Jan 1886 with the Needham child.} [Jaffrey, 25 Feb 1884; adjudged 6 Mar 1884]

165. Samuel Leshure, Keene, sixty-five years old, single, was never married. Has resided in Keene since 1 Jan 1870. Committed to Almshouse at Westmoreland 4 Jan 1884 and discharged 17 Mar 1884. [Keene, 4 Jan 1884; adjudged Apr T 1884]

166. Julius Lyons, Keene, French, born in France, 30 years of age. Came to Keene in Oct 1883. Has a wife and three children, ages of children: 6, 2, and a few months old. Has no friends in this country. Is sick and unable to work and hence compelled to ask for relief. [Keene, 16 Feb 1884; adjudged Apr T 1884]

[57] 167. Mary A. Mansfield, Keene, Irish, born in this country, age 31 years. Married John Mansfield in 1876. Resided in Boston until 1877 when we moved to Bellows Falls, VT. Her husband is 30 years old. Have 3 children, viz: John, age 4 years; Mary; and Edward, 1 year old, the 17th of Nov 1883. Her husband has deserted her and refuses to provide for herself and children. He is keeping a billiard saloon here in Keene and sells liquor, a miserable man. {1885} Both parties gone out of the state. Has a brother, Larie Mansfield at the Almshouse.[18] [Keene, 15 Nov 1883; admitted Apr T 1884]

168. James Morse, Hinsdale, French, born in Saint Elule, Canada, 35 years old. Wife and four children, age of wife 28 years. She was born in the same place that I was. Came direct from Canada to Hinsdale where we have been some 10 months. Names of children and their ages, viz: Mary, 5 years; John, 3

---

[18] See #40, page 14.

years; Joseph, 2 years; and Eliza, 3 months. [Hinsdale, 31 Dec 1884;[19] adjudged 17 Jan 1884]

169. James Murry, Keene, Irish, born in Ireland. Came to this country 35 years ago, age 65 years, nearly. Have lived in Keene since I came to America. Married, wife 62 years old. Four children, viz: Mary, 29 years; James, 28 years; Lizzie, 23 years; and Michael, aged 18 years. Only one residing in Keene, Lizzie. None of my children are able to provide for our support. Have a sore leg that disables me and hence the cause of my request for relief. [Keene, 4 Apr 1884; adjudged Apr T 1884]

[58] 170. Lizzie Mallry, Keene, born in Bristol, RI, 29 years of age. Married; has not resided with her husband for four years last past. His name is James. Two children: Frank and Lizzie. [Keene, 1 Nov 1883; adjudged Apr T 1884]

171. Reuben Nash, Chesterfield, American. Has resided in Chesterfield since 1860, 80 years old. Wife Eliza T., age 78 years, died 11 Apr 1883. Assisted in the burial of his wife. Had been previously aided 1867 or 1868 in the burial of a son. {30 Jun 1866} Applies for relief. [Chesterfield, 29 Mar 1884; admitted Apr T 1884]

172. Mrs. John Parker, 2d, Richmond, French. Has resided in Richmond more or less of the time for the last eight years. Has five children, all dependent. Her husband left home in Dec 1883 and has not been heard from since. She was to go to Lowell, MA with her children, where she has friends and is sure she can get work and support herself. [Richmond, 2 Jan 1884; adjudged Apr T 1884]

---

[19] Date transcribed as written in original. This is probably "1883."

Cheshire County Paupers
1885-1900

[59] 173. Mary Pippin, Marlborough, French, born in West Farnum, PQ, 23 Aug 1839. Resided there until 1868. Married Joseph Pippin. Came to Marlborough in 1883. Husband was born in PQ in 1846. My husband, she says, is now sick and unable to work. Seven children, oldest less than 15 years and the youngest is not four years old. They are desirous of going back to Canada. Gave overseer of the poor authority to assist the family to return to their home in Canada. [Marlborough, 2 Feb 1884; adjudged Oct T]

174. J. W. Pierce, Keene, American, b. in Keene, 49 years old. Married; wife: Cordelia Ingram of VT, age 40. Six children, viz: Charles, 25 years; Hattie W., 21 years; Fred E., 20 years; Sarah E., 18 years; Herbert C., 13 years; and Lone E., 10 years. None of my children are able to support me. Resided in Keene since 1875. [Keene, 20 Mar 1884; admitted Apr T 1884]

175. Mary E. Phillips, Keene, French, born in Canada, 42 years old. Married; husband John, more than 20 years ago. Five children: oldest 17 years, youngest 3 years. Resided in Keene since 1871, most of the time. Husband left her about 1 ½ years ago. Has a divorce from him. Work seating chairs and my oldest child works in the mill. {17 Jul 1886} Daughter married and resides in Worcester. Applies to have her mother come and live with her. Transportation for herself and 3 children furnished. [Keene, 8 Apr 1884; admitted Apr T 1884]

[60] 176. Jane A. Page,[20] Fitzwilliam, American, born in Jaffrey, 36 years old, the 7th Nov 1883. Father's name, Jonathan Page, resides in Fitzwilliam. Has been assisted by the town of Jaffrey for nine years last past. Becomes a county charge under the new pauper law of 1883. Never married. Is badly afflicted with corrupt sores all over her body. Her nose

---

[20] See #123, page 41.

Cheshire County Paupers
1885-1900

has been almost entirely eaten away. [Fitzwilliam, 3 Nov 1883; admitted Oct T 1883]

177. Fred Pooler, Keene, French(?), about nine years old. Father, Chas. Pooler is about 30 years old, is a very intemperate man, supposed to be living in New York City. His mother resides in Boston and is about 30 years old. Sometimes sends a little clothing to her boy, but does not contribute very much. The parents formerly resided in Keene. His mother was an American and the daughter of Abner Hill of Swanzey. [Keene, 6 Jan 1884; admitted Apr T 1884]

178. Eli Richardson, Keene, American, born in Stoddard and resided there until 1880. Since then has resided with Elijah Mason of Surry, age 48 years, the 11th Oct 1883. Is not very bright, claims that Mason owes him for labor. Sent to Almshouse 28 Jan 1884. {Discharged 21 Apr 1884. Gone to Alstead to reside with a farmer.} [Keene, 15 Mar 1884; adjudged Apr T 1884]

[61] 179. Adelia Jolly, Jaffrey, French, born in Canada, 22 years old, the 23rd of last Feb. My father's name is Lewis and mother's name is Lois. They reside in Jaffrey. Never married (?). Have one boy, Arthur Russell, born 25 Nov 1882. She is now pregnant with child, that she claims was begotten last February by Frank Harley, who she claims has left Jaffrey and gone to Providence, RI. Sent to County Almshouse, where she was confined and after having recovered from confinement was discharged. [Jaffrey, 9 Nov 1885; admitted after Oct T 1885]

180. Lucius Davis, Gilsum, American, 50 years old in June 1885. Has resided in Gilsum for 28 years last past. My father died, he states several years ago. Was assisted by the public for many years. His mother is still living and is supported by the county. Has a small homestead in Gilsum, is at this time sick

Cheshire County Paupers
1885-1900

Rheumatic fever. {10 Nov 1891} Said Davis is receiving $6.00 per month pension. [Gilsum, 12 Dec 1885; admitted after Oct T 1885]

181. Ann Merrifield, Troy, American, 55 years old. Never married. Has resided for many years with Reuben Gibson. She is now sick and unable to earn her support and therefore Gibson applies for aid. She is a sister of Simeon Merrifield and also of Mrs. Maria Wyman. {30 Jan 1886} Mrs. W has been an inmate of the County Almshouse. [Troy, 15 Dec 1885]

[62] 182. John Crato, Roxbury, French, born in Canada, 34 years old. Has resided in NH about 5 years. Have 3 children, viz: Delia, born 19 Apr 1871; George, born 14 Dec 1872; and John, 18 Jan 1875. Wife living, name Delia. Her father's name is Frank Pluff. [Roxbury, 15 May 1875; admitted after Apr T 1875]

183. Delia Russell, Marlborough, French, born in Montreal, 23 Feb 1863. My father's name is Lewis Jolly and my mother's Saloma. Resided in Oakland, MA from 1 Jan 1873 to 1875; in Fitzwilliam to 1878; in Mason, NH to 1879; in East Jaffrey to 1881; in Fall River, RI to 1882, when I married Joseph Russell; soon after moved to Harrisville and remained there until 1883 when her husband left her, and she has known of whereabouts since.[21] She came to Marlborough to reside in Nov 1883. Her husband was born in Canada about the year 1857. Applies for aid on a/c her support to bury her child, as to pay the expenses. [Marlborough, 22 Mar 1884; adjudged Apr T 1884]

184. Margaret Ruffle, Keene, American, born in Surry, 52 years old. Married; name of husband Samuel. Has one

---

[21] Transcribed as written in the original. Probably she had **not** known of his whereabouts for some time.

Cheshire County Paupers
1885-1900

daughter residing in Ashburnham, MA. Has resided in Keene more than 40 years. Receives a pension of ninety-six dollars per year. Has not a very good character. [Keene, 8 Apr 1884; admitted Apr T 1884]

[63] 185. John Robbins, Hinsdale, French, born in Three Rivers, Canada. Came from Canada four years ago. He is 29 years old, never resided in the United States prior to four years ago. Has seven children. [Hinsdale, 29 Nov 1883; admitted 13 Feb 1884]

186. Lucius D. Reynolds, Winchester, American, born in Orange, MA (?). Married about 20 years ago and resided in MA until 1880 when he came to Winchester to reside. Wife died in the spring of 1883 of consumption. Children went to live with his father in Orange, MA. His wife was born in Winchester and was the daughter of Charles Moulton. Has always been poor. [Winchester, 1 Nov 1883; admitted after Oct T 1883]

187. Mary Shortell, Keene, Irish, born in Ireland, 70 years old. Was married to William Shortell in Ireland. Have no children. Have resided in Keene about 35 years. Have had some relief for several years past. [Keene, 4 Apr 1884; admitted Apr T 1884]

[64] 188. John Sharker, Keene, French, born in Canada, 58 years old. Married, wife born in Canada, 38 years old. Two children: Julia, 11 years, and Peter, 7 years old. Resided in Keene, Rindge, and Jaffrey. Was aided in Keene. Was adjudged and aided in Keene in 1882 or 3. [Keene, Jaffrey; admitted Apr T 1884]

189. Kate Stack, Walpole, Irish-American, born in Providence, RI, 3 Aug 1853. Married, husband born in Rockingham, VT 15

49

Cheshire County Paupers
1885-1900

Nov 1850. Was married in Athol, MA 7 May 1876. Came to Walpole to live in 1882. Three children, viz: John F. and Edward, age 7 years; Bernard, age 2 years. Husband deserted her a short time ago, and being pregnant and unable to work she calls for some relief. {Admitted to Almshouse 6 Mar 1884. James A., born 13 May 1884. Her other children are at his father's in Walpole.} [Walpole, 18 Feb 1884; adjudged Apr T 1884]

190. Ida J. Willard, Keene, born in Athol in 1856 and is 28 years old. Married Dennis A. in April 1876. Has not resided in NH over two years. Two children: one two years and the other six months of age. Only ask for relief temporarily. [Keene, 21 Mar 1884; admitted Apr T 1884]

[65] 191. Mary Ann Willis, American, born in Alstead, about 22 years old. Has resided in Winchester since she was about 6 years old. Was the daughter of Wilber F. Willis,[22] who came to Winchester to reside in 1868 and remained there until 1879. The mother of Mary A. Willis was the daughter of John Hale of Winchester who died prior to 1860. Wilber F. Willis deserted his family in 1879 and where he is now, no one knows. Mary Ann Willis, the mother of the above named girl died in 1881. {This girl has a feeble intellect and not capable of caring for herself. Admitted to Almshouse 16 May 1884.} [Winchester, 5 Mar 1884; adjudged 6 Mar 1884]

192. Sarah P. R. Smith, Rindge, American, 88 years old. Husband died in 1862. Has resided with Benj. F. Danforth, Jr., for eight years last past. Has a son residing in Rindge. She has been aided by the town to the amount of $2.00 per week and her son to the amount of $1.00 per week. [Rindge, 23 Nov 1883; admitted 7 Dec 1883]

---

[22] See also #1297, page 436.

Cheshire County Paupers
1885-1900

193. Tom Shaw, Hinsdale, English, born in Hurddivefile[23], Yorkshire, England, 23 years of age. Has been in America two years; came direct to Hinsdale. Has been nine months married, age of wife 23 years. She has been in this country one year only. Neither my parents or her parents ever resided in this country. [Hinsdale, 22 Dec 1883; admitted 17 Jan 1884]

[66] 194. Lottie Thomas, Stoddard, American, born in Colebrook, NH and is 42 years old. Resided in C nearly 17 years, and in Nashua about 22 years, and in Stoddard about 4 years. Married Mark Smith of Nashua in 1860 and lived with him about eight years when said Smith obtained a divorce from her, and in 1874 she married Joseph Thomas of New Haven, CT with whom she lived about six months and then he returned to New Haven where he now resides. Has children, but no minor children. [Stoddard, 5-20 Mar 1884; admitted Apr T 1884]

195. John Algat Turnquest, Keene, Swede, born in Sweden 17 years old. Has resided in Keene the last nine months. Has been in this country about one year. Parents never resided in this country. Father's name is John, resides in Stockholm. Wants work, asks for relief only until he can get work. Gave him work at J. B. Abbott until a place was secured for him at Barton Aldrich's in Westmoreland. He is smart, but not truthful and trustworthy. {1885} Remained at Mr. A's only a part of the season, when he left and his whereabouts are now unknown. [Keene, 5 Jan 1884; admitted Apr T 1884]

196. Eliza V. Vigar, Jaffrey, French (?), born in Plattsburg, NY, 48 years old last April. Married Chas. Vigar in Montreal, Canada. Husband still resides there. Has three children: Lizzie, born 12 Jun 1872; Georgia A., born 13 Oct 1876; and

---

[23] Possibly Huddersfield.

Cheshire County Paupers
1885-1900

John, b. 24 Mar 1881. Has resided in Jaffrey only nine months. [Jaffrey, 21 Jan 1884; admitted 1 Feb 1884]

[67] 197. Jonas Wight, Keene, American, born in Dublin, 61 years old. Married and has one minor child. Names: wife, Lucretia A., age 43; child, Mabel, age 8 years. Has always resided in Dublin and Harrisville until he came to Keene 8 years ago. {1885} Gone from Keene. Wife sustains a bad character. Since the date of the affidavit she has given birth to a pair of illegitimate twins. [Keene, 10 Nov 1883; admitted Apr T 1884]

198. Seth Withington, Chesterfield, American. Has resided in Chesterfield since 1 Jan 1870 to date, is seventy years of age. By reason of poor health is obliged to apply for relief. {Admitted to the Almshouse 7 Dec 1883; discharged 24 Apr 1884, and readmitted 25 Dec 1884. Died 26 Jul 1885.} [Chesterfield, 26 Nov 1883; admitted 7 Dec 1883]

199. Henry Clay Allen, Fitzwilliam, American, born in Fitzwilliam 12 Nov 1829, and is now 53 years old. Married and has two children. His wife died 27 Apr 1864. Has lived in various places in New England and NY since 1 Jan 1870. Children, both of age; one married, neither able to render any relief. His father died in Troy in 1871, aged 78 years. Calls for relief by reason of sickness. [Fitzwilliam, 17 Sep 1883; admitted 12 Oct 1883; escaped 16 Oct 1886]

[68] 200. Isabella C. Allen, Jaffrey, American, born in Reading, MA. Has resided in Jaffrey and Troy for more than 20 years. She is the daughter of John A. Allen. Records do not show that any relief was rendered. The case was probably withdrawn. [Jaffrey, 4 Sep 1883; admitted 16 Oct 1883]

201. Perrin Applin, Marlow, American. Has resided in Marlow since 1850, is 80 years old. Married to his last wife in _____.

Cheshire County Paupers
1885-1900

She died in 1869. Has been supported by the town of Marlow since 1872. Becomes a county charge under the new pauper law of 1883. {1885} Admitted to the Almshouse 2 Nov 1884. Died 12 Jun 1885. Body removed to Marlow for burial. [Marlow, 19 Oct 1883; admitted Oct T 1883]

202. Mary M. Baker, Winchester, American, born in Winchester and has always resided there, age 47 years. Lives with her brother Chas. S. Baker. She is feeble in body and mind, and not capable of caring for herself or earning her living. Her parents are living but aged and dependent upon their son Chas. S. She has been aided by the town every year since 1870. [Winchester, 1 Nov 1883; admitted Nov 1883]

[69] 203. Pheba Bean, Marlborough, French, born in Corvensville, PQ, age 45. Came to Marlborough in 1883. Husband died in Jun 1882. Has five children, viz: Pheba, 22 years; Frank, 16 years; Peter, 13 years; Charles, 11 years; and Adelia, 5 years. [Marlborough, 28 Sep 1883; admitted 5 Oct 1883]

204. Barney Burns, Keene, Irish, found dead in the Police Station. Never resided in Keene so far as known by City Marshal who has resided in said city more than thirty years. [Keene, 26 Oct 1883]

205. Frank Carr, Marlborough, born in England, 29 years old. Came to America about 19 years ago. Has resided in Warren most of the time since he came to this country. [Marlborough, 11 Sep 1883; admitted Oct T 1883]

[70] 206. Bridget Carey, Keene, Irish, resided in Keene for 23 years last past, age, 60 years. Widow; husband died about ten years ago. One child, Michael, age 25 years. He does not work much and therefore cannot aid his mother but very little. [Keene, 29 Sep 1883; admitted 12 Oct 1883]

Cheshire County Paupers
1885-1900

207. Albert R. Corey, Gilsum, American. Has resided in Gilsum since 1866. Married to Sarah Jane McCoy in 1869. Her age is 42 years. One child 13 years old. Wife has been insane and was in the Hospital at Concord for treatment for several months in 1883 or 1884. He deserted his wife about the time she was committed to the hospital. His whereabouts are unknown. {Apr T 1885} Child died a year or more ago. Sarah Jane Corey died 11 Oct 1886. [Gilsum, 18 May 1883; admitted 5 Oct 1883]

208. Ann Crabb, Winchester, Irish, born in Ireland. Came to America about 25 years ago. 45 years old. Married, husband's name William Crabb. Has never resided in any town in NH but W. Mr. C left his family since three weeks ago and went, as he told his children in search of work, and has not been heard from since. Three children, viz: Willie, 10 years; George, 7 years; and Michael, 12 years. Has no means of support except by her own labor, is at work at this time in one of the mills at Ashuelot at 75 cents per day. [Winchester, 8 Oct 1883; admitted Oct T 1883]

[71] 209. Edgar E. Decamp, Walpole, father of Charles Decamp, a minor who was drowned in the Connecticut River 12 Sep 1883 and buried at the expense of the town. Came to Walpole to reside in 1882. Applies on account of the expenses incurred for the burial of his son. [Walpole, 10 Oct 1883; admitted 22 Oct 1883]

210. William Duplex, Rindge, French, born in Keene, 34 years old. Have resided, he says, in Jaffrey and Rindge since 1870; for the last 8 years in Rindge. Married; wife's name Selina LaClair, age 23 years. Four children, viz: Mary Jane, 7 years; Sophia, 5 years; Freddie, 4 years; and William, 1 year. His

Cheshire County Paupers
1885-1900

father moved about 1874 from Jaffrey to CT. [Rindge, 24 Jul 1883; admitted 22 Oct 1883]

211. Elvira Douglass, Marlborough, American, born in Westmoreland, 29 Apr 1818, and resided there until 1840; to Marlborough to live about 1871 and have resided here since. Widow, husband died during the War, 12 May 1864. Rec'd a pension of $96 per year which she thinks is not sufficient to support her. Lives with her sister's family, Mrs. Haradon.[24] Applies for no relief only when she is unable to work. [Marlborough, 20 Oct 1883; admitted]

[72] 212. Peter Duprey, Harrisville, French, born in Canada, age 42 years. Married; seven children, viz: Delia, 12 years; Emery, 10 years; George, 8 years; John, 6 years, William, 4 years; Ella, 2 years; and Meddie, 8 months. Came to America about twenty years ago. Came to Harrisville to live in May 1883. Wife is in very poor health, unable to work, and much of the time he has to stay at home to take care of the children and his wife. He has the reputation of being a hard working man. [Harrisville, 28 Sep 1883; admitted 5 Oct 1883]

213. Dennis Enwright, Troy, Irish, born in Ireland, 45 years old. Has resided in Troy since about 1877. Married Ellen Hill in 1862. She was born in Ireland, is 47 years old. She is insane, and therefore he is obliged to call for relief. Overseers of the poor in Troy instructed to remove Mrs. E to the NH Asylum for the Insane 29 May 1883. {1884} Died 2 Oct and her body was taken to Troy for burial. [Troy, 8 Oct 1883; admitted Oct T 1883]

---

[24] See #263, 373, 651 and 686 for other persons staying with Mrs. Lucinda Haradon.

Cheshire County Paupers
1885-1900

214. Rufus D. Field,[25] Winchester, American, born in Winchester 15 Feb 1851. Went from home when he was about 12 years of age. Married Susan E. Robbins 26 Nov 1873, since which time he has resided in Winchester and Chesterfield. Her father's name is Daniel E. Robbins. He has resided in Chesterfield for many years. She will be 26 years old, the 21st of Nov 1883. She deserted her husband and does not now live with him. Has three children, viz: Charles E., 9 years; Frank H., 7 years; and Frederick R., 5 years. Charles E. was admitted to Almshouse 25 Aug 1884. Frank H. lived with Mr. Fullam of Winchester, and Frederick R. was taken to the Home for Little Wanderers, Boston. He is quite smart but the other two are below par. [Winchester, 22 Oct 1883; admitted Oct T 1883]

[73] 215. Mary Fisher, Hinsdale, American, taken from the Almshouse, Brattleboro, VT by Jos. E. Randall to keep until 18 years old; will be eighteen 15th of Nov 1883. She was an illegitimate child, and her mother now resides in Brattleboro, VT. Application for relief is made to the town by reason that she is pregnant and expects to be confined in Jul next. She alleges who the father is, made complaint against him. Recovered $200 for the support of the child. He subsequently married the girl after having got her into trouble the second time. [Hinsdale, 29 May 1883; admitted Oct T 1883]

216. Mahala Girard, Keene, French, 27 years old. Married, husband's name is Charles, age 28 years. Two children, viz: George Albert, aged 6 years and Frank Joseph, aged 3 years. Mrs. G's parents have resided in Keene for several years. Her father's name is Frank Gero. Her husband has recently left her, and she does not know where he is. Being very destitute and without means to earn a support for herself and children, she

---

[25] See #1161. See also #432 and 1329.

has been forced to call for relief. [Keene, 1 Aug 1883; admitted Oct T 1883]

217. Emma J. Graves, Westmoreland, American. Has resided in said Westmoreland more than 15 years. Age 32 years. Her parents both died prior to 1872. She is living with a family by the name of Jas. G. Greeley in W and the county pays for her board. [Westmoreland, 13 Oct 1883; admitted Oct T 1883]

[74] 218. Henry Hall, Westmoreland, American, born in Westmoreland, 81 years of age, unmarried. Has always resided in Westmoreland. Has been supported by the town since 1878. Has been married, but his wife is dead. [Westmoreland, 16 Oct 1883; admitted 17 Oct 1883]

219. Sally Hemmingway, Jaffrey, American, 96 years of age, widow. Husband Luther Hemmingway died in 1872. She was married to Mr. H in 1867. She will be 97 in Jan next. [Jaffrey, 15 Oct 1883; admitted 17 Oct 1883]

220. Edwin Jackson, Chesterfield, American, about 38 years of age, single. Has a residence in Montgomery, VT and a mother and brother residing in Richford, VT, they having recently moved from Montgomery. Has recently been at work for J. M. White of Chesterfield. Is insane. Has been in the Asylum at Brattleboro, at two different times under treatment. Committed to the Almshouse, the selectmen of Montgomery, VT notified. Committed to the Asylum at Brattleboro on request of selectmen of M to whom a bill of costs was sent and by them paid. [Chesterfield, 31 Aug 1883; admitted Oct T 1883]

[75] 221. Mary Jones, Troy, Irish, born in Ireland, 39 years of age. Married, husband's name is Edward, age 34 years. Resided in Troy from 1874 or 1875 to 1878 or 1879; then in Akron, OH, and since 1883 (April) have resided in Troy. Her

*Cheshire County Paupers
1885-1900*

husband deserted her and neglects to aid in her and the children's support. Has four children by Jones, viz: Willie, age 10 years; Mary, age 9; Ella, age 4; and Lizzie, age 2. She is sick with consumption and under a physician and nurse's care. Sent Kate Ryan from the Almshouse to take care of her. She died 188__. Children are admitted to the Almshouse 17 Mar 1884; the 3 oldest discharged 9 Apr 1884, the youngest 4 Jul 1884[26].

222. George M. Kingsley, Fitzwilliam, American, born in Colton, St. Lawrence Co., NY, age 39 years. Came from NY state to Fitzwilliam in 1882. Married, has a wife and 5 children living. My children's names are as follows: Berton, age 13; Eltha E., age 11 years; Ida, age 4; Ella, age 2; and Mabel, age 5 mos. Elthea E. and Ella have been very sick with typhoid fever. Mr. K. has fits and can work only part of the time. Mrs. K is nearly worn out taking care of the children during their sickness. [Fitzwilliam, 3 Oct 1883; admitted 12 Oct 1883]

223. Peter Louzen, Marlborough, French, born in Culberth, PQ 20 Apr 1851. Parents names, Albert and Mary. Married Agnes Wilcox in 1869. Came to M in 1879. Five children, the oldest 13 years and the youngest one year. [Marlborough, 3 Dec 1883; admitted 13 Feb 1884]

[76] 224. Luther Lawrence, Winchester, American, age __. Insane, committed to the Asylum in 1871 and has been supported by the town to the present time. Under the recent pauper law he becomes a county charge. Amos Lawrence of Richmond is a brother. Has several children. Been married twice. Mrs. Gunn of Keene was his last wife. {1885} She obtained a divorce and married Gunn and later obtained a divorce from Gunn and married Abbott Wright of Keene.

---

[26] No date of application or admittance given.

Cheshire County Paupers
1885-1900

{1886}Lawrence died at the Asylum 6 Jan 1886. Body removed to Westport for burial. [Winchester, 22 Oct 1883; admitted Oct T 1883]

225. Edward F. McGravey, Rindge, Irish-American, born in Taunton, MA 16 Apr 1865. Father came from Ireland. His name is Peter. His (Edward's) mother died 9 Jun 1875. Edward was sent to the State Primary School at Monson in August 1877 and remained there until 1880 when he came to Rindge. His father now resides either in Taunton or Milford, MA. Applies for relief by reason of inability to earn his support at this time. [Rindge, 11 May 1883; admitted 22 Oct 1883]

226. Joseph Palladee,[27] Marlborough, French, born in St. Hison, PQ, 57 years old, the 15th day of Dec last. Married, name of wife Louisa, age 55 years. Have no children. Wife able to earn her support, but cannot her own and husband's. He is shiftless and lazy. Goes to Troy to live. From Troy he was assisted to friends in MA, who he thought might take him in, but he remained only a short time. On his return he was sent to the Farm. {See #101} His wife resides in Marlborough and supports herself. [Marlborough, 8 Aug 1883; admitted 5 Oct 1883]

[77] 227. Margaret Rafferty, Winchester, Irish, born in Ireland. Came to W two years ago last April, age 40 years. Widow; husband died nine years ago. Four children: a daughter residing in Brooklyn, NY, 22 years old, and a daughter in Keene 21 years old, and two, 13 and 10 years old residing with her in Winchester. The one residing in Brooklyn is married. Since the death of her husband she has been entirely dependent upon her daily earnings for support. She is now sick and unable

---

[27] Labeled "old affidavit." See also #1391, page 466.

Cheshire County Paupers
1885-1900

to work and therefore dependent and obliged to call for relief. [Winchester, 21 Sep 1883; admitted Oct T 1883]

228. Johannah Sheehan, Keene, Irish, born in Ireland and came to this country in 1871. Was married in 1871 to Patrick Sheehan. He died in 1880. Always lived in Keene since landing in this country. Four children, viz: Nellie, age 10; Bessy, 8 years; Maggie, 6 years; and Timothy, 2 years. [Keene, 1 Jun 1883; admitted Oct T 1883]

229. Abner Stanley, Jaffrey, American, 81 years old last April. Since 1 Jan 1870 have lived in Winchendon, MA and Fitzwilliam, NH 5 years, and then came to Jaffrey and has since resided there. Has been assisted by the town of Troy, April 1883, where he had gained a settlement prior to 1870. [Jaffrey, 15 Oct 1883; admitted 17 Oct 1883]

[78] 230. Horace R. Thurston, Charlestown, NH, born in Deerfield, MA, 60 years old. Moved to Jaffrey from Claremont 20 Dec 1882 and remained there until 8 Mar 1883, when he was assisted by the selectmen of said Jaffrey to move to Charlestown with his family, a wife and one son. The next day after arriving at Charlestown he applied for relief. Aid was rendered and a claim made against Cheshire Co. to pay the cost of the same. Cheshire Co. being liable by reason of the aid furnished to transport him into Sullivan Co. {See affidavit dated 9 Mar 1883} [Jaffrey]

231. Bertie L. Willard, Winchester, American, born in Hinsdale, 23 Apr 1874. His father George Willard died in NY in 1880. His mother Ella Phelps Willard died in Winchester in 1878. She was the daughter of Maria Clark of Winchester. Bertie is now living in the family of Albert Putnam in Winchester. He is a cripple and is obliged to use a crutch. The town of Winchester had been paying $1.50 per week for his

Cheshire County Paupers
1885-1900

support since Apr 1882. [Winchester, 23 Oct 1883; admitted Oct T 1883]

232. William Welch, Winchester, American, born in Hinsdale 27 Apr 1811. Has resided in Orange, MA most of the time since 1869, where he has a wife, two sons and a daughter residing, but not of sufficient ability to support him. Has been in W only a few days. Applies for admission to our Almshouse. {Admitted to Ch. Co. Almshouse 25 Apr 1883; discharged 18 Jun 1883. Readmitted 5 Sep 1884; discharged 5 May 1885.} [Winchester, 24 Apr 1883; admitted Apr T 1883]

[79] 233. Susan A. Nash, Walpole, American, born in Sullivan, NH and is twenty four years old. Married Chauncey W. Nash when I was sixteen years old. Has resided in Walpole most of the time since her marriage. Has three children, viz: Alice A., born 22 Apr 1874; Henry H., born 27 Jan 1876; and Oscar W., born 25 Oct 1877. All born in Walpole. My father was Dauphin Spauldin, 2d of Sullivan. He moved to Keene about 1860. Was in the War of 1861 and died in the Service. My mother's name is Susan R. She married Chas. Derby of Westmoreland, some 14 years ago, and is now residing with her husband in Westmoreland. C. W. Nash has deserted his family and neglects to support them and his whereabouts at the present time is unknown. Susan A. Nash and two of her children, Alice A. and Henry H. were admitted to the Almshouse 4 Oct 1881. Alice A. was sent to the Home for Little Wanderers, Boston 7 Nov 1881 and her mother was discharged and went to reside with her mother, where she was confined. {She was readmitted 7 Aug 1882 and discharged 23 Aug 1882. Her babe, now about 2 years old was placed in a family by the name of Brown in East Westmoreland. Good reports are rec'd concerning Alice and her home. Mrs. N has acted badly, has given birth to a child since she was discharged from the Almshouse in 1882.

Cheshire County Paupers
1885-1900

{Oscar W. never came to the custody of the courts} [Walpole, 1881; admitted 1881]

235[28]. Julia A. Emerson, Keene, American, born in New Ipswich, NH, age 72 years. Her parents died when she was quite young. Was married to Chauncey W. Emerson in 1833. Had two children: the oldest died young, the other married a man by the name of Bristol and resides in Albany, NY. She is an invalid. Mr. Emerson died in Albany, NY in 1876 leaving her, his wife no means of support. Has lived in Mr. Pond's family in Keene for some time past, they being kin to her. {1885} Mrs. Emerson died at the Co. Farm where she was admitted 12 Nov 1879, on 10 May 1885, age 78. Her body was forwarded to her daughter in Albany, NY. [Keene, 27 Sep 1879; admitted Oct T 1880]

[80] 237. William Weeks, Winchester, American, born in Warwick, MA in 1807. Since 1870 have resided in Hinsdale five years and Saratoga, NY two or three years and in Winchester since 1880. Has two children living, aged 36 and 39 years. {1884} His sister aids in his support to avoid having him taken to the Almshouse. Lives with Lyman H. Fisher. Died in Winchester. [Winchester, 1 Nov 1882; admitted 1 Dec 1882]

238. Alivia S. Whitney, Jaffrey, American, 67 years old last June. Was married to John S. Whitney in 1865, came to Jaffrey to reside in 1871 and has since resided there. [Jaffrey, 12 Apr 1882; admitted Apr T 1882]

239. James Williams, Alstead, American, born in Pembroke, 55 years old. Has been engaged in giving concerts ever since he

---

[28] The last entry took up the space allotted for #234. Following this entry, there is no #236.

was large enough to travel, but is unable to follow the business longer applies for admission to the Co. Almshouse. Admitted 7 Feb 1883 and discharged 28 Apr 1883. [Alstead, 6 Feb 1883; admitted 24 Feb 1883]

[81] 240. James A. Troller, Walpole, Irish, born in Ireland. Came to VT in 1879. Has resided in Walpole most of the time since. Is 40 years old. Married Maggie Armstrong in Ireland. Five children, viz: William J., age 9; James A., age 7; and Maggie, age 2. The other two children are in Ireland with their grandparents. Had the misfortune to break his leg on the 5th of June last, and hence, calls for relief, having no means to support his family. [Walpole, 15 Sep 1882; admitted Oct T 1882]

241. Carrie Truax, Hinsdale, born in Jay, NY, 22 years old. Married, husband has recently left her. Has one child living, age 3 years. Her or her husband's parents never resided in NH. Her father resides Schrom Rivers, NY. Wants temporary relief.[29]

242. Rose Scott, Marlborough, American, born in Bangor, ME, age 37 years. Has two children, viz: Alice B., age 15 and Francis A., age 4. Husband died 10 Apr 1879. Was recently burnt out; am now on my way to friends in South Vernon, VT. The fire left me destitute. {Ordered the overseers to aid her if thought worthy.} [Marlborough, Feb1883; admitted Feb 1883]

[82] 243. Orinda Beckwith Metcalf, Gilsum, American, age 72 years. Married Richard Kimball Metcalf in 1830. Divorced from him in 1845 or 1846. Had three sons. The youngest when last heard from was in Wisconsin. His age is 43 years. Since she was divorced from her husband she has made it her home

---

[29] No date of application or admittance.

Cheshire County Paupers
1885-1900

with Joseph M. Chapin[30] of Gilsum. [Gilsum; admitted Oct 1881]

244. Oliver Chapin Beckwith, American, age 66; resided with Joseph M. Chapin. Parents both died in Alstead. Weak in body and mind. {Died 30 Sep 1889.} [Gilsum; admitted Oct 1881]

245. William Bowers, Troy, English, born in London, England, age 40 years. Came to T about 1880 and has resided there since. [Troy, 2 Mar 1883; admitted 9 Apr 1883]

[83] 246. Chas. Brown, Swanzey, French, born in Canada, age 33 years. Came into NH about twelve years ago. Married about five years ago; two children: Joseph H., age 4, and Rosa A., 1 ½ years. Neither of his parents ever resided in NH. His wife is 22 years of age. Her maiden name____. She was born in Orange, MA. [Swanzey, 6 Feb 1883; admitted Apr T, 1883]

247. Lucius Bates, Keene, American, b. in West Chesterfield, MA. Has resided in NH about 12 years. Was at Westport, Swanzey ten years. Parents never resided in this state. Married to Julia M., age 28. Children: Edwin J., age 8; Archie B., age 6; and Chas. A., age 1. Mrs. B's parents, Andrew J. and Rosina A. Crown, have resided in Keene some 3 or 4 years; in no other place in this state. [Keene, 24 Oct 1882; admitted Oct T 1882]

248. Richard C. Blake, Keene, American, age 77 years; resided in Keene since 1860. Never married. Was temporarily at Westmoreland when he was taken sick and forced to apply for aid. {1883} Fell or was thrown from a wagon and broke his thigh, and has been confined to the bed since at Mr. Wyman's

---

[30] In the original his name was given as "Joseph M. Chapen" in Orinda's affidavit and "Joseph B. Capin" in Oliver Beckwith's (#244). The 1880 census in Gilsum shows him as Chapin.

house in the west part of Keene. [Keene, Westmoreland; admitted Jul 1882.]

[84] 249. Ellen Bushey, Winchester, born in Bristol, VT where she resided until she moved to W in 1882. Her father is dead and her mother never resided in NH. Age 17 years, never married. Has one child, an infant name Arthur Hill (?). Alleges that Arthur Hill of Bristol, VT is the father of her child, a boy born the 29 Nov 1882. Is residing with her sister, Mrs. Barrus. Is desirous to return to her mother in Bristol, VT, and wants means to pay the cost of her confinement and expenses to Bristol. The requested aid furnished. [Winchester, 9 Dec 1882; admitted 2 Feb 1883]

250. Harriet L. Bartlett, Hinsdale, formerly resided in Cornish and Claremont. Has resided in various places in Cheshire County since 1874 or 5. Married, husband Chas. C., died in Hinsdale 9 Jan 1881, where we came to live in Apr 1879, 53 years old. Has two children, viz: Edgar C., age 18 years and David N., age 15 years. Both sick with malarial typhoid fever, and hence is obliged to call for aid. Before her husband died he purchased a place in Hinsdale for $1800 and only $575 of the amount has ever been paid. The place is mortgaged and could not be sold at this time for enough to the claim upon the place. [Hinsdale, 2 Jan 1883; admitted 5 Jan 1883]

251. Ellen Crotto, Marlborough, French, born in Granby, Canada East, 7 Sep 1867, and resided in said Granby until May 1882 when she came to Marlborough. Her father Alfred Crotto died in Grand Isle, VT about 1867, and her mother Josephine now resides in Granby, PQ. [Marlborough, 16 Oct 1882; admitted Oct T 1882]

[85] 252. Whitney Barrett, Hinsdale, American, born in Hinsdale, age ___ years, father of Charles Barrett, who died 19

Cheshire County Paupers
1885-1900

Sep 1882, and whose age is about 20 years. Application is made for assistance in paying the funeral expenses of Charles, the father being too poor to pay the same. [Hinsdale, 6 Oct 1882; admitted Oct T 1882]

253. Lilla J. Bingham, Stoddard, American, born in Gilsum, 22 years of age. Married in Jun 1875 to Joseph S. Bingham. Has resided in Stoddard and Gilsum to date. Husband has left her and therefore she is forced to call for aid. Three children, viz: Gracie M., age 6; Miles J., age 4; and George A., age 6 months. Mother's name Ellen M. Brown; father's name Rodney J. Mrs. B is a daughter of Osman McCoy of Gilsum. Her husband, Joseph S. is 31 years old and a son of Chas. W. Bingham, who has resided in G since 1860. [Stoddard, 22 Apr 1882; admitted Apr T 1882]

254. William H. Butterfield, Rindge, American, born in Peterborough, age 78 years, widower. Has resided in Ashburnham and Rindge since 1 Jan 1870. Wife died in Apr 1854. [Rindge, 20 Dec 1882; admitted 6 Mar 1883]

[86] 255. Mary Carter, Hinsdale, America. Has always resided in the NE states, age 42 years. Husband left her about four months ago and she does not know where he is. Has seven children under 21 years of age, viz: Ezra, age 13; Joseph, age 11; Willie, age 9; Olive, age 8; John, age 5; Ellen, age 3; and Jennie, age 7 months. Has been married about 22 years. My husband is 42 years old. [Hinsdale, 7 Jan 1882; admitted Apr T 1882]

256. Mary Cahill, Walpole, makes an affidavit that John Cahill and John Ahern were both natives of Ireland and came direct to their place in April last and went to work in the Paper Mill and that on the 6th day of August last, both were drowned in the Connecticut River, neither were married and neither possessed

Cheshire County Paupers
1885-1900

property sufficient to pay the expenses of burial. Cahill was 18 years old and Ahern 17 years. [Walpole; allowed the cost of burial expenses]

257. Ellen Costine, Walpole, Irish, born in Ireland, age 27 years. Single, parents never resided in this country. Father died about 16 years ago; mother still living, resides in Ireland. She came to America about 3 ½ years ago. About fourteen weeks ago she was thrown from a wagon and broke her leg and since has not been able to perform any manual labor. Has one brother residing in this country. [Walpole, 22 Oct 1882; admitted Oct T 1882]

[87] 258. Lawrence Currier, Hinsdale, French, born in Qubeck(sic), Canada, about 19 years old. Parents both dead; father died three years ago last July in Rutland, VT, a week before Lawrence came to H. He is single, partially blind and unable to earn his support. [Hinsdale, 19 Feb 1883; admitted 24 Feb 1883]

259. Josannah H. Chipman, Keene, American, age 39 years, married. Husband Edward S. is an agent for the Warner File Works, is 50 years old. Has gone at this time to Holyoke. Have resided in Cheshire County nearly 20 years. Four children, viz: Lulu May, age 13; Grant E., age 11; Daisy, age 3 years; and Bertie, age 9. Applies for aid to move to Holyoke where husband is at work, but has not means to pay expenses of moving his family. [Keene, 31 Jan 1883; admitted 2 Feb 1883]

260. Edward Comer, Keene, Irish, born in Ireland, age 32 years. Came to America in 1866. Has resided in Keene in all about 5 years. Parents never resided in this country. Wants means to go to St. Louis, Missouri, where he claims to have friends. Claims for transportation rejected. [Keene, 24 Oct 1882]

Cheshire County Paupers
1885-1900

[88] 261. Mary Carr, Marlborough, born in Lowell, MA, age 29 years, the 15th of last August. Parents never resided in this state. [Marlborough, 10 Sep 1883; admitted Oct T 1883]

262. Margarette Delphy, Winchester, French, born in Canada, 78 years old. Came to the United States about seventeen years ago. Has been married but her husband is dead; died before she came to the US. Has son Joseph Delphy with whom she resides. [Winchester, 2 Jan 1883; admitted 5 Jan 1883]

263. Edwin Doolittle, Winchester, American, born in St. Johnsbury, VT in 1809. Married, wife living, age ____ years. Since 1870 he has resided in Keene three or four years in Hinsdale two years, and in Brattleboro, VT from 1875 to 19 Oct 1882, when he was aided by the overseers of the poor of Brattleboro to move to his nephew's in Winchester. He states that he received $25 to assist him to move. Was at the Poor Farm in B for sometime before he came to W. Wife has had a slight shock. Supported at Harry Eames' in Swanzey for a time, then went to live with the Haradon's[31] in Marlborough. {1886} Edwin Doolittle died, Tuesday, 26 Jan 1886. [Winchester, 6 Dec 1882; admitted 3 Mar 1883]

[89] 264. Joseph Drake, Hinsdale, b. in VT, age 20 years, single. Father: Charles, somewhere in VT, don't know where. He was in Castleton, VT, the last I knew anything about him. He has since gone from there. My mother never resided in NH. [Hinsdale, 24 Nov 1882; admitted 11 Dec 1882]

265. Kate Donovan, Keene, Irish, born in Ireland, age 45 years. Married John Donovan in Ireland. Came to this country in

---

[31] For other people who stayed with the Haradons, see #211, 373, 651 and 686.

Cheshire County Paupers
1885-1900

1871. Has resided in Keene since that time. Three children, viz:[32] Her husband was killed on the railroad 27 Oct 1882. My or his parents never lived in this country. [Keene, 20 Dec 1882; admitted 7 Apr 1883]

266. Henry Dubois, Winchester, French, born in Canada, age 27 years. Married and has one infant child. Came to Winchester about six weeks ago. Parents never lived in the United States. [Winchester, 7 Sep 1882; admitted 6 Oct 1882]

[90] 267. Oscar T. Frink, Chesterfield, American, age 46 years. Has resided in Chesterfield since 1870 with the exception of one year in Keene. Has been married and has two sons, but his wife does not reside with him, having obtained a divorce. She resides in Keene with her two sons, viz: Eddie O., age 14, and Westley L., age 12. Served in the late civil war and was honorably discharged. [Chesterfield, 20 Sep 1882; admitted 6 Oct 1882]

268. John Foley, Keene, Irish, age 19, born in this country but his parents were both born in Ireland. Has always resided in Putney, VT. Came to Keene to attend Fireman's Muster, and when starting for home while standing on the platform of the car, he lost his balance and fell between the cars, and the trucks passed over his hands and both had to be amputated. His folks are poor and reside in Putney, and hence he applies for aid to pay his board, etc. [Keene, 19 Sep 1882; admitted Oct T 1882]

269. Elvira Allen, Westmoreland, American, born in Surry, 20 Mar 1815, age 67 years. Was never married. Resided in Westmoreland from 1860 to 1874 and then in Burlington, VT 3 ½ years, then in Westmoreland where I still live. Her father

---

[32] No children listed in original.

Cheshire County Paupers
1885-1900

David Allen died in 1855. Is now residing with her brother-in-law Henry B. Hall. Has two brothers, Noah and David, residing in Burlington, VT, and two sisters in the north part of Keene. {Admitted to Almshouse 20 Jan 1883 and discharged 6 Jun 1884. 30 Jan 1886 is living with H. B. Hall, Westmoreland.} [Westmoreland, 25 Dec 1882; admitted 2 Feb 1883]

[91] 270. George Geisick, Harrisville, German, born in Germany, age 35 years. Came to America nine or ten years ago. Never resided in NH until he came to work upon the Manchester & Keene RR. Froze his feet in some way. Parents never resided in this country. Applies for relief until he is able to work. [Harrisville, 14 Mar 1883]

271. George Grenier, Winchester, French, came from Canada. Married; wife died in Aug 1881. Very poor, no means to pay bills incurred on account of sickness and death of wife. [Winchester, 14 Apr 1882; admitted Apr T 1882]

272. Emily T. Howe, Jaffrey, American, 85 years old in Feb last. Married Enoch F. Howe in 1835. Resided in Aurilens, MI twenty-three years and in Lansing, MI, 18 years. She came to Jaffrey in 1881. Her husband is at Aurilens, MI and dependent upon charity. Was in good circumstances at one time, but Mr. H became very intemperate; want and dependency followed. She is blind or nearly so. John M. Farnum of Keene is a nephew and Mrs. Stephen L. Randall, a niece. She other relatives in Jaffrey.[33] {noted later} Admitted to the Almshouse 20 Jun 1884. [Jaffrey, 22 Sep 1882. Admitted Oct T 1882]

[92] 273. Mary F. Howe, Jaffrey, American, born in NY and always resided there prior to 1881, age 40 years. Married; name

---

[33] Transcribed as written in the original.

Cheshire County Paupers
1885-1900

of husband Eliakim Howe, age 41 years in July last. He was born in NY and never lived in this state before we came to Jaffrey in 1881. He is now insane and at the Asylum at Concord. They have two children: Thadie is 16 years, and Lottie, 13 years old. {23 Aug 1889} Application for help renewed. At Nathan B. Rowe's, Swanzey. [Jaffrey, 21 Oct 1882; admitted Oct T 1882]

274. Lucy D. Sawtell, Jaffrey, American, age 79 years last Mar. Widow; husband died 1 Mar 1859. [Jaffrey, 11 Jul 1882; admitted Oct T 1882]

275. Roxanna Holmes, Winchester, American, born in MA, 72 years old. Was married to Alvin Holmes of Middlefield, MA and died in Michigan about two years ago.[34] Neither ever resided in NH until she came to Winchester to visit her daughter Matilda J. Lewis the 27 of Apr last and where she was taken sick with a fever. Mrs. Lewis applies for relief in taking care of her mother, she being unable to support her without assistance. [Winchester, 6 Jun 1882; admitted 7 Jul 1882]

[93] 276. Mary Hammond, Keene, born in VT, age 29 years. Married Frank Hammond in 1867. He deserted her in 1881. They came to Keene to live in 1869 and have since resided here. They have four children, aged respectively 14-10-8 and 5 years. She is at her mother's with one child. Her maiden name was Mary Oliver and her father died in 1857, and in 1879 her mother married Charles Boovier. [Keene, 3 Mar 1882; admitted 10 Mar 1882]

---

[34] Transcribed as written in the original. Presumably Alvin died in Michigan.

Cheshire County Paupers
1885-1900

277. Geo. E. Keizer, Sullivan, born in Nova Scotia, age 23 years. Parents never resided in NH. [Sullivan, 19 Mar 1883; admitted 3 Apr 1883]

278. Patrick O'Keefe, Keene, Irish, born in Ashburnham, 19 years of age. Has resided with Mary A. Ryan since he was five years old. His father is residing in Fitchburg, MA and is very poor. Application is made for assistance by Mrs. Ryan by reason of his sickness. [Keene, 17 Sep 1881; admitted Oct T 1881]

[94] 279. Caroline King, Hinsdale, German, born in Germany, 61 years of age. Widow of T. King who died in Hinsdale 25 Jan 1882. Came to Hinsdale in 1881. [Hinsdale, 24 Feb 1882; admitted Apr T 1882]

280. Isaac Jolly, Keene, French decent (*sic*), born in Plattsburg, NY, 41 years old. Has lived a greater part of his life in MA. Has lived only a short time in Cheshire County since 1870. Married; his wife is 31 years of age. Her parents never lived in this country. Call for aid by reason of sickness. [Keene, 1 Feb 1883; admitted 2 Mar 1883]

281. Sarah A. Kelton, Winchester, American, adopted daughter of Wheaton and Mary Ann Kelton. Has lived with them since she was a year old. Her adopted parents were married in 1826. Mrs. K was 77 years old, the 27 Nov 1882. [Winchester, 4 Apr 1883; admitted Apr T 1883]

[95] 282. John LaBounty, Hinsdale, French, born in Keysville, NY, 38 years old 12 Apr 1882. Came to Hinsdale about nine years ago, never resided in any other town in NH. Has married 12 years ago last Oct. Seven children, viz: Denie, 11 years; Georgianna, 8 years; Matilda, 6 years; Rosana, 4 years; Wilford, 3 years; Mary Louisa, 1 year; and Agnes, 2 months. His father

Cheshire County Paupers
1885-1900

Peter LaBounty has been assisted by the county. [Hinsdale, 25 Aug 1882; admitted 1 Sep 1882]

283. Tyler Lincoln, Westmoreland, American, born in Westmoreland, 77 years of age. Unmarried, a mason by trade. {noted later} Admitted to Almshouse 8 Dec 1882. Died 5 Mar 1884. [Westmoreland, 18 Nov 1882; admitted 1 Dec 1882]

284. Mary Livingston,[35] Walpole, American, born in Walpole and claims to be 96 years old, but is probably not so old. She is feeble mentally and physically. Unmarried. She had two illegitimate children, both dead: one died in the army, and by special act of Congress she draws a pension as a dependent mother, and it is her sole means of support. She has distant relatives residing in Walpole and Somerville, MA. {Admitted to the Almshouse 15 Dec 1882.} {Died 4 Oct 1885 and her body taken to Walpole for burial.} [Walpole, 30 Sep 1882; admitted 1 Dec 1882]

[96] 285. Joseph Mountainor, Keene, French, born Canada, age 30; came to NH in 1880 for the first time. Came to Keene in 1882. Married; wife's age 18; child, an infant. Our parents never resided in the United States. [Keene, 10 Mar 1883; admitted Apr term 1883]

286. Sarah T. Martin,[36] Hinsdale, American, born in Bath, NH, 67 years old. Widow; husband, Truman C., died in Bradford, VT about 3 years ago at the Poor Farm, where he had been about 14 years. He was born in Bradford. I have resided in Hinsdale all the the time since 1870. [Hinsdale, 24 Feb 1882; admitted Apr term 1882]

---

[35] See # 53, page 18.
[36] Original appears to be "Marlin," but according to the 1880 census for Hinsdale, it is "Martin." See also #724.

Cheshire County Paupers
1885-1900

287. Nellie A. Martin,[37] Keene, born in Norwich, VT where her parents now reside, 25 years old. Her own mother is dead, and her father is married again. Her parents have not resided in NH since 1860. Never married, applies for relief on account of sickness. [Keene, 29 Apr 1882; admitted 10 Mar 1882]

[97] 288. Ella L. Nickerson, Keene, American, born in Sutton, MA, 28 years old. Married Horace M. Nickerson, 15 Oct 1871 at Oxford, MA. Resided in Hinsdale about 6 years and Swanzey, two years, since 1870. Her husband died in Keene, 14 Dec 1882. Two children, viz: Sarah W., age 6 years; Willie F., age 4. Her husband was 49 years old. He was born in Rhode Island. [Keene, 29 Dec 1883; admitted Apr term 1883]

289. Charles Parker, Swanzey, American, born in Hardwick, MA 14 Aug 1814. Has always made Boston his home since he was 25 years old. Came to Swanzey only temporarily. Has been married and had three children, all dead. His mother died in Hinsdale, NH in 1871 and his father in 1872. They had resided in Hinsdale some 6 or 7 years. [Swanzey, 22 May 1882; admitted Apr term 1882]

290. Laura A. Pierce, Chesterfield, American; lived in Westmoreland and Chesterfield since 1860, age 42 years; never married. [Chesterfield, 3 Apr 1882; admitted Apr term 1883]

[98] 291. Patrick McManus, Harrisville, Irish, born in Ireland, 29 years old. Married, wife resides in Ireland. His parents never resided in this country. Is now sick and hence applies for relief.[38]

---

[37] Name appears to be "Marlin" in original, but the 1880 census for Hinsdale gives the name as "Martin."
[38] No date given for application or admittance.

*Cheshire County Paupers
1885-1900*

292. Arthur Proux, Marlborough, French, born in Canada, age 27 years. Never resided in NH until Nov 1881. Unmarried; father and mother never resided in this country. Unable at this time to provide for himself. [Marlborough, 22 Dec 1882; admitted 5 Jun 1883]

293. Joseph Powers, Winchester, English, born in England, age 52 years. Came to this country in 1875. Has usually resided in Boston in the winter and traveled about the country summers, working at his trade, repairing umbrellas. Called for relief by reason of sickness. [Winchester, 6 Oct 1882; admitted Oct term 1882]

[99] 294. Florence M. Perkins, Keene, American, born in South Royalton, VT, age 25 years. Father's name Horatio M. Perkins; her mother's name was Mary Ann. Her father died when she was 14 years old, and her mother when she was about 6 years old. Her parents never resided in NH. She is pregnant and if delivered alive will be an illegitimate child. She has made an affidavit in which she alleges by whom she is pregnant. Has had one or two illegitimate children. States that her father was supposed to have been murdered in Athol, MA. Admitted to the Almshouse 16 Jan 1883. {Discharged 16 Aug 1883, a place having been secured for her and her child, when she could work and earn her board and clothing. Sometime in the fall she married O. L. Nash of Swanzey and lived with him until sometime in January when she left him and came to Keene. From Keene was admitted to the Almshouse again, as Florence Nash 17 Jan 1884 and discharged 19 Sep 1884 to go to Haverhill, MA to work where later her child was taken and placed in the Orphan's Home in that city. Since she came back to Cheshire County and is residing with her husband.} [Keene, 15 Jan 1883; admitted 2 Feb 1883]

Cheshire County Paupers
1885-1900

295.[39]

296. Walter E. Porter, Hinsdale, born in Lyden, MA in Jul 1881. His mother died in Lyden, MA in Aug 1881 when Walter was about five years old. His father is French and claims to have been born in Middlebury, VT. He came to Hinsdale to live in Oct 1881. Walter was left with Mr. G. H. Frederick, his mother's brother. Sometime about the first of May 1882, Charles Porter, the father of Walter, went to Brattleboro to reside and since has refused to support his boy. Hence application is made by Mr. Frederick for aid to keep him. {Admitted to Almshouse 24 Oct 1882. On 27 Jul 1885 Walter E. was placed in a house in Marlboro, VT.} [Hinsdale, 7 May 1882; admitted 27 May 1882]

[100] 297. Mary Patnode, Marlborough, German, born in Albany, 17 Nov 1864. In 1872 came with my father Mike Patnode to Irony (*sic*), Clinton Co., NY to live. In 1880 came to Swanzey to reside in the family of George Patterson, a cousin; from there came to Marlborough to work in the mills and to live in the family of Frank Pluff. Has applied for help by reason of sickness. Her father resides in Irony, NY. [Marlborough, 1 Nov 1880; admitted Apr term 1881]

298. James L. Parks, Richmond, American, age 48 years. Has resided in Brooklyn, NY most of the time until 1869. Resided in CT and NY from 1869 to Dec 1881 when he came to Richmond, NH to live with his sister Elmira L. Shove. Admitted to the Almshouse 13 Apr 1882 and discharged 6 Jul 1882. {Readmitted 14 Dec 1882. He was never married. In some way his mind appears to be damaged. Died 2 Mar 1890 at County Almshouse and buried in County Cemetery.} [Richmond, 8 Apr 1882; admitted 2 Jun 1882]

---

[39] Space allotted taken up by last entry.

Cheshire County Paupers
1885-1900

299. Isaac W. Rogers, Keene, American, age 56 years old last Dec. Came to Keene in Aug 1882 with two sons, viz: Henry E., age 19 and Calvin R., age 18. Has never resided in any other town in NH. Has been twice married; both living, but does not live with either. Illegally married to his second wife, the mother of his two children. He claims his oldest son is lazy and afflicted with the evils of self-abuse, and that he is unable to support him. [Keene, 19 Feb 1883; admitted 24 Feb 1883]

[101] 300. John M. Reed, Winchester, American, born in Keene, age 48 years last Mar. Resided in Keene until age 20; traveled with a circus and lived in various places, but has always regarded Keene as his home. Married some 12 years ago; wife's name Annie T. She belonged in Maine where she has relatives living. They have five children, viz: William, age 11; John, 9; Mary, 6; Annie, 4; and an infant. Sickness and inability to work necessitates him to call for relief. {John M. died 1884.} [Winchester, 2 Nov 1882; admitted 11 Dec 1882]

301. Heber Riel, Jr., Winchester, French, born in NY and resided there until he came to Manchester, NH in 1880. Age 40 years. Was married thirteen years ago last March. Four children, ages respectively 12-10-6 and 4 years. His father Heber Riel, Sr.[40] has resided in W some 3 years. [Winchester, 20 May 1882; admitted 27 May 1882]

302. Mary C. Riel, Winchester, French, born in Troy, NY, age 27 years. Never resided in NH prior to coming to Winchester about four years ago. Has been married and her husband is dead. His name was Peter. "My parents nor my husband's parents," she says, "never resided in NH." She has four children, viz: Peter, age 6; Wilfred, age 4; Cordelia, age 2; and

---

[40] See # 44, page 15.

Cheshire County Paupers
1885-1900

Emma Phoeba, age 6 months. [Winchester, 29 Jun 1882; admitted Oct term 1882]

[102] 303. Mary Rineau, Richmond, French, age 50. Married; husband's name Eustin. Has one son; his name is Eustin, age about 10. Her husband left her; neglects to contribute to her support or his son. Came to Richmond before 1870, resided 12 years. {16 Apr 1881} Admitted to the Almshouse with her son. Discharged 4 Apr 1883 to go to live with Mr. Reynolds of Westmoreland. {1885} Eustin goes to reside with Mr. Farr, Park Hill; mother still at Mr. R's. [Richmond, 12 Apr 1881; admitted Apr term 1881]

304. Fanny Richards, Dublin, American, born in Hebron, NH age 23 years. Resided in Milford, NH from 1868-1878. Was married in Milford 17 Jun 1877 to Chas. E. Richards; divorced from him 24 Apr 1880. Has one child, viz: Charles W., born 21 Jul 1878. Came to Nelson, NH in 1879, rec'd some assistancewith her mother while residing in Nelson. Aided in Hillsboro County. Her mother's name is Josephine Percival. Moved from Nelson to Harrisville then to Dublin in 1880. {1885} Remarried to _____ Mrs. Percival has gone to reside with her son in Providence, RI. See Letters.[41] Mrs. P's age is 70. [Dublin, 22 Apr 1881; readmitted; adjudged in Nelson, 1879]

305. Leonard T. Roby, Marlborough, American, born in Nashua, 1 May 1824. Single. Resided in California from 1852-1871. Lived with George Tilden of Marlborough most of the time since. He is brother to Mrs. Tilden. In 1879 he had a shock since which time he has had fits and his mind seems to be badly damaged. Has a sister residing in Keene and several

---

[41] Though the original text says "See Letters," no accompanying letters were found by author. See also #36, page 12, and #1424, page 477..

*Cheshire County Paupers
1885-1900*

relatives in Nashua. {Admitted 16 May 1882 to Almshouse. Died 29 May 1884; burial in Nashua} [Marlborough, 29 Apr 1882; admitted Oct term 1882]

[103] 306. Harriet Royce, Keene, American, born in Weathersfield, VT, age 48. Has resided in Keene all of the time since 1860. Parents never resided in NH. [Keene, 7 Apr 1882; admitted]

307. Mary Sweeney, Winchester, Irish, b. Mayo Co., Ireland, age 17. Came from Ireland in 1882 to Winchester. Mother died 14 years ago. [Winchester, 18 Sep 1882; admitted 6 Oct 1882]

308. George D. Scott, Chesterfield, American. Age 39 years. Married; name of wife, Nancy A. Three children, viz: Bertie G., age 8; Ida D., 5; Agnes D., 2.[42] His father's name was Adolphus; mother Diantha (Stearns). Owen Burn and Mary were the names of Mrs. Scott's parents. Has not known the whereabouts of her father for nine years. Her mother died some 18 years ago. [Chesterfield, 24 Jun 1882; admitted 7 Jul 1882]

[104] 309. Phoeba (Wilder) Stevens,[43] Walpole, American, born in Sullivan, age 81. Has been married three times. Her first husband was William Parker of Keene; second husband was Joseph Wheeler of Keene; third husband was Joseph Stevens of Alstead. Owned a small place in Alstead in 1872. In 1878 she put her money into the hands of Charles Derby who agreed in writing to maintain her, but the agreement being defective he could not be held; she only lived with him about one year. In 1880 she went to reside with Mr. George Wilson of Walpole where she was taken sick and relief applied for. Later it was shown that she had a settlement in Keene and was

---

[42] See also #810, page 273.
[43] See #466, page 157.

supported by said city of Keene until the passage of the pauper law which took effect 11 Sep 1883. Under this law she became a county charge and was removed from Mr. Porter's in Alstead, where she was supported by the city of Keene to the County Almshouse 8 Oct 1883. [Walpole, 29 Mar 1880; admitted Apr term 1880; readmitted Oct term 1883]

310.[44]

311. Roswell Burnham, Westmoreland, American. Father of William Burnham, 15 years of age and inmate of the State Reform School; relief is asked to pay his board at the school, etc. [Westmoreland, 29 Nov 1879; admitted Apr term 1880]

[105] 312. Rose Bouvier, Keene, French, born in Canada, 19 years old, wife of Lewis Bouvier, who was also born in Canada. Husband deserted her in Apr 1880 and went to Colorado. Never resided in NH prior to 29 Sep 1880. [Keene, 29 Oct 1880; admitted Oct term 1880]

313. Ellen Collins,[45] Nelson, Irish, born in Ireland, 40 years old. Married; husband does not provide for his family. They have five children: the oldest 16 years and the youngest three years. Claims to have suffered for the want of food and clothing. [Nelson, 21 Jun 1881; admitted Oct term 1881]

314. Elvira Carlton, Winchester, American, 63 years old, wife of Sidney Carlton. He neglects to provide for her support. Is unkind and treats her badly. He is a brother of Judge Carlton of Winchester. Has relations in Keene and Fitzwilliam. One son Frank P. Carlton resides in Winchester. His father is 73 years old. [Winchester, 18 Apr 1881; adjudged Apr term 1881]

---

[44] Space taken by last entry.
[45] See also #886, page 298.

Cheshire County Paupers
1885-1900

[106] 315. William F. Whitcomb, Marlborough, American, born in Swanzey, 16 Jun 1850, 29 years of age, single. Has resided in Marlborough and the state of MA for the last 19 years. Father was born in Swanzey and his mother (Eunice A. Collins) in Marlborough. Mother is dead and his father has been an inmate of the County Almshouse since 16 Jun 1873; the son after 29 Apr 1880. {Brother, father and son were afflicted with fever sores and in 1881 each had a limb amputated. The father died 3 May 1881, and William was discharged 2 Jul 1881; has since married. Father's name is Cyrel Whitcomb.} [Marlborough, 9 Apr 1880; admitted Apr term 1880]

316. Bryan Lindergan, Keene, Irish, born in Ireland, 62 years of age. Came to America in 1839; resided Hoosac Falls, NY from 1866 to 1880; went to Portland, ME and resided until the 8th of Sep 1880 when he came to Keene. Married and wife died 1 Dec 1879 at Hoosac Falls, NY. One son who resides in Keene, age 26. Has friends in Hoosac Falls, NY that are willing to assist him, if he will return there. Gave him assistance to Hoosac Falls. [Keene, 6 Apr 1881; admitted Apr term 1881]

317. Daniel Lynch, Winchester, Irish, born in Ireland, age 28. Came to America in 1867. Has resided six years in Manchester, since 1867 and in no other place in NH over one year. Parents never resided in this country. On the 10th of Oct was severely injured upon the railroad at Winchester, which resulted in the amputation of one limb. Having no means, has been obliged to call for help. [Winchester, 16 Dec 1878; admitted Apr term 1879]

[107] 318. Nora Anna Madden, Keene, Irish, age 18. Father applies for aid by reason that she is pregnant with child, which she alleges was begotten at the city hotel, Keene by A. R. Williams, a runner for gas fixtures. Sent to the Almshouse 4

Cheshire County Paupers
1885-1900

Feb 1881 and there maintained at the expense of the city until discharged 21 Mar 1881. She was confined 5 Feb 1881. [Keene; town pauper]

319. Rufus J. Foster, Troy, American, 54 years of age. Has resided in Troy, Richmond, and Swanzey. Has been married, wife is dead. Has two children: a daughter and son. Has several sisters and a brother. Two sisters reside in Troy. {Admitted to the Almshouse 12 Oct 1880. Died 15 Oct 1885. Body sent to Troy for burial.} [Troy, 9 Oct 1880; previously adjudged]

320. Julia M. Brown, Keene, American, born in Sullivan, 61 years old. Has resided in Keene with the exception of a few months for twenty-two years last past. Has recently had one limb amputated. Died 13 Feb 1886 at Keene. [Keene, 7 Aug 1882; admitted Oct term 1882]

[108] 321. Lucy P. Pickering, Winchester, American, born in Swanzey, 69 years old. Has resided in Winchester since 1854. Has been married; husband died in 1870. Has a daughter Almira Pickering who is 45 years old and resides with her. She lives upon a little place owned by her husband's brother Loring Pickering who resides in California. {Elmira Pickering died 21 Mar 1888.} [Winchester, 23 Oct 1883; admitted Apr term 1884]

322. Alice Blais, Hinsdale, French, born in Canada, 49 years old. Married; husband 39 years old; refuses to support his family. Has four children, viz: Rosa St. Peter, age 11; Lewis Blais, age 8; Alfred, age 5; and Faretense, age 2. {Rosa St. Peter} It is claimed that she has in the hands of a guardian in Canada $5000 to $6000. This is a daughter by a former husband. [Hinsdale, 22 Dec 1885; admitted 1 Jun 1885]

Cheshire County Paupers
1885-1900

323. Rowland Gould, Winchester, American. Wife; has no children. He has been blind for a great many years. Gould died. His wife survives him and is maintained by the county. [Winchester; adjudged prior to 1861]

[109] 324. Roselthia Keyes, Alstead, American, born in Littleton, NH 23 Feb 1836. She is demented and incapable of supporting herself. She has a mother, a sister and two brothers living. Her mother and one brother reside in PA, near Bradford; one brother resides in Alstead. The sister, Mrs. Bartlett, resides in East Unity, NH. Her father is dead. {20 Oct 1891} The brother, who resides in Alstead, is a shiftless, worthless person. The mother and brother who reside in PA; their condition is unknown. [Alstead, 10 Nov 1885]

325. Charles A. Seward, Keene, American, 34 years old. Has a wife and three children. Was admitted a county pauper in Apr term 1880. Age of children: 9, 7, and 4. His father has been assisted by the county. [Keene, 13 Jul 1885]

326. Simon P. Wilcox, Marlborough, French decent (*sic*), born in St. Cutbert, PQ 4 Jul 1844, where he resided with his parents, Andrew and Mary Wilcox, until Apr 1864. Came to Marlborough in Apr 1870 and has lived there since, except for about two years that he resided in Swanzey. Was married in 1868; has seven children; the oldest sixteen, the youngest three. [Marlborough, 14 Jan 1886; admitted after Oct term 1885]

[110] 327. George F. Brown, Troy, born in Portland, ME, 28 years old. Single. Parents never resided in NH. He has been here only since the 14 Jan 1886. Being sick, he is compelled to ask for relief. Ordered to County Almshouse 13 Feb 1886. Father is insane and resides at South Windham, ME; his mother is dead. [Troy, 26 Jan 1886]

Cheshire County Paupers
1885-1900

328. Louisa Armstrong, Hinsdale, born in Winchester, age 61. Has resided in Hinsdale since she was two years old. Her husband Alpheus H. was in the 14th NH Vols; has been dead 21 years last Sep. She receives a pension of ninety-six dollars a year. [Hinsdale, 2 Feb 1886; admitted 5 Feb 1886]

329. Fred P. Cutler, Troy, 67 years old. Unmarried. Served in the War of 1861-65, was honorably discharged from the US Army 26 Mar 1863. Would like to enter the Soldier's Home. [Troy, 3 Feb 1886; admitted after Oct term 1885]

[111] 330. Fidelia Tellia, Marlborough, French, born in Nicolet, PQ, 14 May 1857. Came to Cheshire County in 1872; resided in Harrisville, Keene, and Marlborough. Married Joseph Tellia 16 Jun 1873. He was born in Canada, 12 Dec 1855. He came to Swanzey with his parents in 1869 where he resided until married. He deserted his family in Jul 1885. Two children: a son and a daughter, ages 10 and 7. [Marlborough, 16 Jan 1886; admitted 5 Mar 1886]

331. Calvin S. Pratt, Richmond, American, about 83 years of age. Married; wife, Lucy Pratt.[46] Natick, MA has paid the sum of $5 a month for his support, but refuses to pay more, and the amount is insufficient. Wrote to the Overseers of the Poor several times, of Natick, several times but rec'd no answer. Ordered the selectmen of Richmond to take him to the Poor House in Natick. Order complied with. His wife refused to go and remains with her brother Converse Martin in Richmond. Conveyed to Natick, MA, the expense paid by the selectmen of Natick. [Richmond, 7 Jan 1886; admitted after Oct term 1885]

332. Julius Picole, Marlborough, French, born in Canada, 20 Mar 1848. Came to Marlborough from there in 1879; has lived

---

[46] See #122, page 41.

there since. Married in 1872. Five children, viz: Julius, age 13; Isabel, age 11; Dennis, age 8; Frank, age 6; and Joseph, age 2. [Marlborough, 27 Jan 1886; admitted after Oct term 1885]

[112] 333. Lucy Miller, (Melo), Keene, French, 25 years old the 12th of Mar. Married Charles Miller (Melo), the 2d May three years ago. Two children, viz: Chas. A., born 19 Jul 1883; and William H., 6 months, the 17th of this month (Mar). Her father and mother Joseph and Rosella Jolly have resided in Keene for the last twenty years or more. They own a small place at the upper end of Washington Street. Her husband has resided in Keene some 5 years and in Winchester about four years. He and his parents moved from New York state about nine years ago. His parents have owned a farm in Winchester for several years past. His father's name is Gilbert Miller (Melo). Her husband is now residing in Brattleboro, VT. This woman and her children appear to have gained a settlement in Keene through her father; her husband not having gained a settlement in NH. [Keene, 10 Mar 1886; not admitted; adjudged after Apr term 1889, under new act of 1888]

334. Julia A. Willis, Alstead, American, wife of George A. Willis. Mrs. Willis has been aided as a pauper heretofore under the name of Julia A. Orne (see #31, p. 11). Her husband and his father have resided in Alstead and other places in Cheshire County. He did not reside with his wife for only some three or four months after he married her. [Alstead, 12 Mar 1886; admitted Oct term 1886]

[113] 335. Ida Harvey, Winchester, American. Father born in New Ipswich, NH. Ida is 24 years old, single, resides with her father Charles L. Harvey. This case was rejected; Chesterfield admitted to liability. [Winchester, 7 Mar 1886; Oct term 1886]

Cheshire County Paupers
1885-1900

336. Joseph Little, Winchester, French, born in Canada, age 43. Has resided in Winchester since 1873. Married; four children, viz: Lora, age 13; Emma, age 11; Joseph, age 7; and Willie, age 5. [Winchester, 9 Mar 1886; admitted Apr term 1886]

337. John Sheehy,[47] Jaffrey, Irish, born in Ireland, 79 years old the 24th of last June. Has resided in Jaffrey for twenty years or more. Admitted to the Almshouse. [Jaffrey, 20 Feb 1886; admitted Apr term 1886]

[114] 338. William and Persis Horton, Alstead, American. Age of William at the time he was admitted was 80 years. Mrs. Horton was 76 years old. Both have resided for some years with Mr. French in the east part of Alstead. {Persis died 10 Dec 1884. William Horton died 6 Nov 1891, age 93, 3 months, 2 days.} [Alstead; admitted Apr term 1878]

339. Polly Hodge, Jaffrey, American, age 81 years in Jul 1883. Husband John Hodge died in Feb 1882, age ___. She now resides with her son Edwin L. Hodge in Fitzwilliam (1 Apr 1885) Has a son by the name of Amasa residing in Templeton, MA. Mrs. Hodge was admitted a county charge at the Apr term 1884. Subsequently in 1885 evidence was furnished the Court, showing that the town of Jaffrey was liable, and not the county for her support. [Jaffrey, 23 Jun 1884; admitted Apr term 1884]

340. Betsey Aldrich, Swanzey, American, born in MA, age 68. Married when about twenty years old and have always resided since my marriage in Cheshire County. My husband died in Swanzey in 1872. Has two children, both married: David S. and Betsey Worster. Is residing with her son in Swanzey. Has an injured foot, and is unable to do much of any work. [Swanzey, 1 Dec 1885; admitted after Oct term 1885]

---

[47] The 1880 census for Jaffrey states his name as "Shahe."

Cheshire County Paupers
1885-1900

[115] 341. Frank L. Thurston, Stoddard [Admitted Apr term 1876]

342. Fanny Ellen Watters, Keene, born in St. Johnsville, NY, age 42. Married; husband's name is Edward A. Watters. He was born at or near Rutland, VT and is 29 years old. Has resided in Keene nine or ten years. No children. Husband has recently left me; don't known where he is. Has no relatives able to assist her. [Keene, 9 Apr 1886; admitted Apr term 1886]

343. Lottie E. Moore, Winchester, American, born in Winchester, age 5. Has one brother (Clarence E. Moore) and 2 sisters. Her mother Eva G. Wheeler has been twice married; first to Fred W. Moore at Vernon, VT 30 Sep 1873; and to Chas. O. Wheeler of Winchester, 25 Apr 1881. Her father's name was George W. Stanford. Her mother married second E. H. Sawtelle of Winchester and she has been aided in Hinsdale by the county where they now resided. Eva G. has 4 children, viz: Clarence E., age 9, now living in Northampton, MA; Lottie E., age 5; Ada M., age 3; and Alice E., 8 months old. Her father Fred W. Moore was drowned at Northampton, MA. [Winchester, 15 Apr 1886; admitted Apr term 1886]

[116] 344. Jerry Dolan, Walpole, Irish, born in Ireland, age 49. Came to the US in 1867. Came to Walpole in 1882 and has ever since resided there. Married 16 years ago to Bridget Marsy. Her age is 45 years. Four children, viz: Eliza, age 15; Katie, age 10; Jerry, age 7; and Thomas, age 5. Wife in poor health for 6 months past, and unable to sit up since Christmas; out of work himself and hence is obliged to ask for relief. [Walpole, 6 Jan 1886; admitted Apr term 1886]

345. Lizzie Doyle, Walpole, Irish, born Ireland, age 45. Came to NJ when quite young. Married Michael Doyle 13 years ago.

Cheshire County Paupers
1885-1900

They came to Brattleboro, VT about 5 years ago, where her husband died about one year ago. Has one child, Mary, age 11 this month (Feb). Has been working in the Fall Mountain Paper Mill until taken sick about four weeks ago, hence applies for temporary relief. [Walpole, 5 Feb 1886; admitted 17 Feb 1887]

346. Denzil M. Streeter, Hinsdale, American, b. in Dummerston, VT, 58 years old, widower. Has one daughter who keeps house for him; works in the factory when able. Army in the war of 1861-65; receives a pension of $2 a month. No aid furnished with which the county was made chargeable; not admitted and entered as a pauper. [Hinsdale, 19 Feb 1886]

[117] 347. Philip Thomas, Walpole, American, born in Westmoreland. Seventy-nine years old, the 28th of May 1885. Resided in Surry many years. Has been married twice. For his second wife, married Clarisa Foster of Walpole about 1866. Has resided in Walpole the last 15 or 20 years. No children. Mrs. Daniel W. Aldrich of Worcester is a sister of his and is paying $1.50 per week toward his board at George H. Gassett's of Walpole. {Ordered to Almshouse 23 Apr 1886. Died 4 May 1886 of paralysis at George H. Gassett's.} [Walpole, 1 Dec 1886;[48] admitted Apr term 1886]

348. Charles Webb, Chesterfield, American, born in Keysville, NY, age 34. Parents reside in Chesterfield; his father's name is Nathaniel. Charles has always resided in NY, except about six years during which he lived in Chesterfield. Last fall he was taken insane and his father went to NY state and brought him to his house in Chesterfield. He is now worse, and he applies for aid in his support and requests that he be sent to the Hospital at Concord. {Sent to NH Asylum for the Insane 11 Feb 1886.} [Chesterfield, 10 Feb 1886; admitted Apr term 1886]

---

[48] Though the original credits this entry as Dec 1886, it is probably 1885.

Cheshire County Paupers
1885-1900

349. W. R. Kenny, Surry, American. Married, has six children, viz: Hattie M., age 12; George, age 11; Jennie, age 10; Ida, age 7; Ella, age 5; and Charles, age 3. He has no settlement, but his wife and children take the settlement of her father in Gilsum. He, in blasting rocks, nearly lost his eyesight by a premature explosion. The above record is incorrect as it states he has no settlement. He has a settlement in Surry, but she and the children have no settlement by reason of illegal marriage to him. {Hattie M. died in Surry 7 Sep 1872.[49]} [Surry; admitted Apr term 1879]

[118] 350. Ephraim Martin, Rindge, American, born in Richmond, age 85. Moved to Westminster, MA in 1821 or 1822 and resided here and at Phillipston until 1882 and since then he has resided in Rindge. Has been married and had children. Receives a pension by reason of the death of a son who was in the service during the late war. Mrs. Willard, late of Rindge deceased, was a daughter. She died several years ago and he has since lived with her husband. [Rindge, 17 Mar 1886; admitted Apr term 1886]

351. Jeremie Cornet, Keene, French, born in France, age 40. Has a wife and two children, ages 6 and 8 years old. Came from France to NH in 29th May 1885. [Keene, 18 Jan 1886; admitted Apr term 1886]

352. Daniel Dillion, Marlborough, Irish, born in Ireland, 40 years old. Never resided in NH until last March. Married; wife's name is Margery. He is sick and poor and hence applies for relief. {Daniel Dillon died 16 Apr 1886.} [Marlborough, 14 Apr 1886; admitted Apr term 1886]

---

[49] The handwritten original may read "1892." It is unclear.

Cheshire County Paupers
1885-1900

[119] 353. Fred M. Perry, Keene, Irish (?), born in Manchester, NH, age 22. Came to Keene in Oct 1884. Went with my parents to Canada when 4 years old and resided 7 years. Then went to NY state and lived until I came to Keene. Parents have always resided in Canada and state of NY since they left Manchester. He is married; his wife is 22 years old. She was born in Canada. Parents never lived in NH. [Keene, 14 Apr 1886; admitted Apr term 1886]

354. Joseph Alix, Keene, French, born in West Farnum, PQ, 39 years old. Was in the service in the war of 1861-65. Belonged to Co. E., 14th Regt CT Vols. Married 19 Jun 1883; no children. Wife has a sister residing in Dublin: Mrs. Ellen Pierce. My wife's maiden name was Emma Whitcomb. She is 19 years old. (See affidavit.)[50] [Keene, Feb 1886; admitted Apr term 1886]

355. James Rorke, Keene, b. Portland, ME, age 21. Married; wife Mary was born in Halifax, NS. Neither his or her parents ever resided in NH. [Keene, Jan 1886; admitted Apr term 1886]

[120] 356. Cuthbert H. and Ella G. Hurd, aged respectively 7 and 5 years, children of Nettie E. Hurd and Horace E. Hurd. Mr. Hurd deserted his family some three years ago; his whereabouts are unknown. Mrs. Hurd, 28 years old, b. Holden, MA; respected to be a nice, industrious woman. Her father (named Prouty) is still living; resides in Warwick, MA; said to be in indigent circumstances. One of the children resides with Ira Prentice; the other with Leonard Bryant of Fitzwilliam. The mother is at work at West Upton, MA, but not being very well is unable to earn enough to support her children; has applied to the town of Fitzwilliam for assistance in taking care of her children in the homes and families in which they are now living.

---

[50] No accompanying affidavit was found by author.

Cheshire County Paupers
1885-1900

{In Apr 1887, no aid asked for Cuthbert H.} [Fitzwilliam, 27 Mar 1886; admitted Apr term 1886]

357.[51]

358. Charles C. Sargent, Keene, American, born in Warner, NH, 1 Jan 1824. Married; wife Hannah M., age 45. One son Alfred G., age 10 and one Charles B., age 18, to whom I have given his time. Have two daughters; both married and reside in Keene, viz: Nellie M. Perkins and Sylvia A. Barry. Was in the service in the late war, Co. K, 5th NH Vols. [Keene, 27 Mar 1886; admitted Apr term 1886]

[121] 359. Joseph Flood, Jaffrey, American, born in Marlborough, age 73 last Oct. Went to Jaffrey to live in 1870. Has no wife living or minor children. { Died 8 Jun 1886.} [Jaffrey, 19 Apr 1886; admitted Apr term 1886]

360. Peter Wood, Westmoreland, American, born in Standish, ME, 2 May 1797, and is in his 89th year of age. Has resided in Westmoreland about 10 years; previously resided in Westminster, VT for 15 years. [Westmoreland, 19 Apr 1886; admitted Apr term 1886]

361. Harry E. Lowell, Keene, born in Marlow, age 18, the 22 Nov next. Parents both living, but not together. Have not lived together since I can remember. Mother had her name changed after she separated from father. His name was Stevens, and he resides, I am informed in Concord. His mother Mary R. Lowell resides in Nashua, NH. Has little property. Has one brother who bears his father's name: Clark D., who lives in Newbury, NH. Harry lived in Keene a while last summer and returned

---

[51] Space taken up by last entry.

here about 4 weeks ago, and was soon after taken sick. Appears to be an honest young man. [Keene; admitted Apr term 1886]

[122] 362. Mary McLaughlin, Keene, Irish, born in Ireland, age 47 on 18 Oct 1886. Married; husband's name William A., age 47 on 3 Nov 1886. One child Hugh, age 13 the 18th of Aug 1886. Reside on Oak Street. Husband was in the war of 1861-65. Honorably discharged. He was convicted of the murder of a Mr. Craig[52] and sentenced to state prison during life. Was pardoned a few years ago; is now blind and helpless. Mrs. McLaughlin owns a house and lot on Oak Street for which she paid $350. Has owned it five years. {Has gained a settlement since for herself and child. He still remains a county charge.} [Keene, 1875; admitted Apr term 1875]

363. John Vigneau, Marlborough, French, born in ___, age 37. Married; wife Sophronia Vigneau, age 24. She is very sick with consumption. {noted later, "con for proof." Mrs. Vigneau died 10 May 1886.} [Marlborough, 7 May 1886]

364. Sadie E. and Charles H. Sperry, Swanzey, ages 11 and 9 years respectively. Father's name is Charles Sperry; mother's, Carrie E., age 40. She was divorced from Charles Sperry in Apr 1884 and married to Amos L. Corey 29 Nov 1884. Her present husband refused to support her children by her first husband. Resided in MA most of the time until she married Mr. Corey. [Swanzey, 7 May 1886; admitted 10 May 1886]

[123] 365. Thomas Mulqueny, Jaffrey, born in England, age 25. Single. Parents reside in Hyde Park, MA. Came to Jaffrey in March last. Applies for relief by reason of sickness. [Jaffrey, 30 Mar 1886; admitted 10 May 1886]

---

[52] The Allen Aaron Craig murder was profiled in *Hard Time in Concord* by author, pages 103-104. See also #1232, page 414, and #1345, page 452.

Cheshire County Paupers
1885-1900

366. Louis Tacy, Winchester, French. Born in NY state, age 31. Married; three children, viz: Maggie, age 7; Louis, age 5; and Lizzie, age 3. Came to Winchester in 1880. Resided in Hinsdale in 1883. [Winchester, 20 May 1886; admitted after Apr term 1886]

367. James W. Arling, Hinsdale, American. Born in Northfield, MA, Jun 1851, age 35. Married; wife Ethel H., born in Ashuelot, NH 20 Aug 1860, daughter of Edward H. Sawtelle of Hinsdale. Three children, viz: Frank W., age 5; Lucy E., age 3; and Florence E., age 1. Name frequently written Arlen. [Hinsdale, 21 May 1886; admitted 30 Jul 1886]

[124] 368. Mary A. Burdett, Swanzey, American, born in Westfield, MA, age 53. Wife of Luke H. Burdett, who resides in MA. Has five children by a former husband, G. S. Stevens, who died 25 years ago, viz: George S., born in 1852; Charles G., born in 1854; Carrie, born in 1856; Arthur F., born in 1858; and Hattie M., born in 1860. Came to reside in Swanzey in Sep 1884. One son and daughter reside with her. {Mrs. Burdett died 5 Mar 1887.} [Swanzey, 29 May 1886; application filed 29 May 1886 by Joseph Hammond; admitted 30 Jul 1886]

369. George Adams, Keene, English, born in England, age 70. Came to America 20 years ago. Has no relatives in this country. Has several brothers in England. Sent from Fitzwilliam to Keene, and from Keene to the Almshouse in Westmoreland. [Keene, 4 Jun 1886; admitted 30 Jul 1886]

370. James O'Keefe, Walpole, born in Ireland, age 32. Came to America when about 12 years old. Father died in Ireland about three years ago; a year later his mother came to this country. Married Margaret Sullivan, age 27. Three children, ages 6 years, 2 years and 8 months respectively. Mr. O'Keefe is

Cheshire County Paupers
1885-1900

insane and in the NH Asylum for the Insane. Cause excessive drinking. [Walpole, 17 May 1886; admitted 30 Jul 1886]

[125] 371. John Dougherty, Keene, Irish, b. Nova Scotia, age 28, the 15th of last January. Married; wife Susan McLear, age 29. Their parents are all dead; his never resided in the United States; hers resided for many years in Keene. No children. Out of work, hence, calls for relief. Is intemperate; has recently served a short sentence in the House of Corrections for being drunk. [Keene, 17 Jun 1886; Apr term 1887, not adjudged.]

372. Josiah T. Swinington,[53] Nelson, American, born in Lyndeborough, NH, age 63. Married; has five children, viz: Emily L., age 14; Walter P., age 11; Leroy A., age 7; Ella M., age 4; and Ida M., age four months. Rents the place on which he resides. Applies for aid by reason of sickness. [Nelson, 5 Jun 1886; admitted 30 Jul 1886]

373. Amasa Davis, Richmond, American, born in Walpole, age 77, single. Enlisted in Co. C, 14th NH Vols in 1862, and was discharged from Stone (Deserter's) Hospital, Washington, DC in May 1864. His papers do not show that he was honorably discharged. Has a daughter in Marlborough and one son in Royalston, MA, and a son in Vernon, VT. On 4 Aug, was carried to Westmoreland to board with Mrs. Lucinda Haradon.[54] {On 31 Aug, it was written: Charles Davis of Vernon and Wallace Davis of Royalston, MA are Amasa's sons. Jane Hale of Marlborough, NH is a daughter. Mrs. Haradon states that said Davis' name is Amos, not Amasa, that he enlisted (her sister Mrs. Douglas thinks) in the 2d NH Regt, and deserted, reenlisted in the 14th NH, receiving a bounty.} [Richmond, 28 Jun 1886]

---

[53] See also #49, page 17.
[54] See also #211, 263, 651 and 686.

Cheshire County Paupers
1885-1900

[126] 374. Reuben C. and Mary Florence Powers, Keene, American, born in Keene, 13 Jan 1878 and 15 Aug 1880, respectively, children of Reuben R. and Mary A. Powers. Father died 13 Jan 1882; mother afterwards married 6 Oct 1884 Frank Dodge of Walpole, NH, is about 30 years old. Her father Galbin resides in North Braintree, MA, manufacturing boots and shoes. Mrs. Dodge since the death of her first husband has behaved very badly, gets very drunk, is now in jail, charged with setting fire to a barn of Henry Dodge on the 12th of Jul. She brought the above named children to Keene and left them with their grandmother, Mrs. Mary A. Powers Stowell and returned to her house in Walpole. The children were in the Home for Little Wanderers in Boston for a short time after their father's death, but have resided with their mother since her marriage to Mr. Dodge. Reported to be bright intelligent children. Their grandmother makes application to the city of Keene for their support. [Keene, 21 Jul 1886; admitted Oct term 1886]

375. Florance Leary, Roxbury, Irish, born in Ireland, age about 44, single. Came to Roxbury last spring to work cutting granite. Worked on stone in Roxbury once before. Has been sick more or less since a year ago; has evidently consumption. Has two sisters and one brother residing in this country. Parents never resided in America. His father is dead. His sister Mrs. Bridget Carr resides at #44 Corey St., Charleston, MA. The other sister Mrs. Mary Sullivan resides at Mt. Sterling, Brown Co., Illinois. His brother resides somewhere in California. Has no relative able to support or aid him. Ordered to the Almshouse. [Roxbury, 29 Jul 1886; admitted 30 Jul 1886]

[127] 376. Ellen S. Holden, Roxbury, age 34. Married; husband left her in 1872. Has been married since, though not divorced. Has two children, viz: Harry A. Fisk, age 11, the 16th

Cheshire County Paupers
1885-1900

of Apr 1886; Jennie Belle (Phillips?), age 1 year, the 15th of Dec 1885. This last child is illegitimate. Her father's name was Joseph Haskell. Parents both dead. Have been dead several years. They resided in Rindge previous to their death. Her husband resides somewhere in MA. Only one child lives with her. She is sick, hence the application for aid. Is keeping house for Dick Cota. [Roxbury, 29 Jul 1886; adjudged Apr term 1886]

377. Henry Eddy, Hinsdale, American. He thinks he was born in Jamaica, VT, age 38. Married; wife's name was Lydia Roberts, West Wardsboro, VT. Five children, three of them living with him. He has been aided by the town of Newfane, VT. Names and ages of children, viz: Flora, age 16; Willie H., age 14; Alvaretta M., age 12; Idella M., age 9; and Rosa A., age 7. Alvaretta and Idella were sent to the Baldwin Place Home in 1884 from the town of Winchester. (See page 49 #147.) The father and one of the daughters were held and sent to the House of Correction, Westmoreland for living together incestuously. {25 Oct 1886} Alvaretta sent to West Townsend[55] to reside with Rev. T. Mackie. [Hinsdale, 4 Aug 1886; admitted Oct term 1886]

378. Joseph Naylor, Harrisville, born in Canada, age 56. Has been married twice. Does not live with his last wife; has not for more than a year. Her name is Mary S. Has children by his first wife, more by the second. Two under 21 years of age, viz: Peter, age 18 and Rosa, age 16. Both were residing in Webster, MA, the last time heard from. Has a brother Charles Naylor residing in Harrisville and with whom he has made his home since last winter. Applies for admission to the Co. Almshouse. Gave Mr. George Davis order to admit him. [Harrisville, 10

---

[55] Original appears to read "W. I. Townsend." See also # 147, page 49.

Cheshire County Paupers
1885-1900

Aug 1886; adjudged after Apr term 1886; escaped 21 Nov 1886]

[128] 379. Maggie Jordon, Keene, Irish, widow, was 23 years of age when she applied for help in 1881. Has two children, viz: Katie, age 5; Marnie, age 2 years old. Her mother Kate O'Brien resided with her. The children are bright, smart appearing children but their mother is a very bad woman and often gets beastly drunk. {Ordered to Almshouse and admitted 31 Jul 1883; discharged 15 May 1884 to go to work for Mr. Green of Westmoreland. Readmitted 21 Aug 1886 with one child.} [Keene, adjudged Apr term 1881; ordered to the Farm from Marlborough, 16 Aug 1886]

380. Kate O'Brien, Irish, widow, lives with her daughter Maggie Jordon. [Keene, adjudged; ordered to Farm from Marlborough, 16 Aug 1886]

381. Charles W. Hinds, Walpole, American, born in Hubbardstown, MA 10 Jan 1813, and is now 73 years old. Married Elizabeth Handy by whom he had two children, viz: Chas. J., born in 1842 and Jarvis H., born in 1844; wife died five years ago. Has resided in Walpole since 1835. {Admitted to the Almshouse 27 Aug 1886.} [Walpole, 13 Aug 1886; adjudged Oct term 1886]

[129] 382. Benjamin Lavine, Keene, French, born in Sherbrooke, Canada, 52 years old in Sept next. Married; wife Delemore, is thirty-six years old. Has six children: Adelia, 11 years; Anna, 6 years; Georgianna, 5 years; Mary, 4 years; Walter, 2 years; and Phillip, seven months old. Their house and all of their household effects were burnt in Westmoreland a few days ago, while they were all absent from it. Mr. L was at the time and is now at work at or near New London, CT. His brother Joseph is taking care of his family and only asks to have

Cheshire County Paupers
1885-1900

some clothing furnished them. [Keene, Aug 1886; admitted Oct term 1886]

383. Margaret Ella Gowdy of Keene, Irish, born in Ireland, 27 years old. Married Edward M. Gowdy of Claremont, NH in Jul 1879. Three children, viz: John Henry, age 6; James Clarence, age 5; and Margy Ella, age 4 years old, in Jun last. Mrs. G came to America ten years ago. Her husband has always resided in Claremont until he came to Keene to reside in Apr 1885. James Gowdy, his brother, resides in Keene and works in the railroad machine shop. Mrs. Stevens, a sister, resides on School Street. Has three brothers and a sister living in the West. Edward M. Gowdy was very intemperate at one time and then reformed and for the last ten years has been steady until about three months ago, when he began drinking and since then has behaved very badly and neglected his family. The last of August he was complained of, tried before the Police Court and sentenced to the House of Correction for two months. [Keene, 25 Sep 1886; application and ___ received; admitted Apr term 1887]

[130] 384. John Jolly, Keene, French, born in Keysville, NY, 46 years old. Married Ellen Sharkee five years ago; she is 20 years old. They have one child, John, two and a half months old. Has a brother Joseph Jolly, living on Washington St. in Keene. Has resided in Keene and vicinity for the last seven years. [Keene, 25 Sep 1886; adjudged Oct term 1886]

385. James D. Lewis, Walpole, American, born in Springfield, NH and is 29 or 30 years of age. His mother Mary G. Lewis is dead; his father Marvin Lewis has married again and now resides in Newport, NH. The said James D. Lewis married Edna Jennings of Unity, NH about 7 or 8 years ago. One child, a boy, 6 years old. Some two months ago (13 Sep 1886) James D. Lewis began to show signs of insanity and has recently been

Cheshire County Paupers
1885-1900

examined and pronounced insane, and committed to the NH Asylum for the Insane. {3 Dec 1890 said Lewis was transferred from the Asylum to the Almshouse. Condition, demented.} [Walpole, 7 Sep 1886; adjudged Oct term 1886]

386. Lovell C. Taft, Richmond, born in Swanzey, 32 years of age. Married, no children. Was committed to the Asylum 8 Nov 1879 where he has been since with the exception of about two weeks. His wife is the daughter of Warner Harris of Swanzey. The said Taft has been under guardianship since 8 Jun 1880, George W. Willis being his guardian. He said Taft had at that time about $800 which has been expended for his maintenance at the Asylum. He has two brothers and two sisters living: a brother and sister in Swanzey, and a brother in Framingham, MA. The residence of the other sister is not known. 3 Dec 1890 transferred from Asylum to Almshouse, condition, demented. [Richmond or Swanzey, 23 Sep 1886; notice of application for aid received 1 Aug 1886]

[131] 387. Louis Chausse, Marlborough, born in Lower Canada, 42 years old, 16 Oct 1885. Married; wife's name, Josephine, age 37. Have five children, viz: Adelia, 13 years old; Eugene, 10 years old; Minnie, 8 years; Emile, 5 years; and William, age 2. Has been running the engine at the Marlborough quarry for the last two and a half years. The works having stopped, he is out of employment and applies for aid to go to Lawrence, MA. [Marlborough, 28 Sep 1886; Oct term 1886, admitted]

388. Horace Page, Keene, American, born in Henniker, 48 years old, the 29th of Dec 1886. Married; does not live with his wife. She is in Concord, NH. Has 5 children, 3 dependent upon him for support; 2 support themselves. Rec'd aid in the town of Dearing (sic) last spring from the County of Hillsboro; was in the service of the US during the late war. [Keene, 18 Oct 1886]

Cheshire County Paupers
1885-1900

389. Nellie I. (Hastings) Mitchell, Keene, born in Belvidere, Illinois, American, 17 years old. Married John Mitchell of Troy, NH, 3 May 1886. Is pregnant with child and liable to be confined any day. Husband neglects and refuses to support or care for her. Is at work at the present time for Levi A. Fuller, Marlborough Depot. Her father is dead; her mother married to Charles F. Grout, George St., for her second husband. Mrs. Mitchell is now living with her mother. [Keene, 18 Oct 1886; admitted Apr term 1887]

[132] 390. Daniel Gilbo, Keene, Irish, born in Ireland, about 40 years of age. Married; wife Mary, 32 years of age or more. Three children, viz: Mary, aged 4, the 3rd of Dec next; Willie, aged 2, the 31st of Jul last; and John Luke, 9 months and one week old. Mr. Gilbo has been in feeble health and unable to work for several weeks past. [Keene, 18 Oct 1886; admitted Oct term 1886]

391. William F. Ruderham, Rindge, born in Boston, 18 years old, single. Parents never resided in NH. Has been very sick; hence the application for relief. [Rindge, 2 Sep 1886; adjudged Oct term 1886]

392. James Doherty, Rindge, born in St. John, NB in Jan 1864, 22 years old. Parents never resided in NH. [Rindge, 10 Sep 1886; adjudged Oct term 1886]

[133] 393. Nancy Pearson, Hinsdale, American, born in Pittsfield, NH in Oct 1816; maiden name Nancy Marston. Married George Pearson of Andover, NH in 1841. Went to Hinsdale to reside in 1883. Her husband born England about 1826 and came to America when 9 or 10 years old. Resided in Pittsfield, ME from 1853 to 1883. {Died in Hinsdale 18 Sep 1886.} [Hinsdale, 17 Sep 1886; adjudged Oct term 1886]

Cheshire County Paupers
1885-1900

394. Gideon Foster, Marlborough, French, age 18 years. Parents came from Canada to Marlborough 17 Apr 1885 and returned to Canada 6 Oct 1886. The boy remained in Marlborough to work. Taken sick with typhoid fever and is at this date 22 Oct 1886 very sick. Hence the application for relief. The boy is well spoken of. [Keene, 20 Oct 1886; adjudged Oct term 1886]

395. Henry Griffin and wife, Gilsum, American, born in Ticonderoga, NY; wife Polly Griffin was born in Underhill, VT and is 44 years old. Mrs. G did have a sister residing in Walpole, NH, said Henry Griffin is 56 years old. [Gilsum, 6 Sep 1886; admitted Oct term 1886]

[134] 396. Antoine Shambs, Marlborough, French, born in Canada, 39 years old. Has resided in Marlborough about one year. Has a wife and six children, viz: Henry, 17 years old; Felix, 16 years old; Clara, 14 years old; Fred, 11years; George, 9 years; and Rosanna, 6 years old. {Antoine S. died 4 Oct and one of the boys 9 Oct 1886 of typhoid fever.} [Marlborough, 4 Oct 1886; adjudged Oct term 1886]

397. Simon W. Todd, Jaffrey, born in Nelson, NH, age 33. Married Lucy T. Allen of Peterborough, NH in 1873. She was 30 years old, 10 Dec 1884. Two children, viz: Lizzie J., born 10 Jul 1874 and Harry A., born 11 Oct 1880. Wife sick and he claims to be poor and unable to support himself and family; continued for proof that Mrs. T did not gain a settlement through her father. [Jaffrey, 3 Jun 1885; admitted Oct term 1886]

398. William Skivington, born in Boston, age 26 years. Married; wife Mary, age 25 years. Has one sister now with him, age 20 years. Has been to Canada to have a surgical

Cheshire County Paupers
1885-1900

operation performed. On his return to Boston his money gave out and when they reached Rutland, where they were furnished with transportation to Keene; Overseer Howland of Keene gave him transportation to their house in Boston. [Keene, 14 Oct 1886; adjudged Oct term 1886]

[135] 399. Mrs. John Bean, Keene, born in Canada, 32 years old. Married; her husband John Bean was born in Canada and is 37 years old. Poor and very destitute; wants means to get to her friends which was furnished by the city overseer of the poor. [Keene, 12 Sep 1886; admitted Oct term 1886]

400. Persis Paine, Westmoreland, American, born in Westmoreland, 74 years old. Was never married. Has always resided in Westmoreland; has several nieces and relatives in said Westmoreland. {Overseers of the poor applied 23 Oct 1886, through Willard Bill, Jr., for an order to take her to the County Almshouse. Order issued to John Works 23 Oct 1886; admitted 1 Nov 1886.} [Westmoreland, 21 Oct 1886; admitted Oct term 1886]

401. Hannah Crouch, Chesterfield, American, 69 years old, when adjudged. Applied for relief by reason of an accident by which she broke her thigh and made her helpless. Resides with relatives in the southeast part of Chesterfield. [Chesterfield; adjudged Oct term 1876[56]]

[136] 402. Mrs. James L. Davis, Gilsum, American, was 60 years old when adjudged; is at this time (Oct term 1886) 83 or 4 years. {Died 10 May 1887 at her daughter's, Mrs. Howard.} [Gilsum; Oct term 1863]

---

[56] Date transcribed as in original. From this point on for several pages the entries are not in chronological order. On page 168, it repeats the date of adjudgment of Hannah's case as 1876.

Cheshire County Paupers
1885-1900

403. Ezra Howard,[57] Hattie M. & Perley E. (*sic*), Gilsum, adjudged while residing in Stoddard. [Gilsum; Apr term 1882]

404. Martha Cobb, Harrisville, American. Admitted to the Almshouse 5 Dec 1888 and was at that time about 67 years old. [Harrisville; adjudged Oct term 1868]

[137] 405. Mary Bigelow, Jaffrey. [Jaffrey; adjudged Apr term 1882]

406. Charles W. Raymond, Jaffrey. [Jaffrey; adjudged Oct term 1880]

407. George Priest, Keene, American. [Keene]

[138] 408. John Buckley, Keene, Irish, 54 years old when adjudged. Wife and one or two children. Is very intemperate; inclined to be lazy. {Had a shock of paralysis in 1885. Died sometime in the winter (?) of 1885-6.} [Keene; adjudged Apr term 1875]

409. Isabelle Sawin, Keene, American. [Keene; adjudged Apr term 1877]

410. Joseph Alex, and wife, Keene. See page119. [Keene; admitted Apr term 1886]

[139] 411. Edmund Brown, Keene, American. Entered Oct term 1886 and a small bill for relief was presented by the city of Keene and paid by the County. Later it was discovered that

---

[57] In the original, the name is given as "Howard Ezra," but according to the 1880 census from Marlow, the name should be "Ezra Howard."

Cheshire County Paupers
1885-1900

Brown is a city pauper and notice of the fact given to Mr. Howland, overseer of the poor. [Keene]

412. Mary Marcott, Keene, French. [Keene; admitted Apr term 1882]

413. Silvia Snow, Keene, American. {Died 25 Sep 1891.} [Keene; admitted Oct term 1879]

[140] 414. Eliza Bates, Keene, American, 55 years old when adjudged; widow. Her maiden name was Perry. Had several brothers and a sister or two. Had one brother who was a prominent railroad man. His name was George W. He died at Malden, MA sometime in 1880, leaving an estate valued at from $50,000 to $75,000. [Keene; adjudged Apr term 1876]

415. Gabriel Rock and wife, French, was 73 years old when admitted. He is blind. His wife leads him about the streets and they subsist principally by begging. They are furnished a small house free of rent by John Drummer. They have been repeatedly ordered to the County Almshouse but they refuse to go. [Keene; admitted Apr term 1868]

416. George Clasby and wife, was 55 years old when adjudged. He is apparently a lazy indolent man and his wife, a daughter of King Chapman of Keene, claims to be an invalid. She married Clasby against the wishes and protests of her parents and friends, and therefore they withhold the relief which they are abundantly able to furnish. [Keene; adjudged Apr term 1885]

[141] 417. Jane Dawson, Irish. Resides with her son-in-law in the south part of Walpole. Was 79 years old when adjudged Oct term 1886. Within the last 2 or 3 years, Mr. Heald, her son-in-law has removed to Keene, Ward 3, and with his son is engaged in the ice business. [Walpole; admitted Oct term 1879]

Cheshire County Paupers
1885-1900

418. Mary Mitchell, Irish, was 80 years old when adjudged. Has children residing in Keene, married. Was burned out in 1878 or 1879, and the Commissioners rebuilt her a small house and took a deed of her house and lot in favor of the county. Her husband is dead. [Keene; admitted Oct term 1879]

419. Samuel Priest, American. When adjudged he was 30 years old. [Keene; admitted Apr term 1880]

[142] 420. John Ryan, Irish. At the time he was adjudged he was 50 years old. Married; wife Mary is a hard working woman, but he appears to be a shiftless lazy fellow. Have at this time seven or eight children. For the last 6 or 8 years, she has done the cleaning at the Court House earning yearly for this work $30 to $50 a year. Resides in ward 4, "Red Row;" rents a house of Faulkner & Colony. [Keene; adjudged Oct term 1886]

421. Frank Gero, French.[58] [Keene]

422. Joseph Palmer, Am., age 38 [Keene; adjudged Oct 1886]

[143] 423. Chas. Anderson, Swedish, born in Sweden; is ___ years of age. Came to Harrisville to work on the Keene and Manchester Railroad, was taken sick and removed to the County Almshouse. {Oct term 1886} Mr. Anderson has remained at the Farm since the date of admission, and does not wish to go away. He has worked steadily and faithfully, and is a good man. [Harrisville; adjudged Apr term 1877]

424. E. L. Barrett, American, born in Hinsdale. Parents still reside there. Admitted to the Almshouse as a town pauper and boarded there several months. He is partially insane. {Readmitted 18 Oct 1888 as a town patient, is at this time

---

[58] See also #216, page 73.

Cheshire County Paupers
1885-1900

(1 May 1891) about 28 years old.} [Hinsdale; town pauper]

425. William L. Bolster, American, b. in Gilsum, is ___years of age, single. Is idiotic and has been from birth. Has been supported at the public expense for many years. {Re-moved to the County Farm 18 Jan 1886. It is claimed that his mother who married John Cole, for her last husband, left the use of $500 to her husband during his life time; at his death the principal is to be used for the support of her son. Wm. L. Bolster: see will on file Probate Office.}[59] [Gilsum; adjudged after Apr term 1875]

[144] 426. A. E. Burpee, American. [Dublin]

427. Chas. Burns, Irish.

428. Eddy Bates, American

[145] 429. Benjamin Crosby, American.

430. John Donnally, Irish.

431. William Eastman, American.

[146] 432. Charles Field, American, son of Rufus D. Has a brother living with Mr. Fullam of Winchester. See #214.

433. John Fitzgerald, Irish.

434. Chas. Flemming, American.

[147] 435. Hosea and Mary Grimes.

436. Rufus E. Guillow, American. See page 17. [Gilsum]

---

[59] Verne Greene checking...

Cheshire County Paupers
1885-1900

437. Alpheus Handy, American, born in ___, 56 years old. Single, is partially insane and at times quite violent, but has not been bad for a number of years. His father Paul Handy resides in Fitzwilliam. Alpheus was in the late war and lost his left arm. He burnt a barn in Fitzwilliam and convicted of the offense and committed to the Asylum as an insane person. He possesses some property and draws a pension of $30 per month and is under guardianship. He was admitted to the Almshouse 3 Dec 1873 on request of his guardian who pays the county $10 per week for his board, and has since 21 Feb 1886. [Fitzwilliam; 13 Nov 1886]

[148] 438. Fred E. Hill, American. See page 54.

439. Amasiah Keyes, American.

440. Jonas Miles, American.

[149] 441. Alvin Martin,[60] American, Richmond, born in Richmond, 77 years old. Admitted to Almshouse 27 Jun 1884. Has a brother Ansel living in Richmond and other relatives. {Died at the Almshouse 19 Jun 1891, buried in County Cemetery.} [Adjudged Apr term 1882]

442. William McCarney, Irish.

443. M. F. Newton, American.

[150] 444. J. C. Plummer, American.

445. Walter E. Porter, French.

---

[60] Original shows the name to be "Marlin," but according to the 1880 census for Richmond, his name is "Martin."

Cheshire County Paupers
1885-1900

446. William Ruffle,[61] American, Keene, born in Keene, and at this time (1 May 1891) he is 64 years old. Has one son William J. Ruffle residing in Keene and two daughters that are married.

[151] 447. Joseph Thompson, American.

448. Ithama Ward, American.

449. Josiah Wilson, American, Swanzey. Has been supported by the County since 1875. Adjudged 26 Jul 1875, was then 58 years old. Admitted to the Almshouse 15 Feb 1882. {30 Nov 1891} Said Wilson is now nearly blind and deaf.

[152] 450. Nancy Ballou, Am., born Surry. Inmate of the NH Asylum many years until transferred to Westmoreland 12 Dec 1877. She at times is violent, hard to control, all of the time.

451. Mary Callahan, Irish, Swanzey. Adjudged Apr term 1871, was then 28 years old. Admitted and discharged from the Almshouse several times. Readmitted 9 Nov 1885 and has since remained there. She is very violent at times. Has a mother and married sister residing in East Swanzey. She owns one half interest in a small place near East Swanzey.

452. Sarah Dickinson, American, Swanzey, born in Swanzey. Adjudged Apr term of court 1870; then 46 years old. Admitted to the Almshouse 1 Nov 1870. Insane, has to have a room by herself. Died at the County Farm.
[153] 453. Deborah A. Fish, American, Hinsdale. Father's name: James; mother's name: Deborah Perham. Her father died when she was about 2 ½ years old, and her mother some 20

---

[61] William Ruffle's divorce in 1875 is covered in *'Til Divorce Do Us Part* by author, page 170.

Cheshire County Paupers
1885-1900

years ago. No brothers or sisters, single. Has one illegitimate child, viz: Julius Hiram Pelkey, born 7 May 1864 or 1865, placed in the Orphans' Home, Franklin in 1867 or 1868. She was admitted the Almshouse, Westmoreland when the institution was first opened 18 Nov 1867, and has been there without vacation all the years since.

454.[62]

455. E. M. Gallagher, Irish.

456. Grace Hale, American.

[154] 457. J. C. Harrison, American.

458. I. S. Holbrook, American.

459. Pattie, American.

[155] 460. Bridget Riley, Irish.

461. Lucy P. Russell, American.

462. Mary E. Russell, French.

[156] 463. Anna Smith, Am., d. at the County Farm Sep 1892.

464. Bridget D. Smith, Irish.

465. Martha Stratton, American.

[157] 466. Phoeba Stevens,[63] American.

---

[62] This number was left out of the sequence.
[63] See #309, page 104.

Cheshire County Paupers
1885-1900

467. Sarah O. (Aldrich) Thayer, American.

468. Mary Whitcomb, American, born in Richmond, is ___ years old, single. Parents reside in Richmond; father's name: Joseph. Has a sister, Mrs. Stephen Williams in Keene, and one in Jaffrey, Mrs. Bailey. Mary, when young, was bright, intelligent.

[158] 469. Rhoda Woodcock, American.

470. Stella Wake, American.

471. Lydia and Abigail Cass, Americans. Lydia Cass died 4 Nov 1886. [Richmond]

[159] 472. George Goyette, Keene (3-4 months), French, born in Canada, 26 years old. Married; wife Josephine Baraby, 28 years old. Children: Louis A.(7 years, 7th Jun) and Frank E. (age 1, last of Mar). Father resides in Montreal, Canada; mother dead. Her parents reside in West Farnham, Canada. Sickly and unable to do any hard work; hence the application for aid. {House, Centre St., corner Midelle} [Keene, 7 Dec 1886; admitted 12 Mar 1887]

473. Albert Weld, Keene, English. Married; wife Jane Weld was born in Canada. His age is 34 years; hers is 29 years. Two children, viz: Willie W. and George M., aged respectively 11 and 8 years. Have resided in NH only a few months. Mr. W's parents are dead; Mrs. W's parents reside in Canada. He has been at work in Skeete factory until taken sick some six weeks ago. [Keene, 10 Dec 1886; admitted 9 Mar 1887]
474. William A. Flagg, Jaffrey, American, born in Fitchburg, MA, 38 years old. Married; wife Ermina C., was the daughter

Cheshire County Paupers
1885-1900

of Luke and Emeline C. Bryant and is 31 years old, 30 Dec 1885. Married 27 Nov 1871. Four children, viz: Lizzie M., born 21 Jan 1873; Robert F., born 4 Apr 1875; Almon M., born 27 Jun 1879; and Ada J., born 10 Nov 1882. Resided in Fitzwilliam from 1873 to 1881; in Winchendon, MA five years; to Jaffrey to reside in Aug 1886. Wife sick. [Jaffrey, 17 Dec 1886; admitted 12 Mar 1887]

[160] 475. Onesime Lamiraude, French, born in Canada, 44 years old. Married; have 3 children, who are minors, viz: Mary Jane, 4 years; Laura, 3 years; and Harry, 1 year old. Resided in Farmington, NH about 12 years since 1 Jan 1870, and only about one year in Ashuelot, NH. Is well spoken of as a man willing to work, when able, and support his family and pay his bill. Is sick at the present time and hence, the application for aid. [Winchester, 25 Dec 1886]

476. Marion G. Bates, born in Hillsboro, NH, age 15 years last Apr, daughter of Mathew Holbrook of Stoddard. Married Francis A. Bates. He was born in Gilsum and is about 43 years of age. [Gilsum, 10 Jan 1887; admitted 3/7/90]

477. Proctor R. Gay, Keene, born in Derby, VT, will be 44 years old next Oct. Married; wife died in Sep, 3 years ago. One child 16 years old, the 26 Aug 1886. Has resided in Littleton, Lisbon, Newport, Concord and Hill, NH since 1 Jan 1870, but in no town in the state over two years in succession. Has been aided in Concord and Hill since last Jun by the county of Merrimack. Was advised by the commissioners of the county to go back to Keene, to which town he was credited when he enlisted into the service. In 1884 he was aided in Keene to go to Penn. {24 Jan 1887} Has been aided in Merrimack County within three months. {This man is evidently a dead beat.} Had notice given in paper of his being a fraud, etc. [Keene, 24 Jan 1887; affidavit filed 24 Oct 1884, but not admitted]

Cheshire County Paupers
1885-1900

[161] 478. Marsden Bishop, Keene, born in Nova Scotia, 46 years of age the 29th of last Jun. Widower; buried his wife some three years ago while residing at Framingham, MA. Has seven children; five minors; four dependent upon him for support, viz: Edgar Truman, 11 years old, the 13 of Mar inst; Abbie Belle, 9 years; Arthur P., 7 years, Feb last; Olive A., 4 years, May 1886; Luella Maud, is 16 years old and taken care of her younger brothers and sister until taken sick. She is now under treatment at the Invalids Home this city. The father requests the four youngest children placed in good home. [Keene, 2 Mar 1887]

479. Mrs. H. L. Carson, Keene, American, born in Bethlehem, NH, 64 years of age. Has been married; husband died in 1862. She has been canvassing to earn her living and that of her mother who is now with her. Came to Keene last Saturday and stopped at Eagle Hotel. Claim to be destitute and without means to pay their bills or leave town. Claim to be residents of Holderness, NH and that town has been their home for many years. Mrs. C's mother Cynthia T. Coffin is 77 years old and her husband died some eighteen years ago. She claims that her husband was well-to-do until failed by the failure of ex-Governor Gilmore. Authorized Overseer Howland to assist them toward home as far as Concord, NH. [Keene, 5 Mar 1887; accepted 9 Mar 1887]

480. Lizzie Moreney, Keene, Irish, born in Ireland. Came to America about 6 years ago; came to NH about 2 months ago. Was married two years ago last month to James Moreney. He returned to the old country the 15 of last Oct; expects him back in May next. Have no children. Am pregnant, expects to be confined within a month or two. Her husband is 22 years old and her age is 26. She wants to go to her aunt's in Watertown, CT; to be sick; has no means to get there. Will have to have aid if she remains here. Has received money from her husband and

*Cheshire County Paupers
1885-1900*

therefore withdraws her application for aid, dated 9 Mar. [Keene, 8 Mar 1887]

[162] 481. Achsah Little (affidavit of Austin O. Adams), Jaffrey, America, age 63 years old, stepmother of Mrs. A. O. Adams and of Rev. J. H. Little, who resided in Jaffrey for a number of years. Her husband died in Lowell, MA 29 Jul 1868. Mrs. L. is afflicted with rheumatism and unable to labor. She resides with Mr. A. O. Adams who does not feel able to support her. [Jaffrey, 7 Mar 1887; admitted]

482. Charles Moore, Rindge, born in St. John, NB, 33 years old. Has always resided in NB until he came to Rindge in 1883. Married; wife Catherine Moore is 31 years old. Neither of our parents ever resided in NH. Children: Mary Ann, age 5; John Andrew, 3 years; and Martha L., 5 months. [Rindge, 9 Feb 1887; admitted]

483. Samuel C. Hudson, Gilsum, born in Gilsum, 64 years old. [Gilsum, 17 Mar 1887; admitted Apr term 1887]

[163] 484. John Loisell, Marlborough, born in Canada, 32 years old. Married; wife Sophia Selline. Four children, viz: Eva, 10 years old; Lena, 8 years old; Glory, 4 years old; and Ida, 2 years old. [Marlborough; admitted 15 Apr 1887]

485. Mrs. Maria Gains and five children, Fitzwilliam. Affidavit incomplete; returned to selectmen. [Fitzwilliam, 12 Apr 1887; 4-13-87, affidavit returned for additional proof]

486. Chas. H. Dougan, Westmoreland, born in Hartford, NY, 31 years old. Unmarried. Has resided most of his life in the states of NY and VT. Parents never resided in NH. Ordered to the County Farm 26 Apr 1887. [Westmoreland, 20 Apr 1887; admitted 23 Apr 1887]

Cheshire County Paupers
1885-1900

[164] 487. Emily C. Allard, Keene, born in Grantham, NH, 43 years old. Married; 5 children, viz: Frank D., 13 years; Amy B., 12 years; Ralph C., age 9; Bruce, 7 years; Grace B., 3 years. Claims to have a house in Pittsford, VT to which place they were furnished transportation. [Keene, 9 Nov 1886; admitted Apr term 1887]

488. Lucius Spear, Keene, born in Quincy, MA, 58 years old. On his way to his house in MA. Destitute of means to pay his lodging and board. Transient. [Keene, 11 Nov 1886; admitted Apr term 1887]

489. Robert Mitchell, Keene, age unknown. Common laborer, has resided in Keene only a short time. Was taken sick and hence his application for aid. Left for parts unknown as soon as he was able to be out. Affidavit of P. Howland taken. [Keene, 11 Apr 1887; admitted Apr term 1887]

[165] 490. John H. Congdon for Willie Winters. Young Winters was brought the Avon Place Orphans' Home, Cambridge, MA, age and place of birth unknown. By order of J. B. Abbott he was taken back to the Home from which he was taken. [Troy, 6 Apr 1887; admitted Apr term 1887]

491. Geo. R. Putnam, Nelson, born in Orange, MA, 28 years old. Married; wife, Mary. No children. Came to Nelson about 1885. Never lived in NH before. Have resided nearly all of my life in Orange, MA. Mrs. Putnam has been sick and the house in which they lived was burned about 1 Apr 1887. Lost everything except the night clothes they had on at the time. His and her parents reside in MA. They have been removed to Harrisville, NH. [Nelson, 8 Apr 1887; admitted Apr term 1887]

Cheshire County Paupers
1885-1900

492. Asa Kempton, Richmond, born in R, 27 Feb 1823. Always resided in R; father resided and died there. Insane for more that 20 years. Lives with his brother Simon Kempton. Died 1 Jul 1889. [Richmond, Oct 1886; adjudged Oct 1875]

[166] 493. George Champane,[64] Swanzey, born in Canada, age 32; wife Elizabeth, 26 years old; one son George, age 4 years. Went from Canada to Gardner, MA to reside about 4 years ago. Neither his parents or the parents of his wife ever resided in NH. Has been at work at the box shop, Wilson Pond, but having only part time work now, he is unable to support his family and therefore asks for aid to return to Canada. [Swanzey, 21 Apr 1887; admitted 23 Apr 1887]

494. Elizabeth Healey, Keene, Irish, born in Ireland, 24 years old. Came to America about 7 years ago and to Keene from Chester, VT last January (1887). Father dead; mother resides in Ireland; sister Mary Lawton living in Providence, RI. Married John Morrison, but he left her nearly 2 ½ years ago. She learned he had a wife living at the time. Recently confined; child lived only a short time after its birth; makes oath that James B. Sullivan of Chester, VT, was the father of the child; he promised to pay all expenses during her confinement. [Keene, 11 Apr 1887; admitted 23 Apr 1887]

495. Chas. A. Siefert, Keene, age 42. Wife Katie, age 30. Two children, viz: Mary K., age 19 and Ida, age 6 years. Out of work; applies for aid to get to Philadelphia where he has a letter to show that he and his daughter can have work. Promises to return the cost of ticket if we will pay for his fare there. Directed Overseer Howland to furnish him a ticket. [Keene, 26 Apr 1887; admitted 26 Apr 1887]

---

[64] See also #892, page 300.

*Cheshire County Paupers
1885-1900*

[167] 496. Dennis A. Phelps, Walpole, born in Londonderry, VT 21 Dec 1836. In January 1856 married Silvia Abbott of said Londonderry; has seven living children, aged respectively 8-10-13-17-24-26-29. Has resided in said Walpole since 1872 or 1873.[65]

497. Mary LaPlant, Keene, born in Barnet, VT, 38 years old. Married Richard LaPlant at Concord, NH in 1873. He was born to the best of Mrs. LaPlant's knowledge in Canaan, NH. He is by occupation a railroad employee on Cheshire Railroad since he came to Keene until recently when he drew his pay in full and left for parts unknown to his wife. He is 31 years old. Have 4 children, viz: John, aged 13, in Jun next; Lewis A., 8 years in Sep last; H. A. and Harvey I. (twins), 5 years, 4 May inst. She applies for aid to pay rent, having been ordered out of her house. [Keene, 9 May 1887; admitted 12 May 1887]

498. Mrs. Elizabeth Wood, Keene, born in Ordensbury,[66] NY, 45 years old. Married; Elijah Wood in 1862. He is 55 years old. Have two children, Mary F. age 24 and Charles, age 17. Husband has been at work in the skate factory until recently; had a little trouble and left. Has gone to Manchester to find employment. Never had to call for aid before. Daughter has been married; husband's name Joseph LaBounty. He is dead. She can have work in a mill at Manchester and the family ask for aid to get there. The boy is at work in Nashua. [Keene, 12 May 1887; admitted 12 May 1887]

[168] 499. Hannah Crouch, Chesterfield, American. Has resided in Chesterfield for a great many years. In 1876 she fell and broke her leg or thigh and since has been aided by the

---

[65] No date of application or admittance given.
[66] Perhaps Ogdensburg is meant.

county. She is now (Apr term 1887) 80 years old. She is a very worthy old lady and is deserving of much sympathy. See page 135. [Chesterfield; adjudged Oct term 1876]

500. Lena Goyette, Keene, French, born in St. Mary, Canada, 21 years old, single. Parents both dead. They never resided in NH. She has resided here some four months. Has been doing housework, but is unable to work now, expects to be confined about the 1st of Jul. She alleges that she was seduced by a young man in Montreal, Canada, that she does not know his present whereabouts. She is now living with her brother George Goyette, corner of Centre and Middle Streets, who is receiving relief for himself and family. [Keene, 14 May 1887; admitted 16 May 1887]

501. Mrs. Mary Lynch, Hinsdale, Irish, born in Ireland, 22 years old. Married; husband Richard Lynch was born in Lawrence, MA and is 25 years old. He has recently deserted his family. Two children: Margaret, 4 years old and John, 2 years. Her husband is intemperate, abuses his family; recently struck his wife's mother and broke her arm. She works in the mill. They have resided in Hinsdale only since last Jul. Came there from Lawrence. [Hinsdale, 16 May 1887; admitted 17 May 1887]

[169]. 502. Joseph Castro, Keene, Irish, 27 years old. Married; wife's name Margaret. She is about 38 years old. One child, Joseph, who will be 4, the 12th day of Jul next. His parents reside in Highgate. Her parents reside in Keene. She gained a settlement through her parents and has been assisted, according to the overseers report in the city of Keene. Having gained a settlement she does not lose it until she gains another. See #817. [Keene, 23 May 1887; admitted after Apr term 1887]

Cheshire County Paupers
1885-1900

503. John Q. Kinson, Keene, American, born in East Ware (*sic*), NH 22 May 1844, and is now 43 years old. Has been married; buried his wife Addie last fall. Has one child living with him, Willie D., age 11 years, last Apr; the other child's name is Jessie F. and she was 16 years old last Feb. He was a member of Co. G, 14 NH Vols in the war of 1861-5. Has resided in Ashburnham, MA for 18 years last past. Was paralyzed about one year and a half ago and has been helpless since. Has been aided in Ashburnham. Came to Keene about the middle of May to avail himself of the act for the benefit of soldiers and seamen, etc., having been ordered to the Poor House in Ashburnham. Has a woman from Boston to keep his house. [Keene, 31 May 1887; admitted after Apr term 1887]

504. James Kenney, Marlborough, born in Boston, MA, 22 years old in Nov 1886. Parents died when he was about 3 years old. Came to Marlborough to reside about the first of Feb 1887. Sick, removed him to the hospital apartment of the House of Corrections, Keene. Has had a run of typhoid fever. No friends or relatives in this country. [Marlborough, 4 May 1887; admitted after Apr term 1887]

[170] 505. Joseph Duplesy, Winchester, French, born in Canada, 36 years old. Married; wife was born in Canada. Have eight children, viz: Simon, age 13; Joseph, age 11; Candace, age 7; Mary, age 5; Johnny, age 4; Phillip, age 3; Victoria, age 2; infant, age 7 months. Have no parents residing in the US. [Winchester, 5 May 1887; admitted after Apr term 1887]

506. Chas. F. Cutting, Swanzey, American, born in Northfield, MA, 8 Apr 1850. Has resided in Springfield, MA and Winchester, NH since 1870. Parents reside at Westport, NH, are poor and unable to take care and support him. [Swanzey, 11 Jun; after Apr term 1887]

Cheshire County Paupers
1885-1900

507. Mary Murphy, Keene, Irish, born in Ireland, unable to tell her age; is probably nearly 70 years old. No relatives, no friends in this county. Has resided for several years in Swanzey at Mr. Asa A. Kendall's. Has a very bad limb that will doubtless kill her sooner or later. She was never married. [Keene, 14 Jun 1887; admitted after Apr term 1887]

[171] 508. Lowell C. Mason, Keene, American, 35 years old. Single; father resides in Keene; mother dead. Has a brother residing in Keene and a sister, Mrs. E. E. Pressey of Worcester. Said Mason is an imbecile and is and has been for some time past living at Wilber's in Surry. [Keene, 20 Jun 1887; admitted]

509. Rufus Foster Whitney, Keene, American, 41 years old; married. Have 3 children, viz: Addison, 17 years old; Charles R., 11 years; Perley E., 4 years. Sent to the Asylum, Concord 25 Jun 1887; died there 5 Jul 1887. [Keene, 5 Jun 1887; admitted after Apr term 1887]

510. Margaret Coy, Hinsdale, Irish, born in Ireland, 62 years old. Came to America 14 years ago; lived in Boston, Salam (*sic*) and Lawrence, MA; in Hinsdale 6 months. Husband died 30 May 1873. Arm broken by her daughter's husband Richard Lynch. [Hinsdale, 4 Jul 1887; admitted after Apr term 1887]

[172] 511. Charles E. Champney, Frenchman. Married; shot his wife 2 Jul 1887; two balls took off edin (*sic*) the back of head; removed to Cheshire County jail. His age about 29 years. Louisa Champney, his wife, is doing well; asks for no further aid. [Fitzwilliam, 5 Jul 1887; admitted after Apr term 1887]

512. Alfred Morse, Marlborough, American, b. in Swanton, VT, 26 years old. When I was 17 years old, then came to Marlborough. Am married; wife's name is Hatty Rivers; have

Cheshire County Paupers
1885-1900

one child 5 months old. [Marlborough, 11 Jul 1887; admitted after Apr term 1887]

512 ½. Alzevine Lamonanda, Frenchman, born in Canada, 45 years old. Came to the United States in 1861. I have a wife and two children. My wife's name is Caroline Lamonanda. My wife was born in Canada and her parents live there now. [Winchester, 25 Oct 1887; admitted Oct term 1887]

[173] 513. Terressa Spitzenberger, North Walpole, born in Germany, 39 years old. Was married to Frank Spitzenberger of Eley (*sic*), VT in Aug 1883; lived there until Mar 1884 when we moved to North Walpole, NH where we lived until the death of my husband 14 Apr 1887. I am in destitute condition with two small children to care for, one boy three years old and one boy 18 months old. [North Walpole, 26 Nov 1887; admitted Oct term 1887]

514. Charles J. Hinds, Keene, b. Winchendon, MA, 7 Mar 1841; am now 46 years of age. I am poor and unable to work by reason of physical disability. I have resided in Keene since 1 Jan 1870, except for the period of about two years. My father is reported to be an inmate of the County Almshouse.[67] My mother died in Walpole some 5 years ago. I have been married but was divorced from my wife some 10 years ago. I had three children: Charles Frederick, William Leonard and Carrie E. Can't recollect their ages. I served in the army of the United States in Co. F, 6th NH Vols, and was honorably discharged. [Keene, 29 Nov 1887; admitted after Oct term 1887]

515. Margaret Cornfield, Hinsdale, born in Ireland, am 70 years old. Came from Canada Aug 1887. I brought with me a grandson Johnnie Cornfield, 13 years old; his father and mother

---

[67] See #381, page 128.

both dead. [Hinsdale, 18 Nov 1887; admitted after Oct term 1887]

[174] 516. Frances C. Bugbee, Jaffrey, born in Hancock, NH 25 Oct 1838. I am 49 years old. I married Charles N. Bugbee Sep 1856. My husband is insane; I have not lived with him for 11 years. My husband was a member of Co. A, 3d VT Vol. I came to NH in 1881. I have never owned any property of any description. [Jaffrey, 18 Oct 1887; admitted Oct term 1887]

517. Leon Boufor, Winchester, born in Canada, 38 years old. Came to the United States about a year ago. My father died when I was about 4 years old. My wife was Adele Gonyou, born in Canada; died in Winchester 30 Sep 1887. I have nine children: Emma, age 18; Georgianna, age 17; Joseph, age 14; Cyrelo, age 12; George, age 10; Mary, age 6; Richard, age 4; Anne, age 2; and Florence, age 1 month. [Winchester, 18 Oct 1887; admitted Oct term 1887]

518. Aleck Granier, Winchester, born in Canada in the district of Quebeck (*sic*)., and 40 years old. Came to Winchester in Apr 1876. My father is now living in Canada and has never lived in the United States. My wife is Annie Nellitt, is 55 years old, was born in Canada; have 6 children: Annie, age 14; Alice, age 11; Philemen, age 7; Leander, age 5; Velcemer, age 3; and Demorest, age 1. [Winchester, 20 Oct 1887; admitted Oct term 1887]

[175] 519. Solomon Ballane, Walpole, County of Cheshire. In Oct 1885, a woman calling herself Nellie E. Johnson of Bellows Falls, VT came to my house and engaged board for her boy Arthur W. Johnson, then about 8 years old for $1.75 per week. She continued to pay his board until about Oct 1886, when she stopped making payments and has paid nothing since. I know nothing of said Mrs. Johnson; she said she was separated from

Cheshire County Paupers
1885-1900

her husband. Nor do I know anything of her husband. [Walpole, 24 Oct 1887; admitted Oct term 1887]

520. Eliza E. Davis, Swanzey, born in Chesterfield, 46 years old. I was married in 1865 to John Nash of Winchester, whom I afterwards learned had a wife living. My first husband's name was James L. Davis, who died in the army. I lived with Nash about 4 years, then moved to MA where we separated. I have 3 children, the youngest is 26 years old. [Swanzey, 21 Nov 1887; admitted after Oct term 1887]

521. Annie Newton, Keene, born in Lebanon, NH, 26 years old, single. I am the mother of Frank Newton, who was born on the 11th day of Dec 1886 in the city of Boston. I am unable to maintain my child; therefore, apply to the city of Keene to support him. My mother has been dead for many years. My father is living, so far as I know. [Keene, 11 Jul 1887; admitted after Apr term 1887]

[176] 522. George H. Page, Swanzey, County of Cheshire. I was born in Leominster, MA and am 57 years old. I was married on 21 Mar 1878 to Mary E. Smith of Worcester, MA, whose parents' home was in the state of NY. I have 3 children: Frank E., 8 years old; George B., 6 years old; and Beloa May, 3 years old. I resided in Leominster, MA in 1870 where I afterwards continued to live 4 or 5 years. [Swanzey, 26 Oct 1887; admitted after Oct term 1887]

523. Edward Moor, Marlborough, born in Canada in the town of Barnston, 55 years old. I left Canada about 15 years ago, came to Claremont, NH. I have a wife and four children named Ellen, age 16; Lizabeth, 12 years; Jerry, 10 years old; Selina, 7 years old. My father and mother have never lived in NH. [Marlborough, 25 Jul 1887; admitted after Apr term 1887]

Cheshire County Paupers
1885-1900

524. Leander Felt, Winchester, NH. My sister Irene W. Felt is old and of poor memory and is unable to support herself. Irene W. Felt was born in Nelson, NH about the year 1814, was never married, came to Winchester with her father's family sometime between the years 1850 and 1860. Irene W. Felt's mother died while her father lived in Sullivan. {Died Nov 1887.} [Winchester, 2 Jun 1887; admitted after Apr term 1887]

[177] 525. Margaret Henderson, Keene, born in Nova Scotia in 1828, 59 years old, widow; buried my husband George Henderson 11 years ago. Have one child George C., 19 years old, the 15th day of last Jul. I furthermore state that my son met with a serious accident by which he had his right foot partly cut off. I am obliged to ask for relief from the city of Keene, being poor and no relatives able to support me. [Keene, 8 Aug 1887; admitted after Apr term 1887]

526. Asa M. Ray, Keene. I was born in Sutton, MA. I am 59 years old, the 4th day of Jan last. I am poor and in need of relief for myself and wife. We came to Hinsdale to live 8 or 9 years ago; remained there 2 years; removed to Westport, NH; remained about 2 years; moved to Keene. Was in the US army, Co. A, 57th MA. Myself or wife have never owned any real estate or taxable property. Reside with their daughter Mrs. Lucius F. Breed. {Mrs. Eliza Ray died 18 Feb 1889, age 56.} [Keene, 18 Aug 1887; admitted after Apr term 1887]

527. William F. Haskell, Keene, born in Boston, MA, 22 Jun 1828. I have been sick since last Jul. I am poor and in need of relief and therefore apply to the city of Keene for such assistance as my condition may require. I am a widower. My wife died some 25 years ago. I have no children, have resided in Stoddard and Keene most of the time since 1870. Was a member of Co. C., 4th NH Vols, and was honorably discharged

Cheshire County Paupers
1885-1900

from the army of the United States in May 1862. [Keene, 2 Sep 1887; admitted after Apr term 1887]

[178] 528. Frank Byron, Marlborough, born in Canada, 39 years old. I came from Canada to Marlborough in the fall of 1885, have never lived in NH before that time. Louisa Byron, my wife, is 33 years old. We were married in Milbury, MA 18 years ago. We have nine children. I do not own any real estate in the United States. [Marlborough, 20 Sep 1887; admitted after Apr term 1887]

529. John P. Fallaize, Marlborough. Say I was born in the Island of Guernsie. I came to Marlborough, NH about the 1st of Jul 1886. I am a single man, 27 years old. My father or my mother never lived in the United States. I am sick and have no money to pay my expenses. [Marlborough, 24 Sep 1887; admitted after Apr term 1887]

530. Emily Massier, Marlborough, born in Canada, 25 years old. Married in Canada to Elicha Massier, who is 32 years old. Came to Marlborough 24 May 1880, have never lived in any other place. We have 4 children:[68] Esther, 9 years; Fred, 7 years; Eli, 2 months. My husband has never owned any real estate. [Marlborough, 20 Sep 1887; admitted after Apr term 1887]

[179] 531. Annie Patnode, Winchester, wife of the late John Patnode who died in this town on 14 Sep last. My husband John Patnode was born in Demorana, NY 1869; he came to Winchester to live about 15 years ago. His father and mother both died when he was a child. [Winchester, 25 Oct 1887; admitted Oct term 1887]

---

[68] Only 3 children listed.

Cheshire County Paupers
1885-1900

532. Edward C. Blanchard, Hinsdale, born in Hinsdale, 63 years old. Married in 1857 to Amanda Stockwell of Boston, MA. My wife is 47 years old. Moved to Vernon, VT in 1868, lived there 6 years; Barnardston, MA 5 years; moved to Hinsdale, NH in Apr 1884. On the evening of 9 Dec 1887 Mr. Blanchard was badly burned by the bursting of a lamp while he was reading. [Hinsdale, 19 Dec 1887; admitted after Oct term 1887]

533. Ira A. Kinson, Keene, born in Ware (sic), Hillsboro County, NH 22 Nov 1841; that I married Annie E. Murdo 22 years ago last Jul; that she is 40 years old the 4th of Jul last. Have seven children, viz: Alfred Decatur, 19 years; Clarence Austin, 16 years; Edgar, 14 years; Henry, 12 years; Claud, 8 years; Ionia Estella, 5 years; Captola Mary, 3 years. I resided in Ashburnham, MA from 1 Jan 1870 to 1886; from 1876 to 1878 in Washington, this state; and in Keene since that date. [Keene, 27 Dec 1887; admitted after Oct term 1887]

[180] 534. Mary E. Hamblet, Keene, daughter of Mr. and Mrs. Oren Hammond of Richmond and Keene, respectively deceased. My mother died at my house in Keene, Oct last; my father died in Richmond, Jun 1885. To the best of my knowledge and belief neither my father or mother have owned any real estate in their own right or personal taxable property of the value of $250. [Keene, 27 Dec 1887; admitted after Oct term 1887]

535. Lucy Prux, born in Canada, 33 years old. Came to Marlborough, NH, the 11th day of Nov 1886. I have two children: one boy Lewis, 13 years old; one girl Florence, 7 years old. My husband died in Canada about 3 years ago. We lived in Manchester, NH, some two years previous to his death. [Marlborough, 30 Dec 1887; admitted after Oct term 1887]

Cheshire County Paupers
1885-1900

536. Delany Ware, Keene, born in Buckland, MA, 83 years old, the 21st of Nov 1886. I am poor and unable to support myself and having no relatives who are liable or able to support me without aid. I came to Keene to reside with my son Dexter D. Ware. My husband John Ware died at Shelburn Falls, MA 16 Jun 1862. I have four children living: Roxana resides at Athol, MA; Sylvester M. whereabouts unknown; Dexter D. above named 48 years old. [Keene, 29 Jul 1887; admitted after Apr term 1887]

[181] 537. Walter Read, Nelson, English, born in London, Great Britain, 24 years old. I came to this country about two weeks ago. I am out of money and obliged to ask for aid over Sunday, when I shall again search for work. [Nelson, 6 Jun 1887; admitted Oct term 1887]

538. Frank G. Farnum, Jaffrey. I am well acquainted with Julia Farwell. She has lived in my father's family for more than 20 years until his death in 1884. Since that time she has lived with my mother and myself. We have lived in Jaffrey all the time to Mar 1886. She has never owned any property of any description since 1870. She never married. She never received any aid from any town or place. She was born in Nelson, NH 28 Jul 1823. She has never owned any property of any description since 1870. [Jaffrey, 5 Jan 1888; admitted after Oct term 1887]

539. Lewis Lapoint, Troy, born in Berkshire, VT, in the year 1847. I was married 25 Dec 1867 to Julia Freeman who was born in Burlington, VT in 1847. I lived in Canada until Mar 1885. I have not lived in any place in NH except Troy. I am not the owner of any real estate nor personal property to the amount of $100. [Troy, 2 Mar 1888; admitted after Oct term 1887]

Cheshire County Paupers
1885-1900

[182] 540. Susan A. Carpenter, born Walpole, 45 years old. My husband's name was James Carpenter, who died the 10th of May 1887. I have seven children, 3 of whom are dependent on me for support: Elmer V. and Ida V., twins, born 29 Mar 1876; and Daisy C., born 23 Nov 1885. Since 1 Jan 1878 I resided in Walpole about 3 years; in Alstead about 4 years; in Marlow about 8 years; in Gilsum, 1 year; and in Keene since last May. We have not since 1 Jan 1870, owned any real estate. [Keene, 27 Dec 1887; admitted after Oct term 1887]

541. Joseph Vigneault, French, Swanzey, born in St. Celestine, Canada, 36 years old. Married to Victoria Richard in 1874 of St. Gregory, Canada, whose parents also live at St. Gregory where they have always resided. I have 5 children, namely, Victoria, 14 years; Willis, 4 years; Ernest, 11 years; Jennie, 8 years; and Glory, 1 year old. I resided in Canada in 1870 when I continued to live for about 12 years when I came to Hinsdale, where I lived about a year. Moved to Newmarket, NH where I lived about a year. I have not owned an equitable interest in $150 of real or $250 of personal estate or paid taxes on that amount. [Swanzey, 28 Jan 1888; admitted after Oct term 1887]

542. Charles MacClaine, Keene, born in Scotland. Has not any father or mother living; never lived in NH. Was sent to the County Farm. [Keene, Oct term 1888]

[183] 543. Michael Kelly, Irish, born in Ireland, 29 years old. Work at Bellows Falls, VT. Married; wife's name is Maru Kelly. Have two children, 16 and 2 years old. Wife insane and taken to the NH Asylum. [Walpole, after Oct term 1887]

544. Willard H. Rumrill, born in Weathersfield, VT, 23 years old. Married; my wife's name is Florence A. Rumrill, born in Canada; 19 years old. Lived in NH about one year. My wife is sick, the reason I call for help. [Gilsum; after Oct term 1887]

Cheshire County Paupers
1885-1900

545. A. G. Shockley, born Kennebunk, ME. Married; wife's name is Matilda Shockley, 49 years old. Have three children: Mary E., 17; Anna G., 16; and Walter W., 14 years old. Lived in Keene 13 years. [Keene; after Oct term 1887]

[184] 546. Herbert Spring, 44 years old, not of sound mind. Has lived for 20 years at Charles Knight's in Westmoreland. Never was married; living at William H. Woodward, Keene. Ordered to County Farm. [Keene; after Oct term 1887]

547. Joseph Gorman, 24 years old. Married; wife's name Mary, 24 years old. Have two children: one 3 years old and the other 1 year. Had my feet badly frozen. Call for temporary aid. [Sullivan; after Oct term 1887]

548. Margaret Camfill, Irish, born in Ireland, about 70 years old. Lived in Canada 40 years; came to this country last August. [Hinsdale; after Oct term 1887]

[185] 549. Rosie Piche, born in Whitehall, NY, 34 years old. Married; my husband's name Edward Piche. Have had two husbands; my first one, Theodore Rivet is still living; had a divorce from him 11 years ago. Have three children: Sarah, 19; Rose, 14; and Peter, 12. Now known as Rose Knowles. [Keene; after Oct term 1887]

550. Julia Coffey. Married; husband's name Daniel Coffey. Have three children: Daniel, 9; Julia, 6; Timothy, 4 years old. My husband is dead; died 2 years ago. Have lived in Keene 25 years. [Keene; after Oct term 1887]

551. George W. Sheldan, 47 years old. Married; my wife's name is Phoeba, who died 20 Jun 1887. Have four children:

Cheshire County Paupers
1885-1900

Eva E., 19; Ella B., 14; Grace G., 11; Herbert E., 8 years old. Have lived in Keene since 1864. [Keene; after Oct term 1887]

[186] 552. Charles H. Wilson,[69] born in Nova Scotia, 41 years old. Have a wife, who is 46 years old. No children. Have lived in Rindge, Jaffrey, Fitzwilliam, Richmond, Marlborough and Keene. Came to Keene last October. Was in the service of the United States in the late Rebellion. Live on Washington Street above Woodbury's Mill. [Keene; after Oct term 1887]

553. Mary Davis of Gilsum. Frances A. Howard, affidavit of Mary Davis; not of sound mind; died from being burnt. [Gilsum; after Oct term 1887]

554. John Tallia, born in Canada. Was married to Josephine Marrones in 1846. I am 84 and my wife is 66 years old. {John Tallia died 21 Jul 1888.} [Marlborough, Apr term 1888]

[187] 555. Fred E. Granger was born in CT, 30 years old. Lived in Keene 5 months. Am married; the name of my wife is Sarah A. Her name before her marriage was Rivet; her age is 19. Her mother's name is Rose Piche.[70] I have one child about sixteen months old. [Keene; Apr term 1888]

556. Sarah E. Breen, affidavit by John H. Rogers, 32 years old, born in Maine, came to Keene in 1876 or 1877. Lived with said Rogers 6 or 7 years. Taken to County Farm. [Surry; after Apr term 1888]

557. Benjamin Clark, affidavit by George K. Wright, has worked for said Wright for ten years. Has lived in Keene for 15 years, living at Hospital at Jail. His daughter paying $1 per

---

[69] See #1189.
[70] See #549, page 185.

Cheshire County Paupers
1885-1900

week for board. {Died 28 Sep 1889.} [Keene; after Apr term 1888]

[188] 558. Kendall B. Bryant, born in Jaffrey, 29 years old. Married Louisa Moultney. My wife had one child by her first husband, Mary Moultney, 5 years old. Has had 3 children by Bryant. Bryant was committed to jail on complaint of his wife for an assault upon her. {Was liberated after several months on account of illness, hemorrhage of the lung; soon after died. Mrs. B. was discharged from Farm where she was admitted 19 Oct 1889 and 22 May 1890; her children 19 Jun 1890.} [Jaffrey; after Apr term 1888]

559. Nancy R. Blanchard, born in Keene, 41 years old. Has a husband whose name is Amos Blanchard, who was born in Stockbridge, VT, is 44 years old. Have 4 children, whose names are as follows: Willie A., 14; J. Henry, 12; Clerance, 10 years; Flora I., 11 months old. [Keene; after Apr term 1888]

560. Mary Kennedy, affidavit by S. M. Herse, was sent to Boston. [Winchester; Apr term 1888]

560 ½. Daniel J. Nevers, Troy, born in Charlestown, NH, 12 Mar 1848. Married Risby Howard 22 Sep 1871. Five children: Bertha, Gertie, Jerome, Enos and Flossie, aged respectively 15, 11, 8, 5, and 2 years. Was a private in Co. 5th NH Vols. {D. J. Nevers dead.} [18 Feb 1888; adjudged after Apr term 1888]

[189] 561. Fred W. Davis, born in Perkinsville, VT in 1855. Have lived in Gilsum, Swanzey and Fitchburg, MA, and Keene. Am married: Clerice E. Plummer. Have had two children, were sick with the scarlet fever. Mrs. Plummer has a residence

in Winchester, therefore the children have the same.[71] [Winchester; Apr term 1888]

562. Thomas Kenyon, born in England, 43 years old. Came to America 11 years ago. Lived three years only in NH; at Tilton 2; one in Suncook. [Hinsdale; Apr term 1888]

563. Mary C. Reyneau, wife of John Reyneau, was married to him 1878 at Sharon, VT. Lived in Sharon, VT, 3 years. Her age is 25; his age is 29 years. Have three children: Emma, 5 years old; Willie, 4 years old; and Johny, 2 years old. They have lived in Richmond 3 years. Were taken to County Farm. [Richmond; Apr term 1888]

[190] 564. James E. Williams, [or Pibbs], 15 years old. Father's name George Williams who lives in MA. His mother was born in Ireland; lives with his unkle (*sic*) John Williams; was injured by the accidental discharge of a gun on Thanksgiving Day, 1887. [Winchester; Apr term 1888]

565. Adelin Laflame, 34 years old; born in Canada. Married 1869 to Nelson Laflame in NY.[72] He died three years ago; has seven children whose names and birth are as follows: Eliza, 12 Jul 1870; Laura, 9 Nov 1873; Frank, 18 Dec 1876; Matilda, 11 Dec 1878; Arche, 20 Nov 1880; Josephine, 5 Aug 1882; and Bertie, 12 Feb 1885. [Jaffrey, after Apr term 1888]

566. Maime Berthiame, born in Canada, 31 years old, came to Marlborough May 1888. [Marlborough, after Apr term 1888]

---

[71] The original gives her name as "Plummer," though that was her name before her marriage to Mr. Davis. See also #1199, page 403.
[72] In the 1860 census for Chazy, NY (Clinton Co.), Nelson is shown as a 1 year old with his parents, Andrew and Mary LaFlam, both aged 30. His sister Mary A., was age 3.

Cheshire County Paupers
1885-1900

[191] 567. Seth Wilber,[73] born in Westmoreland, 80 years old; not married, always lived in Westmoreland. Taken to the County Almshouse Jul 1888. [Westmoreland, after Apr term 1888]

568. William A. Bugbee, 26 years old, son of Francis C. Bugbee, a county pauper, adjudged Oct 1887. [Jaffrey, after Apr term 1888]

569. Malachy Brien, 68 years old, born in Ireland, lived in America five years, unmarried. Taken to the County Almshouse Oct 1888. [Keene, after the Apr term 1888]

[192] 570. James H. Daggett, 58 years old, born in Waterville, VT; am married, have ___ children; was in the Army and honorably discharged. {Died 1890.} [Walpole, after Apr term 1888]

571. William H. Fuller, 38 years old, born in Boston, MA. Married; wife's name Sarah Ann. Her maiden name was Sarah Ann Chace, 39 years old, born in MA. Seven children: William H., 9 years old; George F., 7 years old; Elisha L., 4 years old; Hattie B., 2 years old and one 2 weeks old. Came to NH Nov 1887. {Ordered from Fitzwilliam to the Almshouse and admitted 2 Apr 1890. He was discharged 19 May 1890 and his wife and children 2 Jul 1890. Ellen M. Fuller, his sister, age 20, admitted same time and discharged 15 Oct 1890.} [Rindge, after Apr term 1888]

---

[73] His name appeared to be "Willie," but the *History of Westmoreland* shows it to be "Wilber." Seth was born in Foxboro, MA, 8 Apr 1808 and died 11 Sep 1888, in Westmoreland.

Cheshire County Paupers
1885-1900

572. Tufill Robbins, born in Canada, 23 years old. Lived at Hinsdale eight years, married to Louisa Ducy of Winchester, NH, 17 years old. [Hinsdale, after the Apr term 1888]

[193] 573. Reuben Gassett,[74] age 60, b. in Townsend, MA. Was in the Army 1 ½ years; married in 1866; has two children: one, 17, and the other 15 years old. Wife living but does not know where she is. He is sick. [Walpole, after Apr term 1888]

574. Carroll Raymond by Hattie E. Cummings, his mother. Born in Winchendon, MA 11 Oct 1875. Father's name was Christopher F. Raymond of Winchendon; was divorced from him 1883. Present husband's name is Benjamin F. Cummings of Fitzwilliam. [Fitzwilliam, after Apr term 1888]

575. Neal Elmore, born in Hinsdale, 50 years old; lived in Keene, 4 or 5 years. Was married to Lizzie Whitney of Warwick, MA in 1867. She died six years ago; had three children, viz: Frank, 18 years old; Oscar, 15 years old; and Florence, 12 years old. Frank and Florence live in Boston, MA. Oscar in Keene. Was in the United States Army 2 years and honorably discharged. [Keene, after Apr term 1888]

[194] 576. Louis Wood, 26 years old, born in MA. Married; wife born, age 27 years; had one child who died recently, only three months old. [Keene; Apr term 1888]

577. Louis Gabounes, born in Minnesota, 78 years old. Came to Keene in 1875 or 1876. Taken to County Farm 13 Sep 1888. Transferred to the House of Corrections in Keene 8 Oct 1890, by reason that he made an effort to poison Marshall F. Newton with Paris Green by putting it into his tobacco. [Keene, after Apr term 1888]

---

[74] See also #82, page 28.

Cheshire County Paupers
1885-1900

578. Simon Dyer, 48 years old, born in Burlington, VT. Married; wife's name Elizabeth. Children's names as follows: Frank, 19 years old; Delia, 17; Melvin, 15; Josephine, 13; John, 12; Julia, 10; Eben, 2, and one by the name of Augdni[75] died from the effects of being burnt which made them ask for help. [Swanzey, after Apr term 1888]

[195] 579. Anna Robbins, Hinsdale, born in Canada, 40 years old. Lived in Hinsdale 5 years. Married; names of children: Silas, 19; Victory, 16; Emmah, 13; Eliza, 10; May, 5; Henry,1. Her husband left for Lowell and has sent for his family; gone to Lowell, MA. [Hinsdale; Apr term 1888]

580. Carroll Raymond by Stephen Batchelder. Same as #574. [Fitzwilliam, after Apr term 1888]

581. Delina Fountain, Walpole, Canaan, NH, 1 Jul 1866.[76] Married; husband's name Peter Fountain, 6 Jul 1880. Her husband left her 6 Jan 1888; not heard from since. Have one child, a girl 4 years old. Her husband was a drinking man. [Walpole, after Apr term 1888]

[196] 581.[77] Peter Borron by Peter T. Borron, his son. Born in Canada, 79 years old; died at Eagle Hotel, Keene, 5 Apr 1888; his son Peter T. Borrin thinks he will be able to pay the expense of burial at the Apr term 1889. [Keene, after Apr term 1888]

582. Alfred Russell, Swanzey by John C. Bourn and George W. Willis. Said Russell came from MA but a short time ago. Was married; had 2 children, the youngest died at Swanzey 28

---

[75] Transcribed as in original.
[76] Presumed to be her birthdate. See also #756, page 255.
[77] Number transcribed as in original.

Cheshire County Paupers
1885-1900

Feb 1888. Mr. Russell and wife soon left town. No further information could be had. [Swanzey, Oct term 1888]

583. Samuel Messiah by Ellen B. Bouvir, born in VT, 20 years old. He shot himself Sep 1888 at the Hotel Marlborough and was cared for there until taken to the Hospital at the jail in Keene. After getting well, left for parts unknown. [Marlborough; Oct term 1888]

[197] 584. Michael McCarty, Irish, born in Ireland, Sep 18___. Married Mary Cragen of Claremont, NH; have four children: Michael, 10 years old; Alice M., 8 years old; John, 3 years old; and James, one year old. His wife's age is 34. Mr. McCarty was sick for a long time and was better, but had a relapse and died. [Walpole; Oct term 1888]

585. Romniso Hill, Richmond, b. in Clerksbury, MA, age 40. Wife died Dec 1887; 3 children. [Richmond; Oct term 1888]

586. Mary J. Hughes, Marlborough, Irish, born in Ireland. Married: husband's name James, born in Ireland. Have five children. Her husband has gone to Barre, VT and is at work. Promises to send money for the support of his family. The children's names and ages are as follows: Michael, 9; Kate, 8; Lizzie, 3; Stephen, 2; and Eddie, seven months old. [Marlborough; Oct term 1888]

[198] 587. Ellen Deyo, Swanzey, born in Irona, NY, 21 years old. Married to John Deyo 1886; one child, 2 years old. Husband been gone four months; does not know where he is. Promises to send money but has not. {18 Feb 1890} Selectmen report that Mrs. D has a second child about 3 weeks old. Husband has returned to Swanzey to live but does not contribute to her support. [Swanzey; Oct term 1888]

Cheshire County Paupers
1885-1900

588. George Millet, Marlborough, born in Canada. Came to America 1882 to the town of Winchester. Married to Caroline Good. They have six children: Mary, 18; Emma, 16; Della, 14; Clord, 12; Carrie, 10; and Rosie, 7 years old. [Marlborough; Oct term 1888]

589. Charles M. Bishop, born in Nova Scotia, 48 years old. Married; name of wife Louisa, 25 years old. Have one child: Eddie, 3 years old. Mrs. Bishop was quite sick the time the affidavit was taken and died a few days afterwards. [Marlborough; Oct term 1888]

[199] 590. Martha Ball, Keene, born in Bristol, England, 44 years old. Married; has five children. Husband gone to Ohio and is at work. Mrs. Ball desires to go to her husband; his name is Charles. The children's names are: Sarah Ann, 18; Isabelle, 13; Martha Elizabeth, 10; Gerdice F., 5; Hatte L., 1 year old. Mrs. Ball and children went to Ohio. [Keene, after Apr term 1888]

591. Thomas Foley of Keene, Irish, born in Ireland, County of Cork, 75 years old. Lived in Keene, 30 years. Married; her name is Hannah, 60 years old; has one child, 30 years old, living in Boston, MA. [Keene, after Apr term 1888]

592. Dexter D. Ware,[78] of Keene, born in Charlemont, MA, 49 years old. Married; wife's name Sarah E., who is fifty years old. No children. Mr. Ware is an invalid, was in the army. He is troubled with cancerous humors; has a pension of four dollars per month. Has lived in Keene for the last eight years. Lives on Winter Street. [Keene; Oct term 1888]

---

[78] See also entry #536, page 180.

Cheshire County Paupers
1885-1900

[200] 593. Louisa B. Holman of Keene, 28 years old, born in MA. Married; husband's name is William H. Holman; one child, Frank Smith, 3 years old by first husband, Edward Smith. Lived in Keene 2 weeks. Says her husband is gone off buying horses. She is living at the house of Mr. Sparks, near Swanzey line. Left Keene. [Keene, after Apr term 1888]

594. William Johnson, Keene by John Kent. Went from Keene to NY. [Keene; Oct term 1888]

595. L. Chebois by Hiram Stowell. Was sent to the County Almshouse, Westmoreland. [Keene; Oct term 1888]

[201] 596. Joseph Duclow, Marlborough, 48 years old, born in Canada. Came to America Apr 1888. Married; the name of his wife is Phoebe, 41 years old. The children's names are as follows: Lydia, 17 years old; Donelda, 9 years old; William, 7 years old; and Sarah, 3 years old. [Marlborough; 2 Nov 1888; adjudged 2 Nov 1888]

597. John Sharkley, Marlborough, born in Canada, 45 years old. Married; name of wife Eliza, 15 years old. Mr. Sharkley had his foot crushed at the stone ledge. [Marlborough, 12 Dec 1888; adjudged 12 Dec 1888]

598. Joseph Coriveau, Marlborough, born in Canada. Came to Marlborough, the 4th Apr 1888. Married; wife born in Canada and came to Marlborough Apr 1888. Mr. Coriveau met with an accident on the railroad 28 Dec 1888; therefore calls for aid to pay the doctor's bill and nursing. Have three children; names as follows: Alace, 6 years old; Eliza, 4 years old; and Willie, 2 years old. [Marlborough; 4 Jan 1889; adjudged 4 Jan 1889]

[202] 599. Mary J. Southwell, born in Nelson, 35 years old, 6 Apr 1888. Married; husband's name John Southwell, born in

Cheshire County Paupers
1885-1900

England, 35 years old. He deserted his wife; is an intemperate man. Have three children: Frank Orrel, 6 years old; John Faniel, 3 years old; and Charles Arthur, one month old. Lives No. 86 Church St., Keene. [Keene; Oct term 1888]

600. Fanny W. Noice and George P. Noice, Richmond. She was born in North Hartford, VT; he was born in Hartford, VT. Fanny W., age 68; George W.,[79] age 39 years. Came from VT to Roxbury one year ago and there to Richmond. Ordered to County Farm; aided, did not go. [26 Jun 1888; admitted Oct term 1888]

601. Charles L. Knowlton of Jaffrey, born in Jaffrey 17 Sep 1844 and is 44 years old. Married Emma E. Wood, 1 Jun 1872; has one son Walter G., 6 years old. Wife died 24 Aug 1882. Mr. Knowlton was in the jail or house of corrections when the affidavit was taken and asks for help for his child. [Jaffrey, 5 Jul 1888; admitted Oct term 1888]

[203] 602. Hannah P. Gould of Marlow, born in Sunapee, NH, 81 years old. Married; husband's name Oliver K. Gould, 85 years old. Lived in Marlow since 1872. Oliver K. Gould died Oct 1892. [Marlow; admitted Oct term 1888]

603. Mary Jane Waters of Gilsum, 23 years old, born in Stratham, NH. Married; husband's name George L. Waters. He was born in Whitehall, NY and is 27 years old. She came to Gilsum to visit friends last Sep. [Leon][80] Does not know where her husband is. Have three children, namely: Fanny E., 5 years old; Hattie May, 4 years old; and George E., 1 year old. [Gilsum, Jan term 1889; admitted Apr term 1889]

---

[79] Original says "George W." though the rest of the entry states his names as "George P. Noice."
[80] The author has no idea what "Leon" has to do with this entry. The name just appears in the text after "last Sep."

Cheshire County Paupers
1885-1900

604. Sophie Smith of Keene, 79 years old, born in Canada, widow. Husband died 8 years ago. Has lived in Keene 5 years. Lives with her son-in-law, Nelson G. Bartlett. [Keene; admitted Apr term 1889]

[204] 605. John Shallum of Marlborough, born in Canada, 77 years old. Married; wife, 74 years old, was born in Canada. Have a son and daughter living in VT who will support them if sent to them. [Marlborough; admitted 9 Jan 1889]

606. Eleanor W. Yardley of Marlborough, born in Marlborough, 39 years old. Was married to Manley R. Yardley, 2 Jul 1870. Three years afterwards her husband left her and has not done anything for her support since. Has one child Ethel B. Yardley, 17 years old. Her mother was supported by the county. She has sued for a divorce and attached for alimony. Her son is at the Orphans Home, Franklin. [Marlborough; admitted 9 Jan 1889]

607. Gilman J. Raymond, Keene, born in Stoddard, NH, 37 years old. Married; wife's name Jennie L., 31 years old, born in NY state. Have five children: Charles M., 7 years old; Eliza A., 5 years old; Anna E., 4 years old; Arthur W., 15 months old. Also, John L. Burpee, the wife's child by her second husband. {Jennie L. Raymond died. Child born since affidavit was taken, sent to Orphans Home in Franklin 6 Nov 1893.} [Keene; admitted 10 Jan 1889]

[205] 608. Samuel M. Bishop, Keene, Littleton, NH, born and is 51 years old. Has lived in VT for the last 25 years. Has a sister living in Lynn, MA; wished help to get there. Was sent along. [Keene; admitted 5 Jan 1889]

Cheshire County Paupers
1885-1900

609. Emily C. Bryant,[81] Jaffrey, 72 years old. Her husband Luke Bryant died 30 years ago. She is sick and wants aid. [Jaffrey; admitted 16 Jan 1889]

610. Peter G. Bryant, Jaffrey, son of Emily C. Bryant, 38 years old. Never married. Sick, the reason he calls for help. Died. [Jaffrey; admitted 16 Jan 1889]

[206] 611. Oscar T. Frink, the same as #267, page 90. [Chesterfield; admitted 19 Jan 1889.[82]]

612. Peter Perry of Keene, born in West Townsand, CT (*sic*), 22 years old. Married; wife Anna, born in Milbury, MA, 21 years old. Lived in Keene 8 months. Subject to fits. Was taken to County Farm. Found that he was living with another man. Wife has left the farm. [Keene; admitted 22 Jan 1889]

613. Daniel J. Murphy of Keene, born in Ireland, 38 years old. Married; wife's name Annie. Has six children: Anna M., 13 years old; May E., 11; John, 9; Patrick H., 6; Elizabeth, 8; Daniel, 3 years old. Wife insane; was taken to the NH Asylum. [Keene; admitted 24 Jan 1889

[207] 614. Joseph Parker Pray, born in England, 27 years old. Married; wife's name Carrie E. Parker, born in Nova Scotia, 23 years old. Have two children: Willie, age two years old, and Eva May, one year old. [Troy; admitted 7 Feb 1889]

615. Mary Grando, Marlborough, born in Canada, 27 years old. Married; husband's name Joseph Grando. He left his wife six weeks ago. Have three children: Addie, 6 years old; Albert,

---

[81] See #474, page 159.
[82] Additional note on this entry says, "No. 90, 6 Oct 1882." This probably refers to a previous pauper book, location unknown to author.

Cheshire County Paupers
1885-1900

3 ½ years old; and [Deru], 2 ½ months old. [Marlborough; admitted 8 Feb 1889]

616. Margaret Tatro, Rindge, 61 years old, born in Scotland. Was married Clement Tatro; he died 1 Apr 1867. Has four children, all of age and married. [Rindge; admitted 14 Feb 1889]

[208] 517.[83] Charles F. Nims, Marlow, born in Sullivan, 59 years old. Enlisted in Co. K, 6th Reg't, NH Vols, 3 Nov 1861; discharged 12 Aug 1863 by reason of disability. Married Ann Howard, mother of the Ezra Howard children, who are receiving aid from the county. [Marlow; admitted 23 Feb 1889]

618. Frederick C. Lang of Marlborough, born in Germany, 45 years old. Enlisted in Co. H, 20th Indiana Reg't; in the service 16 months, then enlisted in Co. C, 1st NH Calvary. Remained in the service until the close of the war. Married in 1863 to Susan S. Holbrook of Nelson. Have seven children: Hattie I., age 21; Edward B., age 17; Anna G., age 16; Earnest C., age 14; Ambrose B., age 13; Fannie M., 8 years old; and Oscar W., 3 years old. [Marlborough; admitted; adjudged Apr term 1888]

619. Mary Ann Aldrich, Richmond, born in Richmond, 70 years old. Never was married; always lived in Richmond. She and her sister lived together alone, many years. Has one sister Mrs. Nahum Cass, residing in Richmond. Admitted to Almshouse 24 Jan 1891. Impulsive and violent at times. [Richmond; admitted 1 Mar 1889]

[209] 620. Louisa M. Hubbard, Keene, born in VT, 53 years old. Have been married and got a divorce from her husband

---

[83] Number transcribed as in original. Children listed are #403, page 136. See also #933, page 314, and #1419, page 476.

*Cheshire County Paupers
1885-1900*

Leonard L. Hubbard about 10 years ago. Was married to him about 28 years ago. Have one child, Idella, 23 years old. [Keene; admitted 8 Mar 1889]

621. John R. Bartlett, Fitzwilliam by Sarah S. Royse, 40 years old, born in VT. Married; wife's name Lizzie, was born in VT, 23 years old. Have 5 children; the oldest is about 4 years old, the youngest an infant. The infant and mother died in Sep 1888. Mr. Bartlett left soon after his wife died. [Fitzwilliam; admitted Apr term 1889]

622. Moulton Whipple, Fitzwilliam, born in Royalston, MA, 55 years old. Has children living in the west. Has lived in Illinois; has a wife living. [Fitzwilliam; Apr term 1889]

[210] 623. Thomas E. Foley, Westmoreland, born in Whitingham, Windham Co., VT, 51 years old. Married. Was a private in Co. E, 11th VT Vols; was honorably discharged. Has a wife and several children, one daughter, who was married to Dennis Sullivan a short time since. [Westmoreland; admitted 12 Dec 1889]

624. William F. Cilley, born in Hillsboro, 37 years old. Married in 1879; 4 children: Ezra, 8 years old; Alice, 7 years old; Eliza M., 5 years; and Elliott C., 2 years old. Wife had 4 children by a former husband. [Stoddard; admitted Apr term 1889]

625. William Galager, Swanzey by Norris C. Carter. Came from Nova Scotia to Swanzey about 22 years old; unmarried. Was sick and called for aid; was sent to the Co. Farm. [Swanzey; admitted 6 Apr 1889]

Cheshire County Paupers
1885-1900

[211] 626. Alfonce Forches, Winchester, born in Canada, 21 years old. Was sick; therefore called for aid. [Winchester; admitted Apr term 1889]

627. Joseph Porey, Winchester, born in St. Greger township, PQ, 32 years old. Was married in 1872 to Shisia Borgan. Have 5 children: Emma, age 13; Annie, age 11; Fred, age 9; Rosie, 7; and Flora, age 3. Mr. Porey is sick and not able to work. He died 19 Mar 1889. [Winchester; admitted Apr term 1889]

628. John Byam, Hinsdale, born in Ireland, 32 years old. [Hinsdale; admitted Apr term 1889]

[212] 629. Peter Gannette, Hinsdale, b. in Canada, 39 years old. Married; wife's name Adaline, b. in Canada, 40 years old. 4 children: Virginia, age 16; Agnes, age 13; Delia, age 12; and Olive, age 3. [Hinsdale; admitted Apr term 1889]

630. Elijah Russett, Swanzey, born in Rexford, Clinton Co., NY, 41 years old. Married to Mrs. Adaline Tissier. Have two children living; wife died 30 Aug 1888. Infant child died 12 Sep 1888. [Swanzey; admitted Apr term 1889]

631. Sarah Stevens, Swanzey, born in Meredith, NH, 74 years old. Married Joseph Stevens in 1833. He died in 1847. Have five children: Ruth A., 55 years old; Sarah L., 52 years old; Martha C., 48 years old; and Burin C., 40 years old.[84] [Swanzey; admitted Apr term 1889]

[213] 632. Emma Hartley of Keene, born in England, 54 years old. Married Joseph Hartley. He died 19 Mar 1889. Has two children: Adolphus, 20 years old, and Mindrell Alice, 23 years old. [Keene; admitted 10 Apr 1889]

---

[84] Though the text says "five children" only four are named.

Cheshire County Paupers
1885-1900

633. Sarah E. Abbott, Keene, b. in Westminster, VT 27 Nov 1849. Married John P. Abbott, 9 Nov 1884; left her; neglected to support her. He was born in Goshen, NH, age 40. Have two children: Frank E., age 11, and Jane E., age 9. Previous to the marriage to Abbott, she married Edward V. Griffith, who was killed 27 Nov 1879. The two children were by her first husband. {Divorced from her husband Oct term 1891. Her name changed to Sarah E. Griffith.} [Keene; admitted Apr term 1889]

634. William Street, Keene, born in Canada, age 38. Married; wife's name Georgeanna, 37 years old. 7 children: Alexandria, 13 years old; Ansitia, 11; Hortense, 8; Ida, 10; Alma, 6; and Archille, 4 years old.[85] [Keene; admitted Apr term 1889]

[214] 635. Louis Gabarees,[86] Keene, born in Canada, 64 years old. Married; May is sixty-four years old. Have four children, living; all grown up. [Keene; admitted Apr term 1889]

636. Frank Brown. Emma V. Mathews, Chesterfield, affidavit of Frank E. Brown, who was sick at Mrs. Mathews house. Came to Mrs. Mathews and sick. His parents died when he was young. Was born in Brattleboro, VT, 27 years old. [Chesterfield; admitted Apr term 1889]

637. A. M. Grover, Chesterfield, born in VT, 40 years old. [Chesterfield; admitted Apr term 1889]

[215] 638. Joseph Boles, Dublin, 70 years old, born in Worcester, MA. Was a private of Co. G, 2d Reg't NH Vols; served three years. Admitted to Almshouse 1890. {Died 5 Nov

---

[85] Though the text states there were 7 children, only six were named.
[86] According to the 1890 NH Veteran's Schedule, his name is Gabouries.

Cheshire County Paupers
1885-1900

1890 at County Almshouse; buried in County Cemetery.}
[Dublin; admitted Apr term 1889]

639. Joseph Menning, Troy, 38 years old, born in Canada. Came to NH six weeks ago. [Troy; admitted 24 Apr 1889]

640. Mabel M. Prescott, Keene, born in Manchester, NII, 11 years old. Was sent to Keene from Tewksbury Almshouse, MA, Dec 1888 by order of state overseer. Her father is living at Groton, MA. She has an uncle and aunt living at Windham, NH. Her mother is dead; died some three years ago. She is now living with C. F. Buffum in Keene. [Keene, 4 May 1889; admitted 17 Apr 1889]

[216] 641. Lawrence Monahan, Keene, Irish, born in Ireland, 78 years old. Came to America in 1864; lived in Keene, 13 or 14 years. Has been married but buried his wife before he came to this country. He is living with Barry Gibbs, his son-in-law who has 9 children. His daughter is dead. [Keene, 25 May 1889; admitted 25 May 1889]

642. John W. Davis, Hinsdale, 41 years old, born in Williamstown, MA. Married Lilly Armstrong of Hinsdale, 21[87] years ago; have 6 children. Their names and ages are as follows: William A., 19; Ada, 14; Marvin A., 12; Frank B., 10; Nettie E., 6; and Susan, 2 years old. He calls for aid because one of the children has cut his arm. [Hinsdale; admitted 7 Jun 1889]

643. Peter May, Dublin, 75 years old, born in Canada. Resided in Dublin 4 or 5 years since 1 Jan 1870. Has children in Worcester and Northampton, MA. Wants money to assist him to them. [Admitted Jul 1889]

---

[87] This number is crossed out with two lines in the original.

Cheshire County Paupers
1885-1900

[217] 644. Tice Low, Westmoreland, born in Toronto, Canada West, age 61. Unmarried. Has resided in the States only about two months. [Admitted 9 Jul 1889]

645. John Gauthier, Keene, born in Canada, 59 years old. Has made Keene his home most of the time since the war. Has been married; wife dead 11 years ago. Has one daughter, Mrs. Fred Mason, who resides on Butler's Court, Keene. Is sick, has nearly lost his mind. Is living at Mrs. Wight's on Washington Ave. [Admitted 9 Jul 1889; final all judgment 30 Aug 1889]

646. Thomas Johnson, Keene, born in Hinsdale, 8 Feb 1805, 75 years old. Has not resided in NH for nearly 50 years. Has lived in various places in MA, making it his home at Marlborough, MA for several years last past. Was never married. Came to NH, expecting to find in Hinsdale or Swanzey some relatives, but learned that they are dead. Applied for aid to go back to Marlborough. Wanted to return from Keene to Hinsdale, and from there to Marlborough, MA. Gave Overseer Howland orders send him to Acton, MA or to County Almshouse. He went away and has not been seen since. [Evidence sufficient but not admitted as said applicant skipped]

[218] 647. Betsey M. Caverly, Hiram L. Caverly, mother and son, Fitzwilliam. Place of birth unknown, ages 46 and 26 respectively. Husband died in 1887; his name was Hiram M. Has depended upon her son for support. He is now sick and therefore Mrs. C, his mother, is obliged to ask for relief. Hiram L. is unmarried. [Affidavit taken 3 Aug 1889; adjudged 30 Aug 1889]

648. Fred Ella, 2d, Winchester, born in Canada, 24 years old. Wife and one child, two weeks old. Came to the US in Nov 1888. Was injured in Jul last while chopping in the woods by a

large stone rolling from a bank above him. Applied to the town for aid 20 Jul, two days after he got hurt. Nationality: French. [20 Jul 1889; adjudged 27 Sep 1889]

649. Mary Cook, Winchester, born in VT, American, age 23. Married; has not lived with her husband since Jul 1888. Husband's name George Cook, age 23. Does not know where he is. Never resided in NH until 2 years ago. Is now living with her husband's uncle Henry Cook. Was injured the 23rd of May last in a scuffle with her husband's brother. {See affidavit.}[88] [23 May 1889; adjudged 27 Sep 1889]

[219] 650. Ellen Conroy, Winchester, born in Ireland, 38 years old last Aug (1888). Came to the US in 1874 and have resided in Winchester from that time to the present, except about 6 months when I resided in Keene. Single; has 2 brothers, one residing in Peabody, MA, and one in said Winchester. Was injured last fall by falling upon the sidewalk and has since been confined to the bed. [18 May 1889. Adjudged 27 Sep 1889]

651. Oren Wilbur, American, Winchester. Has resided with Mrs. Lucinda Haradon for the past 15 years or more.[89] At Marlborough and more recently at Westmoreland. {Died 6 Apr 1889.} [Adjudged Apr term 1873]

652. Robert Turnstall, Winchester, born in England, 66 years old. Came to America about 37 years ago. Married; came to Winchester with his wife 2 Apr 1889. Her name is Elizabeth; she was 52 years old in Apr 1889. Have one daughter Mrs. Samuel Kelley, who resides in Winchester; one son Timothy A., age 16, who also lives in Winchester; and one son who is married and resides in Brookfield, MA. Mr. and Mrs. T are

---

[88] No additional affidavit was located by author. See also #1463, page 490.
[89] For others who stayed with Mrs. Haradon, see #211, 263, 373, and 686.

Cheshire County Paupers
1885-1900

both in feeble health and unable to work all of the time. [Affidavit taken 27 Aug 1889; adjudged 27 Sep 1889]

[220] 653. George Nallette, Winchester, born in Halifax, Canada, age 44 years. Came to the US in Jan 1883. Married; wife and 6 children, viz: Mary, Emma, Adelia, Clora, Annie and Rosa, aged respectfully (*sic*) 19, 17, 16, 13, 10 and 8. Have resided in Ashuelot ever since they came to the US, except 2 years that they lived in Marlborough, NH. Oldest daughter Mary was confined 23 Aug 1889; she alleges that Albert Chandler is father of her child and that his whereabouts are to her unknown. It is also unknown to the selectmen of said Winchester. She, the daughter, is willing to be committed to the Almshouse. [23 Aug 1889; adjudged 27 Sep 1889]

654. Ebenezer Hackett, Westmoreland, born in W, 23 Sep 1820, age 69. Has always resided in Westmoreland. Widower; unmarried since 1859. Has been aided by said town of W for 15 years last past. Has a sister Electa D. Stewart, living in Lunenburg, MA. {Died at County Farm 28 Sep 1889.} [Affidavit taken 30 Aug 1889; adjudged 30 Aug 1889]

[221] 655. Joel Lemorand, Marlborough, born in Canada; nationality: French; 31 years of age. Parents never resided in the US. Married to Cloe Durant 29 Jun 1887. Said applicant came to Marlborough 29 Apr 1889. Never resided in any other town in this state. Mrs. Lemorand's father died 11 years ago. Have no children. [Affidavit taken 22 Jul 1889; adjudged 30 Aug 1889]

656. Warren J. Burgess, Fitzwilliam, born in Royalston, MA, 27 years old, son of Myric Burgess of Richmond, and Rozella Tolman, whose maiden name was Foster; said Warren J. was born out of wedlock. Eliza, wife of Warren J. is a native of North Brookfield, MA. Have 2 children: Walton Eaton, son of

Cheshire County Paupers
1885-1900

the wife Eliza; and Minnie Agnes Burgess, aged respectively 5 years and 10 months. [17 Oct 1887; no evidence of being adjudged]

657. Joseph Durant, Keene, born in Canada, French nationality, age 30. Wife Malvina, 22 years of age. 5 ch: Fred, age 5; Malvina, 2; Louis, 1; Rosetta, 10; Joseph, 8 years of age. Came to Keene in 1871. Has resided in several towns in the county from 1 to 3 years. Father died in Harrisville in 1877; mother now lives in Marlborough. Wife was the daughter of Antoine LaBounty. [13 Apr 1888; no evidence of being adjudged]

[222] 658. Louis Sidello, Nashua (?), born in Canada, 60 years of age. Resided in Canada 12 years, Whitehall 46 years and in Nashua, 2 years. Single. [9 Apr 1888; no evidence of being adjudged]

659. Eliza Driscoll, Walpole, born in Cork County, Ireland, 70 years of age. Came to this country when 32 years of age. Husband Morris Driscoll died about 17 years ago. He was a native of Ireland. Has resided in Walpole for 15 years last past. No children living. Her husband had 2 children by his first wife, still living. [19 Feb 1889; no evidence of having been adjudged]

660. Ellen O'Brien, Keene, born in Ireland, 50 years of age. Widow; husband died 8 years ago. Has 3 children dependent on her for support, viz: Margaret, age 26, non compos and not capable of doing anything; Katie, age 13 last Dec; and Lawrence, age 10, the 10th of Feb inst. Has resided in Keene for the last 27 years. The house and lot which I occupy is mortgaged to Faulkner & Colomy for nearly what it will sell. [29 Feb 1889; adjudged 19 Sep 1889. See No. 675]

Cheshire County Paupers
1885-1900

[223] 661. Kate Lee, Keene, born in Swanzey, about 35 years old. Married; does not live with her husband nor has she for a year past or more. He resides somewhere in MA. Her parents are, it is believed, both dead. She has resided at Virgil A. Wright's in Keene, until she was taken to the NH Asylum for the Insane where she is now supported. She came to Keene from Jeffersonville, MA. [10 Nov 1888; adjudged 19 Sep 1889]

662. James W. Greenwood, Keene, born in Dublin, 5 Mar 1820. Married; wife Mary C. born in Roxbury, NH, 5 Jul 1820. One child, daughter, married name Sarah L. Spaulding. They depend upon the daughter and husband for care and support, but not being able to maintain them, the city of Keene have rendered some relief. Settlement lost in Keene under law passed 14 Aug 1889. [21 Jan 1888; rejected, City of Keene being liable for their support; adjudged 19 Sep 1889]

663. Mrs. Jerry Donovan, Keene, born in Ireland, 45 years of age. Widow; husband Jerry died some two years ago. Has resided in said Keene for 15 years last past. Own a small place on Foster Street, which is mortgaged. Has six children dependent upon her for care and support, viz: John, Daniel, Cornelius, Jeremiah, Timothy, and James, aged respectfully (*sic*) 14, 12, 10, 8, 7, and 6 years. Have been assisted by the city. Settlement in Keene lost under the law passed 14 Aug 1889. Later, found to have a settlement in Keene. [21 Feb 1888; rejected, having a settlement in Keene]

[224] 664. Emma G. Graves, Keene, born in Hinsdale, NH, American, 43 years of age. Was married in 1866 to Oliver C. Graves, who is about three years older than his wife. She was divorced from him about three years ago. Has resided in Keene ever since she was married. Has 2 children dependent upon her for support, viz: Florence E., born 10 Mar 1873, and Alice E.,

*Cheshire County Paupers
1885-1900*

born 28 Feb 1881. Settlement lost under act passed 14 Aug 1889. [21 Jan 1888; rejected, has a settlement in Keene]

665. Andrew P. Webber, Nelson, born Maine, 47 years of age. Enlisted in the 9th Reg't Maine Vol and served five years in said regiment and the 2d Maine Cavalry. Married; name of wife Fanny. 2 children, a boy and a girl, viz: Amy F., and Ivory O., aged respectively, 14 and 11. Resided in Maine from the close of the war until 1875; in Albany and Conway in this state until 1887, when they removed to Nelson. Health poor, unable to do much work, been confined to his bed most of the time since last Dec. [23 Aug 1889; adjudged 2 Sep 1889]

666. Mattie R. Sullivan, Westmoreland, born in ___, 20 years old, the 20th of Jul last past. Married 23 Nov 1887 to Dennis G. Sullivan, who is now residing in Chesterfield. Has one child, Lilla E., born 2 Oct 1888. Husband born in Boston in 1861; resided there until 3 years of age; removed to Dummerston, VT, where he resided 21 years; since in Westmoreland. On the 24th of Jul last past, her husband carried her to her father's house with her child and since neglects and refuses further support. Her father Thomas E. Tobey is furnished with relief from the county. [2 Sep 1889; adjudged 27 Sep 1889]

[225] 667. Julia A. Mead,[90] Alstead, born in Clarendon, VT in 1833 and am 55 years of age (10 Dec 188) (*sic*). Married John H. Mead of Alstead 13 years ago last month; lived with him six to eight years and was then divorced. Has one daughter Myra J. Resided in Alstead until about 4 years ago; since then she has lived in VT, Westmoreland, Marlborough, Keene, and Swanzey. Is now residing in Swanzey. Has been aided by said town of Alstead. {Died in Keene 16 Jul 1893.} [6 Feb 1889; adjudged 13 Sep 1889]

---

[90] See also #1009.

Cheshire County Paupers
1885-1900

668. Margaret Condon, Irish, Walpole, born in the County of Cork, Ireland, 42 years of age. Came to Springfield, VT at the age of 19. Married William Condon, 20 Apr 1870. He died the 12th of Nov 1882. Has 7 children, 5 girls and 2 boys, aged 18, 14, 13, 12, 10, 9, and 7. Has been aided by the town of Langdon since 1882 until the act of 14 Aug 1889, changing the time of settlement. [11 Sep 1889]

669. Ann Mahar, Irish, Keene, born in Ireland. Came to this country in 1848. Married twice; last husband died 14 years ago last April. One daughter Ellen, 33 years old, not bright. Has resided in Keene for 20 years. Owns and resides in a small house on Elm Street. [11 Sep 1889; adjudged 19 Sep 1889]

[226] 670. Elmira Smith, American, Keene, born Springfield, VT, 24 Sep 1844, and shall be 46 years old the 24th of this month. Married; husband Erastus Smith was born in Acworth, NH and is fifty-eight years old, was a private in 14th NH Vols. Two children: a daughter and a son. Husband had two children by a former wife. [11 Sep 1889; adjudged 19 Sep 1889]

671. Lucretia Cummings, American, Keene, born in Sullivan, 37 years old. A widow; Frank W. Cummings, her husband, died the 11th of Aug 1886. 4 children: Harrison A., Lena A., Ora A., and Arthur W., aged respectively 16, 14, 12, and 6 years of age. Her husband was 33 years old when he died. [11 Sep 1889; adjudged 9 Sep 1889]

672. Catharine B. Hastings, American, Keene, born Lancaster, MA. Will be 46 years old the 9th of Oct next. Single, has resided in Keene 34 years or more. Has one sister, Mrs. Aaron Ellis of Keene. [11 Sep 1889; adjudged 19 Sep 1889]

Cheshire County Paupers
1885-1900

[227] 673. Edward Ballou, American, Keene, born in Keene, 28 years old the 24th of Jul last. Single; has been an invalid, afflicted with a spinal difficulty for more than 9 years, during which time he has been aided by the city of Keene. Has resided in Winchester for more than 8 years before coming to Keene, which was in Aug 1888. Was treated at the MA General Hospital in Boston for several weeks in 1888. Father died some 20 years ago; mother is living in Marlborough at the present time. [11 Sep 1889; adjudged 19 Sep 1889]

674. Ellen Waters, Scotch, Keene, born in Montgomery, NY, 41 years old, the 17th of Aug last. Married; husband Edward Waters was born in Rutland, VT and is about 30 years old. No children. Poor health and inability to work is the cause given for asking for relief. [11 Sep 1889; adjudged 19 Sep 1889]

675. Ellen O'Brien, Irish, Keene, born in Ireland, about 50 years of age. Widow; husband died 9 years ago last March. Six children, 2 are taking care of themselves and 4 are at home and partly dependent upon the mother for support. Names: Maggie, who is not bright, is 27 years old; Annie A., Katie E., and Lawrence J. are aged respectively 18, 15, and 13 years old. Owns and resides in a small house on Island St. [11 Sep 1889; adjudged 19 Sep 1889. See No. 660]

[228] 676. Patrick O'Connor, Irish, Keene, born in Ireland. Came to America 42 years ago, 73 years old, widower. Has 2 children living. Does not know the whereabouts of either. Disabled by a broken limb for several years past. Has resided in Keene ever since he came to this country except for a few weeks at a time. [12 Sep 1889; adjudged 27 Sep 1889]

677. George Esty, American, Keene, born Peterborough, NH, 64 years old, the 5th day of Jun last. Resided in Keene for 25 years last past. Widowed; wife died 12 years ago. No children.

Cheshire County Paupers
1885-1900

Applies for aid by reason of being physically unable to earn his living. [13 Aug 1888; adjudged 19 Sep 1889]

678. Sarah Davis, American, Nelson, about 55 years old. Has been married; husband Elliot Davis[91] was sent to state prison in 1877. While in prison his wife procured a divorce. Has several children. She resides with one in Nelson. Has been aided by the town of Sullivan from 1880 to 14 Aug 1889, when she lost her settlement there by virtue of an act passed 14 Aug 1889. [12 Sep 1889; adjudged 19 Sep 1889]

[229] 679. Francis P. Eastman, American, Keene, born in Livermore, Maine, 78 years old, the 31st of last Mar. Widowed. Has one son Hiram Eastman; owns and resides in a small house on George St. [19 Sep 1889; adjudged 19 Sep 1889]

680. James Frances, American, Keene, born in Sterlin Village, CT, 28 years old, the 15th of Jul last. Married; has a wife and one child, viz: Rose, 21 years old and Lilly, 4 months old. Has resided in Dover for 20 years last past. Parents dead; parents of his wife reside in Dover. Is on his way to Perkinsville, VT with wife and child. Has a job assured there. Is out of money and can get no farther; hence the application for aid. Overseer of city poor directed to secure passage for said Frances and family to Perkinsville and charge the same to the county, and to send bill to Overseer of Poor of Dover for collection for the county. [24 Sep 1889; aided but not adjudged]

681. Mabel Griffith, American, Keene, born in Surry, 31 years old, the 6th of April last. Widow; husband Irving Griffith died some 3 years ago. Has three children: Freddie I., Mertie M., and Della A., aged respectively 10, last Feb; 5, last Oct; and 3,

---

[91]The case against Elliott Davis is discussed in *Hard Times in Concord* by author, page 216.

Cheshire County Paupers
1885-1900

last Oct. Mrs. G's maiden name was Carpenter. [24 Sep 1889; adjudged 27 Sep 1889]

682. John Donovan, Irish, Keene, born in Ireland, about 60 years of age. Married; wife Hannah is fifty years old. Two children, dependent, viz: Mary Ellen, 16 years old, and Daniel, 14 years old. One daughter married and living in MA. Has resided in Keene for the last 25 years. Owns a house and lot, subject to a mortgage on Foster St. [21 Feb 1888; adjudged 23 Sep 1889]

683. Sarah J. Howard, American, Keene, born in Ashburnham, MA 1813, 74 years of age. Husband, Amos Howard died 9 years ago, the 6th of last Sep. No dependent children; resides with her daughter Sarah A. Howard. Has resided in ____ with the exception of 2 years since 1853. Settlement lost in Keene under the act of 14 Aug 1889. [21 Feb 1889; adjudged 27 Sep 1889]

684. Gilman Whitcomb, American, Marlborough, born in Marlborough in 1805. Has always resided in said Marlborough, age 84. Received a stipend from Hon. Rufus S. Frost of $20 per year; lost his settlement in M under the act of 14 Aug 1889. {Died 12 Feb 1892.} [31 Aug 1889; adjudged 27 Sep 1889]

[231] 685. Nathan H. and Hattie S. Johnson, American, Richmond, born in Wendall, MA, 29 years old. Married; wife Hattie S. was born in Winchester and is 25 years old; maiden name Cole. One child, Etta May, 2 years, 10 months. The parents of Hattie S. reside in Winchester. [12 Aug 1889; affidavits examined and said family adjudged 27 Sep 1889]

686. Henry C. Billings, American, Keene, born in Keene, is about 35 years old. Single; father and mother both living. Reside on West St. Is afflicted severely with a nervous

difficulty. Has been supported by the city of Keene. Lost his settlement under the act of 14 Aug 1889. Is living with Mrs. L. Haradon in Westmoreland.[92] {Died at Mrs. Lucinda Haradon's 23 Sep 1891. Body taken to West Keene Cemetery for burial by friends.} [24 Sep 1889; adjudged 27 Sep 1889]

687. Peter Posey, Canadian French, Hinsdale, born in Three Rivers, Canada, 44 years of age. Married; wife ____. Have 8 children, viz: Arthur, 15; Rose, 13; Dona, 10; Eddie, 8; Joseph, 5; David, 3; Edmond, 2 ; and Regina, 6 weeks old. Have resided in Hinsdale ever since they came to the US. The oldest boy having cut his leg is the reason for asking for aid. [16 Jul 1889; 25 Sep 1889; Oct term 1889 adjudged]

[232] 688. Johnnie Canfield, Canadian French, Hinsdale, born in Canada in Dec 1873 and is 15 years of age. His mother died at Johnie's birth and his father some two years later left for California, where it is supposed that he died. Neither of his parents ever resided in NH. He came to Hinsdale to live with his aunt in Aug 1886. The name of his aunt is Margaret Rafferty. [13 Sep 1889; adjudged 17 Oct 1889]

689. Harvey Ballou, American, Keene, born in Surry, 29 Mar 1824 and is now 65 years old. Married; does not live with her. Her name is Mary E. Califf Ballou; supposition is that she is living in NJ. Separated in 1873. Had two children: George H. and Clara, aged respectively as near can be ascertained, 25 or 26 and 23 or 24, and that they live somewhere in NJ. {Died at the Almshouse 22 Dec 1892.} [4 Oct 1889; adjudged 17 Oct 1889]

690. Eliza M. Burroughs, American, an indigent daughter of a soldier, Hinsdale, born in Hinsdale in 1851 and is now 38 years old. Her father died in 1865; belonged in Co. F, 11th VT Vols.

---

[92] For others who stayed at Mrs. Haradon's, see #211, 263, 373, and 651.

Cheshire County Paupers
1885-1900

Her mother is still living, named Mary Goodnough; resides Brattleboro, VT. Has been aided every year since 1 Jan 1880 by said Hinsdale. [8 Sep 1889; adjudged 15 Oct 1889]

[233] 691. Stephen M. Whipple, American, Richmond, born in Richmond, 51 years old. Has been married; last wife sued and got a divorce. Has resided a greater part of his life in Richmond. [30 Sep 1889; adjudged 17 Oct 1889]

692. Laura H. Pierce, American, Chesterfield, born in Westmoreland, 53 years old last Mar. An imbecile. Father Jabez Pierce living and resides in said Chesterfield. [15 Oct 1889; adjudged 15 Oct 1889]

693. Ada L. Harvey, Winchester, born in Chesterfield. The evidence shows the town of Winchester liable for her support.[93]

[234] 694. Julia E. Wilder, American, Walpole, born in Walpole, 22 years old (26 years old, see affidavit of 27 Sep 1889). Single; her father was a soldier, died at City Point, the year before the war closed. Her mother Emily Wilder is 55 years old. In 1866 she married her first husband's brother Charles Wilder. Said Julia is subject to fits and is unable to care for herself. {Died 17 Oct 1891.} [26 Dec 1888; 27 Sep 1889; adjudged 16 Oct 1889]

695. Aurilla Predum, Hinsdale, born in ____, age 34. Was married 4 Jul, 19 years ago. Lived with said husband until 18 Sep 1888 when she left him; does not know where he now is. Came to H 16 May 1889. Husband's age is 43. Has 4 children, only 3 with her, viz: Ella, Mary and Thomas, aged respectively 11, 7 and 4 years. Oldest child Eliza is 17 years old and is living in VT. [21 Aug 1889; adjudged 16 Oct 1889]

---

[93] Date of application not shown.

Cheshire County Paupers
1885-1900

696. Jessie Pearl Southwick, American, Keene, b. in Worcester, MA, 6 Dec 1885, illegitimate; mother's name Julia E. Phelps; father's Edmund M. Southwick. The mother, it is supposed, resides somewhere in Springfield, MA with or near her parents. The father, it is thought, lives in Lancaster, MA. See affidavit for particulars.[94] [4 Oct 1889; adjudged 17 Oct 1889]

[235] 697. Anna R. Dodge, American, Keene, born in Vergennes, VT, 40 years old, widow. Husband Frederick Dodge died 6 Feb 1882. He was a member of Co. D, 18th NH Vols. Has one daughter Helen S., aged 15 years. [5 Oct 1889; adjudged 17 Oct 1889]

698. James M. and G. S. Stone, American, Swanzey, born in ___. Father, Norris C. Stone died in Winchester; mother, Sarah E. resides in Winchester. Admitted to the Almshouse 23 Oct 1889; transferred to the NH Orphans Home, Franklin 2 Oct 1890. [2 Oct 1889; adjudged 17 Oct 1889]

699. Esther Whitcomb, American, Keene, born in Chesterfield 8 Sep 1815, 74 years of age. Has resided in Keene for 8 or 9 years last past. Has been married; husband Silas Whitcomb died 4 Aug 1876; no children living. [5 Oct 1889; adjudged 17 Oct 1889]

[236] 700. Sidney Carlton, American, Winchester, born in West Dorset, VT, 81 years old last Jun. Married; wife Elvira Poland, age 72. Has a son in Orange, MA, pays for his mother's support. Has one son in Winchester, married and has a family. Has 5 daughters living; all married. Admitted to the Almshouse 16 May 1890. [8 Oct 1889; adjudged 17 Oct 1889]

---

[94] No other material found on this entry.

Cheshire County Paupers
1885-1900

701. Samuel Strafford and Fidella Strafford, his wife, American, Winchester. Mr. Strafford, 82 years old; Mrs. Strafford, 76 years old. He was born Readsboro, VT and she Belchertown, MA. He has resided in Winchester for 21 years and has no children of his own; was married about 12 years ago. She has 4 children by first husband, who died 14 years ago last Jan. None of her children reside in NH. [10 Oct 1889; adjudged 17 Oct 1889]

702. Edwin Davis, American, Gilsum, born in Sullivan, 30 years old. He and his parents were declared paupers in 1864 and aided. [14 Oct 1889; adjudged 15 Oct 1889]

[237] 703. John Morris, French, Fitzwilliam, born in Three Rivers, PQ, 46 years of age. Married; wife Ella A. Morris, age 25 years; 3 children, viz: Freddie, age 7; Lucinda, age 5; Arla, age 2. Said Morris being sick is forced to ask for some relief. [10 May 1889; adjudged 15 Oct 1889]

704. Henry Knowlton, American, Dublin, born in Framingham, MA, age 72 years. {Died 11 Mar 1891.} [30 Sep 1889; adjudged 15 Oct 1889]

705. James A. Dyton, American, Winchester, born in NY, age 48. Came to Winchester in 1876. Served in Army of the US in the 35th NY and 14th NY Artillery. Claim of $21 allowed at the Oct term of Court 1889. [Adjudged 2 Apr 1890]

[238] 706. Polly Potter,[95] American, Fitzwilliam, born in Fitzwilliam, 30 Aug 1803 and is now 86 years of age. Has resided in Fitzwilliam since 1 Jan 1880, except about 1 year in 1884 and 1885. [14 Oct 1889; not adjudged. Adjudged]

---

[95] See also #716.

Cheshire County Paupers
1885-1900

707. Tama Davis,[96] American, Fitzwilliam, age 85, widow of Chauncey Davis, Sr., late of Fitzwilliam and stepmother of Chauncey David, Jr., of Fitzwilliam. {Died 24 Jul 1890.} [14 Oct 1889; adjudged 17 Oct 1889]

708. Benjamin J. Crosby, American, Surry, born in Surry, age 34. Father and mother reside in Surry. Has one sister Mrs. Cole living in Keene and two in MA. He is at this time an inmate of the NH Asylum for the Insane. Has been supported by the town of Surry for 6 or 8 years or more, either at the County Almshouse or the NH Asylum. Has an uncle and an aunt insane and supported at the Almshouse. His mother is insane. [17 Oct 1889; adjudged 17 Oct 1889]

[239] 709. James Dunbary, Irish, Winchester, born in Ireland, 77 years old. Has lived in this country 23 years and in Winchester for 22 years. Has one daughter Mrs. David Dugan, who resides in Winchester and one son in Brattleboro. Both are poor and unable to care for him. [12 Oct 1889; adjudged 18 Oct 1889]

710. Mattie A. Caswell, American, Keene, born in North Wayne, ME, 33 years old. Married; husband William A. is 32 years old. He deserted her in Aug last. Has resided in Claremont for the last 9 years, except for a few months at a time. Has two children: Luella Bell Phelps, by a former husband, age 9; and Alton Earl, age 2. Has friends in Claremont; came to Keene only a few days ago to get work. Wants to return to C with her children. Gave her aid to return home. [14 Oct 1889; not adjudged]

---

[96] In the vital records of Fitzwilliam, her name was given as Tamar. She was the stepmother of Chancy David, Jr., according to the *History of Fitzwilliam*.

Cheshire County Paupers
1885-1900

711. Mary Gregwon, French, Harrisville, born in St. Morris, Canada and is 35 years old. Was married to Frances Gregwon at Peterborough 21 Nov 1875. Husband killed on the railroad 1 Nov 1884. Has 6 children, viz: Mary, Palmer, Clara, Lodie, George and Vangie, aged respectively, 13, 12, 10, 8, 6, 5. Has been supported by the town of Harrisville since the death of her husband. [29 Sep 1889; adjudged 18 Oct 1889]

[240] 712. Sadie C. Crossfield, American, Keene, born in Keene, age 23 years. Father's name Charles; mother Abbie. Her father died several years ago and her mother is somewhere in MA. She was for several years an inmate of the NH Asylum for the Insane and supported at the expense of the city of Keene, Said Sadie has been boared (*sic*) for a year or two past at Mrs. Daniel Twitchell in East Swanzey at the expense of the city. [18 Oct 1889. Adjudged 19 Oct 1889]

713. George H. Ellis, American, Roxbury, born in Keene 10 Mar 1833, 56 years old. Has resided in Roxbury since 1870. Marrion L., his wife, is 40 years old. They have 11 children, viz: Perley W., Cyrus K., Olive M., Ida M., Wilmer G., Elmira L., Bertie S., Olive M., (?), Clara M., Charity M., and Daniel K., aged respectively 22, 20, 17, 13, 15, 12, 10, 8, 7, 5, 4. {Infant born since the affidavit and statement above was made, and died on or about 2 Sep 1890.} [22 Oct 1889; adjudged 23 Oct 1889]

714. Emma Shaver, French, Marlborough, born in Canada and is 42 years old. Widow; husband died in Jan 1887. Has 3 children, viz: Charlie, Martha and Lena, aged respectively 15, 12, and 8 years. [30 Sep 1889; adjudged 16 Oct 1889]

[241] 715. Elvira Deeth, American, Rindge, born in ___, age ___. Said Elvira has been supported by the town of Rindge for a year or two past at the county farm. Her husband Moses S.,

Cheshire County Paupers
1885-1900

died in Rindge in 1881 or 1882. Died at County Farm Oct 1889, body removed by friends and buried in Marlborough. The said Elvira Deeth had two children by her first husband, viz: Elizabeth Farrar and ___. [16 Oct 1889; adjudged 16 Oct 1889]

716. Polly Potter,[97] American, Fitzwilliam, born in Fitzwilliam 30 Aug 1803. Has always resided in Fitzwilliam except for about one year 1884 or 5, when she resided in Rindge. Has had real estate until recently in Fitzwilliam. Marked as "duplicate." [14 Oct 1889; not adjudged. See affidavit. Adjudged.]

717. William H. Blanchard, a dependent soldier, American, Fitzwilliam, born in Parrisville, NY, 48 years of age. Married; wife Hannah B. is 45 years old. She was born in said Fitzwilliam. Resided in Quincy, MA from 1880 to 1883. Was a soldier in the late war, a member of Co. ___, 6th VT Vols. [14 Oct 1889; adjudged 2 Nov 1889]

[242] 718. Carrie M. Larabee, Fitzwilliam, born in South Freedom, ME, age 21 years. Parents never resided in NH. Father died 6 years ago in ME. Has been living in Marlborough, came to Fitzwilliam only a few weeks ago. [11 Nov 1889; adjudged 15 Nov 1889]

719. Uriah Mosher, Keene, born in Nova Scotia 11 Apr 1837, 52 years of age. Married; wife Eliza E. (second wife) was born in Annapolis Co., Nova Scotia and is about 30 years old. Has 7 dependent children, viz: Henry, by his first wife; Arthur, Kenneth, Maud, Uriah, Nellie and Josee, aged respectively 17, 13, 11, 7, 5, 4 and 3. Has just buried an infant child. {Wife died 10 Nov 1889.} [4 Nov 1889; adjudged 15 Nov 1889]

---

[97] See also #706.

Cheshire County Paupers
1885-1900

720. Walter S. Pollard, American, Keene, born in Bridgwater, VT, 7 Sep 1854, and is 35 years old. Married; wife Martha E. (Howard) is 29 years old and was born in Gilsum. Three dependent children, viz: Winnee May, 9 years old; Willie H., 6 years old; and Annie L., age 2 years, 6 months. Buried one child about 2 weeks ago. {Annie L. died Nov.} [9 Nov 1889; adjudged 15 Nov 1889]

[243] 721. Frank C.[98] and Joanna Aikens, American, Keene, born in Fairlee, VT, 37 years old, 23 Nov 1889. Married; wife Joanna Valentine is about 19 years of age. Were married 30 May 1889. They reside with his father Enoch Aikens; is intemperate. Mrs. Aikens is of French nationality. [8 Nov 1889; allowed 15 Nov 1889]

722. Lawson Hill, American, Swanzey, born in Swanzey, 72 years old. Has resided in Swanzey for the last 23 years. Unmarried. A friend furnishes house rent and garden free of cost. {Died 10 Jan 1891.} [14 Oct and 24 Oct 1889; adjudged 15 Nov 1889]

723. Reuben G. Howe, American, Stoddard, born in Acworth, 49 years old. Widowed; has had two wives: Mary Whittemore, who died in 1874 and Angelia E. Jefts of Lempster, who died in 1883. Has 4 children, only two minors, viz: Willie W. and Johnie A., aged respectively 12 and 6 years of age. [26 Aug 1889; adjudged 15 Nov 1889]

[244] 724. Sarah T. Martin, American, Charlestown, born in Bath, NH, age 73. Resided in Hinsdale after 1866 for 14 years and then after an absence of ¾ of a year, she returned to Hinsdale and resided 7 years. Has resided in Charlestown since the 24th day of Jun 1889. The facts are she did not gain a

---

[98] See #859.

settlement in Hinsdale. Sullivan County Commissioners claim that Cheshire County is liable for her support. Cheshire County Commissioners claim that the proof furnished is not sufficient to establish its liability. [15 Sep 1889; not adjudged]

725. Ada L. Spaulding, American, Chesterfield, born in Chesterfield, 18 Mar 1862. Has been supported by the town of Chesterfield since May 1887. Father living and resides in Chesterfield. [14 Oct and 17 Oct 1889; adjudged Dec 1889]

726. R. R. Evans, American, Winchester, born in VT, 81 years old, last Feb. Widowed. Has resided in Winchester for many years last past. Has children, but they are not able to care for him. [16 Oct 1889; adjudged 25 Oct 1889]

[245] 727. Joseph Blanchard, French, Nelson, born in Canada, 39 years old. Came to VT when 16 years of age and from there to Marlborough, NH about 2 years ago. Married; wife Mary L. born in Canada, 32 years old. One child Minnie, 3 years old. [16 Oct 1889; adjudged 12 Dec 1889]

728. Cornelius Driscoll, Irish, Keene, born in Ireland, about 40 years of age. Married; wife Hannah L. is about 34 years old. Have 8 children, viz: John, James, Jeremiah, Dennis, Daniel, Michael, Mary and Margaret, aged respectively 13, 12, 10, 6, 4, 2 and 1 year, 9 months, and 2 months. {Mary died 15 Sep 1890, and Michael died 19 Sep 1890 of diphtheria.} [25 Oct 1889; adjudged 12 Dec 1889]

729. Josiah Clark Stebbins,[99] American, Keene, born in Jaffrey, 21 years old, the 23rd Mar last. Single; father Josiah Stebbins resides in East Jaffrey. Said applicant is trying to get aboard of

---

[99] See also #872, #900 and #1354.

Cheshire County Paupers
1885-1900

a freight train, being intoxicated, fell and lost one arm by being run over. [26 Oct 1889; adjudged 12 Dec 1889]

[246] 730. Henry McManus, Fitzwilliam, birthplace unknown, about 42 years old. Has resided in Fitzwilliam a great part of the time for the last 20 years. Has been an inmate of the Worcester Insane Asylum. Was discharged a short time since. Is now quite violently insane. Has been committed to the NH Asylum for the Insane. Single; father was drowned in Troy several years ago. [24 Oct 1889; adjudged 12 Dec 1889]

731. Burchstead, Monahan, Burns, and Young of Gilsum. Transient, affidavits not sufficient to prove the liability of the county. [6 Nov and 11 Nov 1889; rejected]

732. Rosie E. Guillow, American, Gilsum, born in Sullivan, 34 years old, the 14th of last Mar. Married; husband Luther H. was born in Gilsum and was 40 years old the 2d day of last Apr. Have been married 19 years and have always resided in Gilsum, except for two summers spent in Stoddard, until they came to Keene, the last of Nov 1886. Have 4 children, viz: Jehial B., Lione P., Blanchie L., and Chester K, aged respectively 18, 14, 5 and 3 years old. Buried a little boy on Oct last. [19 Nov 1889; adjudged 12 Dec 1889]

[247] 733. Ann H. Centre (Sentre), Keene, born in Greenwich, state of NY, 1 Jun 1830, 59 years old. Widow; husband John H. died two years ago, the 7th of last Apr at Windhall, VT. We had resided there for 6 years or more. Came to Swanzey the 12th day of Jan last and to Keene, the 9th of May. Has 3 minor children, viz: Charles H., Emmaette, and Lilla B., aged respectively 20 (the 20th of Feb last), 12 (the 10th of Jul last), and 9 (the 11th of Mar last). Has one, Markey, 14 years old, bounded out until he is 21 years old. Has six grown up, taking care of themselves. [19 Nov 1889; adjudged 12 Dec 1889]

Cheshire County Paupers
1885-1900

734. Bridget Clark, Irish; husband, American; Hinsdale, born in Northfield, MA, 33 years old. Married; husband Edward A. Clark was born in Hinsdale, and is 30 years old. Has always resided in Hinsdale. Have 3 dependent minor children, viz: Fred Leslie, Edith Jane and C. Prentiss, aged respectively 9, 7, and 2 years. Parents of both dead, except the mother of Bridget. {22 Oct 1891} Two children born since this case was adjudged. [25 Nov 1889; adjudged 12 Dec 1889]

735. Winnie Lally, Irish, Winchester, born in Ireland, 22 years old, the 15th of last Aug. Came to America in 1882. Married; husband John Lally is 29 years old. Deserted his wife a short time ago. They were married the 27th of Sep 1887. Her parents reside in Ireland; his in Ashuelot. Have one child Michael J., 16 months old. [2 Dec 1889; adjudged 12 Dec 1889]

[248] 736. May E. Gould, American, Walpole, born in Providence, RI, the 14th day of Mar 1853. Married Frank Gould at Brattleboro in May 1886. Have resided in N. Walpole since 12 Mar last. The 14th of Sep last her husband was committed to the Windham County jail. His parents are not living. Her parents reside in Atkins, Windham County, VT. {10 Jan 1890} Ordered to Almshouse. [3 Dec 1889; adjudged 18 Feb 1890. Waiting evidence]

737. Catherine Reardon, Irish, Keene, born in Ireland, 70 years old next Aug. Has resided in Keene for 36 years last past. Widow; husband Michael Reardon, died some 12 years ago. No children living. {12 Dec 1889} has gained a settlement in Keene by possessing $250 of personal estate since 1 Jun 1880; four years in succession. Money deposited in Cheshire Prov. Inst. [6 Dec 1889; 12 Dec 1889, has a settlement in Keene]

Cheshire County Paupers
1885-1900

738. Morris Custello, Gilsum, transient, 34 years old. Came from CT. Has left town. [Affidavit defective, not adjudged]

[249] 739. Daniel Jameson, Jaffrey, 13 years old. Does not know where he was born. Parents once lived in Goffstown. Came to Jaffrey to live with Charles H. Chapman, some four years ago. He, Chapman, took me from the Hillsboro County Farm at Wilton. He was taken from said Chapman's by the Overseer of the Poor, J. W. Fassett, on account of cruel treatment. {Ordered to the Farm 7 Jan 1890.} [12 Dec 1889]

740. James Kenney, Troy, born in Boston, 23 years old. Married; wife Annie was born in Keene and is 22 years of age, and her parents still reside in said Keene. His parents he thinks are dead. Her father's name is John Grogan. Has lived in Keene for the last 20 years. One child, viz: Grace E., 5 months old. County liable for James Kenney's support, but the proof is insufficient to show the liability of county to support his wife and child. [20 Dec 1889; adjudged]

741. Rindia A. Frame, American, Keene, born in Dublin, NH, 29 years old, the 13th of Oct 1889. Widow; husband James K. was born in Harrisville, and was 29 years old, the 2d day of Nov last. He died the 22nd day of Nov last. Have three children: Walter L., Grover C., and Lewis J., aged respectively 7, 4, 7/12 years old. Her husband resided a greater part of his life in Harrisville. His parents still reside there. {Grover C. died.} [20 Dec 1889; adjudged 28 Dec 1889]

[250] 742. Ascelia A. Proux, French, Marlborough, born in Canada, 32 years old. Married Ashley Preau, 16 years ago. Her husband died the 5th of Oct 1889. They went to Marlborough to live in 1887. Has 5 children, 2 of them are in Canada with their grandfather, viz: Merrit, aged 9 years and Samuel, aged 4 years. Those living at home are Arselia, 14 years old, Frank, 12

years, and Clara, 6 years old. [24 Dec 1889; adjudged 27 Dec 1889]

743. Franklin Fairbank, American, Roxbury, born in Keene, 68 years old. Married; wife Adeline H. resides in Marlborough with her daughter Mrs. Harriet Hodskins. Have 2 children; the other daughter Laura Thayer resides in said Marlborough. He is an inmate of the NH Asylum for the Insane. Owns a small place in Roxbury. Has been supported for 7 or 8 years past by the city of Keene. Settlement lost under the act passed last August. [27 Dec 1889; adjudged 27 Dec 1889]

744. Elbridge E. Jewell, American, Winchester, born in Winchester, 51years old. Married in 1868 to Emma M. Thomas, West Boston, MA. One child Susie E., 22 years old. Does not live with his wife and daughter. They reside with her aunt and apply for no relief. Was a member in the 2d NH Regiment of Volunteers. [23 Dec 1889; adjudged 27 Dec 1889. A dependent solider]

[251] 745. Caleb Philbrick, American, Roxbury, born in Sutton, NH, 73 years old, the 7th of Oct 1889. Has been married twice. Last wife living has not lived with her for five years last past. Has six children, all of age and none of them able to aid him. Rather shiftless. [27 Dec 1889; adjudged 18 Feb 1890]

746. Mary Mahoney, Walpole, born in Ireland, 49 years old. Landed in America the 15th day of May 1889; came directly to Walpole. Husband died in Ireland, 23 Dec 1881. Have 5 children; oldest is married, name Ellen Flannery, age 29; Bridget, age 21; Michael, age 19; Hanora, age 17; Mary, age 12. Hanora has been sick a long time. Calls for help for her two youngest daughters. {Hanora died (?)} [4 Jan 1890; adjudged 18 Feb 1890]

Cheshire County Paupers
1885-1900

747. Charles Smith, dependent soldier, Marlborough, born in Fitzwilliam, 68 years old. Has resided in Marlborough 24 years. Married; wife Harriet is ___ years old. He served between 2 and 3 years in the army. [3 Dec 1889; adjudged 18 Feb 1890]

[252] 748. Sarah E. Debell, alias Stone, Winchester, born in NY, 41 years old last June. Came to W when she was 2 years old. Was adopted by John G. Dingman. Has been married four times: first, to John W. Rumrill; second, to Orrin J. Davis; third, to Norris C. Stone; fourth, to Fred DeBell. She claims that DeBell had a wife living when he married her and that the marriage was not legal, and therefore she refuses to live with him. Had two children by Rumrill, Davis and Stone: 2 by Stone at Almshouse. She is very much broken. Is living with her adopted parents. Her first husband, Rumrill, died from an injury rec'd in the service of the US. Has applied for a pension. [30 Dec 1890; adjudged 18 Feb 1890[100]]

749. Ella D. Longever, Keene, said Olive Lamphere was born in Lyme, NH, 16 years old last June. Parents reside in Lyme. Mrs. Longever resides in Keene and is her sister. Olive came to Keene the last of June or the first of July last. Was taken sick with diphtheria about the first of Nov and had to have some relief which was furnished to those taking care of her. Make claim on Grafton County for the amount of relief furnished said county being liable for the support of her parents and she being a minor. [3 Dec 1889; adjudged 18 Feb 1890]

[253] 750. Ephraim Tyrrel, American, Dublin, born in Hancock, NH, 75 years old. Has always resided in H until he was brought to Dublin, the 3d day of Feb 1889 to board with his

---

[100] Date transcribed as in original, but it is presumed that application was made in Dec 1889.

sister by the selectmen of Hancock. Hillsboro County acknowledges its liability and sends order in payment of all relief furnished Cheshire County. [12 Oct 1889; Hillsboro Co. appears to be liable, 6 Mar 1890]

751. Willie A. Towne, American, Keene, born in Fitzwilliam 8 Feb 1865. Married; wife Fanny M. was born in Troy, 24 years old. One child Oscar Alfred, 3 months old. Married the 23rd Jun 1889. He came to North Dana, MA where his mother now resides. Her father Albert Pratt lives in Troy. [2 Jan 1890; adjudged 18 Feb 1890]

752. Oliver L. Nash, American, Troy, born in Chesterfield, 59 years old. Widowed; has been married two times. Has children by each wife. Alice M., wife of George H. Kenney, was born in Keene, the 19th Jan 1866. Harry J. was born in Winchester 2 Mar 1869. Calvin A. was born in Swanzey 4 Jan 1872. Married for his second wife, Florence M. Perkins, a county pauper. Was aided by the county while his first wife was living in Winchester. Has 2 children by his first wife, viz: Orrisa L. and Warren A. Warren is dead. She had an illegitimate child before she married Nash. Nash served Co. F, 6th Reg't NH Vols. {31 Dec 1889} Florence died in Troy. [9 Jan 1890; adjudged 18 Feb 1890]

[254] 753. George H. Kenney, American, Troy, born in Walpole, NH, 29 years of age. Married; wife Alice M., a daughter of Oliver L. Nash, age 24. Two children, viz: I. Mabel, born 2 May 1884, and George Avery, born 18 Apr 1889. [9 Jan 1890; adjudged 18 Feb 1890]

754. William J. Lane, American, Keene, born in Dover, NH, 39 years old. Has resided in Rochester the last two years. Father Joseph Lane is dead. [It appears that Strafford Co. is liable]

Cheshire County Paupers
1885-1900

755. Abner Fisk, American, Keene, born Chesterfield, 76 years old. Married; wife Mary L. born in Holland, MA in 1818. Has resided in Keene since Sep 1888. Prior to coming to Keene they lived in New London, CT, 7 or 8 years and in Palmer, MA about the same time. [10 Jan 1890; adjudged 24 Feb 1890]

[255] 756. Delia Fountain, Walpole, born in Canaan, Grafton Co., NH, the 18th day of Jul 1866. Was married to Peter Fountain 6 Jul 1881, resided in Canaan until May 1884. Then came to North Walpole. In Oct 1887 they removed to Westminster, VT. Husband deserted his wife 6 Jan 1888. Two children, one born 16 Jun 1884; the other 10 Sep 1888. Husband was born in Canada. See page 195. [13 Jan 1890; adjudged after Apr term 1888]

757. Erford A. Clark, American, Keene, born in Keene, 34 years old. Married; wife Alice M. born in Surry and is 34 years old. Two children by a former husband, Joseph Thompson, who is supposed to be residing in California for the last 8 or 9 years. Children: Frank L., 14 years old and Bertie W., 9 years old. Clark married Mrs. T some 7 years ago. Have resided in Keene since. Clark recently cut his finger which after a time had to be amputated and later his arm had to be near his shoulder. [10 Jan 1890; adjudged 18 Feb 1890]

758. Bertie G. Greeley, American, Westmoreland, born in Brattleboro, VT, 15 years old last Sep. Neither his father or mother George W. and Mary Greeley have lived in any town in NH since 1 Jan 1880. Said Bertie has lived with Otis Hutchins in said Westmoreland for the year last past. His grandfather on his father's side was James M.; on his mother's Marston Witham. Paternal grandmother Harriet Greeley. Whereabouts of his father and mother are unknown. [1 Feb 1890; adjudged 24 Feb 1890]

*Cheshire County Paupers
1885-1900*

[256] 759. Harry Parker, American, Gilsum, born in Hartford, CT, 29 years old. Resided in said Hartford, CT for about 25 years. Came to Gilsum for work. Being disappointed in getting a job and without money he calls for temporary relief. [28 Jan 1890; adjudged 24 Feb 1890]

760. John Chambers, American, Gilsum, born in Quincy, MA, 28 years old. Resided in Q until he was about 25 years old; came to Gilsum for work. Without money, could get no work and therefore asked for temporary relief. [28 Jan 1890; adjudged 24 Feb 1890]

761. Mary J. Allen, American, Keene, born in Saratoga, NY, 32 years old. Married; husband William L. was born in Wallingford, VT, 33 years old. No children. Neither ever resided in the state prior to 1886. Mrs. A's father is dead; mother lives in Stonnybrook, NY. Her husband's parents are both dead. [23 Jan 1890; adjudged 24 Feb 1890]

[257] 762. William J. Ruffle,[101] American, Keene, born in Keene, 24 years of age. Married; wife Hattie L. is 23 years old. Two children, viz: Carl William, 2 years old; the other an infant, 6 days old. Mrs. R was born in Lincoln, ME. Father at County Almshouse; mother resides at Baldwinville, MA. [10 Jan 1890; adjudged 24 Feb 1890]

763. Fred Elmon, American, Keene, born in Hinsdale, age 26. Married; wife Emily A. was born in Lodi, Wisconsin, 23 years old. Two children, viz: George A., 2 years old, the 10th of Jan ult.; and an infant only a few days old. Elmon's parents are both dead. They always resided in Hinsdale. Mrs. E's parents have no settlement in NH. Evidence shows that said Elmon has a settlement in Hinsdale. [20 Jan 1890; settlement in Hinsdale]

---

[101] See also # 446, page 150.

Cheshire County Paupers
1885-1900

764. Edna A. Nims, American, Keene, b. in Sullivan, age 46 last Oct. Married; husband George H. Nims is about 50 years old. Have not lived together for the last 13 or 14 years. Four children, viz: Archie Wallace, age 21, last Sept; Edith V., age 19, last Aug; Blanche A., age 17, last Jul; and Harrington D., age 14 last June. The first 3 earn enough for their own support. Mrs. Nims has always until now supported herself and children, but of late she has been subject to fits and is unable to labor as much. Her husband resides in town and is a miserable wretch. [23 Jan 1890; adjudged 24 Feb 1890]

[258] 765. Putnam H. Foley and Edna R. Foley, Keene, b. Rochester, VT, 35 years of age. Married 4 years ago last Aug; not lived together since the 11th of Nov last. Husband born in Brandon, VT, age 33. No children by Foley; 2 by former husband. She does not ask for any relief. Application made in his behalf by Mrs. Wilson on Colorado St. with whom he boarded. [24 Jan 1890; not adjudged; application withdrawn.]

766. Ida Harvey, American, Chesterfield, born in C, 11 Feb 1862, 28 years old. Single. Has resided in Winchester since 1878 with parents; father's name Chas. L. Harvey. Has been in very feeble health for several years. The town of C has given some assistance in her support for 4 or 5 years. Her father having gained a settlement there prior to 1880, lost under the act of the 14th Aug last. [1 Feb 1890; 24 Jan 1890, action postponed. See affidavit.[102] Adjudged 1 Nov 1894]

767. James Trainor, Gilsum, b. in New Haven, CT, age 28. Has lived in New Haven nearly all his lifetime. Is here temporarily in search of work. Only applies for temporary relief. [1 Jan 1890; adjudged 24 Feb 1890]

---

[102] Affidavit #335, page 113, is a previous application for aid.

Cheshire County Paupers
1885-1900

[259] 768. John Greenway, English, Keene, born in Cornwall, England, 71 years old, the 3d of last January. Single; has been married; wife Grace died about 3 years ago. Two children, viz: Richard, who resides in Westerly, RI and George, who resides in Milford, CT. Has resided in Keene for the last 14 or 15 years. [28 Jan 1890; not adjudged; city liable]

769. Edgar N. Harrington, American, Keene, born in Troy, NH, 37 years old. Married; Isis E. (Nash), his wife has deserted him. One child Bertha L., 10 years old. His father, he thinks, resides in Amsterdam, NY. Mother has been dead twenty years or more. [5 Feb 1890; adjudged 24 Feb 1890]

770. Gilbert Field, American, Keene, born in Swanzey, 67 years old. Single. Has resided in Keene for 25 years last past. Weak minded. [12 Feb 1890; adjudged 24 Feb 1890]

[260] 771. Emily M. Rumrill, American, Winchester, 50 years old, single. Came to Winchester, the 5th of last Sep to visit her sisters Mrs. Thomas Rumrill and Mrs. George W. Notts. Was taken sick about 20th of Jan and having no means was obliged to call for aid. {Died 22 Dec 1890.} [12 Feb 1890; adjudged 24 Feb 1890]

772. Amelia Blanchet, French, Keene, born in Canada, 35 years of age. Married; husband Joseph Blanchard or Blanchet, was born in Canada, is 34 years old. Three children, viz: Eva, 13 years old; Arzelia, 11 years old; and Flora, 10 years old. Husband has been at work in the Harness Factory, got into a little trouble and left. Has gone in search of work. She wants to get means to go to Woburn where she has friends who she is sure will help her. No aid rendered. [14 Feb 1890; applicant left town; not adjudged 24 Jan 1890]

Cheshire County Paupers
1885-1900

773. Almira M. Phillips, American, Harrisville, born in Kingston, NH, 27 Apr 1849. Married; husband Albert M. One child, viz: Mary W., born in Portsmouth in 1881. Was married the 14th Feb 1879. Lived in Portsmouth about 15 months when her husband left her and she has not heard from him since. She continued to live in P until Jan 1889 when she came to Harrisville to live. [10 Feb 1890; adjudged 27 Mar 1890]

[261] 774. Hiram W. Eastman, American, Keene, born in Northfield, MA, 59 years old. Married; Lizzie N. was born in Northfield, MA, is 47 years old. Five children,[103] viz: Edward W., age 22; Herbert A., age 19; Frank P. age 18; Harry, age 10 years. All at home except the oldest. Has resided in Keene most of the time for 27 years last past. [17 Feb 1890; adjudged Apr term 1890]

775. John Mason, Canadian, Marlborough, born in Canada, 37 years old. Married about ten years ago to Georgianna Lascomb. She was born in Canada, age 28 years. Two children, viz: Harry, age 10 and Willie, age 7 years. Has resided in M only since Sep. [17 Feb 1890; adjudged 24 Feb 1890]

776. Grace O. Hale, American, Swanzey. Father was born in Richmond 3 Nov 1828. Married Abigail Comstock 24 or 25 years ago, when she was granted a divorce from her husband Otis D. There were 3 children born to them, 2 now living, viz: Perley LaForest and Grace O. The custody of these children was given to the father. Grace O. was on application of her mother declared insane and committed to the NH Asylum for the Insane, and supported by the town of Swanzey. Later she was removed to the County Almshouse, Westmoreland and has been supported by said Swanzey. [29 Oct 1889; 24 Jan 1890, not adjudged]

---

[103] Only 4 children listed in affidavit. See also #46, page 16.

Cheshire County Paupers
1885-1900

[262] 777. Ezra Shantley, Canadian, Hinsdale, born in St. John's, Canada East, 52 years old. Married; wife Gusta Shantley is about 40 years of age. Seven children (see affidavit for names and ages).[104] [3 Mar 1890; adjudged 27 Mar 1890]

778. George O. Harvey,[105] American, Keene, born in Jamaica, VT, 50 years old in Feb. Married; wife Ann S., born in Jamaica, VT, 52 years old. Five children, only one minor, viz: Clara E., age 10. Owns a small place in Winchester. Probably settlement in Winchester. [17 Jan 1890; rejected 27 Mar 1890]

779. Laura P. Bell, American, Keene, born in Clarendon, VT, 38 years old. Married; husband Abraham Bell was 26 years old in March. He cleared out some two weeks ago, and nothing has been heard from him since. His father Frank Bell resides in Winchester. Has children. [10 Mar 1890]

[263] 780. George W. Shattuck, American, Marlborough, born in Albany, NY, 15 Apr 1842. Married 10 Jan 1880; wife Sarah A. White was born in Marlborough, 29 Mar 1858. Has been twice married. Two children, viz: Perley E., age 16, by his first wife; Albert G., age 7. Was a soldier in the late Rebellion and wounded in line of duty. [10 Mar 1890; adjudged 27 Mar 1890]

781. George Garrett, French, Chesterfield, born in Canada, 24 years old. Father resides in Canada. Paul Garrett, a brother, resides in Chesterfield. Said George, while at work in the woods on the 4th of March last, broke his leg. Affidavit imperfect, said applicant not adjudged 27 Oct 1890. Additional proof filed and the case reexamined and adjudged. The said George Garrett was removed to Winchester by the overseers of

---

[104] No affidavit found with these records.
[105] See also #981, page 330.

the poor of Chesterfield, and the cost charged to the county. [29 Mar 1890; not adjudged; 27 Oct 1890, adjudged]

782. Charlotte A. Kelly, Winchester, 27 years old, daughter of Mrs. Robert Turnstall. Married; husband ____. Have four children: Michael, 9 years old last Oct; Robert, 7 years old last Jan; Samuel, 4 years old last Sept; and baby, 2 weeks old. Husband never lived in this state until 2 years ago. [3 Apr 1890; adjudged 29 Jul 1890]

[264] 783. Abigail Rice, American, Nelson. Widow, 79 years old. Husband died in Hancock, NH more than 19 years ago. Has made Hancock her home until Feb 1889 when she came to Cheshire County and has made it her home with Mrs. A. C. Tarbox, her granddaughter. {Died 6 Oct 1890 at Arthur C. Tarbox's in Nelson.} [1 Apr 1890; adjudged 15 Apr 1890]

784. William B. Beach, Hinsdale, born on the Flat Brook, Nebraska, 67 years old or thereabouts. Has been married, is now a widower. Claims to be a Madoc Indian, a medicine man. Is evidently a fraud. {Ordered to the Farm. Admitted 22 Apr 1890; discharged 7 Jun 1890} {In Jun 1890, evidence of his having served as a private in Co. I, 22 Reg't NY Vols was filed and on the next day he was discharged from the County Farm and taken to West Swanzey by Mrs. Luman Seaver.} {12 Nov 1891} Wife and 3 children living, viz: Mary E., wife; Mary E. Rogers; Fanny A. Blood; Willie E., reside in Providence and Woonsocket, RI. Mrs. Beach says that her husband was born in NJ. Readmitted to Farm. [12 Apr 1890; adjudged 15 Apr 1890]

785. Peter Mulgreen,[106] Irish, Marlborough, born in Ireland, more than 60 years old. Came to America in 1850. Widowed;

---

[106] According to the 1870 census of Nelson, his surname is Mulgrew.

*Cheshire County Paupers
1885-1900*

wife died in 1876. Came to M in 1888. Was supported at the Cheshire Co. Almshouse for some 6 months in 1880. Admitted again in 1890. [15 Apr 1890; adjudged 17 Apr 1890]

[265] 786. John Hussey, Irish, Keene, not born in this country, about 30 years of age. His parents reside in Ireland. Single; know of no relatives residing in this country. Sick and unable to make a statement. Affidavit made Patrick Tonghey with whom said Hussey has boarded more or less of the time for 7 years last past. [8 Apr 1890; adjudged 15 Apr 1890]

787. Henry Cook, brother of John H. Cook. John H. states that his brother came to NH from Platsburg (*sic*), NY in Mar 1886 and has resided since in Keene and Winchester. Married; wife resides in P from whom he was divorced in 1886. Has three minor children, viz: John, age 12, living in P; Joseph, age 20, resides in Malone, NY; and Mary, age 16, living in P. Said John H. died at the house of his brother in Winchester 1 Apr 1890. [12 Apr 1890; adjudged 15 Apr 1890]

788. Matilda McGinnis, Irish (French), Keene, born in Canada, 29 years old. Married; husband William was born in Canada, 31 years old. Two children, viz: Rosa, age 7; Roselbeau, age 5 ½. Expects to be confined soon. Husband has deserted her, leaving her very destitute. Has worked at the Pottery in Keene. Resides Baker Street. {After confinement, Mrs. McGinnis and children were forwarded to CT, the whereabouts of her husband being found to be there.} [21 May 1890; adjudged 29 Jul 1890]

[266] 789. Delia Lawan,[107] American, Keene, born in Milton, VT, 40 years of age. Married; husband Raymond Lawan was born in Canada and is 48 years old. Seven children, viz:

---

[107] According to the 1870 census for Hinsdale, the surname is Laware. The text says 7 children, but only 6 are listed, with only 5 ages listed.

Cheshire County Paupers
1885-1900

Chas. H., Nelson, Josephine M., Ephraim, Rosa Bell, and Gertie Ellen, aged respectively 19, 13, 11, 6, and 6/12. The oldest child is of age. Have resided in Keene for 8 years last past. [Jun 1890; adjudged Jun 1890]

790. Lonnie Deering, American, Swanzey, born in Washington, VT, 24 years old the 18th of Aug next. Married; husband Munroe Deering was born in East Bethel, VT and is 28 years old or thereabouts. His parents are both dead. Her father is dead but her mother resides in Chelsea, VT. Two children, viz: Earnest and Bertie, aged respectively 5 and 3 years of age. Husband left her, and she knows not where he is. She has been ill for sometime and her mind is not right. Committed to the Asylum 17 Jun 1890. [18 Jun 1890; adjudged 29 Jul 1890]

791. Harvey Barney, American, Alstead, born in Lempster, 27 Apr 1804, 86 years old. Widowed; was married in 1824. Wife died in 1878. Resided in Cornish from 1 Jan 1880 to Apr 1884, then in Marlow until Feb 1887. [2 May 1890; adjudged 29 Jul 1890]

[267] 792. Bathsheba Holt, American, Troy, born in Wayland, MA, 72 years old. Widow, under guardianship of Edmund Bemis of said Troy. Has resided in Troy and Gardner, MA most of the time since 1 Jan 1880. Has a settlement in Wayland, MA under its laws and having been born there can be removed to said town of Wayland. {Mrs. Holt appears to have a settlement in Wayland, MA and was removed there by Mr. and Mrs. Bemis 29 Jul 1890 by direction of Com. Abbott.} [7 Jun 1890; adjudged 29 Jul 1890; action rescinded]

793. Octavia King (?), Rindge, born in the town of Georgia, VT, 9 Aug 1857, daughter of Eugene and Louisa LaClair. Parents born in Canada. Married at Winchendon, MA, 16 Oct 1874, to Barney King who was born in Quebec, Canada. From

Cheshire County Paupers
1885-1900

1875 to 21 Nov 1888 resided in Chelsea, MA; since in Rindge. Her husband has been absent from her much of the time, and all of the time for the last 15 months. Three children, viz: Barney, born 15 Jan 1881; Melvin, born 29 Oct 1884; and Mabel, born 27 Apr 1889. [15 Jul 1890; adjudged 29 Jul 1890]

794. Joseph Burcham, American, Westmoreland, born in Colchester, CT, Feb 1813. Has resided in Westmoreland all of the time since 1 Jan 1880. Has been married twice; last wife Huldah W. died in Nov 1888. Possessed of a home and lot in said Westmoreland in which said Burcham holds a courtesy right during his life. Was a private in Co. A, 4th Reg't NH Vols. Receives a pension of $8 per month. Has no minor children. Has several married: Mrs. Joseph Doolittle of Keene; Mrs. Shedd of Fitchburg, MA; Mrs. Emerson of Leominster; are his daughters. Said Burcham under the guardianship of J. B. Abbott of Keene. [20 Jun 1890; adjudged 29 Jul 1890]

[268] 795. Charles Plasteridge, American, Keene, born in Northfield, VT, 37 years old, 10 Sep 1889. Married; wife Jennie E. was born in Walpole, NH, 33 years old. One child, viz: Etta, who will be 5 years, 2 Aug next. Has been failing in health for 6 years last past. Has shown symptoms of insanity for several years. Has recently been committed to the NH Asylum for treatment. Parents Amasa and Mary A. Plasteridge reside on Church Street in Keene. Said C. P. has resided in Ohio most of the time of 14 years last past. [21 Jul 1890; adjudged 29 Jul 1890]

796. [108]

797. Avery Bryant, American, Swanzey, born in West Springfield, MA, 59 years old. Married about 1849 to Sarah A.

---

[108] Entry left blank.

Cheshire County Paupers
1885-1900

Morey. Has resided in the town of Swanzey since 1 Jan 1880. Served in the US Army during the late war. Receives a pension of $8 per month. Wife purchased a small place in said Swanzey for $500 and took a deed in her own name which she has held more than four years and paid all taxes. Query: does her title to more than $150 of real estate give him a settlement? Oct term of court decided that the town is liable. See affidavit. {Avery and wife dead.} [3 Mar 1890]

[269] 798. Jennie B. Wilber, American, Dublin, 16 years of age, the 30th day of last Jul. Married George Wilber of Keene in Feb last; that he has deserted her. Father E. F. Whitaker was born in Bethel, VT; mother Jane E. was born in Hinsdale, NH. Age of father 62 years; mother, 55 years. Parents have resided in Dublin for the last 3 or 4 years. She now resides with her father. He and his family lived in Swanzey from 1882 to 1886. [26 Apr 1890; adjudged 21 Oct 1890]

799. W. H. Calkins, American, Swanzey, born in Swanzey, 53 years old. Has resided in Swanzey since 1880. Married to Ellen A. Pratt in 1884. Has been married before. Have the following minor children, viz: Edward, 18 years old; Nahun, about 17; Christie, 15; Irus, 10; Charles, 8; Horace, 4; Forest, 2 . Was 3 years in the service of the US. [31 Mar 1890; adjudged 24 Oct 1890]

800. Willard R. Graves, American, Keene, born in Guilford, VT, 8 Jun 1828. Has been married twice. Had one child by his first wife; more by the last. Second wife Miss Reynolds of Richmond was born in Hancock and is 49 years of age. Served 13 months in Co. F., 4th Reg't VT Vols. Receives a small pension. Wife owns a house and lot on Court Street, valued at $1200. [26 Jun 1890; adjudged Oct term]

Cheshire County Paupers
1885-1900

[270] 801. Silas Whipple, American, Fitzwilliam, 79 years of age, born in Fitzwilliam or Richmond. Has resided in Brookfield, MA from 1875 to 1887 and since then in Fitzwilliam. Single. Insane and in very feeble condition. Living with his sister Elvira Allen of said Fitzwilliam. [22 Sep 1890; adjudged 21 Oct 1890]

802. Elizabeth A. Fletcher, English, Roxbury, born in Bolton, Lancanshire, England, 25 years of age. Married; husband Thomas W. Fletcher is 29 years. Deserted his wife; his whereabouts unknown. Was married in Glasgow, Scotland in 1883. Two children: William E., age 5, born in Ballardvale, MA; and Gertrude E., born in Lowell, age 4. Mother of said Elizabeth resides in Bolton, Lancanshire, England. Her husband's father also resides at Lancanshire. [10 Apr 1890; adjudged 21 Oct 1890]

803. David Bandeen, French, Marlborough, born in Canada, 38 years of age, Married; wife Christina, 17 years of age. Two children, one by former wife, viz: Agnes, 9 years of age; Alice, 2 years old. Married last wife two years ago. {Ordered to Co. Farm, Sep 1892. Died at the Almshouse 9 Oct 1892.} [11 Oct 1890; adjudged 21 Oct 1890]

[271] 804. Darius Newell, Irish, Marlborough, 61 years old. Has resided in Marlborough many years. Served in the US Army in the late Rebellion. Married in 1853; wife Mary Ann is 53 years old. Has 13 children, living, 4 under 21 years of age, viz: Everett W., 18; Kate D., 17; Italie A., 13; Lee M., 11. The three youngest are living at home. Said Newell has had a paralytic shock. [16 Oct 1890; adjudged 21 Oct 1890]

805. John Bell, French, Harrisville, born in Canada, 52 years old. Melvina Young, his wife was born in Canada, 42 years old. Have 12 children , living, 11 under 21 years of age, viz:

Cheshire County Paupers
1885-1900

Louisa, 20, married and lives in Westminster, VT; Phoeba, 18, lives in Westminster; Jane, 15; Ada, 13; Zoa, 11; Fred, 8; Anna, 7; Lizzie, 5; Ellen, 3; Minnie and Lillie, twins, age 16 months. [7 Oct 1890; adjudged 22 Oct 1890]

806. Mary Goodrow, Marlborough. Married; husband George Goodrow, alias Dolfise Goodrow, age 27. Date of marriage 24 Aug 1888. Said Mary was 21 years old 25 Dec 1889. One child, George, one year old. Husband in jail at Woodstock, VT. Has lived in Hillsboro County for more than a year prior to coming at Cheshire County where she applied for relief within a few weeks. Hillsboro County liable, but no claim made as selectmen had paid her fare to Canada. Treated as a transient. [27 Sep 1890; adjudged 21 Oct 1890]

[272] 807. Mary E. Johnson, Cranswick H. Johnson, Hinsdale, born in Nova Scotia, 26 years old. Married in Nova Scotia 13 Sep 1884. Came to Hinsdale in 1889. Two children: Agatha, born 23 Jan 1885, 5 years old, and Jessie, 14 Apr 1890, 4 months old. C. H., husband of Mary E. was admitted to the Almshouse 18 Aug 1890. Escaped 24 Aug 1890. [18 Aug 1890; adjudged 1 Sep 1890]

808. Angeline Breau, French, Jaffrey, born in Veryfield, Canada, 26 years old. Married to John O'Neil; lived with him about two years when he died, leaving me one child; came to NH and after about 3 years married Joseph Breau, Jr. of Jaffrey. Lived with him about 2 years. {10 Sep 1890} He then deserted said applicant, leaving her with one child and since has had one born to her, that is at this date about two or three weeks old. Husband does not contribute to her support or that of the children, viz: William O'Neil, age 5, last Aug; Joseph Breau, age 1 year, 9 months; and Charles Breau, age 3 weeks. [10 Sep 1890; adjudged 23 Oct 1890]

Cheshire County Paupers
1885-1900

809. Theresa Spitzenberger,[109] German, Walpole, born in Germany, 21 Jun 1853. Went to England in 1880; to NY in 1882; to the Ely Mines, VT; a few weeks later was married to Frank Spitzenberger. Moved to Bellows Falls, VT; late in the spring of 1883 and the fall of the same year to North Walpole. Her husband died there in Apr 1887. Furnished some relief by the county. Two children, both boys; one born 2 Oct 1884; the other 29 Apr 1886. On 16 Jun 1890 had a shock of paralysis. Has a sister in Bellows Falls with whom she is now living. [3 Sep 1890; adjudged 23 Oct 1890]

[273] 810. Agnes D. Scott, American, Chesterfield, born in Chesterfield 2 Nov 1879. Father G. D. Scott was a soldier in Co. F, 14th NH Vols. Served from Aug 1861 to Jul 1865; died in the NH Asylum 20 Jul 1883, age 41. Mrs. Scott's maiden name was Nancy A. Burns. She was born in VT. She now resides in Putney, VT; dependent upon her labors for support. Agnes resides with Asa F. Farr. [Adjudged 27 Oct 1890]

811. Mary S. Pelkey, Keene, born in Whitehall, NY, 40 years of age. Married Anthony Pelkey in 1868. Resided West Swanzey and Spragueville from 1880 to 1884; in Keene since husband deserted her the 15th day of Jan 1890. Four children: John E., age 20, resides in Winchendon, MA; Charles A., 17, lives at home and works in Burdett's shop; Mabel, 14, and Ida May, age 7; last two live at home. Own a small place in north part of city, but is mortgaged for all that it is worth. Anthony in Co. G, 5th VT Reg't. [1 Sep 1890; adjudged 2 Sep 1890]

812. Delia LaPoint, French, Keene, born in Whitehall, NY, 16 Dec 1860, 29 years of age. Father and mother both dead. Father's name was Michael Harrigan. Married Willie LaPoint 10th of May, 4 years ago. Had two children; buried one the 9th

---

[109] See also # 513, page 173.

Cheshire County Paupers
1885-1900

of Sep last; the other Willie was 2 years old the 5th day of last May. Husband intemperate; can not live with him, he is so bad. [1 Oct 1890; adjudged 23 Oct 1890]

[274] 813. John Baufor, French, Winchester, born in Canada, 20 years old. Went to Winchester to live 5 years ago. Parents reside in Canada; have never lived in the States. Has been at work in the Ashuelot Mfg Co.'s mills. Was taken sick with a fever about three weeks ago. Single man. [10 Nov 1890; adjudged 3 Feb 1891]

814. Amy A. Tower, American, Keene, born in Harrisville, 21 years old. Married J. H. Tower 28 Aug 1888. One child, J. Wesley, 10 months old. Her parents reside at the present time in Nelson. Her husband is 37 years old. Is an inmate of the House of Corrections for crime. Has been employed as a barber by Ira D. Gates. [7 Nov 1890; adjudged 4 Feb 1891]

815. Victoria Perry, French, Keene, born in Canada, 28 years old, the 12th day of last Apr. Married; husband Fred R. Perry was born near Boston, is about 40 years old, son of Francis A. Perry of Keene. 3 children; husband intemperate, treatment of family cruel. Is said to be an inmate of the House of Corrections in Lowell, MA for cruel treatment of his wife and on her complaint. Mrs. P's father is dead; her mother lives with her in Keene. [1 Nov 1890; adjudged 15 Jan 1891]

[275] 816. Isaac C. Hadley, American, Keene, born in Moretown, VT, 8 Jun 1831. Single. Has resided in Keene for the last 8 or 9 years. Was a private in Co. D, 2d MA Vols; enlisted the 10th of May 1861; discharged in Sep 1861. Receives a pension of $2 per month. Has a brother Edwin W. living in west part of Swanzey and a sister Rebecca J. Holman in Winchendon, MA. [5 Aug 1890; adjudged 15 Jan 1891]

Cheshire County Paupers
1885-1900

817. Margaret Casey Custare, Irish, Keene, born in Lyme, Grafton Co., NH, 4th Jul 1842. Has lived in Keene for the last 19 years. Has been twice married. Married John Casey when she was about 18 years old. He died 9 May 1877. By him she had 7 children, 3 dead, 4 living, viz: Ellen, George, William, and Edward, aged respectively 23, 21, 18, 14. Married Joseph Custare 13 Mar 1882. Had one child by Custare, viz: Joseph, age 7. Present whereabouts of husband unknown. Resides on Grove Street. Wife, city; husband, county. [8 Nov 1890. City pauper; husband adjudged Apr term 1887. See #502]

818. Fred L. Searle, American, Keene, born in Dublin, in the district subsequently annexed to Harrisville, 23 Sep 1858, 32 years old. Married; wife Jennie was born in England, 25 Jan 1852. No children. His parents Fred A. and Salome C. reside in Keene. Mrs. S's father is dead; her mother resides in Taverstock, England. His health is poor and therefore unable to work sufficiently to support himself and wife. [20 Nov 1890; adjudged 15 Jan 1891]

[276] 819. Joseph Conway, French, Hinsdale, born in St. Anne, Canada, 44 years of age. Has resided in Wilton, NH for 10 years prior to the 26th May 1890, and in Hinsdale since May 26th 1890. Married; Mary his wife was born in ____. Seven children, viz: Joseph, Frank, May, Rosa, John, Adrew (*sic*),[110] Eddie, aged respectively 19, 18, 16, 15, 11, 8, and 4 years. It appears from the affidavit that the applicant is a Hillsboro County charge. {1 Jan 1891 found to be a Cheshire Co. charge.} [6 Nov 1890; adjudged 2 Apr 1891]

820. Delia Lane, American, Hinsdale, born in Philadelphia, PA, 32 years old. A widow. Has resided in CT, VT, and MA for 10 years last past and more until 10 Aug last, when she removed

---

[110] Handwriting particularly unclear, could be "Adsend."

Cheshire County Paupers
1885-1900

from Bernardstown to Hinsdale. Husband died 10 Jan 1885 at Hartford, CT. Has 4 children: Horace G., Munroe H., Mabel M. and William, aged respectively 17, 16, 13 and 12 years. The two oldest support themselves. William met with an accident; hence, the call for aid. [8 Nov 1890; adjudged 1 Jan 1891]

821. George P. Ward,[111] American, Troy, born in Ashburnham, MA, 64 years old. Previous to 1883 resided in West Swanzey and since 28 Jul 1883 in Troy. Married; wife was born in Ashburnham, MA and is 68 years old. Has served in the army of the US. Was a veteran of Co. F., 14th NH Vols.[112]

[277] 822. John Duffee, Irish, Keene, born in Ireland, 61 years old the 10th of Nov 1890. Widowed; 3 children living in Boston, MA. Keep house together, not married, names, viz: John, Ann and Rachel, aged respectively 27, 24, and 20 years or thereabouts. Came from Ireland about 6 weeks ago. Was never in America before. Has not seen his children since he came. Was injured by a fall at Watertown, NY and is now on his way to Boston. Wants aid; ordered to Farm. Skipped and has not been seen since. [28 Nov 1890; adjudged 15 Jan 1891]

823. Henry Willard, American, Alstead, age 73 years. Taken from Langdon in the County of Sullivan, to said County Almshouse, where he is now, 8 Jan 1891. Has been ordered from said Almshouse to the Almshouse at Westmoreland. No information as to relatives. {Admitted to Almshouse, Westmoreland, 16 Jan 1891. Discharged.} [3 Oct 1890; adjudged 15 Jan 1891]

824. Caroline Clark, American, Marlborough, age 65 years. Widow; buried husband 35 years ago. Has resided in

---

[111] See #857 and 1024.
[112] No application or adjudgment dates given.

Cheshire County Paupers
1885-1900

Marlborough for 19 years last past. Five children living; youngest 36 years old. Residence of either not stated in affidavit. [25 Nov 1890; adjudged 15 Jan 1891]

[278] 825. Joseph Van Ness, French, Keene, born in France, 70 years old, 30th Jun 1890. Married; wife Julia born in Ireland, age 57 in Jul last. Six children living, 3 in Keene, unmarried with father. Two daughters married and reside in Keene. Owns a small place on Marlboro Street. Has resided in Keene since 1859. [6 Dec 1890; settlement in Keene]

826. Wilhelmina Johansen, Swede, Keene, born in Sweden, 25 years old. Came to the US 2 years ago last Jun. Father and mother both reside in Sweden. Single; in trouble, pregnant, expects to be sick before long. Ordered to and conveyed to Almshouse. {13 Jan 1891} Gave birth to child. [19 Dec 1890; adjudged 22 Dec 1890]

827. Frances Gamlin, Canadian, Jaffrey, born in Canada, 92 years old. Came from Canada to the US 2 years ago. Widow; husband died in Canada. Resides in Jaffrey with a family by the name of Demuris. {Frances Gamlin of Jaffrey died 19 Feb 1893 at Jaffrey.} [17 Dec 1890; adjudged 1 Jan 1891]

[279] 828. Ann E. Hart, American, Stoddard, born in Pembroke, NH, age 63. Widow; husband Charles Hart died in 1870. No minor children. Has resided in Westminster, VT 6 years, since 1880 and 4 years in East Hampton, MA. Affidavit does not show the residence of her relatives. [23 Dec 1890; adjudged 1 Jan 1891]

829. George H. Kimball, English, Keene, born in Manchester, England, 38 years old. Came to the US when about 11 years old; resided at Colchester, VT with his parents about 10 years; lived in Burlington, VT 3 years; came to Keene to live in 1883.

Cheshire County Paupers
1885-1900

Has resided in Keene since, except for about 1 year and a half. Parents both dead; has no near relatives living. One of his legs troubles him badly and unfits him to earn his support in full. [1 Jan 1891; adjudged 15 Jan 1891]

830. George O. Dow, American, Keene, born in Brandon, VT, 60 years old. Married; wife Emma G. was born in Ticonderoga, NY, 40 years of age. Four minor children and one emancipated and married, residing in Keene. Names and ages of the others, viz: Eldridge N., age 16; Myrtle M., 14, last Dec; Eva, 6 years, last Nov; Agnes Jane, 3 years, the 21st of last Jul. Have resided in Keene about 3 years. Prior to coming to Keene to live he resided in Sullivan, this county nearly 20 years. Served in Co. F, 5th VT Vols from 1861 to 1865. [6 Jan 1891; adjudged 4 Feb 1891]

[280] 831. Nellie Graves, American, Winchester, born in Chesterfield, 42 years old. Married; husband Joseph Graves was born in NY state, 55 years old, the 25th day of Dec 1890. They were married in Jacksonville, VT where Mr. G has resided since he was 9 years old until he came to Winchester to live 5 years ago last Feb. Has three illegitimate children, viz: Helen L. Hill, born in Searsburg, VT 24 May 1874, 16 years old; Bell Burrell, 7 years old, 7 Apr 1890; Henry Hill, 12 years, 19 Oct 1890. Helen and Henry's father's name was George Hill, of Chesterfield. He died about 12 years ago. Bell's father died about 6 years ago. Her daughter Helen is sick with consumption. The relief petitioned for is for Helen L. Hill. [7 Jan 1891; adjudged 15 Jan 1891]

832. [113]

---

[113] Entry left blank.

Cheshire County Paupers
1885-1900

833. Mary A. Towne,[114] American, Rindge, 51 years old, the 29th day of Mar 1890. Widow of Solomon F. Towne, who died in Rindge, the 26th Jan 1890. Married in Petersham, MA 8 Apr 1869. Came to R about 1878. Son Frances L. lives in R, age 20, the 26th Jan 1890. Family was aided in Rindge in 1885. Mrs. Towne and son sent to the town in MA where they belong under Chap. 83, sec. 13. [3 Jan 1891; adjudged 4 Feb 1891]

[281] 834. Levi Son, American, Troy, born in Worcester, MA, 35 years of age. Married; wife Mary Jane, born in Nova Scotia, 32 years of age. From 1 Jan 1880 to May 1882 resided in the state of Maine; came to Fitzwilliam in 1882, resided there until 1888. In the spring of 1888 moved to Roxbury; in Mar 1889 to Marlborough; then to Fitzwilliam; summer of 1890 moved to Troy. Five children, viz: Joseph Alexander, born Jun 1880; Mary Jane, born Oct 1881; Mary Louisa, born Jul 1885; Mamie, born in May 1886; Levi, born Aug 1889. [18 Dec 1890]

835. Delima Valede, Keene, born in Canada, 26 years old. Married; husband, 28 years old, name Alfred. Three children: Alfred, 7 years old; Lora, 5 years old; and Lydia, 3 years old. Husband deserted family and neglects to provide for them. Mrs. V and family ordered, and removed to the County Almshouse, 28 Nov 1890. Discharged and forwarded to her sister in Providence, RI, 28 Feb 1891.[115]

836. Noble T. Smith, American, Alstead, born in Washington, VT, 1 Aug 1847, 43 years of age. Married 30 Nov 1878; wife died 24 Oct 1890. Affidavit does not show names and ages of wife and children. Children all dead; died of diphtheria.[116] [26 Nov 1890; adjudged 4 Feb 1891]

---

[114] See also #62, page 21.
[115] No dates of application or adjudgment given.
[116] In the original, the word "diphtheria" is crossed out.

Cheshire County Paupers
1885-1900

[282] 837. Herbert E. Piper, American, Richmond, born in Northfield, VT, 34 years old. Married; wife Stella M. Brown of Weathersfield[117] Bow, NH. Three children: Mattie M., age 10; Bertie E., age 6; and Eddie C., age 4. Report says the family was sent from Royalston, MA to Richmond; that they were paid $300 to leave and the man that conveyed them to NH was paid $500 by the officials of the town of Royalston.

838. George F. Hopkins, American, Chesterfield, born in Chesterfield, 53 years old. Single; served about 3 months in the army of the US in the late war; character bad. Report says he enlisted and skipped 4 or 5 times during the war of the rebellion, having secured each time a bounty or substitute money. {P.S. Has been married but does not live with his wife, she having secured a divorce. Reported to be living in Keene.} [7 Jan 1891; adjudged 4 Feb 1891]

839. Arthur J. Brooks, American, Hinsdale, born in Middletown, CT, 39 years of age, 29 May 1890. Married; wife Addie D., maiden name Perham. Four children, viz: Bertie, age 11 years; Winfield, 10 years; Walter, 7 years; Eva, 5 years, and Mabel, 2 years. Resided in Hinsdale from 1 Jan 1880 to Aug 1882; in Harford, CT (*sic*) from Aug 1882 to Nov 1886, when the family removed back to Hinsdale. [8 Dec 1890; adjudged]

[283] 840. Fred J. Pierce, American, Harrisville. Parents reside Goffstown, is about 27 years old. Single. Has a brother and other relatives in Goffstown. Insane, taken to NH Asylum by S. D. Bemis. Has always resided in said Goffstown until he came to Harrisville about 3 years ago. His taxes have been

---

[117] The letters VT and H are crossed out in the original record. No dates of application or adjudgment are given.

abated there, therefore has gained no settlement there. Parents fairly well off.[118]

841. Clough Gonyon, French, Keene, probably born in Canada, 36 years old. Married; wife Mary is about 27 years old, born in Canada. 5 children, viz: Archie, 9 years; Johnie, 5 years; Lena, 6 years; Mary, 3 years, and Ella, 18 months. Came to Keene from Ottawa, Canada. Calls for relief by reason of sickness. Not adjudged, no claim, affidavit incomplete. [22 Mar 1890]

842. Mary Jane Gordon, American, Troy, born in Auburn, NH, 24 years of age. Married Charles P. Gordon in Auburn 17 Feb 1883. Said Charles P. was born in Raymond 25 Dec 1856, 33 years old. Does not know the present whereabouts of her husband, he having deserted her. Has 3 children, viz: Malvina E., age 6; Edna, 4 years; and Mary Jane, 18 months. Calls for aid by reason of being abandoned by her husband. [13 Jun 1890; adjudged 20 Oct 1890]

[284] 843. Emma Packard, American, Keene, born in New Salem, MA, 34 years of age. Married; husband Charles Packard was born in Erving, MA and is at this time residing somewhere in said state. They were married 17 years ago. Two children, viz: Estella, 12 years and Clarence, 10 years old next Feb. Mrs. P's parents reside with her in Keene. Her mother's name is Emma Halstat. Her husband's parents reside in Erving, MA. [2 Oct 1890; adjudged 25 Oct 1890]

844. Azubah Britton, Keene, American, born in Surry, ___ years old. Married; husband Benjamin Britton, age ___ years. Born in Surry. No children. Husband has one son by his first wife, viz: Benjamin H. Britton of Gilsum. [25 Sep 1889; adjudged Oct term 1889]

---

[118] No dates of application or adjudgment given.

Cheshire County Paupers
1885-1900

845. Ralph S. Thornton, Walpole, American, birthplace unknown, age 8. Went to live with Frank H. Parker, 3 Jul 1890; employed to board said boy by his father Willis Thornton of Bellows Falls, about age 30. Later, said Willis went away with a woman and has not since been heard from, nor has he paid the boy's board. Boy's mother is dead; her name before she married Thornton was Starkey. [7 Aug 1890; not adjudged]

[285] 846. Abraham Bell,[119] Fitzwilliam, American, birthplace unknown, age 27. Married; wife Laura V. is 39 years old. She has 2 children by a former husband L. Kent to whom she was married in 1882 and lived until 1888, when Kent abandoned her. Married Bell in Jul 1888. One child by Bell, viz: Elvira E., age 9 months. Children by Kent: Jessie M., age 8 and Alfred J., age 3. {16 Feb 1891} Ordered to Farm, to await farther (*sic*) proof. Admitted. Discharged 2 Mar 1891 with his family. [21 Jan 1891; adjudged 3 Mar 1891]

847. Jane St. John, Rindge, French Canadian, born in Georgia, VT in 1842; maiden name Hayes. Married Joseph Peter St. John in 1866. Resided in Manchester, NH 1867-1889, except for a short time in adjoining towns; moved to Rindge in 1890. Husband has deserted her and children 17th Jan. Seven children, viz: Frank, 17; George, 14; Charles, 12; Lovina, 9; Louisa, 7; Jane, 4; and Eva Bell, 1 ½ years. No relatives in Manchester, who are willing to aid her. [26 Jan 1891; adjudged 4 Feb 1891]

848. Edgar E. Clark, Keene, American, born in Keene 18 Dec 1856, 35 years old. Has resided in Keene a greater part of his life until about 1886 when said Clark went to Jacksonville, FL to live, and remained there until 1890. Parents dead. C. H. Clark of said Keene is a brother. Has a sister Lelia Clark

---

[119] See also #779, page 262.

Cheshire County Paupers
1885-1900

residing in Worcester, MA. Claims to have a settlement in Keene by having an equitable interest in more than $250 in personal estate for more that 4 years since 1 Jan 1880. Ordered and removed to Almshouse to await farther (*sic*) proof. Not adjudged; discharged from Almshouse, left for parts unknown. [31 Jan 1891]

[286] 849. Luther March,[120] Keene, American, born in Alstead, 24 May 1845, 45 years old. Single; never married. Parents both dead. Achsah March, Luther's mother, was admitted to the Almshouse in 1868 and died 1 Jul 1883. Father died in Marlow a few years before his wife was sent to the Almshouse. Said Luther has always lacked force and has never been able to earn more than his support. Has resided in Walpole for 8 or 10 years last past. [21 Jan 1891]

850. Henry S. Hathorn, Keene, American, born in Bridgewater, VT, 12 Aug 1828, 62 years old. Married; wife Mary J., 55 years old, born in Cornish, NH. 2 children, both married: Alice A. and Eliza A. Eliza married a man by the name of Martin and resides in Hinsdale. Mrs. H resides with her. Said Henry does not live with his wife for some reason. [5 Feb 1891]

851. Mathew Lanigan, Keene, Irish, born in Lowell, MA, will be 15 years old next Apr the 27th. Father, born in Hinsdale, MA,[121] is 52 years old. Mother born in Lowell, is 40 years old. Came to Keene about 5 years ago. Said Mathew is non compos; cannot read nor talk sense. Is violent at times and has to be confined. Has 5 brothers and sisters, viz: Andrew T., age 17; James, 10 years; Lilla, 9 years; May, 7 years; and Nellie, 3 years old next May. Sent to the Farm 11 Feb 1891. Condition, idiotic. [14 Feb 1891; adjudged 3 Mar 1891]

---

[120] See also #907.
[121] This is probably supposed to be Hinsdale, NH.

Cheshire County Paupers
1885-1900

[287] 852. Delima Simons, Keene, French, mother of Rosanna Simons. Said Rosanna was born in Canada, 13 years. Father Clafse[122] Simons is 46 years old; mother 48 years old. Came to this state from Canada in 1887. Mother complains that Rosanna is obstinate and stubborn, had her brought before the Police Court, and she was sentenced to the State Industrial for 2 years. [16 Feb 1891; adjudged 3 Mar 1891]

853. George A. Debell,[123] Winchester, American, born in Winchester, 33 years 1 Oct 1890. Has always lived in Winchester. Married; wife Florence A. was born in Colerane, MA, 28 years old 21 May 1890. Her father's name was Aaron Worder. Her mother married Henry Cook of Winchester some 6 years ago. Six children, viz: Cora, 8 years old, 19 Mar 1890; Della, 6 years, 3 Mar 1890; Arthur, 5 years, 3 Nov 1890; Maud, 4 years, 18th Jan last; Homer, 2 years 26 Jul last; and Clister,[124] 1 year, the 25th Feb 1891. [14 Feb 1891; adjudged]

854. Maria L. Bragg, Hinsdale, American, born in Sunderland, VT, 45 years of age. Married in Mar 1883 to Randall N. Bragg. No children. Randall N. was born in the township that is now Mt. Washington, Berkshire Co., MA 9 Aug 1846 and will be 45 years old next Aug. Mr. and Mrs. B have resided in Hinsdale since Dec 1890. [2 Feb 1891; adjudged 3 Mar 1891]

[288] 855. James Conway, Winchester, born in Taunton, MA, 28 years old, the 4th Jul last. Has lived a greater part of his life in the state of MA. Married; wife Nellie Fowler, 29 years old, the 12th of last, 1890. Her parents are both dead. Were married in Manchester 4 years ago. No children. He had friends in

---

[122] Transcribed as in the original.
[123] See #1098.
[124] Perhaps "Calista."

*Cheshire County Paupers
1885-1900*

Greenfield, MA. They were on their way to G when Mrs. C was taken ill at Winchester and on account of her illness they are obliged to ask temporary relief. Sent to Greenfield, MA by Overseer Slate. [3 Mar 1891; adjudged 2 Apr 1891]

856. Lizzie S. Hall,[125] Winchester, American, born in Hinsdale, 34 years old. Married Henry H. Hall of Keene in Mar 1874. Have not lived together for nearly 10 years. He was granted a divorce from me about 2 years ago. Two children, viz: Herman H. Hall, 13 years old in Jan last, and Gracia M. Hall, 11 years old in Feb last. The son resides in Wardsboro, VT and the daughter with her. Rec'd aid from the county about 10 years ago in Chesterfield. Resides with Henry L. DeBell, who married a daughter, (about 13 years old). [7 Mar 1891; readjudged 22 Jun 1891]

857. George P. Ward,[126] Troy, American, born in Ashburnham, MA, 64 years old. Married; wife was born in Ashburnham and is 68 years of age. Has served in the army of the US, Co. F, 14th NH Vols. Has resided in Troy since 28 Jul 1883. See #821, page 276. [4 Mar 1891; adjudged 2 Apr 1891]

[289] 858. Louis Bourrett, Alstead, French, wife born in Gilsum, 4 Feb 1857, 34 years old. Her name is Laura E. He was born Canada in 1848. Five children: Louis D., 18, last Aug; Gracie, 16; Harvey, 11; Mamie, 10 years old; Albert, 6 years. Returned to overseer of poor for correction. [Filed 4 Mar 1891; adjudged 7 Apr 1891]

859. Frank C. Aikens, Keene, American. Wife aided in 1889. See affidavit #721. Enoch Aikens, father of Frank, makes this application for aid by reason that his son, having rec'd an injury

---

[125] See #157.
[126] See also #1024.

Cheshire County Paupers
1885-1900

in the service of the Fitchburg Railroad was brought to his father's house for care. Report is that the Fitchburg Railroad Co. pay the doctor's bill. [Filed 4 Mar 1891; adjudged]

860. Severine Masse, Marlborough, French, born in Canada, 33 years old. Married; husband Charles Masse was born in Canada, 36 years old. Two children, viz: Henry, 9 years old, and Charles, 2 years old. From 1884 to Feb 1887 resided in Walpole and since the last date they have resided in Marlborough. Apply for aid by reason of Mr. M's health. {18 Mar 1891} Chas. Masse died at Marlborough. [7 Jan 1891; adjudged 15 Jan 1891]

[290] 861. Solon Wheeler, Stoddard, American, born in Keene, 47 years old. Married Abby J. Heath of Marlow in Dec 1872. She died in Nov 1887. Married Mary Shupple in Mar 1890 with whom he now lives. Three children dependent, viz: Ellen, 11 years; Alice, 6 years; and Louisa, 3 years. Removed to Stoddard in Nov 1890, from Bolton, MA where he has lived for more than 10 years last past, and rec'd aid every year. Present wife is 38 years old. [Filed 9 Mar 1891; adjudged 2 Apr 1891]

862. Preston Clark, Fitzwilliam, American, 41 years old. Married; wife Sarah M. is ___ years old. Was married 22 years ago. Six children, viz: Everett, age 13; Nettie, 14; Arthur F., 11; Walter, 9; Bessie V., 7; and Carrie, 5. Removed from Troy to Fitzwilliam in 1890. [16 Mar 1891; adjudged 2 Apr 1891]

863. James M. Bates,[127] Winchester, American, born in Landsgrove, VT, 68 years old, 20 Dec 1890. Married Lucy Whittimore of Winchester in 1862. Three children, namely Rosa E., age 15, 8 Jul 1890; Dasie M., age 8, 2 Jul 1891; and

---

[127] See #127 and 863. See also #1011.

Cheshire County Paupers
1885-1900

Bertha L., 10 years, 10 Oct 1890. Mrs. Bates was 47 years old last Feb. [24 Mar 1891. See #865]

[291] 864. Thomas O. Sullivan, Keene, Irish, born in Ireland; will be 55 years old in Apr next. Has been married; wife Bridget died in Oct 1883, in Charlestown, NH. Has one child, Helen, married; husband's name is Edward Fitzsimmons; thinks they live in Rutland, VT. Came to Keene from Lowell, MA yesterday with view to obtaining admission to the Soldier's Home, he having served in Co. B, 14th NH Vols which was largely composed of men from Cheshire Co. Admitted to the sick rooms at the House of Correction for a few days. [25 Mar 1891; adjudged 2 Apr 1891]

865. James M. Bates,[128] Winchester, American, born in Landsgrove, VT, 68 years old, the 20th Dec 1890. Married Lucy Whittimore of Winchester in 1862. Three minor children, namely: Rosa E., age 15, Oct last; Burtha L., 10 years, Jul 8th, last; Dasie M., 8 years, 2 Jul last. The family have resided in Keene, Swanzey and Winchester since 1 Jan 1880. [24 Mar 1891; adjudged 2 Apr 1891. See also #863]

866. Millie L. McCurdy, Keene, American, born in Dublin, NH, 25 years old. Always resided in said Dublin until she came to Keene to live in 1885. Married George McCurdy about 4 years ago. Her husband died 16 Nov 1890. Father has been dead 11 years. Her mother is living a widow in Dublin, NH. She owns a small place there. Mrs. McCurdy has two children, viz: Robert H. McCurdy about 3 years old; Chester Arthur, 15 months old. Has one brother residing in Boston. Husband born in Lowell, MA and was 35 years old at death, and nearly always lived in Keene. Not adjudged, whereabouts unknown. (29 Oct 1891) [27 Mar 1891; not adjudged]

---

[128] See #127 and 863. See also 1011.

*Cheshire County Paupers
1885-1900*

[292] 867. Lucy B. Robbins, Rindge, American. Notice rec'd from Dr. C. P. Bancroft, Supt. NH Asylum for the Insane, 2 Apr 1891 that the means of support in case of Miss Lucy B. Robbins has failed, and the county becomes liable under Ch. 10, Sec. 20. [2 Apr 1891. See Gen. Laws, Ch. 10, Sec. 20]

868. Asenath Goodhue, Marlow, American, born in ____, 37 years old and of unsound mind, unable to earn a living. Father is dead; her mother resides in Marlow, and she lives with her. Has a brother in Marlow, Augustine Goodhue. Was injured when about 20 years old and has not been of sound mind since.[129]

869. Samuel C. Towne,[130] Richmond, American, born in Claramont (*sic*), Sullivan County, 7 Dec 1833. Widowed; wife Catherine S. R. Ellenwood was born in Acworth, 26 Mar 1838, was 46 years old when she died. Has one daughter, Nellie H. Prescott, 31 years old. Resides in Richmond. Went to Richmond to live with his daughter in Jan 1885. Was a private in Co. G, 9th NH Vols, enlisted 13 Aug 1862; discharged 13 Aug 1865. [31 Mar 1891]

[293] 870. Sadee Hatt, Troy, Nova Scotian. Husband Joseph Hatt was born in Nova Scotia, is 29 years old. Married 3 Oct 1887. Came to Troy from Nova Scotia 8 Oct 1887. Have three children, viz: Almira, 2 years, 9 months; Warren, 18 months; and Walter, 3 months. Husband is now sick with typhoid fever and has been unable to work for 5 weeks. Parents of either never lived in this country. [18 Apr 1891; adjudged 18 Apr 1891]

---

[129] No dates of application or adjudgment given.
[130] See also #903.

Cheshire County Paupers
1885-1900

871. Edwin J. Townsend, Walpole, American, born in Alstead, 47 years old. Married; wife Sabra D. Barnard, born in Watertown, MA. Two children, 4 and 6 years old. Resided in Alstead until he was 22 years old. [Adjudged 22 Jun 1891]

872. Josiah Stebbins,[131] Jaffrey, American. See page 245 and affidavit 729, pertaining to J. Clark Stebbins, which shows the liability of the county to support said Josiah Stebbins.

[294] 873. Marshall S. Whipple, Chesterfield, American, born in Winchester, NH in 1820. Unmarried. Enlisted in the 13th Ohio Reg't in 1862; discharged in Jun 1865. [4 May 1891]

874. Joseph Parrault,[132] Troy, Canadian, born in Canada, 62 years old. Married; wife Julia was born in Canada and is 44 years old. Came to Troy from Otter River, MA in Mar 1889. Five minor children, viz: Henry, 14 years old; Nettie, 10; Mary, 12; Felix, 7; and Adeline, 3 years. Sickness obliges the family to ask for relief. [29 Apr 1891; adjudged 5 May 1891]

875. Smith B. Taft, Hinsdale, American, born in Swanzey, 32 years old, 16 Aug 1890. Adjudged Apr term 1877. Has been an inmate of the County Almshouse. Authorized the Selectmen of Hinsdale to send him to the MA General Hospital for treatment of his arm. See L. Bk. For particulars.[133] [30 Apr 1891; adjudged Apr term 1877, 5 May 1891]

[295] 876. Mary Bigelow, Keene, English, born in Liverpool, England, 59 years old, the 7th of last Mar. Married; husband George Bigelow was born in Whitingham, VT, about 59 years old. No children. Husband deserted his wife some 14 years

---

[131] See also #900 and #1354.
[132] See also #1026.
[133] The author has not been able to discover the location of this book.

Cheshire County Paupers
1885-1900

ago, and has not since contributed to her support. Has not resided in Keene only about 3 months. [3 Apr 1891; adjudged 22 Jun 1891]

877. Horace H. Hall, Stoddard, American. Came from Hancock to Stoddard and has worked for Eben Stacy. Was aided while residing in Hancock by Hillsboro County. Single, about 65 years old. Has lost one arm. {Died in Stoddard, 27 May 1891.} [16 May 1891; adjudged 22 Jun]

878. Dolphus Seveyer, Troy, Canadian, born in Canada, 24 years old. Married; wife Virginia, born in Canada and is 23 years old. Came to the US to live in 1882. Has lived in NH and MA since. Have one child, 21 months old. [2 Jun 1891; adjudged 22 Jun 1891]

[296] 879. Louisa Monty, Keene, American, born in Highgate Falls, VT, 33 years old, 8 Jun 1891. Married; husband Henry William Monty was born in Ripon, Wisconsin and was 34 years old 3 Apr last. Has 5 children, all dependent, viz: Julia E., age 14, 20 Apr last; Henry, age 8, 22 Sep last; Arthur, age 7, 24 Jul inst; Fredy, age 4, 30 Jul inst; Carl Alvin, age 15 months, 26 Jun inst. Husband dissipated and neglects to support his family. His parents reside in Glenn Falls, NY and my father is dead, but my mother lives at Brockport, NY. [13 Jun 1891; adjudged 22 Jun 1891]

880. Ignacas Begai, Walpole, Russian Polander, born in Russia Poland. Came to this country in Apr 1889. Has a wife and children in Russia Poland. By reason of sickness is obliged to ask for relief. Sent to County Farm from which place he escaped and has not since been heard from. [17 Jun 1891; adjudged 4 Aug 1891]

Cheshire County Paupers
1885-1900

881. Charles Boardman, Keene, American, born in Los Angeles, CA, 31 years old. Single. Never in NH prior to yesterday. Has been tramping, evidently. He is rather a mistery (*sic*). Claims to have spent a greater part of his life on the Pacific Coast. Sent to County Farm upon his own application. [18 Jun 1891; adjudged 4 Aug 1891]

[297] 882. Esther McDonald, Harrisville, Canadian, born in Canada, 41 years old. Married Octave McDonald Aug 1889. Has three children by a former husband, viz: Exelia, 17 years old, born in Canada; Josephine, 15, born in Canada; and Henry, 12, born in Canada. She came from Dracut, MA about 2 years ago. Husband resided in Harrisville, 10 years or more. She is afflicted with an ovarian tumor. Removed to one of the hospital rooms in House of Correction, Keene, to have an operation performed. {Attended by Dr. Prouty, Twitchell and Thurston. Died soon after the operation.} [19 Jun 1891; adjudged 7 Oct 1891]

883. John Cotto, Keene, born in Plymouth, NH, 48 years old. Widower. Two children, residing in Dover, viz: William, age 24 and Daniel, age 22, both single. Disabled by reason of rheumatism and unable to earn his support, and he therefore applies for admission to the County Almshouse. Permit issued. [21 Jul 1891; adjudged 4 Aug 1891]

884. Benjamin Grovner, Fitzwilliam, American, born in Fitzwilliam, 75 years old. Has no father, mother, sisters or brothers. Feeble and poor, unable to earn his own support. Order issued to the overseer of the poor to remove to the County Farm. Order complied with. {7 Sep 1891}Died and buried at County Farm. [4 Aug 1891; adjudged 7 Oct 1891]

[298] 885. George O. McCollister, Keene, American, born in Marlborough, 28 Feb 1838, 53 years of age. Married; wife

Cheshire County Paupers
1885-1900

Sarah C. was born in Marlborough and is 48 years old. Have two children, viz: Harry E., age 24 years and Willie G., age 14. Harry E. resides in Boston and is employed at Jordan & Marsh's. Willie lives at home. Mrs. McCollister has a mental difficulty that requires her removal to the Asylum. Mr. McCollister claims he is unable to pay the expenses at the hospital and therefore applies for relief. {1 Sep 1891, at the hospital.} [13 Aug 1891; adjudged 7 Oct 1891]

886. Ellen Collins, Keene, Irish, born in Ireland, about 50 years old. Married; husband Lawrence Collins was born in Ireland, age not known. Resides in Nelson. Has been married about 30 years. Five children: 3 boys and 2 girls; 3 boys, minors; one of them dependent. Has had some domestic trouble and Mrs. C. left home and went to Fitchburg to stop with her daughter, but she was unwilling to support her. Sent her back to Nelson. [22 Aug 1891; not adjudged]

887. Anna Barton, Keene, Irish, born in Ireland, 25 years old, the 7th of last Apr. Married; husband Thomas E. Barton was born in Vergennes, VT and is 28 years old. No children living; have buried two. Parents live in Newton, MA. Husband's parents reside in Providence, RI. Husband intemperate, out of work and is at this time unable to contribute very much toward her support. She asks for help to pay the bills incurred in the burial of her child some 4 weeks ago. [29 Aug 1891; adjudged 7 Oct 1891]

[299] 888. James C. McClearn, Keene, Nova Scotian, born in Nova Scotia, 47 years old, the 14th of last Feb. Single. Has resided in Keene for the past 4 or 5 years. Has been an employee of the shoe shop. An intemperate man. Had the misfortune to break his leg a few weeks ago. Has since occupied a room in the pauper department of the House of

Correction. Has no relatives in this state. [5 Sep 1891; adjudged 7 Oct 1891]

889. Oscar Monty, Marlborough, Finn, born in Finland, Russia, the 7th Dec 1859, 32 years old. Married; has a wife and 3 children living in Finland. His wife's name is Hannah. His parents are dead. Nearest relative in this country is Eddie Erikson, Marlborough. Had his arm badly broken by a stone from a blast in the stone ledges when he was at work. Admitted to one of the rooms in the pauper department of the House of Correction. [5 Sep 1891; adjudged 7 Oct 1891]

890. Jones S. Hale, Swanzey, American, born in Middlebury, VT, 2 Apr 1832, 59 years old. Single; has been married and had one child, May Bell Hale, now at County Farm. She that was his wife resides in Fitzwilliam, having married again. Present name Asenath Ward. No divorce to his knowledge. Has his right leg so badly injured recently by the cars at Marlborough Depot that it had to be amputated. Admitted to pauper department, House of Correction, Keene, for care and treatment. [5 Sep 1891; adjudged 7 Oct 1891]

[300] 891. Terance Cunningham, Troy, American, born in Middleborough, VT, 45 years old. Has never resided 6 months at a time in any town in this state. Father never resided in NH. [4 Sep 1891]

892. George Champaign, Keene, Canadian, born in Canada, 35 years old. Married; wife Eliza B. (Morris) was born in Canada, is about 45 or 46 years old. One child living: George, 8 years old. Came to Keene to live in the spring of 1888. Resided in Swanzey some 3 years since 1880, was assisted in said Swanzey. Possesses a small house and lot on Knight Street, about ½ acre of ground, valued at less than $100. {8 Dec 1891} Sent to Almshouse. 10 Dec had an operation performed upon

Cheshire County Paupers
1885-1900

his shoulder; joint and several pieces of bone taken out. Operation performed by Dr. Prouty of Keene and Dr. Craig of Westmoreland. [23 Sep 1891]

893. Alexander Bouter, Troy, Canadian, born in Canada, age 59. Married; wife Mary born in Canada, age 55. In the War of the Rebellion, 7th Maine Reg't. Resided in Keene and Troy for last 10 years. Has children, but no minors. {Moved to Harrisville; died at H.} [27 May 1891; 29 Sep 1891]

[301] 894. Abner Fisk,[134] Keene, American, born in Chesterfield, 13 Apr 1813, 78 years old. Married Mary L. Smith, still living; think she is 73 years old, and that she was born in Holland, MA. Two children, both of age and living: William A. resides in New London, CT, and Sarah M. married William A. Garfield and resides in Keene. [13 Oct 1891]

895. George Towns, Winchester, American, born in ___, age ___. Has a settlement in Winchester. Has been in the NH Asylum for the last 3-4 years. Taken from the Asylum by Levi Saben to the Almshouse, Westmoreland. [Private patient]

896. Alfred J. Champagne, Chesterfield, Canadian. Committed to the State Industrial School, Manchester 13 Jun 1890 by E. R. Locke, having been sentenced by the Court.

[302] 897. Henry Blake, Marlow, American, born in ___, 26 years old. Widowed; married Nellie Miller in 1889, age 19. She died 14 Mar 1891. Two children: Clifford Blake, age 2; the other an infant. Said Blake's father Charles A. Blake resided in Surry for many years last past, to the date of his death 2 years ago. An imperfect affidavit was filed Apr term of court 1891. [21 Oct 1891; adjudged 22 Oct 1891]

---

[134] See also #755, page 254.

Cheshire County Paupers
1885-1900

898. Ellen L. and Simeon Mason, Keene, American, born in Grafton, VT, 51 years old, the 15 of last Sep. Husband Simeon Mason was born in Westmoreland in the said county of Cheshire and was 66 years old last May. Have one child Zua A. Mason, 15 years old last May, is now at Gilsum, working in factory. [22 Oct 1891; not adjudged, city charge]

899. Jens Sofus Peterson, Keene, Denmark, born in Copenhagen, 19 years old and a few months. Parents both dead. Single. Came to the US last Mar. Has been sick with fever during he was assisted by the city of Keene. [22 Oct 1891]

[303] 900. Josiah Stebbins,[135] Jaffrey, American. See entry 729. Said Josiah Stebbins is father to J. Clark Stebbins. [Oct term 1891]

901. Harriet L. Kidder, Keene, American, born in Walpole, NH, 18 Aug 1820. Has resided in Greenwood, Illinois for 16 years last past with a brother. Came to Keene 11 Sep 1891 to her sister's, Mrs. Gardiner C. Hill. Her brother's wife came in charge of her from Illinois to Keene. Dr. Hill claims that her mind is not right and applies for aid and authority to commit her to the Asylum at Concord. Inquisition or examination held and said woman committed to the Asylum 13 Sep 1891. Dr. Hill reports that she had $60 in cash with her, which he took and deposited in the Bank, and that she has at his house a trunk containing clothing, especially dresses, enough to last as long as she lives. [27 Oct 1891; adjudged]

902. Julia Stevenson, Chesterfield, American, born in Winchester 18 Aug 1831. Widow; husband Ira died the 24th

---

[135] See #729, #872 and #1354.

Cheshire County Paupers
1885-1900

day of Aug last, 86 years old. Was born in Swanzey. Has resided in Chesterfield since 1886. [adjudged 28 Oct 1891]

[304] 903. Samuel C. Town, Richmond, American, born in Claramont (*sic*). See #869, page 292.

904. Mrs. Scovell, Westmoreland, American, born in ___. Admitted to Almshouse as a private patient upon application of her guardian Leonard Wellington. Mind weak. C. M. Scovell of Westmoreland, a son. {Died 25 Sep 1891.} [private patient 19 May 1891]

905. Mrs. Helen E. Hoyt, Winchester, American, born in Attleboro, MA in the year 1856. Married Fred S. Hoyt in 1878; husband's age, 37 years, 30 Nov 1890. Came to Winchester 3 Nov 1890. Have 5 minor children, viz: Helen May, 12 years, last May; Elliot Dix, 11 years, last Sep; Ruby Emma, 9 years, last Sep; Vina Faith, 6 years, 18th of last Nov; David Frederic, 4 years, last Feb. Owner of no real or personal estate, neither of them. Husband published a paper for a time in W, but it did not prove a success. Husband now in Athol, MA. Wants aid to move there. See letter to L. Satave L. Bk.[136] [Filed 5 Nov 1891; adjudged]

[305] 906. Mary J. Barlow,[137] Keene, English, born in England, 50 years old. Husband Nathaniel A. was born in Ticonderoga, NY, 68 years old. Private Co. I, 5th NY Vols. Six children, 2 minors: Arthur J., 19 years, and LeRoy, 17 years. [Filed 6 Nov 1891; adjudged Oct term 1891]

907. Luther March, Westmoreland, American. See page 286, #849. [Filed 6 Nov 1891; adjudged 6 Nov 1891]

---

[136] Author has not located this letter or book.
[137] See #908.

Cheshire County Paupers
1885-1900

908. Mary J. Bigelow, English, Keene. This should be Barlow. See above, #906. [Filed 7 Nov 1891; adjudged]

[306] 909. Paul Lachint, Walpole, German, born in Berlin, Germany, will be 25 years old this month. Single. Has always resided in Germany until 28 Jun 1890. Came to Bellows Falls, VT, 27 Mar 1891; in Oct following he went to North Walpole to visit a fellow countryman and remained a few days; returned to Bellows Falls 29 Oct. He returned to his friend's house in North Walpole, sick with consumption. [Filed 14 Nov 1891; adjudged 18 Nov 1891]

910. Spenser Peal, Walpole, Englishman, about 39 years old. Came to this country about 6 or 7 years ago. Has been in the employ of the VT Valley and Sullivan Co. RR. Has resided in Walpole for the last 4 or 5 years. 14 Oct 1891 he was injured by falling, breaking his arm and jaw so severely that he has been sent the MA General Hospital for treatment. Has no relatives in this country; is destitute. Has spent his earnings nearly as fast as he got them. Has no family, is a single man. [Filed 14 Nov 1891; adjudged 18 Nov 1891]

911. Zephire Martell, Marlborough, Canadian, born in Canada 19 years old. Single. Came to this state in Oct 1890. Prior to coming to NH, had resided in Canada. Parents both reside there. Said Martell was taken violently ill at the house of William Getty in Marlborough, and being destitute, was obliged to apply for relief. [Filed 9 Nov 1891; adjudged 18 Nov 1891]

[307] 912. Mary J. Bigelow, Westmoreland, American, born in Westmoreland 20 May 1835. Married to George Bigelow 6 Mar 1858. Said George Bigelow was divorced from his wife about the year 1867. She, Mary Bigelow, has never remarried. Since her divorce she has resided in Brattleboro, Bellows Falls

Cheshire County Paupers
1885-1900

and for 2 years last past she has lived with her brother Nathaniel Amidon in Westmoreland. Has no means; has been assisted by the town of Rockingham. Is afflicted with disease of the mind that incapacitates her earning her support. [Filed 6 Nov 1891]

913. Michael K. Lynch, Richmond, Irish, born in Ireland, 76 years old. Widowed. Has children. Resides with Mrs. George M. Bowen of Richmond, a daughter and with whom he has lived nearly all of the time since 1 Jan 1880. [Filed 24 Nov 1891]

914. Everett A. Davis, Hinsdale, American, 46 years of age. Wife and one child. Child farmed out to Chas. S. White of Grafton, VT. Town liable for their support. He was admitted to the Almshouse 22 Apr 1891, and his wife was admitted later. [138]

[308] 915. Axel N. Johnson, Westmoreland, Swede. Admitted to Almshouse 13 Jan 1891. Discharged 17 Feb 1891. No affidavit taken. [not adjudged]

916. Mary Doyle, Keene, Irish, age 60. Supported by the city of Keene at $2.50 per week. Transferred from the State Asylum, Concord to the Almshouse, Westmoreland, 29 Oct 1890. [town pauper]

917. George Lunderville, Fitzwilliam, American, born in Keene, 26 years old. Father and mother both dead. His mother was Margaret Ruffle, a resident of Keene. He has a bad sore upon one leg that is liable to cost him his leg. Ordered to the Almshouse upon his own application, and entered 30 Nov 1891. [Filed 30 Nov 1891]

---

[138] No date of application or adjudgment.

Cheshire County Paupers
1885-1900

[309] 918. John Ryan, Keene, Irish, born in Ireland, 43 years old, the 29th of last Apr. Came to America in 1868. Single. Parents never resided in this country. Father dead; mother lives at Carrigan Shore, Ireland. Has lived in Keene about 5 weeks. [Filed 2 Dec 1891; adjudged 1 Mar 1892]

919. Frank Woods, Troy, Canadian, born in Canada, 38 years old. Wife Hannah B. born in Canada, 32 years old. Came to NH in Apr 1890, to Troy. Never resided in any town in this state except Troy. Has resided at Otter River, MA. Has 8 children, viz: Mary, age 16; Frank, 14; Henry, 12; Clark, 9; Sadie, 7; Mabel, 5; Joseph, 3; and Emma, 14 months. [Filed 5 Dec 1891; adjudged 1 Mar 1892]

920. Byron O. Marvin, Winchester, American, born in Alstead, 48 years old last Sep. Served in the army, 6th NH Vols from 21 Oct 1861 to 1 May 1864. Has resided for the last 2 or 3 years in Athol and Orange, MA. Has recently come to Winchester. Married; does not live with his wife. Does not know where she is. [Filed 15 Dec 1891; adjudged 1 Mar 1892]

[310] 921. Joseph Gates, Keene, Nova Scotian, born in Nova Scotia, 44 years old, the 4th of last Jul. Widowed; wife Mary Kelley died 3 years ago or more in Halifax, NS. Came to the states soon after. Has resided in the vicinity of New Bedford most of the time since coming to the states. No relatives in this country. Makes application for admission to the county almshouse and was sent there 18 Dec 1891. [Filed 18 Dec 1891; adjudged 1 Mar 1892]

922. Lydia K. Cutting, Winchester, American, wife of Samuel Cutting, who died in Winchester 6 Feb 1892. He was born in Northfield, MA, 62 years old. Was a soldier, belonged to the 36th Reg't MA, private. A member of John Sedgewick Post in Keene, but did not keep up his dues. Lydia K. Cutting, 47 years

*Cheshire County Paupers
1885-1900*

old; have one child George W. Cutting, 10 years, 21 Feb 1892. [Filed 23 Feb 1892; adjudged 1 Mar 1892]

923. Mary Ellen Peruss,[139] Hinsdale, French, born Keene, 18 years old, 3 Feb 1873. Has lived in H since 1876. Father died at Keene when she was about 3 years old; mother soon after. [Filed 13 Jan 1892; adjudged 17 Mar 1892]

[311] 224.[140] Jerry Lower, Keene, was born in Highgate, VT, 65 years old. Married Rosie Flag in Burlington, VT in 1869; she is 40 years old. Children: Antwine, age 19 years; Mary, 13; Freddie, 10; Rossie, 8; and Ellen, 3. [adjudged 29 Mar 1892]

225. Thomas Pratt, Walpole, Am., born in Boston, MA 6 Feb 1861. Father was George Pratt, a native of Ireland. Married in Boston 1859; died Apr 1870 in NY. Said Thomas Pratt was taken to the NH Asylum from Walpole, 19 Feb 1892. [Filed 3 Mar 1892; adjudged 29 Mar 1892]

926. Joseph Paul, Winchester, born in NY, 39 years old. Married 8 years ago; wife Mary A. Paul, 28 years old. Children: William Pratt, 7; Hellen J., 4; Mary A., 2 years old. Moved to Winchester Sep 1891. Was not a soldier. [Filed 17 Mar 1892; adjudged 5 Apr 1892]

[312] 927. Charles Bertram, Marlborough, French Canadian, born in Canada, 45 years old. Married; wife Cordelia Bertram was born Canada, 41 years old. Came from Canada to M 17 Apr 1886. Have 6 children: Rosa, age 16; Emma, 10; Ellen, 8;

---

[139] See also #952, page 320.
[140] This entry number and the next transcribed as written in original. See also #1072, page 360.

Cheshire County Paupers
1885-1900

Clara, 6; Agnes, 3; Alba, 1 year old. Family has been sick. [Filed 26 Feb 1892; adjudged 5 Apr 1892]

928. Lottie Rockwood, Keene, born in Fryeburg, ME, 1856. Father's name was Ripley Farrington, who died in 1872. Has been married; husband's name H. P. Rockwood, who was born in Lewiston, NY. Died in 1889. Has 2 children: Edward C., 14; Florence E., 9 years old. [Filed 24 Mar 1892; adjudged 5 Apr 1892]

929. George Medcalf, Marlborough, born in Rindge, 62 years old. Married in 1854 to Emily S. Peirce and divorced 12 years ago. Married again about 1886 and also divorced from her one year and a half after marriage. Has 3 children: Lawrence, 36, who is living in Nashua; Ada M. Hadley, 21, living in Rindge; one adopted by John Price. [Filed 25 Feb 1892; adjudged 5 Apr 1892]

[313] 930. Israel Passano, Fitzwilliam, French, born in 1842, 47 years old. Married; wife Cora Passano, 30 years old. Has 4 children: Edward N., 12 years old; Alta M., 10; Walter L., 5; and Freddie, 3. Not a soldier. He is sick, therefore calls for aid. [Filed 18 Mar 1892; adjudged 5 Apr 1892]

931. Laura S. Farr, Winchester, Am., born in Westminster, MA, 63 years old. Was married when 15 years old to Filetus Ballou of Richmond in 1866 or 1867. He left her and married another woman about 1872. She married William Farr; he died in 1890. In Jul 1891 she moved to Winchester. Has one son born in Arberndale (*sic*), MA, Ira F. Ballou, 44 years old. Her last husband had a small place in Wendall. Mr. Farr was not a soldier or sailor. [Filed 6 Jan 1892; adjudged 5 Apr 1892]

932. Ella L. Hartwell, Winchester, Am., 38 years old. Married; husband's name Charles H. Hartwell, 40 years old. Have one

child by the name of Asa J. Hartwell, 8 years old. Lived in Winchester about one year. Charles H. Hartwell was not a soldier or sailor. Ella L. Hartwell has two children by a former husband, Horace W. Nickerson, a soldier in the late war. Children: Sarah W. Nickerson, age 15, and Willie F. Nickerson, age 14. Mrs. Hartwell's father's name Asa Ray, a county charge.[141] [Filed 11 Feb 1892; adjudged 5 Apr 1892]

[314] 933. Etta Pollard, Keene, Am., born in Marlow, age 24; lived there until she was fifteen years old. Married Charles Pollard in Jun 1887, but he left her after one month and has not aided her since. Etta Pollard has one child by a former husband; adopted by a family in Troy. The former husband's name is Albert Barns, who is about 35 years old; living in Stoddard and married again. Mrs. Pollard's father Ezra Howard is dead, was formerly a county charge, living in Gilsum and Marlow. {Died Mar 1892} Dead. [Filed 29 Mar 1892; adjudged 8 Apr 1892]

934. Alba Chapin, Swanzey, Am., born in Littleton, NH, 63 years old. Lived in Swanzey about 8 years. Single. He had a paraletic (*sic*) shock and was taken to the County Almshouse, Westmoreland. He lived about 8 years with Edmond Stone of Swanzey. {May 1892} Died at Almshouse. [Filed 20 Jan 1892; adjudged 6 Apr 1892]

935. Josephine Morrin, Jaffrey, French Canadian, born in Canada. Married; husband's name Edmond Morrin. He has deserted his wife and gone to Canada. Have three children, names and ages are as follows: Josephine, 6; Pierse, 4; and Eugene Morrin, 2. The youngest is under the doctor's care having been badly burned, therefore she asks for assistance. [Filed 11 Jan 1892; adjudged 8 Apr 1892]

---

[141] See also #526, page 177.

Cheshire County Paupers
1885-1900

[315] 936. Anson S. Harrington, Winchester, Am., born in Northfield, MA, 20 years old and died in Winchester 28 Dec 1891. [Filed 31 Dec 1891; adjudged 11 Apr 1892]

937. Henrietta Devilaire, Keene, 68 years old, French, born in Quebec. Came to Keene Jul 1879. Has three nephews living in Keene. [adjudged 13 Apr 1892]

938. Mary Manigan, Keene, Irish, born in Ireland, 71 years old. Came to the US 6 years ago. Her husband never lived in this country, but died in Ireland. She is now living with her daughter Mrs. Daniel Coffe, feeble and unable to support herself. [adjudged 13 Apr 1892]

[316] 939. George Campfield, Winchester, Irish, born in Ireland, 74 or 75 years old. Was married 25 years ago to a Mrs. Butler of Otter River, but has not lived with her for 21 years; has not any children; was not in the army or navy. Ordered moved to County Farm, 2 May 1892. [Filed 30 Apr 1892; adjudged 6 May 1892]

940. Richard Blair, Harrisville, French, born in NY, Essex County, 28 years old. Came to Peterborough this state about 6 years ago, lived in Peterborough about 4 years, then made Harrisville his home with his father and mother. Was married 4 years ago, but has not lived with her for nearly 3 years. She resides at West Peterborough. Have not any children. Was badly burned at a fire in the town of Hancock on 11 Apr 1892, and by his orders was carried to his parents in Harrisville. [Filed 4 Apr 1892; adjudged 6 May 1892]

941. Rebecca Whitcomb, Fitzwilliam, American, 90 years old. Single, and has not any children. [Filed 3 May 1892; adjudged 6 May 1892]

Cheshire County Paupers
1885-1900

[317] 942. John B. Young, Hinsdale, French, born in Canada, 24 years old. Married; have two children: Addeline, 19 months old, and Laura, 6 months. Call for aid on account of sickness. [Filed; adjudged 6 May 1892]

943. William Perry, Keene, American, born in Keene, 22 Jun 1824, about 68 years old. Has lived in RI; Foxboro, MA; and Saratoga, NY. Came to Keene 17 May 1892. Was married in 1863 to Isabella Glass; have one child: Ernest R. Perry, 18 years old. His wife and child are now living at Newport, RI. Was not a soldier sailor (*sic*). Charles Perry of Keene is a brother of William Perry. Applied for admittance to County, the Almshouse; admittance granted 20 May 1892. [Filed 20 May 1892; adjudged 20 May 1892]

944. Jennie S. Wilder, Winchester, 59 years old. Widow of Ivory P. Wilder, who was born in Dublin, NH, and was 77 years old when he died 18 May 1892. Two daughters married. Ivory P. Wilder had three brothers: one living in Keene, one in Marlborough and one in Peterborough; and one sister living near Boston. Ivory P. Wilder owned property valued at $700, when he died in Vineland, NJ; also Jennie S. Wilder expects $500 from her brother; therefore Jennie S. Wilder promises to pay the bill for the care and burial of her husband. [Filed 20 May 1892; adjudged]

[318] 945. John Laseaker (or Andrew Lasick), Hinsdale, Polander, born in Poland Russia, Europe, 22 years old. Came to the US 10 Mar 1891 and worked for Amasa B. Davis of Hinsdale. He is single. Was taken insane 24 May 1892 and taken to the County Almshouse and was sent to the Asylum 31 May 1892. To be treated at the expense of the state. [Filed 24 May 1892; adjudged 24 May 1892]

Cheshire County Paupers
1885-1900

946. Lena C. Coleman, Keene, American, 28 years old. Came to Keene from Londonderry, VT 29 Nov 1890. Was married to William Coleman, 1887. He died Feb 1889 in NYC. Has one child, daughter of said William Coleman, 3 years old, and one male child, 11 days old. Lena C. Coleman testifies that the male child was the son of Darius Chamberlain of 75 Davis St., Keene. {Mrs. Coleman has left Keene and the child is now at Mrs. Mary Southwell's, Church St., Keene.} [Filed 26 Apr 1892; adjudged 24 May 1892]

947. Louisa Valley, Keene, French, born in Canada, Sep 1864. Was married to Joseph Montery when 14 years old, lived with him until he died in 1885. Had one child by said Montery, about 14 years old. Married Kendall Bryant of Jaffrey in 1886; lived with said Bryant 3 years until he died. Had 3 children by said Bryant, 2 now living: Josephine, 5 years; William, 4 years. Married Albert Valley about 2 years ago; lived with him 6 months, when the said Albert Valley left her. [Filed 24 May 1892; adjudged 24 May 1892]

[319] 948. Joseph Kober, Winchester, German, born in Germany, 31 years old. Married; wife, 29 years old. Lived in this country 13 years. Lived in Winchester 4 years. Has been married 3 years; have one child: Ellen Kober, about 1 year old. Joseph Kober was taken to the NH Asylum the last of May 1892. [Filed 3 Jun 1892; adjudged 3 Jun 1892]

949. Samuel H. Seaver, Richmond, American, 65 years old. Was married to Emma F. Whitney Oct 1877. Have not any children. Lived with his wife about 6 months when they separated. He is sick and therefore calls for aid. [Filed 20 May 1892; adjudged 3 Jun 1892]

950. William Street, Keene. Married; wife's maiden name, Bell Sumner; was married in 1883. Have 2 children: Ada Bell,

Cheshire County Paupers
1885-1900

7 years old; and Gracie, 1 year old. [Filed 17 Jun; adjudged 17 Jun 1892]

[320] 951. Almon Lamont, Marlborough, French, born in Canada, 32 years old. Came to US in 1891. Married; wife's maiden name Louisa Abar; has been married 6 years. Have three children: Eli, 8 years old; Eugene, 3 years; and Alfred, 7 months old. He has a bad knee, cannot work. [Filed 4 Jun 1892; adjudged 17 Jun 1892]

952. Mary Ellen Perusse, Hinsdale, French, born in Keene, 3 Feb 1872, 19 years old. Lived in Keene about 1 year; lived in Great Falls, NH, 2 years; have lived in Hinsdale since. She is not married but has one child: Ellen, born 23 Feb 1892. [Filed 22 Jun; adjudged 22 Jun 1892]

953. Alace M. Stacy, Hinsdale, American, 35 years old, born in Hinsdale. Married 22 Dec 1872 to Edward Stacy at Brattleboro, VT. Husband deserted her about 2 months ago. The names of the children are as follows: Edward, 18 years old; George, 16; Lottie, 12; Julie, 10; Josephine, 8; Mary A., 5; Esther E., 3; and James, 5 months. [Filed 4 Aug; adjudged 11 Aug 1892]

[321] 954. Thomas C. Shortell, Westmoreland, Irish, born in Concord, NH, 10 Jul 1822. Was married to Mary Vincent 1852. She died in 1860. Has 2 sons, does not know where they are. Mr. Shortell was ordered to the County Farm in Jul 1892. [Filed 11 Aug; adjudged 19 Aug 1892]

955. Agness Ella Knapp, Hinsdale, American, born in Newfane, VT, Apr 1875. Lived in Hinsdale about 2 years. She has a father living in Newfane, VT, George W. Knapp. Agness Ella Knapp died 24 Jul 1892. [Filed 4 Aug; adjudged 19 Aug 1892]

Cheshire County Paupers
1885-1900

956. Nellie M. Fuller, Swanzey, born in West Stockbridge, MA, 26 years old. Has lived in Swanzey about 2 years. Has not any father, mother, brother or sister living. {Died in Aug 1892 at Swanzey.} [Filed 20 Jul; adjudged 19 Aug 1892]

[322] 957. Emeline Shaw, Keene, American, born Fort Ann, Washington County, NY, 24 Nov 1842. Was married to Reuben Shaw about 30 years ago; he died 7 years ago. They have had 9 children, 8 are now living: Emma E. Lang of Lomton Springs (*sic*), NY; Pheba J. Davis of CA; Esther A. Clark of CA; Merritt H. Shaw of North Rupert, VT; John O. Shaw of Winchester, NH; Ida M. White at Keene; Kate B. Shaw, also in Keene; and Ernest M. Shaw of N. Rupert, VT. [Filed 19 Aug; adjudged 19 Aug 1892]

958. Lyman G. Kilburn, Winchester, American, 50 years of age. Had been married; has not lived with his wife for 18 years; does not know whether she is living or not. Has had 3 children, the youngest is more than 21 years old. Was in the army, enlisted in a VT reg't. Lyman G. Kilburn died Jul 1892. [Filed 4 Aug; adjudged 2 Sep 1892]

959. Sam Parrent, Troy, French, born in Canada, 25 years old. Married; wife's name Matilda Parent, born in Canada, 27 years old. Came to Troy Dec 1890. By reason of sickness, they call for aid. Have 5 children: Alberteen, 6 years; Wilder, 4; Joseph, 2; Eva, 1 ½ years; and infant, 3 months old. {3 children died Sep 1892.} [Filed 20 Jul 1892; adjudged 2 Sep 1892]

[323] 960. William F. Reed, Richmond, born in Amherst, MA, 54 years old. Married Oct 1879 to Mary [Boestr]. Have 3 children: Nellie E., 7 years; Frank R., 3; and the infant, one week old, Olive K. Wife, 36 years old; she died 25 Aug 1892. Came to Richmond Dec 1891. Infant child died Sep 1892. [Filed 13 Sep; adjudged 16 Sep 1892]

Cheshire County Paupers
1885-1900

961. Jacob Wheeler, Rindge, born in South Dorset, VT, 2 May 1857, 35 years old. Married to Rosa DeLane; she died in 1883. Second wife Abby M. Gyle.[142] Moved to Rindge Apr 1892. Wife, 25 years old, 28 Jun 1892. One child: Frederick H., 5 years old. [Filed 12 Sep; adjudged 16 Sep 1892]

962. John C. Short, Keene, 16 years old, born in Bennington, VT. Father and mother both dead. Has four brothers living in Acworth, NH. Calls for aid because his hand was cut while working in the shop in Keene. {Gone to Hoosic Falls, NY 8 Oct 1892.} [Filed 2 Sep; adjudged 7 Oct 1892]

[324] 963. Ellery Venne, Troy, French, born in Canada, 23 years old. Not married. Insane; was sent to the County Farm, remained about one month. Was ordered to the Insane Asylum for remedial treatment. Taken from Asylum to County Farm. [Filed 16 Sep 1892; adjudged 7 Oct 1892]

964. Charles W. Richardson, Surry, American, born in Keene, 15 Jul 1892,[143] son of Samuel Richardson of Keene. Married; wife's name Hattie M. Kenney. Have 2 children: Fred E., 3 years; and Flossie L., 21 months. Mrs. Charles W. Richardson died Sep 1892. [Filed 24 Oct; adjudged 24 Oct 1892]

965. Jennie Bushey, French, 37 years old, born in Canada. Came to this country when 12 years of age. Married Joseph Bushey when 16. Three children: Bertie, 14; Henry, 8; Earnest, 17 months old. Joseph Bushey left his wife about 6 years ago. [Filed 2 Sep; adjudged 25 Oct 1892]

---

[142] Handwritting is unclear here. This surname may be incorrect.
[143] Date transcribed as in original.

Cheshire County Paupers
1885-1900

[325] 966. Samuel Hosley, born in Whitington, VT, 20 Nov 1823. Lived there until Oct 1887 when he came to Keene where he has since lived. {Died.} [Filed May 1892; adjudged 1 Dec 1892]

967. Joseph Moran, born in Canada, Marlow, French Canadian, 33 years old. Lived in the States about 20 years. Married; wife's name Eliza Shorty. Have one infant child, female. [Filed 1 Dec 1892; adjudged 1 Dec 1892]

968. Warren A. Thayer, Swanzey, American, born in Winchester, NH, 35 years old. Married 27 Sep 1886 to Josephine M. Norcross, who is 22 years old. One child, 4 months old. Mrs. Thayer's father's name is Nelson Norcross and lives in Harrisville. [Filed 23 Nov 1892; adjudged 20 Jan 1893]

[326] 969. Amanda C. Clark, Hinsdale, American, born 10 Oct 1853 in CT. Married; first husband's name Jerome Armstrong. Lived with him 7 years when they separated. Then she married George W. Foster; lived with him 2 years, then separated. 25 Jul 1892, she married Warren I. Clark, then came to Hinsdale. First husband's children are as follows: Henry A. Armstrong, 22 years old; Joseph M., 20; Estalle, 16; and Nellie, 14. [Filed 3 Nov 1892; adjudged 20 Jan 1893]

970. Edward Fitzgerald, born in Ireland, 42 years old, Keene, Irish. Married; wife's maiden name May Coffee. Moved to Keene Sep 1891. Wife died 9 years ago. Have 2 children: Shemas, 12 years; and Maggie, 10. Was sentenced to House of Correction 3 months for being drunk. Therefore could not care for his children. Is a tailor by trade. He states that he owned real estate to the value of $400 in Winchester but the records do not indicate that he was there long enough to acquire a residence. [Filed 1 Oct; adjudged 20 Jan 1893]

Cheshire County Paupers
1885-1900

971. Peter T. Marrion, Keene, 40 years old. Married; wife's maiden name Alice Allen (35). Four children: George, 18 years; Annie, 16; May, 14; and Harold, 12. Moved to Keene from Troy in 1880 and lived in Keene since. Harold Marrion is at the State Industrial School at Manchester. Peter T. Marrion is a barber and works at his trade in Keene. [Filed 3 Jan 1893; adjudged]

[327] 972. Charles S. Fenton, Keene, 25 years old. Married; wife's maiden name Sadie Berman, 20 years old. Have one child: Benny, 18 months old. Came from VT to Keene last Sep. [Filed 3 Jan 1893; adjudged 20 Jan 1893]

973. Asa Robbins, Nelson, American, born in Nelson, 77 years old last Apr. Single, unable to work; therefore calls for aid. {Died 20 Dec 1896 at the Farm.} [Filed 3 Feb 1893; adjudged 3 Feb 1893]

974. Aaron H. Horton,[144] 26 years old, unmarried, born in PA. Methodist minister. Insane; taken to the Asylum for Insane. [Filed 28 Jan 1893; adjudged 3 Feb 1893]

[328] 975. Alfred Lang,[145] Keene, 31 years old, born in Finland. Came to this country last Jun. Married and has 3 children. His wife and children are in Finland. He is at the City Hospital, Keene, a part of one foot will have to be amputated. [Filed 3 Feb 1893; adjudged 3 Feb 1893]

976. John D. Tiffany, Keene, 42 years old. Married Mary Ann Conway. One child: John J., 17 years old. Said John J. Tiffany is at the State Industrial School, Manchester. Moved from

---

[144] The name "Edgar M. Thompson" is crossed out.
[145] "Ed Ericksen" crossed out.

Cheshire County Paupers
1885-1900

Boston to Keene Oct 1892. [Filed 3 Feb 1893; adjudged 3 Feb 1893]

977. Sybel A. Thayer, Swanzey. Her husband is dead, whose name was Eli Thayer. He died 25 Jul 1862. He was a private in Co. E, 2 NH Vols. Sybel A. Thayer receives a widow's pension of $12 a month. Said Sybel A. Thayer had an attack of paralysis and is entirely helpless. [Filed 3 Feb 1893; adjudged 17 Feb 1893]

[329] 978. Oscar J. Bordwin, Keene, 68 years old. Has been married twice. First wife's maiden name Eliza Markes, by which he has 2 children under age: Albert, 20 years, and Carrie, 18 years. His first wife is dead; died about 12 years ago. His second wife's name Lela Cole, by which he has no children, but she had one child by a former husband: Anna, 14 years old. Has taken the name Bordwin. [Filed 3 Mar 1893; adjudged 3 Mar 1893]

979. Annie Erickson, Keene, 37 years old, born in Sweden. Came to the US 1889. Came to Keene Jan 1893. Was married to Eric Erickson in 1883. Have three children: Annie, 8 years; Carrie, 6; and Elisa, 1 years old. Her husband left her about 18 months ago. [Filed 3 Mar; adjudged 3 Mar 1893]

980. Elizebeth Larson, Marlborough, born in Denmark, 23 years old. Came to this country May 1892. Single; neither of her parents ever lived in this state. She is stopping at the house of H. C. Johnson of Marlborough and is sick. [Filed 3 Mar; adjudged 3 Mar]

[330] 981. George W. Colomy, Swanzey, born in New Durham, 34 years old. Married to Ella J. Harvey of Winchester, 26 years old. Has one child: George D., 7 years old. Wife's father name George O. Harvey of Winchester, who is a county

Cheshire County Paupers
1885-1900

charge. Was a veteran of the US army. George W. Colomy is in poor health; therefore calls for aid. [Filed 4 Jan; adjudged 3 Mar 1893]

982. Harry H. Tillison, Westmoreland, born in Everett, MA, 16 years old. Not married. Came to Westmoreland Oct 1889. Father and mother both dead. Has one half brother living in Gilmanton, NH; one own sister and a half sister living in Beverly, MA. Affidavit returned and no aid granted. [Filed 13 Feb; adjudged 3 Mar 1893]

983. Anna F. Lang, Troy, born in Germany, 31 years old. Have lived in the US about 12 years. Not married. Her parents never lived in this country. She is sick and therefore calls for aid. [Filed 21 Feb; adjudged 3 Mar 1893]

[331] 984. Daniel Fannagan, Jaffrey, born in Ireland. Came to America in 1848. Have no family living. Wife and children died soon after the war. Enlisted into US service in 1862: Co. G, 3rd MA Cavalry. Served until the close of the war. He is living alone in the west part of the town. [Filed 17 Mar; adjudged 17 Mar 1893]

985. Martha B. Scott, Alstead, born in Lempster, 16 Nov 1818, 74 years old. Unmarried; was married to Samuel T. Scott, 21 May 1848; he died 20 Aug 1882. [Filed 3 Mar; adjudged 17 Mar 1893]

986. Frank E. Davis, Keene, born in Acworth, 42 years old. Has made Charlestown, NH his place of residence since 1871. Was never married. Has one brother living in Bellows Falls, VT; a sister in Charlestown. Calls for aid because he has a sore hand. Was sent to the County Farm 17 Mar 1893. [Filed 17 Mar; adjudged 17 Mar 1893]

Cheshire County Paupers
1885-1900

[332] Etta Baylis, Keene, 42 years old. Have lived in Keene 35 years. Was married to Edward Baylis in 1870. Have one child: Effie, age 12. Edward Baylis died in Keene in 1890 and was about 56 years old, and lived in Keene for 40 years. He came from England. [Filed 17 Mar; adjudged 17 Mar 1893]

988. Watson S. French, Keene, 29 years old, born in Hartland, VT. Came to NH to live 1889. Was married to Flora Eddy in 1881. Have 3 children: Winforn E., 11 years old; Wilford H., 8; Lura Bell, 6; Has been divorced from the said Flora about 4 years. Wilford is living in Londonderry, VT; the other two are in Keene. [Filed 3 Mar; adjudged 17 Mar 1893]

989. Mary A. Perry, Keene, 44 years old. Was married to Albert Perry in 1868. He left his wife about 1 year ago. Have 4 children: Melinda, 15 years; Georgie, 9; Mary, 6; and Jennie, 4. [Filed 17 Mar; adjudged 17 Mar 1893]

[333] 990. Sylvanus Robbins, Keene, 76 years of age. Married; wife, 31 years old. She was born in Granby, VT. They have been married about 13 years. One child. Mr. Robbins is a Methodist minister. They were ordered to the County Farm. [Filed 20 Jan; adjudged 23 Mar 1893]

991. Freeman Hebert,[146] Troy, born in Canada, 45 years old. Married; wife Julia, born in Canada, 44 years old. Five minor children: Tommy, 17 years; Napoleon, 15; Eddie, 12; Freddie, 8; and Josephine, 4. They have lived in Troy since Apr 1889. Calls for temporary aid on account of sickness in the family. [Filed 27 Mar; adjudged 30 Mar 1893]

992. Joseph Cleywod, born in Canada. I am 28 years old, am married and have 2 children: Lora, 3 years, and Alma, 4

---

[146] See also #1026.

months. Neither of my parents nor my wife's parents ever lived in NH. My wife's maiden name Jennie Fish. I came from Michigan about 3 years ago, and I never had lived in NH before. [Filed 23 Feb 1893; adjudged 4 Apr 1893]

[334] 993. Mrs. Isabella Carney, Keene, 31 years old; maiden name Connelly; married James Carney in Nov 1886. Four children as follows: John D., age 5; Mary, 4; James, 2; Isabella, nine months. Parents had been dead a number of years previous to my marriage. [Filed 4 Apr 1893; adjudged 4 Apr 1893]

994. Harriet J. Griffith, Keene, 49 years old. Divorced in 1889. Have three children, all over 21 years of age. To the best of my knowledge, I have no relatives living; neither anyone liable to care for me. [Filed 17 Mar 1893; adjudged 4 Apr 1893]

995. Joseph Gookey, Hinsdale, 36 years old, born in Canada. 1 Jan 1880 was living in Harrisville, moved to Hinsdale in 1888. Never owned any real estate or personal property. Have four children as follows: Willie, 9 years; Emma, 7; Fred, 5; and baby, 2 weeks old. [Filed 18 Jan 1893; adjudged 5 Apr 1893]

[335] 996. Mary A. Coughlin, born in Northfield, MA, 16 years old. Her parents have never lived in NH. The said Mary A. Coughlin has no residence in this state [of ever has had has] a residence in MA and has been sent there to be supported. [Examined and adjudged 8 Apr 1893]

997. George D. Surprise, Richmond, born in Essex, NY, 40 years old. Have 4 children: Mary M., 6 years; Julia, 5; Alice, 3; and George M., 2 years. I came from York state[147] in 1882, lived in MA 9 years; in NH 1 year since 1880. [Filed 5 May 1893; adjudged 5 May 1893]

---

[147] Presumably, New York State.

Cheshire County Paupers
1885-1900

998. Joseph Demarco, born in Italy, 43 years old. Married, but family never lived in this country. Came to NH 21 Apr 1893. Said Demarco is very sick and asks for temporary assistance. [Filed 5 May 1893; examined and adjudged 5 May 1893]

[336] 999. Eidith Walcott, Swanzey, born in Holden, MA, 36 years old. Was married in 1876 to Alexander Clark; had one child, now 15 years old. Was married to Harvey Walcott in 1885 in RI, by whom I had only one child, that is living: Marion, 7 years old. My husband was a soldier in the US army, volunteer in 21st MA reg't, served 3 years. The child Marion and the Walcott boy Harvey, age 11, sent to Little Wanderers Home in Boston. Ada, daughter of Harvey by first wife. [Filed 5 May 1893; examined and adjudged 5 May 1893]

1000. Emma Peterson, Hinsdale, 42 years old, born in Williamstown, MA, 21 Apr 1851. 1 Jan 1880 living in Hinsdale, continuously lived in Hinsdale up to the present time. Married 22 years ago to John Peterson. Said husband never gained a settlement in any town by paying a poll tax seven years in succession, owning any property, either personal or real. My parents died when I was a child. (signed W. H. Butler, clerk). [Filed 5 May 1893; examined and adjudged 5 May 1893]

1001. John Kinnirey, Walpole, born in Ireland. Resided in the US 24 years; lived Walpole the years, 1869-72; moved to Burlington, VT and lived in VT about 20 years; removed to Walpole on or about 1 Nov 1892. I have 4 children under the age of 21: John, age 4; Henry, 12; William, 9; and Joseph, 3. Have never paid any tax, other than a poll tax. [Filed 8 May 1893; examined and adjudged 19 May 1893]

[337] 1002. Octavia Antiene Bayou, 37 years old. Married 19 years ago. My husband died last Apr. Have 7 children, as

Cheshire County Paupers
1885-1900

follows: Joseph, 13 years; May, 12; Delia, 9; Orgius, 7; Alfred, 5; Theodore, 3; Leander, 9 months old. We moved to Keene in Apr 1893, never lived in NH previous to that. We came from the state of NY, have no relatives able or liable to aid me in my support. [Filed 30 May 1893; examined and adjudged 2 Jun 1893]

1003. Edward O. Cobleigh, 78 years old. Have made my home in Keene for the last 26 years. Since 1880 I have not owned any real estate, neither have at any time had any personal property. I was married 24 years ago. My wife previous to our marriage had six children, all of which are living and have families. I am sick and unable to earn my support. Neither myself or wife have any relatives able or liable to aid in our support. [Filed 2 Jun 1893; examined and adjudged 2 Jun 1893]

1004. Mrs. Hattie P. Hastings, 35 years old. Married to Fred E. Hastings in 1879. Have since lived with him until 1 Apr 1893. Have five children as follows: Carl, 9 years; Lizzie, 12; Bertha, 8; Allie, 5; and Everett, 3 years old. My name previous to my marriage was Hattie Sawyer. We owned property to the amount of $800 for 3 years. Have lived in Keene since 1887. The said Fred E. Hastings never served in the army or navy; is about 33 years of age. [Filed 2 Jul 1893; examined and adjudged 21 Jul 1893]

[338] 1005. Victoria Drollette, widow of Frank Drollette, lately deceased. I am 21 years old, married to said Drollette about 3 years and 9 months ago. We have one child about 3 weeks old named Rosella. Said Drollette came to NH from NY about 6 years ago and went to Swanzey which I think was the first time he lived in NH. My father's name was Frank Durant, who has been dead about 15 years. [Filed 2 Jun 1893; examined and adjudged 2 Jun 1893]

Cheshire County Paupers
1885-1900

1006. Woodbury J. Nims, 71 years old. Married to Lois Wright in 1850, who is now living with me. We have two children: Charley, about 40 years old, and Georgie, about 30. Have lived in Keene since 1879. Since 1880 I have not had $150 worth of real estate or $250 worth of personal estate. I have no relatives able to aid us in our support. {19 Jun 1893} Died at Almshouse. [Filed 2 Jun 1893; examined and adjudged 2 Jun 1893]

1007. Joseph Lemire, Jaffrey, born in Canada, where I always lived until 8 months ago. I now live in Jaffrey; have never paid a tax in the US. Have 9 children, as follows: Adelbert, age 17; Joseph, 16; Clophire, 15; Clodia, 14; Manda, 11; Evangeline, 9; Denis, 6; Cadies, 4; and Arliam, 2. Now in need of assistance. [Filed 19 May 1893; examined and adjudged 2 Jun 1893]

[339] 1008. Abbie C. Crossfield, born in VT, 50 years old. Went to MA when I was about 4 years old, lived in MA until I was married 5 Jun 1866 to Charles H. Crossfield, then moved to Keene. Have 2 children[148]: Kendall, 18 years, and Caroline M., 16 years. Have no real or personal estate. My husband died in 1884. [Filed 16 Jun 1893; examined and adjudged 16 Jun 1893]

1009. Frank E. Turner, Alstead, born in VT, 1853. Living in Bellows Falls, 1 Jan 1880; lived there until 1 Jan 1889; went to Brattleboro, lived one year; moved to Alstead. Have never been a soldier or sailor in the service of the US. Married in 1884. My wife died in 1890, was married again in 1891 to a daughter of John Mead. Have 4 children: Lula, born in 1886; Susie, born 1888; Frank H., born 1890; and Clement, born 1893. My wife is a daughter of Julia Mead.[149] See affidavit, page 225. [Filed 16 Jun; examined and adjudged 16 Jun 1890]

---

[148] Another child is #712, page 240.
[149] See #667, page 225, and #1037, page 348.

Cheshire County Paupers
1885-1900

1010. Gideon Noel, Westmoreland, born in Canada, 19 Aug 1854. Lived in Canada until 1888 when I came to this country. Lived in Marlborough, Hinsdale, Chesterfield and about 3 years in Brattleboro, VT. Came to Westmoreland in Sep 1892. My wife was born in Canada. Have 2 children: Regina, age 6, and Rosa, age 2. {noted later} Died in Westmoreland; family returned to Canada. [Filed 1 Jul 1893; examined and adjudged 7 Jul 1893]

[340] 1011. Albert A. Lewis, 25 years old. My father formerly lived in Swanzey, went west 7 years ago. My wife Rose E. Lewis was the daughter of James M. Bates,[150] age 16. My wife's father is dead. Mrs. Bates was living in Winchester at the time of his death. [Filed 2 Jun; examined and adjudged 7 Jul 1893]

1012. Colten C. Bailey, Stoddard, 58 years old, born in Windsor, VT. My wife died in 1885. Lived in VT in 1883. I lived in MA in 1885 since then have lived in Stoddard. Was a soldier in Co. E, 1st VT Cavalry. Never received aid before. [Filed 26 Jun 1893; examined and adjudged 7 Jul 1893]

1013. Pauline C. Simpson, born in Sweden, 1869. To MA in US in 1887. Came to Keene in 1892 where I have since resided. Married in 1891 to Charles S. Simpson. My husband left me about the year 1893. My husband told me he was born somewhere in NY; don't know the residence of his parents. My parents resided in Sweden at the time I came to the US and do now. [Filed 28 Jun 1893; examined and adjudged 7 Jul 1893]

[341] 1014. James D. Graves, born in Whitingham, VT, 30 years old. Always lived in VT until 4 years ago when I moved

---

[150] See #127, 863, and 865.

to Winchester, NH, where I now live. My wife's name is Nellie O. Graves, age 44. She has 3 children by a former marriage, all of age. I was married to Mrs. Nellie O. Ballou, who was divorced from Joseph Ballou on 7 Oct 1884. We have one son by this marriage: Arthur J., 7 years old. [Filed 19 Jun 1893; examined and adjudged 27 Jul 1893]

1015. Robert T. Aldrich says Annette Cook, born in Whitehall, NY, 47 years old. Widow; husband unknown. Has lived in Westmoreland 18 years and died there. [Filed 5 Jun 1893; examined and adjudged 21 Jul 1893]

1016. Gilbert T. Stevens, Walpole. On oath say that Nicholas Wade, an old man about 70 years old, came to my house and wanted work. I took him in and for the last year he has lived with me. Said he was born and always lived in East Bridgewater, MA until 2 years ago when he went to Greenfield and there to Walpole. [Filed 4 Aug 1893; examined and adjudged 4 Aug 1893]

[342] 1017. Maria L. Bridges, Surry. On oath say that Charles Hardy is my son who had no legitimate father, who was born, 18 Dec 1864 at Marlborough. My son has made it his home with me to this time. Charles is a non compos person and incapable of taking care of himself. {The above named Charles Hardy was drowned at Westmoreland 13 Aug 1893.} [Filed 4 Aug 1893; examined and adjudged 4 Aug 1893]

1018. I[151] hereby certify that Charles Howard came to work for me on or about 28 May 1893. Should think he was about 28 years old. Had no property of any kind; has not paid poll tax 7 years in succession since 1 Jan 1880. On the afternoon of 4 Jul

---

[151] Record does not indicate who was giving this information.

*Cheshire County Paupers
1885-1900*

was killed by the cars. [Filed 25 Jul 1893; examined and adjudged 4 Aug 1893]

1019. William P. Rugg, born in Nashua, 44 years old. Married Mary McGovern in 1882 in South Boston. Have 2 children: Mary Margaret, about 6 years old, and Susan Clara, little more than 2 years old. [Filed 18 Aug 1893; examined and adjudged 18 Aug 1893]

[343] 1020. Earnest Stacy, 47 years old. Married to Alice Davis of North Hinsdale in 1871. We have 7 children: George, about 19 years old; Alice, about 15; Pearl, about 12; Josephine, about 8; Agnes, about 7; Esther, about 5; and James, about 1 ½ years old. My wife is about 37 years old. [Filed 31 Aug 1893; examined and adjudged 1 Sep 1893]

1021. Carl Swenson, 24 years old, born in Sweden. Came to this country 6 years ago, coming directly to Keene where I have since lived. Have one boy living, 5 weeks old: Oscar L. My father is still living in Sweden. [Filed 31 Aug 1893; examined and adjudged 1 Sep 1893]

1022. Nelsen H. Andrew, 32 years old, born in Champlain, NY, where I lived until I came to Keene about the middle of Jul 1893. Married Minerva Scrow about 13 years ago. I have 3 children: Minnie, about 12; Mary, about 6; and Adolphus, about 3. My father and mother are both dead. The parents of my wife are both living at Champlain, NY and have always lived there or near there. [Filed 31 Aug 1893; examined and adjudged 1 Sep 1893]

[344] 1023. Benjamin Marcaux, born in Canada, 19 years old. I came into the US 3 years ago. Single and have no parents. This affidavit was made in Mar last 1893, and put on file and

was lost, this being a copy. [Filed in March; adjudged 1 Sep 1893]

1024. Eunice H. Ward, Troy, widow of George P. Ward. See page 288, No. 857. Page 276, No. 821.

1025. Minnie M. Hill, American, born in Marlborough, 30 Apr 1872, the daughter of George W. Hill of Marlborough. My mother's name was, I think, Naomi White. My father died in 1879; my mother soon after. Married Fred Whitcomb and went to MA to live. I have one child, born 25 Aug 1893. The father of the child is Walter Cobb. [Filed 16 Sep 1893; examined and adjudged 6 Oct 1893]

[345] 1026. Thomas Parrault, Frenchman, born in Otter River, MA, 9 Jun 1869. Married; wife Maria Heberts, born in Manchester, NH, 8 Aug 1873. Came to Troy spring of 1889, lived until Oct 1892; moved to Otter River, lived until 3 Jul 1893; returned to Troy. My wife's father's name is Freeman Heberts. My father's name is Joseph Parrault. For parent's residence, see pages 294, 333.[152] [Filed 25 Sep; examined and adjudged 6 Oct 1893]

1027. Demars Raymond, Frenchman, born in Canada, 42 years old. Have 3 children as follows: Alsead, age 18; Olivan, 17 years; and Mary, 15. Never lived in this state until we moved to Marlborough about 1 year ago. [Filed 25 Sep; examined and adjudged 10 Oct 1893]

1028. Clara E. Parmenter, American, born in Chesterfield, 58 years old. My first husband John W. Parmenter died in Chesterfield 8 Aug 1862. I am now living with my second husband. I am the mother of Clara E. Parmenter who is 33

---

[152] For parents' affidavits, see #874 and 991.

Cheshire County Paupers
1885-1900

years old, born in Keene. [Filed 20 Jul; examined and adjudged 4 Aug 1893]

[346] 1029. David Thornton, African, born in Kentucky, 22 years old. Came to Boston when I was quite small. Lived in Boston until I came to Winchester 4 years ago. My parents never lived in this state. Married to Ida M. White about 8 months since. She had 2 children: Girtie and Nora, about 1 year old. Girtie, 3 years old is dead. [Filed 1 Sep 1893; examined and adjudged 17 Oct 1893]

1030. Frank A. Bryant, American, born in Richmond. Came to Winchester when I was about 10 years old, where I have lived most of the time since. I married Mrs. Hattie M. Button of Winchester. I am 30 years old; my wife is 31. She had one boy by a former marriage. His name is Albert C. Button, 8 years old. I had 2 children: Ernest G., 2 years old, and Viola E., 11 mos. [Filed 15 Jul 1893; examined and adjudged 17 Oct 1893]

1031. Susan A. Reed, American, born in Westfield, VT, 30 years old. Married to Joseph Reed 17 Aug 1882, and have lived in Andover, VT since that time until 1 Dec 1892. Have 6 children: William H., 10 years; Ernest, 8; Ida, 7; Emma, 5; Vicar, 3; and Edward, 1 year old. [Filed 4 May; examined and adjudged 1 Oct 1893]

[347] 1032. Ella F. Monroe, American, born in Walpole in 1867. Lived there until I was 18 years old. Married Fred Monroe in 1885; he died 5 Nov 1890. Came to Keene, Nov 1892. [Filed 25 May 1893; examined and adjudged 25 Oct 1893]

1033. Alvena Bennett, 36 years old. Was married to George H. Bennett, about 7 years ago. I have 4 children, 2 by a former husband, as follows: Joseph Croshea, age 14; Richard Croshea,

Cheshire County Paupers
1885-1900

11; Alvena Bennett, 3; and Lizzie Bennett, 1. My first husband Joseph Croshea died 10 years ago in Fitchburg, MA. My present husband is 30 years old. My father is living but has no property. [Filed 15 Sep; examined and adjudged 1 Oct 1893]

1034. Frances Traxler, 19 years old, born in Marlborough. Lived there until I was 9 years old. My father died 8 years ago, at which time he lived in Dublin. My mother now lives in Harrisville. I was married to Perly Traxler in Mar last and by him have one child: Bertrice Pearl, about 9 weeks old. My husband now in Chesterfield. He is about 23 years old. He came to Keene in Nov 1891.[153] [Filed 1 Feb 1893; examined and adjudged 1 Oct 1893]

[348] 1035. Frank A. Poole, American, 35 years old, born in Pembroke, NH. Was adopted by Samuel Poole, Surry when I was 6 weeks old. Lived with him until I came to Keene, 13 years ago. I married Emma Knight in 1880 and we have 3 children: Vernie M., age 12; Elmer, 8; and Bessie, 6. [Filed 3 Nov 1893; examined and adjudged 3 Nov 1893]

1036. Henry A. Herrick, Stoddard, American, 38 years old, born in Lyndeborough. Married in 1881 Lisia Wilson. I received aid from Hillsboro County when I lived in Greenfield about 5 years ago. [Filed 10 Nov 1893; examined and adjudged 19 Nov 1893]

1037. Frank E. Turner, Keene, American, 50 years old. In 1880, lived in Bellows Falls, VT, where I lived until Jan 1889; moving from there to Brattleboro, where I lived until Apr 1891; moved to Walpole, staying there a few months; went to Alstead; to Keene in Sep last. In 1884, married Alta M. Larrabee; she

---

[153] Pearley F. Traxler and Gertrude Gilson had a daughter Beatrice P., born 13 Nov 1892 in Keene, according to the 1892 *Keene Annual Report*.

Cheshire County Paupers
1885-1900

died in Nov 1890. We had 3 children: Luna J., age 7; Susie Q., 5; and Frank Draper, age 3. [Filed 10 Nov 1893; examined and adjudged 17 Nov 1893]

[349] 1038. Edward Keats, born in England, 45 years old. Married in 1882. She is 36 years old. Have 6 children: Harold, age 10; Fred, 9; Lawrence, 7; Teddy, 6; Clara, 5; Thomas, 2. Three children by a former marriage: Willie, age 19; Alfred, 17; and Ernest, 16. [Filed 15 Dec; examined and adjudged 15 Dec 1893]

1039. William O. Carkin, Marlborough, born in Tyngsboro, MA, 57 years old. Am father of Isaac A. Carkin, now sick with a fever. I have one daughter, Ada J. Carkin, 18 years old. [Filed 1 Oct 1893; examined and adjudged 15 Dec 1893]

1040. Charles B. Rice, American, born in Cambridge, MA, 1 Jul 1870. Came to Keene about 1 month ago and by reason of sickness am obliged to ask for temporary aid. [Filed 15 Dec 1893; examined and adjudged 15 Dec 1893]

[350] 1041. John Nelson, born in Denmark, 2 May 1869. My parents reside in Denmark. Have lived in NH about 2 months. [Filed 15 Dec 1893; examined and adjudged 15 Dec 1893]

1042. Shurburn P. Hale, American, born Rindge, 1831. Single; was married to Emma Stevens about 5 Jan 1858; was divorced from her about 19 years since. Have always lived in Rindge; have never paid taxes in any town, except Rindge in this state. [Filed 1 Dec 1893; examined and adjudged 15 Dec 1893]

1043. Orpha C. Noonan, 32 years old, born in Fort Ann, NY. Lived there until I was married 9 years ago to Thomas Noonan. Lived in this state about 4 years. On account of the death of my

Cheshire County Paupers
1885-1900

husband, I asked for aid in his burial. [Filed 20 Nov 1893; examined and adjudged 30 Nov 1893]

[351] 1044. Thomas Lawrence, born in Spane (*sic*), 4 Dec 1842. Lived 2 years then went to West Indies Islands. Was there one year, then went to Canada, where I have since resided. My family are there now. I left Canada 1 Dec 1893; came to Keene. [Filed 28 Dec 1893; examined and adjudged 28 Dec 1894]

1045. Clarinda L. Gerard, American, born in Langdon, NH, Sep 1844. Married Louis Gerard in 1860. He was a soldier of VT. He afterwards enlisted in NY Reg't. Since that time have heard nothing from him. About 1870 I received aid from Cheshire County. [Filed 21 Dec 1893; examined and adjudged 16 Jan 1894]

1046. Cyprien Filiault, Frenchman, born in Canada, 31 years old. Came from Canada to Manchester when I was 17 years old. My wife Phoebe Filiault lived in Manchester when I married her 11 years ago. Lived about 3 years; went back to Canada when I was 20 years old and remained there until Aug 1892, when we came to Winchester. I have 4 boys and 3 girls: Alexander, age 8; Elvina, 7; Edmond, 6; Ida, 4; Aldea, 3; Henry, 1 ½; and Dena, one week old. My wife's mother lives in my family. Also a niece of my wife. Her name is Clara Champagne, 15 years old. [Filed 17 Jan 1894; examined and adjudged 19 Jan 1894]

[352] 1058.[154] Alvin W. Withame, (hospital affidavit), born in Lowell, ME in 1863. Lived until I was 18 then went to West Stewartstown, NH. My father died when I was 6 months old. My mother is not living. I came to Roxbury 20 Jun 1893,

---

[154] Number transcribed as in original.

Cheshire County Paupers
1885-1900

where I have lived since. [Filed 10 Oct 1893; examined and adjudged 19 Jan 1894]

1048. Clement Gwinn, Frenchman, born in Canada, 61 years old. I came from Canada to Harrisville 25 years ago. Then I returned to Canada where I stayed until about 11 months since, when I came to Winchester where I have since lived. Have no family. {This man has returned to Canada.} [Filed 17 Jan 1894; examined and adjudged 19 Jan 1894]

1049. Alexander Feloe, Swanzey, Frenchman, born in Canada, 46 years old. Always lived in Canada until about 8 years ago, when I went to Manchester, NH and lived 2 years. Then I moved back to Canada where I was until last May. I came with my family to Swanzey. We have 9 children as follows: Alexander, age 16; Leoneda, 15; Eveline, 13; Delina, 11; Clara, 9; Henry, 8; Albert, 5; Alden, 4; and Arthur, 15 months old. Have had sickness in my family and an unable to work. [Filed 6 Jan 1894; examined and adjudged 19 Jan 1894]

[353] 1050. Mary Vigneau, Winchester, French. Am wife of Peter Vigneau, 47 years old. My husband is 47. Was married 26 years ago in Canada. Born in Canada and lived there until he was 17, when he came to NH and lived in Canaan, Claremont, Hinsdale, Ashuelot. We have 6 children, namely: Clara, 17 years; Martin, 14; Peter, 13; George, 10, Abbott, 7; and Willie, 3 years old. The child of Clara was born and died when a few days old. My daughter Clara expects to be confined soon and we are obliged to call for aid. [Filed 17 Jan 1894; examined and adjudged 19 Jan 1894]

1051. Mrs. John Foster, Keene, 35 years old. My name was Julia Bennett previous to my marriage to John Foster. My husband is 42 years old. We have 5 children: Annie, who is married to Joe Tatro about 2 years ago, is about 20 years old;

Cheshire County Paupers
1885-1900

Malvina, 16; Alice, 11; Rosa, 10; Johnnie, 5. Have not lived in NH since 1883 until last fall. [Filed 8 Jan 1894; examined and adjudged 16 Jan 1894]

1052. John Belletete, Jaffrey, Frenchman, born in Canada, about 60 years old. Lived in Canada until about 4 ½ years ago when I moved York state about 6 months, then I came to Jaffrey where I now live. Have no wife living but have one daughter and one son with me. The son, aged 18, died this morning 2 Jan 1894, and am obliged to ask for aid in his burial.[155] [Filed 4 Jan; examined and adjudged 16 Jan 1894]

[354] 1047.[156] Dolphia Guillmette, Frenchman, born in Canada, 29 years old. My wife is 23. We have 3 children as follows: Orvila, 5 years; Henry, 2; and Rosa, 9 months. My father is dead; my mother is in Canada and is poor. My wife's parents are in Ashuelot; name is John Bergnon. I moved from Canada to Ashuelot about 4 years since. [Filed 19 Jan 1894; examined and adjudged 19 Jan 1894]

1053. Frank Sharkey, Keene, 58 years old. Was married to Lucy Coster in 1869. We have 9 children as follows[157]: Arthur, 17 years old; Fred and William, 18; Mary, 15; Delia, 12; Laura, 10; Jessie, 4; and Matoon, 2 years old. Never lived in NH until Aug 1891 where I have since lived. [Filed 1 Jun 1894; examined and adjudged 16 Jun 1894]

1054. Julia Gakey, born in France 1845. Lived there until 1884, then came to North Adams, MA. Lived there 6 months, then moved to NY; lived there about 4 years, then came to

---

[155] According to the 1894 *Jaffrey Annual Report*, Joseph Belletete, son of John, died 1 Jan 1894.
[156] Number transcribed as in original.
[157] Only 8 children named in document.

Cheshire County Paupers
1885-1900

Keene, where I have since lived. [Filed 5 Jun 1894; examined and adjudged 16 Jun 1894]

[355] 1055. Emma Brunell, Troy, French, born in Canada, 29 years old. Married Moses Brunell, who was born in Canada, 30 years old. My husband has left me. Never lived in NH until Jun 1893. I have 3 minor children: Henry, 10 years; Eddie, 6; and Clara, 2. [Filed 4 Jun 1894; examined and adjudged 16 Jun 1894]

1056. Frank Houle, Rindge, French, born in Canada 1859. In 1880, I married Louisa Dargant in the same town I was born. Never lived in NH until about 3 years ago. I have 5 children as follows: Albert, 11 years; Louisa, 7; Gena, 5; Julia, 7; and Robetin, 1 year old. [Filed 8 Jun 1894; examined and adjudged 19 Jun 1894]

1057. Hannah Harley, Hinsdale, 60 years old, born in Ireland. Came from York state to Hinsdale in 1888, where I have since lived. My parents never came to this country. [Filed 10 Oct 1893; examined and adjudged 19 Jan 1894]

[358] 1059. Nelson Beshaw, Hinsdale, French, born in Canada East about 1825. Left Canada, 35 years old; came to MA and continued to live in that state until I came to Hinsdale to live in 1891. My wife is dead. I have two children, both living in MA, age 25 and 27. [Filed 25 Jan 1894; examined and adjudged 2 Feb 1894]

1060. Arthur T. Dupree, Nelson, born in Lowell, MA, 9 Mar 1879. His mother came from Lowell; her name was Maria Davis; his father is unknown. The said Arthur Dupree is now at the State Industrial School. [Filed 1 Jan 1894; examined and adjudged 2 Feb 1894]

Cheshire County Paupers
1885-1900

1061. Tuffield Patterson, Swanzey, French, born in Alburg, VT, 40 years old. In Oct 1881 I moved to Swanzey and have lived in Swanzey and Chesterfield continually ever since. I have 7 children as follows: Willie, 10 years old; Henry, 9; Bessie, 7; John, 5; Eddie, 4; Birdie, 2; and Lucy J., 8 months old. I ask for aid on account of breaking my leg. [Filed 20 Dec 1893; examined and adjudged 9 Feb 1894]

[357] 1062. Peter Paridis, Troy, French, born in Canada, 38 years old. Married; wife born, Canada, 35 years old. Never lived in NH previous to 24 Oct 1893. I have 6 children. Their names and ages are as follows: Mary, 14 years; Eava, 12; Fred, 7; Devry, 5; Ned, 2; and infant, 3 days old. [Filed 2 Feb 1894; examined and adjudged 10 Feb 1894]

1063. Edward J. Doyle, Dublin, born Jaffrey, about 42 years old. Unmarried; lived in Dublin from 1880 to 1885. When he was removed to Concord Insane Asylum, remained there until Dec of that year. His expenses being paid by the town of Dublin since that time. He has lived a portion of the time in MA. {Taken to the Asylum at Concord with others May 1904.} [Filed 3 Feb 1894; examined and adjudged 9 Feb 1894]

1064. Eugene Raulaugh or Rollet, Hinsdale, French, born in France, 48 years old. Never lived in NH until Apr 1892. Lived in Winchester 14 months until Jun 1893 when moved to Hinsdale, where we have since lived and now reside. My wife's age is 44. My children's names and ages are as follows: Eugena, 18 years; Rose, 15; Paul, 13; Mary, 9; Charles, 7; and Louis, 16 months. We are out of work and need aid. [Filed 9 Feb 1894; examined and adjudged 9 Feb 1894]

[358] 1065. Harry S. Asher, Keene, 48 years old. I have a wife, Lena Collins, age 24; married in 1889. Have no children. I think her parents are living. Came to live in Keene in Jun

Cheshire County Paupers
1885-1900

1893 where we have since lived. [Filed 28 Feb 1894; examined and adjudged 1 Mar 1894]

1066. Edward E. J. Shanessey, Marlborough, born in Manchester, 34 years old. Was married 4 Jul 1887 to Mary Sheeny, born in England, 25 years old. Neither of her parents ever lived in this country. I have 4 children: Lillie May, 5 years; Katie, 3; Ruby Etta, 2; and William Edward, 4 months. Came to Marlborough to live in 1893. [Filed 1 Mar 1894; examined and adjudged 1 Mar 1894]

1067. John McGregger, Jr., 62 years old. Married Ellen Cornell in 1853; she is about 60 years old. We have one child John McGregger who is about 30 years of age; does not reside in this state since 1888. I have lived in Hinsdale; Greenfield, MA; and Keene. Have lived in Keene since 1880 6 or 7 years. Have owned for about 20 years a small place on Dover Street. I paid $700 and paid all taxes assessed thereon. {The above named real estate is deeded to Ellen McGregger, wife of John; she belongs to city of Keene. } [Filed 10 Feb; examined and adjudged 16 Mar 1894]

[359] 1068. William Nolen, 65 years old. Married to Catherine Sullivan about 20 years ago. We have no children. My wife died 5 years ago. Lived in Keene since 1880, 3 or 4 years. I went to California, stayed until 1889; I returned to Keene where I have since lived. [Filed 10 Feb 1894; examined and adjudged 16 Mar 1894]

1069. John Shaver, 37 years old. Married in Jul 1881 to Louisa Durant, who is about 28 years old. We have 3 children: John Herbert, 8 years; Lovisa May, 4; Peter Alfred, 2. Moved to Swanzey in Nov 1893. Mrs. Shaver's father is dead; the mother

Cheshire County Paupers
1885-1900

is now living in Marlborough, NH.[158] [Filed 10 Feb 1894; adjudged 1 Mar 1894]

1070. Joseph Martell, 47 years old. I married Hattie LeRose in 1885; she is 24 years old. We have 3 children: Ernest G., 7 years; Clarence J., 2 years; and Florence H., 6 weeks. We moved to Keene Apr 1890. Never lived in NH before. [Filed 10 Feb 1894; examined and adjudged 16 Mar]

[360] 1071. Clifford McDonald, Hinsdale, 41 years old, born in Canada. In 1880, lived in Harrisville, continued to live there until 1883; moved to MA, lived 3 years; returned to Harrisville where I lived until Apr 1893; moved to Hinsdale. I am single; my wife is dead. Have 8 children as follows: Agnes, 18 years; Dora, 16; Jennie, 15; Christie, 12; Alburt, 10; Willie, 8; Florence, 6; and Ernest, 3 years old. [Filed 12 Feb 1894; examined and adjudged 16 Mar 1894]

1072. Rosa Lower, Keene, 45 years old. Married to Jerry Lower 1870. We have 5 children as follows: Antoine, 20 years; Mary L., 14; Fredy M., 11; Rosa, 10; Ellen, age 5. Lived in NH since the fall of 1890. [Filed 12 Feb 1894; examined and adjudged 1 Mar 1894]

1073. Charles E. Whitney, Fitzwilliam, born in Surry 29 Apr 1850. Married; have 10 children living, 6 of whom are living at home with me: Nellie L., 11 years; Susie, 9; Gracie, 6; Gertrude, 4; Harry, 2 ½; Hattie, 6 months old. One girl, age 17, in Chesterfield the last I heard from her. Milton, age 14, living with Dr. Waterman; two boys in Chesterfield, ages 10 and 15.

---

[158] The annual report from Marlboro shows John Shover and Marie Louise having a child born 23 Oct 1887. John Shover and Louise Durant had a son Peter A. born 19 Aug 1891, according to the 1891 report.

Cheshire County Paupers
1885-1900

Have lived in NH since Jun 1892. [Filed 26 Feb 1894; examined and adjudged 28 Mar 1894]

[361] 1074. Alivine Bastarache, born in St. Barnaby, Quebec on 3 Aug 1846. Married to Joseph Bastarache, 28 Apr 1862. Never lived in NH until Oct 1892. [Filed 15 Mar 1894; examined and adjudged 16 Mar 1894]

1075. William Bigwood, born in England, 31 years old. Married and have 4 children as follows: Amber G., 11 years; George A., 9; Hattie E., age 4; and Willie, 2 years. Moved from MA to Richmond but a short time ago. [Filed 7 Mar 1894; examined and adjudged 16 Mar 1894]

1076. Emma Tibbetts, 49 years old. Married; have one child, Bessie J., who is sick, age 12. Resided in Keene until Jun 1886; lived in Brattleboro, VT until Mar 1894; moved to Fitzwilliam. My husband left me on 6 Aug 1887. [Filed 27 Mar 1894; examined and adjudged 28 Mar 1894]

[362] 1077. Charles G. Stevens, Richmond, born in Southampton, MA, 40 years old. Married; wife's name was Abbie Richardson of Keene; married 7 Jun 1892. Have one child, 6 months old, Willie A. I came to NH in 1884; lived in Swanzey 3 years; lived Richmond one year; in Winchester 11 months; Alstead, one year; Richmond, 6 months; Keene, 6 months; then to Richmond where I live at the present time. [Filed 28 Oct 1893; examined and adjudged 4 Apr 1894]

1078. George Sharkey, Keene, 25 years old. Was married to Susie Wall in Nov 1892. Have one child, not named, 2 months old. My wife is 22 years old. I came to Keene to live 4 years ago from VT. Never lived in NH before. My wife's father is dead and my mother lives in Canada. [Filed 3 Apr 1894; examined and adjudged 3 Apr 1894]

Cheshire County Paupers
1885-1900

1079. David Pelto, Keene, 35 years old. Was married to Florence Bascomb in 1881, who is 25 years old. We have 5 children as follows: Wilmer, 11 years; Florence, 9; Eddie, 7; Nancy, 5; and David, 3 years. Came to Keene from NY state in Jun 1892; have never lived in NH before. [Filed 3 Apr; examined and adjudged 3 Ap 1894]

[363] 1080. Salina Brooks Pollard, Keene, 29 years old. I married Peter Pollard in 1880, who is 33 years old. We have 3 children: Silvia, 11 years; Willie, 5; and Nora, 1 year old. My husband left me in search of work and have heard nothing from him. We lived in NY state until Aug 1893, when we moved to Keene. Never lived in NH before. The parents of my husband are both dead, but mine are both living in the state of NY. [Filed 3 Apr; examined and adjudged 3 Apr 1894]

1081. Gideon Hilie, Hinsdale, French, 26 years old, born in Canada East. In 1880 was living in Swanzey; lived there about 3 years. From there went back to Canada where I lived a short time, then returned to Swanzey; stayed a few months; went to Keene; lived about 1 year; back to Canada; stayed about 6 months; went to VT, where I lived a short time; back to Canada; stayed about 1 ½ years; went to Springfield, MA. Never lived in any one place long enough to gain a residence. Have a wife; maiden name Eliza Genyer. One child, 18 months old. [Filed 5 Apr 1894; examined and adjudged 5 Apr 1894]

1082. Henry J. Pratt, Winchester, born in Shutesbury, MA, 79 years old. My wife's name is Sarah H. Pratt. Mrs. Pratt receives a pension of $12 a month on account of a son who died in the late war. Have always lived in MA. The above named Pratt ordered to Farm, if aid continued. [Filed 11 Jan; examined and adjudged 6 Apr 1894]

Cheshire County Paupers
1885-1900

[364] 1083. Ira W. Russell, Keene. Personally acquainted with Polly H. Ballou. She is 84 years old, a widow. She has lived in Cheshire County for the last 15 years, living in Keene about 6 years; the balance of the time in Surry and Walpole, about the same time in each place. Her husband has been dead about 18 years. [Filed 4 Apr; examined and adjudged 18 May 1894]

1084. Mary E. Newton, Keene, born in Charlestown, NH, 11 May 1865. Lived there until I was 15 years old. Moved to Bellows Falls, VT with my mother. My father died in 1879. Lived in Bellows Falls 2 years. Then married Harry Newton; lived with him 1 year. Moved to Walpole; lived there 3 years; moved back to Bellows Falls and lived 1 year. Then he left me and have not seen him since. Have 2 children: Hubbard H., 5 years, and Fannie M., 3 years old. [Filed 11 Apr; examined and adjudged 11 Apr 1894]

1085. Edward Baker, Keene, born Middlebury, VT, 2 Nov 1845. Married; have 3 children, named: Ida May, age 9; Edgar, 7; and Arthur, 14 months. I lived in VT until Mar 1893, when I moved to Keene where I now live. [Filed 4 May; examined and adjudged 4 May 1894]

[365] 1086. Daniel Twitchell, Swanzey, 71 years old, born in Richmond. Came to live in Swanzey about 17 years ago. Continued in Swanzey most of the time since. Married Menirva Freeman of Hartland about 40 years ago, but has not lived with her for about 10 years. Have 6 children, grown up. [Filed 4 May; examined and adjudged 4 May 1894]

1087. Taylor E. Hill, Winchester, American, 52 years old, born in Chesterfield. Lived there until 1885; went to Kansas; lived until I came to Winchester in 1888, where I have since resided. I have a wife and one child; married 4 years ago; wife, native of VT. My child 10 months old; name is Gardner T. Hill. I was a

Cheshire County Paupers
1885-1900

soldier, served in Co. F, 14th NH Regiment. [Filed 4 May 1884; examined and adjudged 1 Jun 1894]

1088. Noel Rocheleau, French, born in Canada, 49 years old. I came to Troy in Jul 1893. Previous to that time I had lived in Otter River, MA, 23 years. My wife is 48 years old, born in Canada. The names and ages of my minor children are as follows: George, 15 years; Charles, 13; Frankie, 7; Napoleon, 5; and Allice, 2 years. [Filed 18 May 1894; adjudged 1 Jun 1894]

[366] 1089. Augusta Pickett, Winchester, born Derry, NH in 1842. I came to Winchester in 1861. I married Lucius Metcalf of Winchester. I lived with him for a time and was divorced. I afterwards married Horatio G. Pickett of Winchester, with whom I lived until his death in Jun 1886. Died at Almshouse. [Filed 4 May 1894; examined and adjudged 4 May 1894]

1090. Christopher Biggie, Winchester, 34 years old, born in Ireland. Came to this country when I was 14 years of age. Lived in NY state 6 years; moved to Winchester, stayed about 6 years; back to NY, lived about 8 years; moved back to Winchester in Oct 1893, where I have since resided. Have a wife and 5 children.[159] My children are as follows: Edmond, age 11; Charles, 8; Bertie H., 5 and Jessie A., age 3. [Filed 4 May 1894; examined and adjudged 4 May 1894]

1091. David L. Whitemore, Winchester, born in Winchester on 18 Aug 1841. Have always resided in said town. Married and have 6 children, named as follows: Nellie E., born 1866; Emma J., born 1869[160]; Herbert, born 1878; Herman E., born 1880;

---

[159] Only names of 4 children listed in original text.
[160] See #1302.

Cheshire County Paupers
1885-1900

Freeman C., born 1884; and Victor S., born 1886. [Filed 18 May 1894; examined and adjudged 18 May 1894]

[367] 1092. Lucy Marble, Rindge. I am Maria Wood and am acquainted with Mrs. Lucy Marble. She came to live with me in 1881 and has continued to live with me since, with the exception of 2 years. She has been married but has not lived with him for several years. Think her age about 45 years. [Filed 18 May 1894; examined and adjudged 18 May 1894]

1094[161]. Daniel Ellis, Keene, 70 years old, born in Richmond. Have lived in Keene 35 years. Unmarried; since 1880 have not owned property in any town long enough to gain any settlement. {Died in Feb 1895.} [Filed 18 May 1894; examined and adjudged 18 May 1894]

1095. Joseph Stevens, Winchester, 52 years old, born in Canada, where I lived until about 1864. I went to VT, lived about 7 years; moved to Winchester, lived 3 years; moved back to Canada, lived a few years; moved back to Winchester, where I have since resided. Have a wife, but no children. [Filed 15 Jun; examined and adjudged 15 Jun 1894]

[368] 1093. Michael McBride, born in Boston, 1827. Always lived in MA until I came to Rindge. Have lived in Rindge for a short time; several different times. Now living in Rindge, am poor and in need of relief. [Filed 1 Jun 1894; examined and adjudged 1 Jun 1894]

1096. Jacob Smith, Westmoreland, born in Russia, 45 years old. Wife's name is Julia, 38 years old. 3 children: Toba, age 12; Charles, 9; and Jennie, 7. Landed in this country in 1892.

---

[161] #1093 appears on the next page.

Cheshire County Paupers
1885-1900

Lived in Westmoreland since Jun 1892. [Filed 28 May; examined and adjudged 1 Jun 1894]

1097. Maria J. Verry, Hinsdale, 21 years old, born in Winchester. Continued to live in Winchester until Apr 1892; moved to Chesterfield and lived there until Mar 1893. I came to Hinsdale and on account of sickness, am obliged to ask for temporary aid. Married; my husband's name William H. Verry. Have 2 children: Frank E., age 5, and Annie C., age 2. [Filed 15 Apr; examined and adjudged 5 Jun (1894)]

[369] 1098. George H. Town, Winchester, 42 years old. Was 15 years old when he came to Winchester, where he resided until 1886, when he was taken to the Asylum at Concord. Taken from Concord to Westmoreland, where he is at the present time. Never was married. His father is dead; his mother is living. The above affidavit was made by his sister. [Filed 18 May 1894; examined and adjudged 18 May 1894]

1098. George A. DeBell,[162] Winchester, 35 years old. Resided in Winchester from my birth up to 1886; moved to Keene where I lived until 1887; in Jul moved back to Winchester, where I have since resided. Married; have 8 children, namely: Cora, 12 years; Della E., 10; Arthur N., 8; Maud L., 7; Herman J., 5; Calista, 4; Eva M., 2; and a baby, 6 months old. [Filed 18 May 1894; examined and adjudged 18 May 1894]

1099. Delina Goulet, Winchester, 15 years old, born in Canada. Always lived there until I came to Winchester in Nov 1893. [Filed 18 May 1894; examined and adjudged 18 May 1894]

[370] 1100. Joseph Pluff, Marlborough, born in VT, 33 years old. Married 13 years ago to Delia Woods, who is 32 years old.

---

[162] See #853.

Cheshire County Paupers
1885-1900

We have 6 minor children: Joseph, 13 years; Henry, 11; Napoleon, 9; Mary J., 7; Nellie M., 5; and Daniel, 1 year old. Injured to my arm, am obliged to call for temporary aid. [Filed 18 May 1894; examined and adjudged 18 May 1894]

1101. Theodore Durant, Swanzey, French, 42 years old, born in Canada. Came to Harrisville 19 years ago, where I lived about 6 years; moved to Keene, lived about 2 years; back to Harrisville, lived about 1 year; moved to Peterborough, lived about 1 year; moved to Harrisville, resided about 4 years; moved to Keene, resided about 2 years; came to Swanzey. Married; wife's name Hellen, who is 40 years old. Have 5 children as follows, living: Joseph, 11 years; Josephine, 8; Fred, 6; Ida, 9; and Lillia, 6 months old. [Filed Sep 1893; examined and adjudged 7 Oct 1893]

1102. Marie Girouard, born in New Brunswick, 28 years old. Single. Never lived in the US until May 1893. My parents live in New Brunswick; never lived in NH. [Received 6 Jul 1894; examined and adjudged 6 Jul 1894]

[371] 1103. Ankust Hill, Marlborough, 26 years old. He first came to NH in 1893. Single; never married. By reason of having broken his leg he is obliged to ask for temporary aid. [Filed 15 Jun 1894; examined and adjudged 15 Jun 1894]

1104. Amelia Antoiniotti, born in Platsburg (*sic*), NY, 33 years old. Came to Keene in 1892. Married; my husband's name Mitchell Antoiniotti; have been married 6 years. Have 2 children, named as follows: Frank A., age 4, and Josephine A., age 2. My husband is 38 years old. [Filed 6 Jul; examined and adjudged 6 Jul 1894]

Cheshire County Paupers
1885-1900

1105. Eugene H. Barrett, Winchester, about 50 years old, born in Winchester. Always resided there. Has no children. [Filed 2 May 1894; examined and adjudged 20 Jul 1894]

[372] 1106. Leopold Herbert, German. Came from Germany about 6 weeks ago to Hinsdale. Born in Germany 27 May 1863. Always lived there until came to this country as above stated. [Filed 4 May 1894; examined and adjudged 1 Jun 1894]

1107. Frederick Bartlett, Walpole, French, born in Canada, 40 years old. I came to NY state when I was 14 years old. From that time until 2 years ago I worked in NY, Kansas, Nebrasky (*sic*), the Dakotas and other states. 2 years ago last fall I came to live in NH and never until then. [Filed 27 Jul 1894; examined and adjudged 27 Jul 1894]

1108. Isaac Champaign, Keene, French, 32 years old, born in Canada. Previous to coming to NH, I lived in VT and NY. Nine years ago I married Emma Prigson in NY; lived in Manchester, NH in 1885 for 3 months; moved to Keene, where I lived 3 years; moved to Bellows Falls, VT, stayed 1 year; moved back to Keene where I have since lived. My wife is 26 years old. Have 4 children: Olive, about 7; Albina, 5; Maud, 3; and Henry, 1 year old.[163] [Filed 15 Sep 1893; examined and adjudged 10 Apr 1894]

[373] 1109. Charles E. Clough, Winchester, 38 years old, born in Dover, VT. Taken from Dover when I was 2 years old to Unity, NH, where I lived until 1889; went to Newfane, VT, where I lived 2 years; moved to Winchester, where I have since resided and now reside. Married; have 3 children. Their names

---

[163] When Henry was born, the 1892 *Keene Town Report* listed his parents as Isaac Chapering and Emma Brigout. The 1894 town report shows a son born 11 Nov to Isaac Champaigne and Emma Pregout.

Cheshire County Paupers
1885-1900

are Edith E., age 12; Edna G., 10; and Winnie, age 8. [Filed 15 Jun 1894; examined and adjudged 3 Aug 1894]

1110. Florence Patch, Keene. I, Mrs. A. L. Lauyen, am acquainted with Florence Patch. She is 8 years old. Her father is living in Cleveland, Ohio; her mother is dead. She has never lived in NH previous to her coming to my home in Oct 1893. [Filed 3 Aug 1894; examined and adjudged 3 Aug 1894]

1111. Herbert Jones, Dublin, born in England, 26 years old. Was never married. I first came to this country in May 1891. My parents never lived in the US. Have never received assistance before from any city or town. [Filed 1 Aug 1894; examined and adjudged 7 Sep 1894]

[374] 1112. Emma Hernois, Troy, born in Canada, am married, am 33 years old. My husband John Hernois, born in Canada, 39 years old. At the present time the residence of my husband is unknown. My husband never lived in NH previous to 1891. The names of my children are as follows: Bertha, 9 years; John, 7; Eva, 5; Annie, 4; Dora, 2; and Rosa, 1 year old. [Filed 9 Aug 1894; examined and adjudged 7 Sep 1894]

1113. John Jolley, Fitzwilliam, 29 years old. My wife's name is Caroline, 25 years old. Have one child named Delia, 5 years old, and one named Delbert H., 3 years old. Lived until 1885; moved to North Adams, MA, lived there 2 years; moved to Nashua, NH in 1887, lived about 2 years; to Bellows Falls, VT, lived 3[164] months; to Fitzwilliam in 1884 and have lived there since. [Filed 26 Aug 1894; examined and adjudged 7 Sep 1894]

1114. Fred Sansea or Alfred St. Cyr, Hinsdale, French, 25 years old, born in Canada East, Province of Quebec. First came

---

[164] Handwriting is poor here. Could be "9" months.

Cheshire County Paupers
1885-1900

to the States 6 years ago last April. Came to Winchester in 1888, lived there until 1890; returned to Canada, stayed a little more than 1 year; moved to Hinsdale where I have since resided. My wife's parents now live in Canada and have never lived in this state. My father lived in this state about 1 year, and no more. Have two children: Henry Sansea, born in 1891, and Eviline Sansea, born in 1893, now 11 months. [Filed 5 Sep 1894; examined and adjudged 20 Sep 1894]

[375] 1115. John LaMountain, Fitzwilliam, French, am traveling to my friends in York state and am sick. [Filed 17 Sep 1894; examined and adjudged 20 Sep 1894]

1116. George D. Baker, Keene, born in West Saulsbury (*sic*), VT in 1888,[165] where I lived until I came to Keene in 1889. Married; wife's name Lula M., 26 years old. Have one child, Nellie, 8 years old. [Filed 7 Aug 1894; examined and adjudged 7 Sep 1894]

1117. Felia Faro, Rindge, French, born in Canada in 1871. Lived there until 1876; then with my father in Marlborough until 1891; since then have lived in Marlborough summers and in Rindge winters. Married in 1890 Ellen Croto of Granby, Canada. Her father was born in Canada, lived there all his life. I have 2 children: Cora, 2 years old, and Clarence, 1 ½ years old. [Filed 10 Sep 1894; examined and adjudged 10 Sep 1894]

[376] 1118. Fannie B. Cummings, Fitzwilliam, wife of Oscar E. Cummings, who is 30 years of age. Married to said Cummings 24 Nov 1891.[166] I came from Quincy, MA some 2

---

[165] Date transcribed as written in original.
[166] The marriage record in the 1891 *Fitzwilliam Annual Report*, lists the bride's name as Fannie B. Merritt, age 22 of Quincy, MA, daughter of Amos Merritt, born Scituate, MA, and his wife Elizabeth, born in Holbrook, MA. Oscar was the son of John F. and Clara B. J. Cummings of Fitzwilliam.

Cheshire County Paupers
1885-1900

years prior to my marriage. Since then have lived in Worcester and Fitzwilliam, but we are not living together. Have 1 child now living: Josiah Kendall Rand, 3 years old. [Filed 20 Aug 1894; examined and adjudged 3 Oct 1894]

1119. Peter Johnson, Swede, born in Sweden in 1854. Came to this country in 1888 to Montana, lived there 3 years; came to Keene in 1892 where I have since lived. Call for help on account of sickness. [Filed 7 Aug 1894; examined and adjudged 21 Sep 1894]

1120. James Henderson, Keene, born in Scotland, 31 years old. Have never lived more than 1 year in any town. [Filed 12 Oct 1894; examined and adjudged 13 Oct 1894]

[377] 1121. Corliss Reux, Keene. Parents are both dead. My mother died in Canada in 1888; father died in PA in 1886. Sent to Reform School. [Filed 12 Oct 1894; examined and adjudged 13 Oct 1894]

1122. Eliza Souls, Keene, 26 years old. Married, do not know where my husband is or has been for more than a year. My husband never lived in NH. I was born in VT, where I have lived most of the time until I came to Keene in Dec 1892. My father lives in Montpelier, VT; my mother lives in Keene. I have 2 children: Darwin, 5 years old, and Mabel, 4 years old. [Filed 18 Oct 1894; examined and adjudged Oct 1894]

1123. Joseph Pregent. Depose and say: born in Canada in 1834. Married; my wife's name Flanie, 37 years old. Have 3 children: Frank, 9 years old; Edward, 5; and Hattie, 3. In 1880 I lived in Allenburg, NY; moved from there to Keene in 1892. I call for help on account of sickness in my family. [Filed 5 1894; examined and adjudged 20 Oct 1894]

Cheshire County Paupers
1885-1900

[378] 1124. Gustave Schilling, Keene, 33 years old, born in NYC. Lived in Boston, MA in 1880, lived there about 3 ½ years; moved to Melrose, MA, lived there 3 years; moved to Cambridge, MA, lived there until 1892, when I came to Keene. Married; have 4 children, viz: Charles, 7 years old; Fred, 6; Pauling, 5; Augusta, 1 ¼ years old. My wife's name Bertha, 26 years old; lives in Keene. Moved here in 1892; never lived in NH before. [Filed 18 Oct 1894; examined and adjudged 18 Oct 1894]

1125. Mike Clark, Hinsdale, now in Keene jail, born in Shannadore (*sic*), PA on 26 Feb 1859. Have never lived in NH until I was arrested at Hinsdale last Jul. Have never been a public charge before. Am single. [Filed 19 Oct 1894; examined and adjudged 19 Oct 1894]

1126. Frank H. Bradbury, Keene, 39 years old. Married in 1877 to Mary S. Low, who is now 34 years old. We have 8 children, as follows: William R., 16; Frank H., 14; John J., 11; Florence R., 10; Edward, 7; Arthur L., 4; Ernest, 2; and Harry, 1 years old. Moved to Keene 27 Oct 1890 from Boston. Never lived in NH before. Have 2 boys in State Reform School: Frank H. and John J. [Filed 20 Oct 1894; examined and adjudged 23 Oct 1894]

[379] 1127. Evenste Therien, Hinsdale, French, 32 years old, was in Canada. Lived Canada 1 Jan 1880 and continued to live there until 1892; moved to Ashuelot, lived there about 1 ½ years; moved to Hinsdale, lived 1 year; back to Ashuelot, lived about 6 months; returned to Hinsdale, where I now live. Married; have 4 children, viz: Cadi Thomas, age 6; Robin W., 4; Horass, 7; and Emilia, 2 months old. [Filed 21 Nov 1894; examined and adjudged 7 Dec 1894]

Cheshire County Paupers
1885-1900

1128. C. Lowell Mason,[167] Surry, American. Lived in Surry since fall of 1886. Has not been taxed for any real estate or paid a poll tax 7 years in succession. Born in Keene 2 Oct 1852; son of Simon Mason of Keene. [Filed 16 Nov 1894; examined and adjudged 16 Nov 1894]

1129. Reconcile E. White, Fitzwilliam, 61 years old. She lived in Fitzwilliam from 1880 to 17 Jun 1883; to Winchendon, MA, lived 3 years until May 1894. Single; born in Fitzwilliam. [Filed 20 Nov 1894; examined and adjudged 7 Dec 1894]

[380] 1130. John B. Hathaway, Jaffrey, born in RI, age 59. Came to NH about 1890, lived about 14 months; moved to Providence for a few months; came to Peterborough, to Sharon in Jun 1892; remained until the following May; moved to Rindge; to East Jaffrey, where I now live. One child, age 14. [Filed 20 Nov 1894; examined and adjudged 7 Dec 1894]

1131. Maurice Cunningham, Irish, Hinsdale, 62 years old, born in Ireland. Was 18 years old when I came to this country; to Hinsdale in 1850. Made Hinsdale my home most of the time until 1882; moved to Winchester, where I have since lived. Married; have 9 children living: John, age 28; Eddie, 22; Mary, 20; Nellie, 18; Lizzie, 17; Hannah, 14; Isabel, 8; Willie, 7; and James, 5. My wife and children all reside in Holden, MA. They left me about 4 years ago. My wife's name is ____. [Filed 5 Dec 1894; examined and adjudged 7 Dec 1894]

1132. Lewis Castor, 68 years old. Always lived in Highgate, VT until I came to Keene in Apr 1894. Married; my wife's name is Sophry, 36 years old. We have 6 children as follows: Eddie, 13 years old; Matilda, 11; Arthur, 7; Phillip, 4; Freddie, 3; and Lizzie May, 8 months old. I call for aid on account of an

---

[167] Name given as Lowell C. Mason earlier (#508, page 171).

injury, my hand. [Filed 9 Dec 1894; examined and adjudged 26 Dec 1894]

[381] 1133. Lewis Castor, Frenchman, Keene, 42 years old. I came from Highgate, VT in 1889; came to Keene in 1890; moved to Surry in 1891; moved back to Keene in 1892; moved back to Surry in 1893; returned to Keene, where I have since lived. Never been aided in any town in NH. Married; my wife is 32 years old. Have 4 children: Charles, 14 years old; John, 12; Addie, 9; and Eva, 2 years old. [Filed 15 Dec 1894; examined and adjudged 16 Dec 1894]

1134. John Kempton and Mary Kempton. I am the mother of John Kempton. Said John was 31 years old last May, born in Richmond, NH. He was about 2 when we went to Winchester, where I have since resided and now reside. Made his home with his parents up the time he was 21. He has been twice married. First wife was Eunice E. York of Chesterfield. He has 4 children by his first wife: Leland S., 10 years old; Elenora E., 8; Henry, 6; and Viola V., 5 years old. [Filed 27 Jun; examined and adjudged 15 Feb 1895]

1135. Lewis Richart, French, Hinsdale, born 2 Feb 1857 in Canada. Went to Claremont, NH, Jun 1880; to Charlestown; to Claremont; left Claremont in Aug 1881; to Bellows Falls, VT, where I stayed 22 months; moved to Walpole, NH in Jun 1883, where I lived until Oct 1885; to Gilsum, where I lived until 1886; to Hinsdale, where I have continued to live to the present time. Have 5 children[168] as follows: Freddie, 12 years old; Rosa, 10; Lizzie, 8; Frank, 4. [Filed 27 Dec 1894; examined and adjudged 15 Feb 1895]

---

[168] Only 4 children are named in original.

Cheshire County Paupers
1885-1900

[382] 1136. Julia Bowiss.[169] I, Andrew Willis of Jaffrey, depose and say Julia Bowiss of Jaffrey is my wife's mother. She is 84 years of age; her husband died in Sharon in 1883. She remained in Sharon until 1891 and then came to Jaffrey where she has since lived. [Filed 1 Jan 1895; examined and adjudged 9 Jan 1895]

1137. Joseph Wallback, English, born in England. Came to this country in Aug 1899 to Trenton, NJ. Lived there until I moved to Keene in 1884, where I have since lived, except about 1 year. Married; wife's name is Mary Buck; in 1868. We have 8 children[170], viz: Mary Josephene, 6 years; John Vincent, 9; Fred Giles, 11; Arthur, 16; and Thomas, 18 years old. [Filed 28 Jan; adjudged 31 Jan 1895]

1138. Orlando Marston, Marlborough, born in England, 34 years old. My wife was born in England, was 33 years of age. Came to America Feb 1892. [Filed 9 Jan 1895; examined and adjudged 9 Jan 1895]

[383] 1139. Joseph Breasseur, French, Jaffrey, born in Canada, 56 years old. I have a wife and 4 children. Wife's name is Mary; children are as follows: Ada, age 17; Rosa, 16; Joseph, 10; and Fred, 8. I removed to Nashua, NH, I think, in 1878 where I lived, with the exception of 2 years, until 1890; moved back to Canada and lived 2 years; came to Jaffrey where I now live. [Filed 6 Jan 1895; examined and adjudged 1 Feb 1895]

1140. Levi Blake, Swanzey, born in Westminster, MA, 30 years old. Lived in Keene in 1880; moved to MA where I lived 4 years, and various other places in MA. I came to Swanzey to live 1st of Sep 1894 where I now live. Have a wife and one

---

[169] Handwriting is poor. This could be "Bowers."
[170] Only 6 children listed in original.

Cheshire County Paupers
1885-1900

child, a girl, 2 months old. Have never before received any aid from any town. [Filed 8 Jan 1895; examined and adjudged 18 Jan 1895]

1141. George S. Dingman, and wife, Winchester. Mary Dingman, widow of J. G. Dingman in 1890. My husband took a child whose name was George S. Brown, who made his home with us from that time until now on to the time of his marriage (Sept 1894). Said George S. Brown never was adopted, although he has gone by the name of George S. Dingman. Said George has left his home; I do not know where he is. Alvena Dingman, wife of George Dingman, 23 years old; went to Westmoreland to live when I was about 2 years old; went to Wakefield to live when about 5 years old; lived until Jun 1893; came to Winchester. My husband has left me. [Filed 9 Jan 1895; examined and adjudged 18 Jan 1895]

[384] 1149. Ellen Gilman, Fitzwilliam, 42 years old, born in Denmark, ME. Single; never lived in NH prior to 3 years ago. Have no relatives in this country that I know of. [Filed 30 Jan 1895; examined and adjudged 31 Jan 1895]

1143. Mary Goulet, Roxbury, wife of Joseph Goulet. Was married at Biddeford, ME in 1881. Said Joseph Goulet, born in Canada, age is 52. My age is 41, born in Canada. Moved to Dublin this state in 1890. In 1893 moved to Roxbury. We have 5 children: Peter J., age 12; Anna, 7; Victoria, 5; Emma, 3; and Edmond, 1 ½ years old. [Filed 30 Jan 1895; examined and adjudged 15 Feb 1895]

1144. Victor Guier, Keene, French, 20 years old, born in Canada. My father died when I was about 1 year old. My mother died when I was a small boy. I came from MA to Keene about 2 years ago. Never asked for aid before. [Filed 15 Jan 1895; examined and adjudged 31 Jan 1895]

Cheshire County Paupers
1885-1900

[385] 1145. Betsey Hendrix, born in Scranton, VT, 68 years old, widow of Benjamin Hendrix. Moved to NH in 1873; to Hinsdale in 1881; to Walpole in 1883; to Westmoreland in 1888. My husband died in 1890. [Filed Feb ___ 1895; examined and adjudged 15 Feb 1895]

1146. Catherine Latellier, Fitzwilliam, 37 years old. Married and have children: Kate, age 20; Archie, 18; and Edmond, 10 years old. My husband Cyrel Latellier is 44 years old and is confined in jail at Keene. Myself and husband were born in Canada. We lived in Richmond, NH, 1 year, and in Fitzwilliam since last May. [Filed 2 Jan 1895; examined and adjudged 2 Jan 1895]

1147. Edward Charton, Jaffrey, born in Canada, 32 years old. Have a wife Albina, aged 27. Two boys: Edmond, age 4, and Archie, 3 months old. Lived in Jaffrey about 20 years. Have never owned or paid taxes on any property. My wife was the daughter of Anthony Avord, formerly of Jaffrey. [Filed 8 Feb 1895; examined and adjudged 15 Feb 1895]

[386] Fred Laflamine, Keene, born in Canada, 5 May 1858. Lived there until 1868; lived in MA about 9 years or most of the time, until last Sep, when I came to Keene. Never was married. [Filed 15 Feb 1895; examined and allowed 15 Feb 1895]

1149. Annie Jutrus, Hinsdale, 28 years old, born in Germany. Left Germany in 1884 and to Philadelphia, PA in Dec of the same year. I lived in the last named place until Sep 1886; moved to state of Michigan, lived until 1889; moved to Canada, stayed until 1892; moved to Hinsdale, where I have since lived. My late husband Joseph Jutrus was born in Canada. Have 1 child: Ellen L. Jutrus, age about 4 months. [Filed 15 Mar 1895; examined and adjudged 15 Mar 1895]

Cheshire County Paupers
1885-1900

1150. Joseph Cota, Keene, 45 years old. I married Carrie Trudo of Bristol, VT 5 years ago. I am living with her now in Keene. By a former wife Rose Perry I had 2 children: Henry, about 13 years old, and Charlie, about 10 years old. Previous to my moving to Milford, NH, 16 Mar 1894, I had always lived in VT. [Filed 15 Mar 1895; examined and adjudged 15 Mar 1895]

[387] 1151. Annie Tacy, Swanzey, wife of Lewis Tacy[171]. My husband is sick in Bennington, VT; aged 39 years, born in Canada; when 1 year old removed to NY state. We were married in 1879. In 1880 removed to Winchester, lived there until 1883; moved to Brattleboro, VT, living there 1 year; back to Winchester in 1884, living until 1890; from Winchester to MA, living there 2 ½ years; to Swanzey, where we now reside. Have 3 children as follows: Maggie G., age 15; Louis, 13; and Lizzie, age 12. [Filed 27 Mar 1895; examined and adjudged 27 Mar 1895]

1152. Charles A. Britton, Keene, American, 72 years old. I moved to Keene in 1878 or 1879, have resided here since that time. I married Mary E. Balch in 1876; she is now living with me and is about 68 years old. Have two children, both more than 21 years of age. [Filed 9 Apr 1895; examined and adjudged 3 May 1895]

1153. Martha A. M. Griffith, Keene, 56 years old. Was married to John Gilman Griffith in 1861. We have one child, Charles G., who is about 30 years old and is now living in Michigan. My husband went west about 1884; since which time he has not lived with me. I ask for aid on account of sickness. [Filed 1 Apr 1895; examined and adjudged 1 Apr 1895]

---

[171] See also #366, page 123.

Cheshire County Paupers
1885-1900

[388] 1154. George P. Campbell, Rindge, 34 years old, born in Stuben, ME in 1861; lived there until I was 19. I came to Rindge, lived 3 years; traveled on the road, canvassing for about 4 years; went to Scarboro, ME, about 3 years. I came back to Rindge and lived here since. [Filed 30 Mar 1895; examined and adjudged 1 Apr 1895]

1155. Delia Capren, Keene, French, 20 years old, born in Canada. Moved to Middlebury, VT, lived 2 years; to Keene in 1893. I am not married. My mother died 5 or 6 years ago. My father is living in Bristol, VT; he has no property. My father came to Bristol about 3 years ago, having always lived in Canada before that. [Filed 25 Mar; examined and adjudged 3 May 1895]

1156. George Trombly, Marlborough, French, born in Canada, 29 years old. Married Georgeanna Tellia, who is 26 years old. Have 4 children, named: Eugene, 7 years old; Lois, 5; Frank, 4; and Dora, 4 months old. I first came to NH in 1883. My father's name is Lewis Trombly. [Filed and adjudged 3 Mar 1895]

[389] 1157. John L. Britton, Keene, American, 91 years old. Married to Sabra M. Tufts in 1859; she is now 54 years old. We have 2 children: Lewis G., age 13, and Jennie C., age 17. I served in the late war 4 years and am drawing a pension of $16 per month. [Filed 21 Jun 1895; examined and adjudged 19 Jul 1895]

1158. Ellen F. Tyrell Bowen, Hinsdale, American, born in Chesterfield, 1 Aug 1858. On 1 Jan 1880 I was living in Hinsdale and have ever since continued to live there. Married to George Bowen at Winchester about 1875; divorced from him within 2 or 3 years after. Have no children living. This

Cheshire County Paupers
1885-1900

affidavit was given by David B. Tyrel. [Filed 30 Mar 1895; examined and adjudged 8 Apr 1895]

1159. Alek Rasmundson, Fitzwilliam, Swede, about 21 years old, born in Gottenburg, Sweden. Came to this country about 3 months ago, landing in Boston. Was injured by the cars in Fitzwilliam on Friday, 28 Jun 1895. Am poor and unable to care for myself. This affidavit was given by H. L. Waterman.[172] [Filed 10 Jul; examined and adjudged 19 Jul 1895]

[390] 1160. Lizzie Fredrickson, Hinsdale, French, wife of John Paul Fredrickson, now of Hinsdale. My parents are both dead. I am 29 years old, have lived in Hinsdale for about 8 years. Never lived in any other place in this state. My husband was 50 years old last April. He has lived in Hinsdale since 1892 and for 11 years prior to 1892 lived in Baltimore, MD. Call for help on account of my husband being sick. [Filed 3 Jul; examined and adjudged 5 Jul 1895]

1161. Rufus D. Field,[173] Winchester, American, 43 years old, born in Winchester. Lived in Winchester until I was 15 years old. My father died in 1884 or 1885. When I was 15, I went to Chesterfield, where I lived most of the time up to 1886; went to Putney, VT, lived until 1894. Have been twice married. My first wife was Susan Robbins of Chesterfield. Had 5 children, 4 living: Charles, age 20; Frank, 19; Fred, 17; and Bessy, 14. Married my second wife, Mary Bragg, of Winchester in 1887. Have no children by this wife. [Filed and examined 2 Aug 1895]

---

[172] Handwriting is unclear. This surname could be incorrect, but Dr. Waterman appears in case #1203.
[173] See #214. His daughter Bessy has a separate file #1329. Son Charles is #432.

Cheshire County Paupers
1885-1900

1162. Thomas Smith, Alstead, born in Dedham, MA in 1861. Have resided in said Dedham to the winter of 1895.[174] On 4 Apr I came to Alstead where I now live with my wife Alice Smith. [Filed 15 May; examined and adjudged 6 Sep 1895]

[391] 1165.[175] Abbie E. Hastings, Stoddard, 41 years old, born in Stoddard. Was married to James E. Reed in 1872, lived in Stoddard until he died in Feb 1895. We had 9 children, 7 are under 21 years old: Lucy, age 16; Clara E., 14; Lillie, 12; Walter W., 10; Grace, 8; Arthur, 6; and Willie I., 2 years old. I was married to Charles Hastings in Apr 1895. [Filed 16 Aug; examined and adjudged 16 Aug 1895]

1164. Lewis Rock, Marlborough, for Addie Madison. I am 71 years old and married; am the father of Addie Madison, the late wife of Harry Madison. She was 41 years old when she died on 10 Jul 1895. She had not lived with her husband for the past 5 years. His residence is unknown. He has never lived in NH; his wife first came to NH in 1891. I am poor myself and was obliged to call on the overseer of the poor of Marlborough for my said daughter. [Filed and adjudged 2 Aug 1895]

1065.[176] Daniel Robbins, Chesterfield, born in Mason in 1830. Lived in Chesterfield since I was 5 years old, up to 1885. Was a soldier in the late Rebellion. Have children as follows: Frank, age 42; Susan, 38; Edgar, 36; Sarah E., 33; Mary A., 32; George, 29; Ida May, 25; Ervin, 22 years old. {Daniel Robbins died Oct 1895. It appears by the affidavit that Hannah, wife of Daniel Robbins, would belong to the town of Chesterfield.} [Filed 8 Aug 1895; examined and adjudged 20 Sep 1895]

---

[174] Transcribed as written in original.
[175] Number transcribed as written in original.
[176] Number transcribed as written in original.

Cheshire County Paupers
1885-1900

[392] 1166. Charles F. Putnam, Jaffrey, born in NY in 1856. Have a wife, aged 36, and 3 children: Flosa, age 4, and twin boys, aged 2 weeks. Have lived in several towns in NH since 1880; have not paid taxes in any town, except Keene, more than 2 years in succession. Married my wife in Lowell, MA. Never lived in NH, until after I married her. [Filed and examined and adjudged 4 Oct 1895]

1167. Herbert A. Hall, Winchester, 27 years old, born in Monson, MA. Never in NH until 1893 when I came to Winchester. My father and mother moved to ___ in 1894. Have no children. My wife's name is Laura A. Hall, born in Rindge, age 22; went with my parents to MA when about 1 year old; lived in MA and VT until 1892. [Filed 16 Aug 1895; examined and adjudged 14 Oct 1895]

1168. Joseph Blodgett, Alstead, 25 years old, born in NY. Have paid poll tax in Alstead 2 years, and am taxed there this year. Never have aided before and call for help on account of injury to my hand. [Filed 15 Sep 1895; examined and adjudged 15 Oct 1895]

[393] 1169. George Hould, Keene, Frenchman, born in Canada, 27 years old. Never lived in NH until 1890. Never owned any real estate to the value of $150, or personal property to the value of $250. [Filed 29 Aug 1895; examined and adjudged 14 Oct 1895]

1170. Nettie Bennett, Richmond, born in Shutesbury, MA, 20 years old. My father never lived in NH. I first came to Winchester eight ___, lived here about 2 years; moved to Hinsdale, lived about 2 years; moved to Richmond, lived 1 year; to Vernon, VT and Northfield, MA, lived about 6 months; back to Richmond, where we now live. Was married to William D. Bennett, Richmond, 1890; lived with my mother

Cheshire County Paupers
1885-1900

until I was married. My husband was divorced from me after living with him about 2 years. I have one child, Lottie B. Bennett, born Jan 1895. [Filed 30 Aug 1895; examined and adjudged 17 Oct 1895]

1171. Julia Foster,[177] Marlborough, French, born in France. Husband John Foster, born in Canada, 48 years old. Have 4 minor children: Alice, age 14; Rose, 11; Johnie, 6; and Josephine, 3 years old. Have not lived in NH since 1880 until 3 years ago, when they came to Marlborough. [Filed 2 Aug 1895; examined and adjudged 2 Aug 1895]

[394] Daniel Bunker, Gilsum, born in Sutton, VT, 57 years old. Have lived since 1880 in Stoddard, 6 years; Surry, 4 years; in Marlow, 1 year; in Alstead, 1 year; and in Gilsum, 3 years. Have one child, Arthur E., 5 years old. My wife's name is Ella Wilder Bunker, born in Marlow in 1860. [Filed 27 Mar 1895; examined and adjudged 15 Oct 1895]

1173. James D. Graves,[178] Chesterfield, born in VT, age 32. Married Nellie O. Grasier of Whitingham, VT. Have lived in NH about 7 years; in Chesterfield since Dec 1894. Never owned property or paid poll tax 7 years in succession. [Filed 30 Apr 1895; examined and adjudged 15 Oct 1895]

1174. Delia Smith or Leware, Keene, 45 years old. Married to Kayman Leware 28 years ago; he died 1 year ago. We had children less than 20 years old, as follows: Gertrude E., 5; Rose Bell, 12; Ephraim1-4 (*sic*); Josephine, 14; and Nelson, 18. On 3 Jan 1895, I was married to Harry M. Smith of Boston, MA, who died about 2 months after. [Filed 7 Oct 1895; examined and adjudged 14 Oct 1895]

---

[177] See also #1051, page 353.
[178] See also #1014, page 341.

Cheshire County Paupers
1885-1900

[395] 1175. George F. Comstock, Keene. Home was in St. Albans, VT. This boy was sent to Reform School by the Police Justice Holmes and is there now. [Filed 7 Oct 1895; examined and adjudged 15 Oct 1895]

1176. Joseph Webb, Marlborough, French, born in Canada, 38 years old. Married 9 years ago, Elizabeth Banshaw, who is 27 years old. We have children as follows: Elizabeth, age 8; Rosanna, 6; Satina, 5; Adeline, 3; and Mary, 1 year old. Came to NH in 1885; lived in Marlborough 2 years; to VT, lived 2 years; moved back to Marlborough, where I have lived since. I have never owned any real estate in NH or personal property to the amount of $25, or paid poll tax 7 years in succession, in any town in this state. Self-supporting for 2 years; came back into the county Jan 1900. [Filed 7 Oct 1895; examined and adjudged 15 Oct 1895]

1177. Frank Jock or St. York, French, Keene, 80 years old. Married some 26 years ago; have 5 children under 21: Mary, 17 years old, is at the Co. Almshouse; Frank, age 18; John, age 20. I do not know where the last two named are. My wife has been dead about 11 years. [Filed 7 Oct 1895; examined and adjudged 15 Oct 1895]

[396] 1178. Charles L. Elgar, Winchester, 46 years old, born in Northfield, MA. Came to Winchester when about 8 years old with my mother. My father died about the time I was born. My mother died about 20 years ago. Have never paid taxes in any town to gain residence. Married; wife's name Adderet[179] Elmore of Dover, VT. Have no children. [Filed 20 Sep 1895; examined and adjudged 14 Oct 1895]

---

[179] Very unclear handwriting.

Cheshire County Paupers
1885-1900

1179. James Sullivan, Jaffrey, English, born in England, 25 years old. Have lived in Jaffrey and Winchendon, the last 5 years. Have a wife, aged 18, and one child, 19 days old. Wife's name Annie L. and beufs[180] Ethel. My wife's father's name Eugene La Close, lives in Rindge. [Filed 2 Oct 1895; examined and adjudged 2 Oct 1895]

1180. Hester Wright, Jaffrey. Lived in Westmoreland since 1873 with the exception of the last 15 months when she has been at Concord Asylum. Her husband died in 1871. [Filed 31 Oct 1895; examined and adjudged 31 Oct 1895]

[397] 1181. Henry Liscord, Keene, 27 years old. Married; my wife's parents live in Templeton, MA; never lived in Keene. We have 2 children: Flossy, 2 years old, and a boy, not named. Asks for aid on account of an injury to my hand. [Filed 3 May 1895; examined and adjudged 1 Nov 1895]

1182. John Gobiel, Jaffrey, French, 28 years old, born in Canada. Have a wife, named Henriette L., and 3 children: Charles, age 4; Clara, 2; and Rosida, 11 months. Married 5 years ago; her age is 26. Her father died in Jaffrey 9 years ago; lived there about 3 years before his death. [Filed 17 Oct 1895; examined and adjudged 31 Oct 1895]

1183. Ephraim Nash, Stoddard, American, 73 years old, born in Gilsum. Married in 1847, Mary Jane Crossfield; died in 1884. Had no children. [Filed 15 Nov 1895; examined and adjudged 20 Nov 1895]

[398] 1184. Charles Baldwin, 72 years old, born in Boston, MA. Since the year 1880, have lived in Keene, Ward 1, excepting the last 9 months, during which time have lived in

---

[180] Very unclear handwriting. Eugene's surname could be LaClare.

Cheshire County Paupers
1885-1900

Stoddard and Marlow. Several years ago I was cared for at the County Almshouse for a while. [Filed 20 Dec 1895; examined and adjudged 25 Dec 1895]

1185. Sarah H. Barry, married James Barry in 1860, with whom I lived 11 years. During that time lived in VT and VA; returned from the latter place in 1871. My husband returning with me at that time; placed me in the Asylum for the Insane at Brattleboro; lived in VT most of the time until 1880. At the present time, am in the Concord Asylum. I have one daughter living, but don't know where my husband was divorced from me several years ago; am about 53 years old. This affidavit was given by Mrs. Chas. Warren, a sister of Mrs. Barry. [Filed 1 Jul 1895; examined and adjudged 2 Jan 1896]

1186. Ambrose H. Piper, 83 years old. Since 1880, have lived in Acworth, Sullivan County, until 1895. Since Feb 1895, have lived with my daughter Lucetta Piper Howe in Gilsum. This affidavit was given by his daughter Mrs. Howe. [Filed 25 Dec 1895; examined and adjudged 2 Jan 1896]

[399] 1187. Allen R. Thompson, born in Poultney, VT, 54 years old. Never lived in NH until 1891; came to Alstead, where I have since lived. [Filed 6 Dec 1895; examined and adjudged 2 Jan 1896]

1188. Orren L. White, Marlborough, 36 years old. 26 Oct 1891 I married Mary E. Fisher of Richmond. We have 3 children, viz: Florence M., age 3; Mattie E., 2; and Charles V., 3 months old. My wife has 2 children by her former husband: Archie E., age 12, and Burton E., age 10. I never lived in this state over 4 years in succession. The above affidavit accepted all but the two oldest children. [Filed 31 Nov 1895; examined and adjudged 2 Jan 1896]

Cheshire County Paupers
1885-1900

1189. Charles H. Wilson, served in the war of the Rebellion, enlisting on or about 19 Nov 1864, in the 112th Reg't NY Vols. For further reference, see No. 552, page 186. [Filed 11 Jan 1896; examined and adjudged 17 Jan 1896]

[400] 1190. Heber Reil, Swanzey, born in Canada, 77 years old. Came to Ashuelot about 15 years ago, where I continued to live 5 or 6 years. Then I came to West Swanzey where I have since resided. I have no wife living. I have 2 sons and 4 daughters, all married and all over 21 years of age. I have never been aided by any town or county. [Filed 14 Jan 1896; examined and adjudged 25 Jan 1896]

1191. David Son, Fitzwilliam, born in Worcester, MA, 37 years old. I came here to reside Mar 1896, am married; wife's name Emma B. Son, age 38. Have one child, Phebe Son, age 9. [Filed 22 Nov 1895; examined and adjudged 2 Jan 1896]

1192. Sarah Willard, Keene, 76 years old. Husband's name George Willard, who died Jan 1893. Since 1880, have lived in Keene, but have not owned any property, neither had my husband. [Filed 6 Dec 1895; examined and adjudged 2 Jan 1896]

[401] 1193. Barney Bushey, Keene, 34 years old, born in NY state. Lived there until I came to Keene in 1892. Married Rosina Barcomb in 1883; she is 29 years old. We have 4 children, viz: Elenor, 11 years old; Delia, 9; Dora, 7; and Mary, 4 years old. My wife always lived in NY until we moved to Keene. [Filed 6 Dec 1895; examined and adjudged 2 Jan 1896]

1194. Orman Hill, Winchester, 28 years old, born in Canada. Always lived there until I came to Winchester, 3 years ago. My parents reside in Canada, always have. I married Pheba Stone of Canada, where her parents reside; always have. We have 3 children, viz: Henry, 2 years old; Orman, 1; and Flora, infant. [Filed 1 Oct 1895; examined and adjudged 1 Oct 1895]

1195. A. J. Harvey, Keene, born in England, 72 years old. Came to NH to live about 1865; lived in Keene about 10 years; moved to Winchester, where I lived about 2 years. [Filed 29 Aug 1895; examined and adjudged 1 Oct 1895]

[402] 1196. Florence Bergeron, Rindge, French, 35 years old, born in Canada. Moved to Rindge with my father when I was 8 years old. Married Michael Bergeron of Fitchburg, MA in 1880. My husband is 37 years old, born in Canada. We lived in Fitchburg until 1890, when we moved to Rindge. My husband died in 1895. I have 5 children, viz: Henry, age 12; Florence, 10; Annie, 6; Ida, 5; and Clemen, 4 years old. [Filed 10 Feb 1896; examined and adjudged 20 Feb 1896]

1197. John Johnson, Hinsdale, Swede, 40 years old, born in Sweden. I came to the US in 1886; have resided in Hinsdale ever since. I married Hilma Boman of Sweden, age 36. We have 5 children, viz: Emily S., 12 years old; John H., 9; Royal W., 7; Willie W., 5; and Hazel C., 1 year old. [Filed 21 Jan 1896; examined and adjudged 1 Feb 1896]

1898.[181] C. E. Adams, Stoddard, born in East Middlebury, VT, 18 years old. Neither my parents nor myself ever resided in this state a year at a time. I am now sick and obliged to ask for aid. [Filed 5 Sep 1895; examined and adjudged 1 Oct 1895]

[403] 1199. Fred W. Davis, Swanzey, 40 years old. Since 1880 I have lived in the following named places in NH: Swanzey, Marlborough, Winchester, Chesterfield, and Keene. Lived in none of the above-named places more than 2 years in

---

[181] Number transcribed as written in original.

succession. I have 2 children, viz: Edna B., age 14, and Bessie L., age 7. I married my present wife Annie A. Waters of Sandersfield, MA 4 Jul 1893. [Filed 30 Jan 1896; examined and adjudged 30 Jan 1896]

1200. Harry Hewins, Troy, 41 years old, born in England. My wife Jane Hewins, born in England, 42 years old. Neither myself or wife ever lived in the US until May 1892. Names and ages of my miner (*sic*) children are as follows: Alfred, age 12; Harold, 10; and Elsie, 4 years old. [Filed 7 Feb 1896; examined and adjudged 17 Mar 1896]

1201. Bert P. Demery, Keene, 27 years old. Married Lena Cummings, who is 20 years old. Have one child, Viola, 2 years old. My father James L. Demery lives in Athol, MA; my mother died in Jan 1893. The father of my wife has been dead 9 years; her mother is now living in Keene. Her name is Lucretia Cummings,[182] now the wife of William Cummings. She owns a small house on Howard Street in said Keene. [Filed 1 Apr 1895; examined and adjudged 2 Oct 1895]

[404] 1202. Lucius Breed, Troy, born in Winchester, 41 years old. My wife is 25 years old, born in Claremont. Her father Charles F. Rumrill lives at present in Unity. I have not paid a poll tax 7 years in succession in any town since 1880. I have resided as follows: 1 year each in Dublin and Winchester; since 1884 lived in Swanzey; moved to Troy, 1895. Children: Frank, age 16; Ina, 14; Fred, 12; Fanny, 7; and Annie, age 6. [Filed 14 Aug 1895; examined and adjudged 1 Nov 1895]

1203. Louis Pullisior, Fitzwilliam, about 34 years old, born in Canada. Came to Fitzwilliam, a transient person, sick and no money or means of support. This affidavit was given by the

---

[182] See also #671, page 226.

Cheshire County Paupers
1885-1900

attending physician H. L. Waterman, MD. [Filed 18 Oct 1895; examined and adjudged 2 Jan 1896]

1204. Michael Clune, Keene, 58 years old. My wife died 4 years ago. I have 6 children, only one being less than 21 years of age, which is Nellie, 18 years old. The rest all live in Lowell, MA. I moved to Keene in 1884, and have lived there since. [Filed 2 Jan 1896; examined and adjudged 2 Jan 1896]

[405] 1205. Fred Short, Keene, 23 years old, born in Great Falls, NH. My father is now living in Augusta, ME, where he has lived 14 or 15 years. My mother is dead. I never received aid before. [Filed 2 Jan 1896; examined and adjudged 2 Jan 1896]

1206. Josie Denno, Chesterfield Factory, wife of John Denno. I was born in Middlebury, VT, 1869; my husband was born in VT, never lived in NH until we came to Chesterfield in 1895. At the present time my husband is in Keene jail; therefore I call on the said town for aid. Have 3 children, as follows: Gracie, age 10; Floyd, 9; Mabel, 6 years old, all born in Middlebury, VT. [Filed 9 Jan 1896; examined and adjudged 1 Feb 1896]

1207. George Nash, Richmond, born in Townsend, VT, 31 years old. Married Celia Austin,[183] resident of Alstead. We have 2 children, as follows: _____, 3 years old and _____, 6 months old. [Filed 27 Jun 1895; examined and adjudged]

[406] 1208. Fabian Wilcox, Marlborough, French, born in Canada, 54 years old. My wife's name is Mary. We came to Marlborough in the fall of 1891; never lived in NH before. We have 2 children, viz: Theodore, age 19, and Minnie, 9 years old. [Filed 6 Mar 1896; examined and adjudged 1 Apr 1896]

---

[183] See also #1353, page 454.

Cheshire County Paupers
1885-1900

1209. Judson Croto, Springfield, MA, born in Canada, 44 years old. My wife is 37 years old, born in Canada. Have lived in NH but 1 year since 1880. I call for aid on account of my son Ephraim, having broken his leg, while coasting, when in Marlboro visiting. [Filed 10 Feb 1896; examined and adjudged 6 Mar 1896]

1210. Hannah Cunningham, Roxbury, 65 years old, born in Unity. When about 16 years of age, married Ebenezer Cummins of Newport, who died in less than 1 year after our marriage. When 19, married Robert Cunningham of Unity, who died in 1884. Since then I have moved from place to place until 1892 when I came to Roxbury, where I have since resided. Have one child living. [Filed 10 Mar 1896; examined and adjudged 20 Mar 1896]

[407] 1211. Emilie Terrien, Winchester, wife of Equrn H. Terrien, who is now in New Bedford, MA. We moved direct from Canada to Winchester 4 years ago, last Jun. Have lived in Winchester ever since. My husband is 34 years old and I am 25 years old. Have 5 children, viz: Oral, age 9; Katie, 7; Bessie, 5; Lidia, 3; and infant, 2 months old. [Filed 26 Mar 1896; examined and adjudged 3 Apr 1896]

1212. Thomas Brickley, Irish. Have lived in Walpole since Aug 1888; previous to that lived in Ireland. [Filed 7 Feb 1896; examined and adjudged 20 Mar 1896]

1213. Orman W. Woods, Alstead, 62 years old. Has had no settlement in Alstead since 1880. Unmarried and so far as we can discover, has had no permanent residence in this state since 1880. He died 16 Mar 1895. This affidavit was made by J. S. Prouty, selectman of Alstead. [Filed 2 Apr 1895; examined and adjudged 1 Jan 1896]

Cheshire County Paupers
1885-1900

[408] 1214. Annie Parmerleau, Troy, French, born in Canada, 30 years old. My husband died in Canada in 1872. He never lived in the state of NH. His and my parents never lived in the US. My children are as follows: Clara, 11 years old; Fred, 9; John, 8; and Frank, 6 years old. [Filed 14 Jan 1896; examined and adjudged 16 Jul 1896]

1215. George Smith, Troy, born in England, 49 years old. My wife Ellen, born in England, 44 years old. I came to America in 1892. I have one son George Smith, born in England, 24 years old, unmarried. He is insane; is in the Asylum. [Filed 7 Feb 1896; examined and adjudged 17 Jul 1896]

1216. Estanestace Bourchard,[184] Gilsum, born in Canada, 77 years old. Was married first, about 1839; she died about 1843. Married second wife in Canada; she died about 1874. Always lived Nashua until last Aug. Have been helped one month, about 2 years ago. [Filed 7 Apr 1896; examined and adjudged 14 Apr 1896]

[409] 1217. Mary Ann Smith, Gilsum, born in Ireland, 40 years old. Married J. M. Smith; he died 4 years ago. Have 4 children,[185] viz: Mary E., 4 years old. [Filed 7 Apr 1896; examined and adjudged 7 Apr 1896]

1218. John McClure, Stoddard, 66 years old, born in Antrim. My wife is dead. I have 2 children: Christina, 17 years old, and David, 15 years old. [Filed 15 May; examined and adjudged 16 Jul 1896]

1219. John Vaughan, born in Greenfield, MA, 38 years old. My wife's name was ____, also born in Greenfield, is 32 years

---

[184] See #1211.
[185] Only one child identified in the original.

Cheshire County Paupers
1885-1900

old. Have never lived in NH. [Filed 14 Apr 1896; examined and adjudged 17 Jul 1896]

[410] 1220. Joseph W. Raymond or Edward W. Moulton of Troy. Have known said Moulton for 17 years; became acquainted with him in Bellows Falls, when he commenced working for me; came to Troy to live in 1891. Has not paid poll tax 7 years in succession in any town in the state. Mr. Moulton's wife died in 1894 and he is now a veteran of the late war. He is now at Concord Insane Asylum. Has one child, Curtis, age 16. [Filed 17 Apr 1896; examined and adjudged 17 Jul 1896]

1221. Rose Winn, Gilsum, daughter of Estancelaer Bouchard,[186] born in Canada, am about 57 years old. Married Moses Winn in Canada. One child, Joseph Winn, about 12 years old. Came from Canada to Nashua about 1887; lived until Sep 1895. [Filed 7 Apr 1896; examined and adjudged 14 Apr 1896]

1222. Henry D. Carr, 39 years old. Always lived in Newport, NH until the fall of 1890 when we moved to Marlow, staying about 1 year; moved South Acworth, where we lived a few months; came to Keene in Jul 1892, where we have since lived. I married Rosie Ann Daniels in 1890. She is 28 years old. Have one child, 8 years old, Frank David. [Filed 13 Apr; examined and adjudged 16 Jul 1896]

[411] 1223. Mary Frezier, Hinsdale, 30 years old, born in Ireland. Came to this country in 1885; came to Hinsdale 1894. Never lived in NH before. My husband was born in England. [Filed 8 Apr 1896; examined and adjudged 21 Aug 1896]

---

[186] See #1216.

Cheshire County Paupers
1885-1900

1224. Isaac Champaign, Keene, son of _____ Champaign, age 75. My father died about 4 years ago. My father and mother lived in Canada previous to their moving to Keene in 1889 or 1890. [Filed 14 Apr 1896; examined and adjudged 14 Apr 1896]

1225. Norman T. Barry, Hinsdale, born in Northfield, MA 29 Jun 1895.[187] Said child was brought to me 23 Sep 1895 and has been with me ever since. The child's mother Mrs. James M. Barry is an actress. She told me she was married 2 Oct 1894 at Salem, MA. The child's father was J. M. Barry and he was an actor. So far as I know, neither have ever lived in this state. [Filed 25 Apr 1896; examined and adjudged 21 Aug 1896]

[412] 1226. Albert Ballou, Hinsdale, 24 years old, born in NY 11 May 1862. In 1880 was living at Adams, MA; continued to live there until Mar 1889; moved to Stafford Springs, CT; lived until Sep 1889; moved to Wales, where I lived until May 1891; moved to Hinsdale, where I have lived since. Was married at Springfield, MA, 30 Oct 1882 to Mary Paro. Both her father and mother are dead. [Filed 13 Apr 1896; examined and adjudged 14 Apr 1896]

1227. Addia E. Kimball, Keene, 45 years old. Was first married to Hyland L. Darren in 1881. He died in Mar 1893. We had three children: Gertrude L., age 9; Grover C., 7; and Charles C. V., 3 years old. My mother has the little girl with her in Newport, NH. The boys are with me. In 1895 I was married to William Kimball; he left in the month of Oct last. [Filed 14 Apr 1896; examined and adjudged 14 Apr 1896]

1228. Rose Linde, Walpole. Is married and has 4 children. [Filed 13 Apr; examined and adjudged 13 Apr 1896]

---

[187] Affidavit prepared by Susan J. Scott.

Cheshire County Paupers
1885-1900

[413] 1229. Oliver Champaign, Keene, 42 years old. Married to Vina ___ in Jan 1881; she is 32 years old. We have 7 children: Oliver, age 14; Isaac, 10; Edith, 6; Frank, 5 months old; Vina, 13; Permelia, 7; Colliss, age 3. [Filed 13 Apr 1896; examined and adjudged 14 Apr 1896]

1230. Frank M. Ballou, Keene, for Charles A. Ballou. I am the father of Charles A. Ballou, age 27. Came to Keene to live in 1881 and have lived here since. Charles received a fall in Jan 1889 from which he has suffered since, not being able to work very much since. I cannot support him any longer and therefore ask for aid. [Filed 13 Apr 1896; examined and adjudged 14 Apr 1896]

1231. Clarra C. Waite, Keene. I, Mrs. J. Lawrence, say I am the aunt of Clarra C. Waite. She is 45 years old. Her mother is dead; her father is living in Keene. J. G. Daniels said Clarra was married to Henry Waite of Haydonville, MA about 1884. After living with him about 2 years, she obtained a divorce. She came to Keene about 1 year ago, and since then has lived with me. [Filed 14 Apr; examined and adjudged 14 Apr 1896]

[414] 1232. Ruth Craig, Keene, widow of Allen A. Craig, age 69, born in Keene. Always lived here. My children are all more than 21 years old. My husband died Aug 1874.[188] I am the grandmother of Florence G. Page, now living with me. Her father William E. Paige, married my daughter Ida Craig in 1878. She is the only child they have. From the time of their marriage to Oct 1890, they lived in Keene. The father left and went to some town in NY state. [Filed 14 Apr 1896; examined and adjudged 14 Apr 1896]

---

[188] The murder of Allen Aaron Craig is profiled in *Hard Time in Concord*, pages 103-104. See also #362, page 122, and #1345, page 452.

Cheshire County Paupers
1885-1900

1233. Frank White, born in Burlington, VT in 1861. Lived there about 28 years; came to Keene in 1889. My parents are not living. Am obliged to ask for aid on account of sickness. [Filed 21 May; examined and adjudged 5 Jun 1896]

1234. Joseph Bouvis, French, born in Canada, 46 years old. I have a wife Delia, age 36; six children: Malvina, age 15; Emma, 13; Willie, 11; Joseph, 9; Flora, 7; and Cora, 5 years old. [Filed 20 May 1896; examined and adjudged 20 May 1896]

[415] 1235. Nettie C. Griffith, Winchester, wife of Wilfred Griffin. He was born in England, 27 years old. Came to America when he was 3 years old. He first came to Winchester to live in 1895. Previous to that he lived in MA. We married 29 Jan 1892; 2 children: babies, aged 8 and 18 months. My father's name is Wilson Carroll. [Filed 5 Jun 1896; examined and adjudged 21 Aug 1896]

1236. Catherine Galliger, Walpole, born in England, age 32. Has been in this country 11 years. Since 1890, have lived in Walpole. My husband James Galliger was born in Ireland, age 36. Came to live in NH first in 1890. My husband has left. I have children as follows: Jennie, age 12; Mary, 10; Katie, 8; Margaret, 6; Bessie, 4; and John, 2 years old. [Filed 5 Jun; examined and adjudged 17 Jul 1896]

1237. Fred W. May, hospital, born in Leominster, MA in 1877. Came to Keene in Mar 1896, where I have since resided. [Filed 6 Jul 1896; examined and adjudged 21 Aug 1896]

[416] 1238. William McDonald, hospital, born in East Randolph, MA in 1855. Lived there until I was about 8; went to Canada, lived about 9 years; to Plymouth, NH, lived about 2

Cheshire County Paupers
1885-1900

years; to Lebanon. Was there 2 years; went to Ashuelot, where I have since lived. [Filed 6 Jul 1896; examined and adjudged 17 Jul 1896]

1239. Ida M. Davis, Gilsum, 41 years old, born in Marlborough. Lived in Marlborough about 16 years. Was married first to Francis Bates;[189] lived with him 5 years in Gilsum; got a divorce from him in 1880. We had one child Forest E. Bates. In 1883, married George W. Davis, lived with until Oct 1895. Have no children by Davis. [Filed 3 Jul 1896; examined and adjudged 21 Aug 1896]

1240. Patrick Smith, tramp cared for at hospital, 39 years old, born in Ireland. Came to America 12 years ago. Never lived in this state. I started from Lowell, MA 22 Jun 1896, in search of work; came to Athol, MA 27 Jun; left Athol for Keene 28 Jun; came to Richmond. Was walking along; was taken sudden with a bad feeling in the head, as if hit, but saw no person about when I was taken. Am now at the hospital in Keene. [Filed 3 Jul 1896; examined and adjudged 3 Jul 1896]

[417] 1241. Lorenzo P. Shepardson, Winchester, born in Warwick, MA in 1835, 65 years old. Was married in 1861 to Miss Eliza Stacy of Philipston, MA. I have 5 sons: Elliott A., William J., Patrick G., Bert E., and Justice F. Shepardson; have 3 daughters: Mrs. Adolph Ramir of Wendall, MA; Mrs. Daniel Verry of Winchester; and Miss Gertrude S. Shepardson. [Filed 3 Jul; examined and adjudged 21 Aug 1896]

1242. Mary Jetts, Jaffrey, 26 years old. Five years ago I was married to Joseph H. Jetts by whom I have 2 children: Eddie, age 3, and an infant daughter, 5 weeks old. Have lived in

---

[189] The multiple marriages of Francis Bates are covered in *'Til Divorce Do Us Part* by author, pages 196-7 and 247.

Cheshire County Paupers
1885-1900

Jaffrey between 2 and 3 years. My husband left me last Sep and have not heard from him since. My husband is 25 years old. His parents live in Lawrence, MA where I think they have lived as much as 18 years. [Filed and adjudged 12 Jul 1896]

1243. Joseph Martenraux, Winchester, 28 years old, born in Canada. I came to Winchester with my parents 12 or 13 years ago; have lived in since. Married; my wife's name was St. Cyr; have one child, 1 years old. [Filed 15 Jul 1896; examined and adjudged 7 Aug 1896]

[418] 1244. Clara A. Thomas, Chesterfield, 75 years old, born in Chesterfield. Since 1880 I have lived in Chesterfield, all the time. I am now sick and unable to do anything toward my support. All the income I have is a pension of $12 a month. [Filed 18 Jul 1896; examined and adjudged 6 Aug 1896]

1245. James C. Brian, Keene, for James P. Brian. I am the father of James P. Brian. He was born 16 Aug 1861; he was never married. When he was about 25, he went west and since then he has lived away from Keene most of the time. To my knowledge, he has no property. On account of my inability to take care of him, he was taken to the hospital for the Insane at Concord, the last of Jun 1899. {May 1904} Was taken back to Concord, at no expense to Cheshire County. [Filed 17 Jul 1896; examined and adjudged 17 Jul 1896]

1246. Joseph Sweeney, Stoddard, 77 years old, born in Charlotte, VT. Came to Stoddard 11 years ago. I have a wife who is 74 years old. [Filed 25 Jul 1896; examined and adjudged 7 Aug 1896]

[419] 1247. George H. Kinney, Alstead, born in Gilsum in 1870. Was living in Surry on 1 Jan 1880; lived in Surry until Aug 1893; moved to Alstead, where I have since lived. Was

Cheshire County Paupers
1885-1900

married in 1891; my wife came from NY about 6 months previous to that time. Have 3 children: Edna, 5 years old; Thomas, 5; and George L., 8 months old. [Filed 21 Aug 1896; examined and adjudged 21 Aug 1896]

1248. Charles E. Houghton, Surry, 41 years old, son of Charles H. Houghton, late of Alstead, deceased. [Filed 21 Aug; examined and adjudged 21 Aug 1896]

1249. Sadie E. Cummings, for Lelela M. Davis, Keene. I was acquainted with Lelela M. Davis, who died in Keene 30 Jul 1896.[190] She was 3 months and 17 days old. The father Edwin F. Davis lived in Bellows Falls, VT. I do not know the maiden name of the mother. To the best of my knowledge neither of them ever lived in the state of NH. The child was brought to me to take care of by the father; the mother having died when the child was about 10 days old. [Filed 21 Aug; examined and adjudged 21 Aug 1896]

[420] 1250. Katie Roche, hospital, born in Westminster, VT 1872. Came to NH about 1892 to Marlborough; lived 1 year; from there to Keene, where I have since resided. My parents are not living. I call for aid on account of sickness. [Filed 21 Aug 1896; examined and adjudged 21 Aug 1896]

1251. Annie Larkin, Keene, 25 years old, born in Dublin, Ireland. Came to this country in May 1890. I ask for aid at the present because I have no money and am not able to take care of myself in my present condition. [Filed 31 Aug; examined and adjudged 7 Aug 1896[191]]

---

[190] The 1896 *Keene Town Report* shows the death of Zelda M. Davis on 30 Jul 1896. She was the daughter of Edwin F. Davis, born in Nova Scotia, and Ella M., born Templeton, MA.

[191] Date transcribed as written in original. Unlikely the request was filed a month after it was adjudged.

Cheshire County Paupers
1885-1900

1252. Samuel Kempton, Richmond, 75 years old, born in Richmond. Was living in Warwick, MA on 1 Jan 1880. Lived there until 1890. Have since worked in the towns of Richmond and Winchester. Have paid no taxes in Richmond or any other town in NH since 1880. I was married to Sarah Pertred in 1850; lived with her 9 years. I left her in 1859. Do not know where she is now. {Dead.} [Filed 1 Nov 1896; examined and adjudged 1 Jan 1897]

[421] 1253. Joseph May, Dublin, 42 years old, born in Bellows Falls, VT. Have lived in Dublin all the time since 1880, with the exception of about 6 months. Have children as follows: Herbert H., age 16; Joseph S., 15; Charles P. 13; Albert B., 10; Josephine L., 9; LeForest I., 8; Orin O., 5; Erwin C., 3; and one who is nameless, 6 months old. My wife is 36 years old. [Filed 8 Sep 1896; examined and adjudged 18 Sep 1896]

1254. Maria Perrault, Troy, born in Manchester, NH, 24 years old. My husband Thomas Perrault or Paro, born in Otter River, 26 years old. My father Freeman Abbott is living in Troy; has lived here for 8 years. The names and ages of our children are as follows: Thomas, age 5; Sammy; and Bertha, 1 year old. [Filed 1 Sep 1896; examined and adjudged 20 Sep 1896]

1255. Jane Gwinne, colored, born in Virginia in 1845; lived until 1861; came to Keene in 1888, where I have since lived. [Filed 22 Oct 1896; examined and adjudged 22 Oct 1896]

[422] 1256. Fred A. Smith, Keene, 27 years old. My father is dead; my mother is living, but has no property. I was married to Lucy Gilman, who is 33 years old. We have no children, but she has a child by her first husband: Eddie, who is 6 years old. My wife's parents are both dead. Came from Walpole to Keene

Cheshire County Paupers
1885-1900

last week. Never have been aided before. [Filed 22 Oct 1896; examined and adjudged 25 Oct 1896]

1257. Alfred Dament, Marlborough, French, born in Canada, 32 years old. Married; my wife's name was Celine Champany, 30 years old. I have 4 children as follows: Dora, age 8; Fred, 7; Arthur, 3; and Flora, 1 ½ years old.[192] I first came to NH 3 years ago last Jul. Neither my parents nor my wife's even lived in NH. I have never received aid before. [Filed 27 Aug 1896; examined and adjudged 1 Oct 1896]

1258. John J. Welch, Hinsdale, born in Northfield, MA 18 Jan 1863, 33 years old. Neither myself or family, have ever been aided before. In Jan 1880 was living in Hinsdale; have lived here off and on ever since. I have a wife and one child: Willie, age 6 years. They now live in CT. [Filed 16 Nov 1896; examined and adjudged 16 Nov 1896]

[423] 1259. Eugenia Dube, Jaffrey, French. Has lived in Greenville the last 8 years, is 25 years old. Her parents never lived in the US. [Filed 6 Nov 1896; examined and adjudged 20 Nov 1896]

1260. Robert Butler, Walpole, born in Amherst, NH, about 55 years old. I went to Rockingham, VT about 1860, lived there until about 1891. When I came to Walpole, lived about 3 years; went to Langdon, Sullivan County, where I lived about 1 year; came back to Walpole, where I have since resided. I have no family. [Filed 30 Nov 1896; examined and adjudged 4 Dec 1896]

---

[192] According to the 1895 *Marlboro Town Report*, the 6th child of Alfred Demont and O. Champanie was a daughter, born 5 Apr 1895.

Cheshire County Paupers
1885-1900

1261. Ada Davis Bosworth, Keene, 21 years old, born South Vernon, VT. Lived there 1 year; Royalston until I was 12 years old; to Keene for 2 ½ years. In Dec 1889 was married to Orrin K. Bosworth of Athol, MA; lived in MA and NH for a few months at a time. My husband left me several years ago. I now call for aid because of my condition. My parents are poor and are being helped at the present time by the county. [Filed 4 Dec 1897; examined and adjudged 1 Jan 1896[193]]

[424] 1262. Edward F. Calkins, Winchester, born in Winchester, 26 years old. Have lived most of the time in West Swanzey until some time in Jan. I moved to Winchester where I now reside. I was married 4 years ago to Sarah Nickerson of Keene. Her father and ___ have been dead 3 years. They did not own any property. Have 2 children: Willie, 2 years old, and George E., now 6 months old. My father William Calkins has received aid through the county as a soldier. [Filed 1 Dec 1896; examined and adjudged 1 Jan 1897]

1263. Elizabeth Keep. Has lived in Keene about 20 years. Has had no property until she came in possession of a small amount of money in a Brattleboro, VT savings bank, 2 or 3 years ago, which is nearly all gone. {14 Nov 1902, signed "A. C. W.": Miss Keep died at the Almshouse, Westmoreland at the age of 92.[194]} [Filed 1 Jan 1897; examined and adjudged 19 Feb 1897]

1264. Lizzie G. Parkhurst, Keene, born in Warwick, MA in 1851. Lived 2 or 3 years; went to Winchester, lived different places in NH and MA for a few months or years at a time. I gained no residence in any one town. Was married in 1890 to

---

[193] Date transcribed as written in original. Likely that the request was filed in 1896 and adjudged in 1897.

[194] The 1902 *Westmoreland Town Report* shows Elizabeth Keep, who was born in VT, died 26 Sep at the age of 92 years, 10 months, and 12 days.

Cheshire County Paupers
1885-1900

Charles Parkhurst. My husband born in Fitchburg, MA. [Filed 1 Sep 1896; examined and adjudged 20 Sep 1897]

[425] 1265. John Fitzgerald, Marlborough, born in Winchendon, MA, 41 years old. My wife Hattie B., 34 years old, born in Ludlow, VT. I first came to NH in the fall of 1893. {John Fitzgerald died at Almshouse.} [Filed 1 Dec 1896; examined and adjudged 1 Jan 1897]

1266. Jennie Goodenough/Greenough, Marlborough, born in Canada, 48 years old, wife of Leon Greenough, who is 50 years old. We first came to this state in Jul 1892. Have lived here since. Have no minor children. [Filed 1 Jan 1897; examined and adjudged 1 Jan 1897]

1267. Joseph Rivers, Marlborough, born in Sheldon, VT, 22 years old. Married; wife's name Jane Sampson, 23 years old. Have 2 children: Joseph C., age 2 ½, and Mary A., 8 months old. My parents came to Marlborough to reside 1880. My parents are poor; my wife's parents came from Canada in 1890, living in NH only 1 ½ years. {14 Nov 1902, signed by "ACW": The above Rivers has 2 children: Joseph and Mary. Supported by the county at Notre Dame Hospital, Manchester, NH.} [Filed 1 Dec 1896; examined and adjudged 1 Jan 1897]

[426] 1268. Mack Johnson, Fitzwilliam, 28 years old, single. Have no relatives in this county. Having been injured I am obliged to ask for assistance. [Filed 1 Jan 1897; examined and adjudged 1 Jan 1897]

1269. Clarence S. Bowen, Stoddard, and wife, am 42 years old, born in VT. My first wife Ida died in 1883. She never had any property in her own right. I married 2nd time Jennie Gamill in 1890. She is 25 years old. Her parents never lived in NH. I have 3 children dependent upon me: Guy, age 16; Freddie, 10;

and Ida, 3 years old. [Filed 12 Jan; examined and adjudged 19 Feb 1897]

1270. John Harrison, Fitzwilliam, 49 years old. Married and have 2 children. Wife and children are not in this country. I am sick and am obliged to call for aid. [Filed 10 Feb 1897; examined and adjudged 5 Mar 1897]

[427] 1271. Alalander Black, Swanzey, 38 years old, born in England or Scotland. Never lived in this state more than 3 years at any one time. Married Nettie Osborn at Boston in 1884. Children as follows: Bessie, age 11; Nettie, 9; Edward, 5; Edith, 2; and William, 9 months old. My wife is 28 years old, born in Boston. [Filed 30 Jan 1897; examined and adjudged 19 Mar 1897]

1271. John McColley, Winchester, born in Fall River, MA, 30 years old. Have never gained a residence by paying poll tax 7 years in succession or owing and paying taxes on $250 personal property; or $150 worth of real estate. I came to Winchester 1 week ago. Was taken sick and was obliged to call for help. [Filed, examined and adjudged 19 Mar 1897]

1272. George Hall, Troy, born in Canada, 47 years old. My wife Sophia Hall, born in Canada, 40 years old. Came to Troy in 1889, have lived until the present time. Have never paid poll tax 7 years in succession in any town in this state, nor on $250 worth of personal property or $150 of real estate, 4 years in succession. [Filed 19 Mar 1897; examined and adjudged 19 Mar 1897]

[428] 1273. Frank Wheeler, Roxbury, 25 years old, born in Plymouth, VT. Am the father of 4 children: Harry B., Orlan B., Bertha M., and a baby unnamed. My wife's name was

Cheshire County Paupers
1885-1900

Barbara E. Green, born in Ireland. [Filed 21 Jan 1897; examined and adjudged 21 Jan 1897]

1274. Family of George May, Fitzwilliam. Said May was born in Canada 1850. Married Mary E., born in VT in 1853. Have 4 minor children, still living. One child, a little girl, age 2 years, died here 14 Jan 1897, named Flossie May. [Filed 15 Feb 1897; examined and adjudged 19 Feb 1897]

1275. Henry M. Parkhurst, Keene, 45 years old. I married Helen E. Grigs about 17 years ago, she being 45 years of age. We have one child: Flora V., 11 years old. Since 1880 I have made my home in Keene. [Filed 2 Jan 1897; examined and adjudged 2 Jan 1897]

[429] 1276. Julius Lourien, Jaffrey, born in Finland, 30 years old. He boards with me, and on account of an accident is unable to work. He asks for aid, being unable to speak English, I give this affidavit for him. His parents never lived in the States. He has no family. {Mat Brala[195]} [Filed 18 Dec 1896; examined and adjudged 18 Dec 1897]

1277. Charles Stenpoise, Rindge, born in Finland. Lived there until 1895, when I came to this country. Have never lived in any one place more than 2 months at a time since I came to this country until I came to Rindge. Have a wife and children in Finland. [Filed 27 Jan 1897; examined and adjudged 5 Mar 1897]

1278. Howard Dexter, Richmond, 44 years old, born in Nova Scotia. Came from there to Richmond in 1892. Have lived here since. Married Sarah Fancy, born in Nova Scotia. She died in Richmond in Jan 1897. Have 3 children: Minnie L., age

---

[195] Handwriting is poor, so this could be a name or illegible note.

Cheshire County Paupers
1885-1900

8; Mary, 2; and Harry A., 4 years old. [Filed 6 Feb 1897; examined and adjudged 15 Feb 1897]

[430] 1279. George B. Perry, Keene, 70 years old. Never married. Since 1880 have made my home in Keene. I have not owned any real estate or had any money in any bank or any other property. {Spring of 1902, signed "W": Mr. Perry died at the Farm.} [Filed 4 Dec 1896; examined and adjudged 1 Jan 1897]

1280. James H. Rowan, Winchester, 40 years old. Lived in Winchester after my birth, all the time until 1884. Since then have lived in different places in MA. I came back to Winchester 7 Mar 1896. Was married in 1887 to Minnie Post of Maine. She died in 1891. Have one child, Mary Elizabeth, who was 9 years old last Feb. She lives with her uncle in MA. [Filed 18 Dec 1896; examined and adjudged 1 Jan 1897]

1281. Julinmory Montpleiseur, Keene, 44 years old. Married in 1879 to Clara Cheney, who died in 1892. We have 5 children who are now living: Alexander, 13 years old; Josephine, 12; Emma, 10; Zuinany, 8; and Dillium, 6. The oldest and youngest are with me in Keene. The others are in Canada. I married Agnes Durues in 7 months after my first wife died. She lived only 7 months. [Filed 1 Dec 1896; examined and adjudged 1 Jan 1897]

[431] Napoleon Belduke, Keene, born in Detroit, MI, 56 years old. Went to Canada when I was 4 years old; lived there until 1860. Came to Concord, NH, lived there until last Aug, when I came to Keene. [Filed 19 Feb 1897; examined and adjudged 5 Mar 1897]

1283. Peter Sharkey, Keene, 48 years old. Married May Rogan, 23-24 years ago. She died about a year after we were

Cheshire County Paupers
1885-1900

married. Then married Sarah Gardner. Children: Albert, age 16; Rosa, 12; Jerry, age 10; Lucy, 4; and Patsey, 6 months old. Came to NH 4-5 years ago, then came to Keene and have since lived there. [Filed 1 Dec 1896; examined and adjudged 1 Jan 1897]

1284. Charles E. Houghton,[196] Surry, born in Uxbridge, MA in 1854, 43 years old. Since 1 Jan have not owned any real estate to any amount. Lived in Keene from 1880 until Jun 1886; then in Providence, RI until Mar 1892. [Filed 16 Dec 1896; examined and adjudged 1 Jan 1897]

[432] Dillon Jacobs, 38 years old, Keene. Married Joseph Jacobs about 14 years ago. He died 8 years ago. Two children: Ada, age 10, and Ida, age 12. The younger is with me; the older in Canada. Came to Keene last Dec. Never lived in NH previous to that time. [Filed 19 Mar 1897; examined and adjudged 19 Mar 1897]

1286. Julius H. Vetter, Gilsum, b. in Germany, age 65. Came to the US in 1852; came to NH about 7 years ago. Have no family. [Filed 5 Dec 1896; examined and adjudged 1 Jan 1897]

1287. Henry D. Sullivan, 31 years old, Keene. Married Eunice Howard in 1890; she is 24 years old. Children: Maude, age 6; Hagen, 5; Fred, 3; and Ethel, 5 weeks old. Mother is dead; father Daniel Sullivan in Lawrence, MA. He never lived in NH, but 2 years. The parents of my wife, Ambrose Howard, Keene; owns a house lot on Carroll Street. [Filed 5 Jan 1897; examined and adjudged on part of husband; wife's residence not settled]

[433] 1288. William W. Pratt, Keene, born in Walpole, 29 years old. My father died when I was an infant. My mother is

---

[196] See also #1248, page 419.

dead. I have never gained a residence in any town by paying a poll tax 7 years in succession, or by owning any property of sufficient amount. [Filed 5 Jan 1897; examined and adjudged 19 Feb 1897]

1289. Maria D. Wheeler, or Fairbanks, Fitzwilliam, 78 years old. Married Dexter Wheeler about 1840; moved to Gardner, MA, lived there 10 years; moved to Michigan, lived there 12 years; buried my husband there. Came to Winchendon and married Mr. Fairbanks; afterward moved to Texas; while there, was divorced from my husband; came east, where I have since lived. Never lived in NH until 1893. [Filed 5 Jan 1897; examined and adjudged 19 Feb 1897]

1290. William Gunn, Swanzey, 90 years old. Lived in Swanzey until 1860; then in Winchester about 10 years; in MA until 1889; since in Swanzey. Married Hannah Austin 1 Oct 1835; died in 1869. Children, viz: Fidelia, died Nov 1836; Andrew A., died 4 Mar 1841; Marrilla A., died 1870; Harriet E., died 1868. Then married Widow Carlton of MA 17 Feb 1872; died 1 Oct 1882. {Dead.} [Filed 19 Mar 1897; examined and adjudged 19 Mar 1897]

[434] 1291. Michael C. Thornton, Keene, 42 years old, Irish, born in Ireland. Came to this country when 14 years old in 1880. I lived in Boston where I lived until 1884 or 1885, then moved to Colorado. Never lived in NH, until 2 weeks ago. My father and mother are both dead. [Filed 1 Feb 1897; examined and adjudged 19 Feb 1897]

1292. Rodolphus Clement, Keene, 79 years old. Married Fidelia Witherel in 1838. She died in 1894. We have one daughter, 50 years old, now living in Westfield, VT. We were living there until 1880, and continued to live there until 1887; came to Walpole where we lived until Nov 1893; came to

Cheshire County Paupers
1885-1900

Keene. My wife died in Keene. I am now getting a pension of $17 per month. [Filed 1 Feb 1897; examined and adjudged 19 Feb 1897]

1293. Arthur Wood, born in Hopkinton, MA in 1866. Lived there 22 years. Came to NH about the middle of Jan 1897. Called for aid on account of sickness. [Filed 19 Feb 1897; examined and adjudged 19 Feb 1897]

[435] 1294. Charles Guinap, Hinsdale, 48 years old, born in York state. In 1888, moved from there to Hinsdale, where I have since lived. I am married; wife is 48 years old; children, viz: George Rowland, age 14, son of my wife; Emma, 11, also daughter of my wife; Kate Guinap, age 9; John, about 5; Lydia, 2; and Joseph, 1 year old. The Rowland children have no settlement anywhere that I know of. I have been a soldier in 96th NY Cavalry. [Filed 3 Mar 1897; examined and adjudged 5 Mar 1897]

1295. Seth Pratt, born in Shutesbury, MA, now of Winchester, 55 years old. Have been married, but have parted. She lives in MA. Have 6 children, all of age but 2: Archie F., age 12, and Laura Pratt, age 14. I lived in Shutesbury all my life until I came to Winchester about 8 years ago. Since then I lived in Richmond about 2 years; in Troy about 6 months; the remainder of the time in Winchester. I was a soldier in the late war, Co. C, 27th MA Vols. I get a pension of $6 per month. [Filed 3 Mar 1897; examined and adjudged 5 Mar 1897]

1296. Alfred La Charity, Hinsdale, 41 years old, born in Canada. Lived there until I came to Hinsdale in 1891. My wife died recently. My parents live in Canada. Have 7 children, viz: Annie, age 17; Ascula, 16; Elmer, 13; Clara, 10; Oclure, 9; Rus, 3; and Albert, 2 years old. [Filed 3 Mar 1897; examined and adjudged 5 Mar 1897]

Cheshire County Paupers
1885-1900

[436] 1297. Wilbur F. Willis, Winchester, 63 years old, born in Alstead. Came to Winchester when a young man; lived there until 16 or 17 years ago. My first wife died a short time before I left Winchester. I married a second time Ellen Hale of Winchester. Have 1 girl, Flossie Annie Diantha, who is 15 years old; one boy Willard, age 8. I came to Winchester in Sep 1895. My wife is nearly blind. [Filed 1 Apr 1897; examined and adjudged 2 Apr 1897]

1298. Mary Milo, widow of John Milo, Rindge, 71 years old, born in Canada. My husband was a soldier in the late war. Before and after the war, he was connected with a gang of wood choppers. We never lived in any one town more than 2 or 3 years consecutively. [Filed 1 Apr 1897; examined and adjudged 2 Apr 1897]

1299. William N. Clegg, Chesterfield or Ellen M. Clegg, wife of William N. Clegg. We were married 3 Jul 1880. Have 2 children: Victor K., age 13, and William L., 21 months old. Lived in said Chesterfield about 3 ½ years; moved to Brighwood (*sic*), MA, lived 6 months; back to Chesterfield, lived 6 or 7 years; moved to Brattleboro, lived about 2 years; back to Chesterfield, where we have since lived. Said William Clegg is about 38 years old. I am 33 years of age. My husband is insane and should be taken care of. {note, dated May 1904: Mr. Clegg was taken with others to the Asylum at Concord. Signed "M"} [Filed 9 Jan 1897; examined and adjudged 28 Jan 1897]

[437] 1300. Louis Pike, Walpole, 45 years old, born in Russia. Have lived in the US 5 years and in Walpole 4 years. Am married; my wife's name is Sarah Pike, 40 years old. Have 5 children, as follows: Bessie, age 17; Willie, 10; Annie, 8; Morris, 4; and Joel, 2 years old. {This family, wife and four

children, were taken to the Farm and one child born after coming to the Farm.} [Filed 1 Oct 1896; examined and adjudged 12 Nov 1896]

1301. Eva B. Ellis, Marlow, 22 years old, born in Alstead. Married Henry Ellis of Gilsum. Have never been helped by any town or county, but my father Joseph Duprias has received aid from Cheshire County. I ask for aid on account of the death of my child. [Filed ___ Apr 1897; examined and adjudged 7 Apr 1897]

1302. Frank Jefts, Winchester, born in Gilsum, 41 years old. Lived in Lempster most of the time since I was 12 years old, until 4 years ago; came to Winchester in 1894. My wife Emma Jefts is 27 years old. She was David Whittemore's daughter.[197] I have 3 children, names and ages are as follows: Mabel E., age 12; Carl E., 6; and Rosa M., 1 year old. I cut my foot while chopping and on that account ask for aid. [Filed 8 Apr 1897; examined and adjudged 15 Apr 1897]

[438] 1303. Charles Pratt, Swanzey, age 60, born in Northfield, MA. Have resided in Hartford, VT most of the time from 1880 to 1892; from Nov 1892 to Nov 1893 in Winchester; since Nov 1893 in Swanzey; and have never had any help from any town before. Married; 2 minor children. Wife is native of VT. I was a soldier in the late war; served in 14th Reg't NH Vols. {Dead} [Filed 7 Apr; examined and adjudged 14 Jun 1897]

1304. Benjamin F. Capron,[198] Marlborough, 49 years old, husband of Ellen L. Capron, who was 46 years old. We have one child: Mary Edith, who is 21 years old. We never lived in NH 4 years in succession and have never been helped by any

---

[197] See #1091.
[198] See also #8, page 3.

Cheshire County Paupers 1885-1900

town in this state, but once, and that was in Fitzwilliam 13 years ago for a short time. [Filed 10 Jun 1897; examined and adjudged 30 Jun 1897]

1305. Mrs. John Lahiff, Keene. Married about 1858. I have since lived with him in Keene. Have no children less than 21 years of age. Said John is about 94 years old, owns a small place on the Swanzey road worth about $800, mortgaged for nearly as much; taxes have been abated. See tax certificate. [Filed and adjudged 4 Jun 1897]

[439] 1306. Fred C. Bishop, Swanzey, 21 years old, born in Swanzey. Lived in Swanzey with my family until I was 14 years old. Have lived in several places in MA and NH since until about 1 year ago, when I came to Swanzey. My father and mother separated about 9 years ago. Married; wife's name was Hannah Day of Leominster, MA, age 22. Have 2 children: Pearl, age 2, and Esther E., 6 months old. [Filed 30 Jun; examined and adjudged][199]

1307. Susan Amidon, Keene, 48 years old. Married to James C. Amidon. 1849. He is now 54 years old. He left me in 1889. We have 9[200] children to whit: Fred P., age 14; James G., 16; Annie K., 19; and Henry H., 20 years old. Neither ever got a divorce, have been aided for the support of myself and family. [Filed 20 May; examined and adjudged 30 Jun 1897]

1308. Alfred Sawyer, Jaffrey. I have been acquainted with Samuel C. Lakin, late of Jaffrey since 1884. He lost his life by fire 7 Mar 1897, and his possessions were destroyed with him. His wife Annie Lakin is insane and is cared for at the NH

---

[199] No year stated.
[200] Only 4 children named in affidavit. The date "1849" was probably the answer to a question asked about her date of birth, since she could not have married James in that year.

Cheshire County Paupers
1885-1900

Asylum for Insane. The last quarter's board was paid by the town of Jaffrey. [Filed 17 Apr 1897; examined and adjudged 4 Jun 1897]

[440] 1309. Mary Holton, Winchester, born in MA, 41 years old. Have lived in Winchester 9 years, with my sister. Have received my support from them through their kindness. Have no property or money; never was married; am blind and unable to work. [Filed 20 Ape 1897; examined and adjudged 4 Jun 1897]

1310. Sarah Ballou, Richmond, 74 years old, born in Troy. Twice married, but both husbands are dead. Have had 8 children, but none of them are living. Have had no property for the last 10 years. {Dead} [Filed 23 Apr; examined and adjudged 4 Jun 1897]

1311. Sarah Sharkey, Lebanon, wife of Peter Sharkey, who is about 35 years old. Came to NH to live in 5 May 1895; lived there until 1 Jun 1896, when came to this town. We have 6 children, oldest boy, age 14; girl, 12; boy, 10; boy, 7; girl, 3; boy, 2 months old. Never have been helped before. [Filed 19 Feb 1897; examined and adjudged 19 Feb 1897]

[441] 1312. Lizzie and Ida Pierce, Keene. I, George E. Poole, am acquainted with Lizzie and Ida Pierce, sisters. Their father's name was George Pierce; they are both dead.[201] Said Lizzie, I think is about 46; Ida, about 5 years younger. Lizzie must have been cared for by the city of Keene for the last 20 years or more at the NH Asylum and city must have taken care of Ida Pierce for the last 5 years certainly. {Lizzie died at Farm.} [Filed 20 May 1897; examined and adjudged 4 Jun 1897]

---

[201] Assuming the "they" refers to both parents.

Cheshire County Paupers
1885-1900

1313. Fred H. Peckins, Troy, born in Ashburnham, 37 years old. My wife was Sarah J. Davis, born in Ashburnham, MA, 28 years old. Never lived (*sic*) until May 1897 when I came to Troy, having always lived in MA. [Filed 20 May 1897; examined and adjudged 4 Jun 1897]

1314. William H. Stone, Fitzwilliam, born in F, 48 years old. Married; wife's name is Rose A. Stone. Children: Hattie M., age 3; Addie, 2; and Henry, age 8 months. Since 1880 I have lived in Gardner, 2 ½ years; Troy, 10 years; and Fitzwilliam, 4 ½ years. [Filed 5 Apr; examined and adjudged 4 Jun 1897]

[442] 1315. Joseph Desalires, Troy, French, born in Canada, 29 years old. Married; wife's name Emma Chicoine, age 27. Since 1887 I have not had an equitable interest in $150 of real estate or $250 of personal property. Have not paid poll anywhere in this state. Names and ages of minor children are as follows: Paul, age 2, and infant, born 10 May 1897. [Filed 21 May; examined and adjudged 4 Jun 1897]

1316. Louis Fortier, Swanzey, French, born in Canada, age 28. Came to the States 18 years ago; went first to live in Ashuelot, where I lived 10 or 11 years; lived in Marlborough, about 1 year; moved to MA, lived 4 years; moved to Bridgeport, CT, stayed 2 years; came to Swanzey about 1 year ago, last fall. [Filed 30 May; examined and adjudged 30 Jun 1897]

1317. Avery Bryant,[202] Marlborough, 67 years old, born in West Springfield, MA. Lived in Swanzey since 1868 to 1891. Have lived in Marlborough since 1891. Married Sarah A. Morey. Never had any children. Was a soldier in MA regiment. {Avery and wife both dead} [Filed 30 Jan 1897; examined and adjudged 30 Jun 1897]

---

[202] See also #797, page 268.

Cheshire County Paupers
1885-1900

[443] 1318. Mary Donovan,[203] Keene, 49 years old. My husband is dead. Have minor children: James, age 15; Timothy, 16 ½; Jeremiah, 18; Cornelius, age 20. I have lived in ___ ever since I was married. For the last 10 years, have been helped by the city of Keene. [Filed 20 May; examined and adjudged 30 Jun 1897]

1319. Hosea G. Pickett, Winchester, born in Winchester. Have lived there all my life, age 73. My wife died 2 years ago. I have no children under age. I have received aid from the town every year since 1890. I owned a small place in Winchester that I deeded to said town for my support 3 years ago. The place was sold at auction for $206. I was a musician in the late Civil War; was a member of the 2nd NH Regiment Brass Band. I receive a pension of $6 a month. [Filed 25 Apr; examined and adjudged 4 Jun 1897]

1320. Sarah J. Winham, Marlow, and Waldo H. Perkins. I am the mother of Ellen J. Winham, who was born Dec 1867. In 1877 she went to Rufus Dodge's in Marlow to live where she removed about 5 years; then worked at various places up to the present time. Since about 1 Jul 1896, she has not been able to work and support herself. I, Waldo H. Perkins, am the legal guardian of Ellen J. Winham, who is confined in the NH Asylum at Concord. Her means of support are all gone. She has no friends or relatives or anyone to care for her. [Filed 6 Aug; examined and adjudged 6 Aug 1897]

[444] 1321. George W. Edwards, Winchester, born in England, 61 years old. Came to America 4 years ago. Have no family. Came to Winchester 25 Aug 1897. Never lived in this state before. Have no property of any kind. [Filed 1 Sep; 1897; examined and adjudged 5 Sep 1897]

---

[203] See also #663, page 223.

Cheshire County Paupers
1885-1900

1322. James A. Blanchard, Hinsdale, am the grandfather of Pauline Crechon, age 11, and Clara Crechon, 9. The said children's mother is dead, Annie M. (Blanchard) Crechon; William Crechon, their father's residence is unknown, having left Hinsdale in 1890. {Spring of 1902: The Crechon children became self-supporting.} [Filed 8 Apr 1897; examined and adjudged 3 Sep 1897]

1323. Peter Liscord, 37 years old, Keene. My first wife died some 6 years ago; my second wife's name Caroline Hould, age 18. Have 2 children: Henry, about 3 years old, and Minnie, about 3 months old. My father John Liscord is living in Keene. My wife's father and mother are living in Canada. Moved to Keene about 2 years ago. [Filed 24 Jul; examined and adjudged 3 Sep 1897]

[445] 1324. Mary Jane Spofford, Keene, 59 years old. Married William Spofford in 1882. He died 28 Jan, last, age 62. Have no children. Lived in Stoddard until about 12 years ago, when we moved to Keene and have since lived in Keene. [Filed 16 Jul; examined and adjudged 17 Sep 1897]

1325. Kate Enwright, Troy, 30 years old. My husband was Thomas Enwright. He died in Troy 1894. Was married in 1885 and have resided in Troy ever since. Have four children as follows: Even, age 10; Nellie, 7; Lizzie, 5; and Marion, 3 years old. {Kate dead} [Filed 9 Apr 1897; examined and adjudged 3 Sep 1897]

1326. Jestin P. Smith, by Arthur J. Holden, Keene. The said Smith died at my house 28 Mar 1897. He was about 35 years of age. To the best of my knowledge his father and mother are both dead. The said Smith came to Keene sometime in Nov last, and do not know as he ever lived in NH before, and had no property. [Filed 14 Apr; examined and adjudged 3 Sep 1897]

Cheshire County Paupers
1885-1900

[446] 1327. John Shackett, Keene, 54 years old. Married to Nancy LaCharity about 7 years ago; 56 years old. No children. Came to Keene in 1894; never lived in NH before, except 1 year in Littleton and other places for a few months at a time. Never aided before. [Filed 15 Apr; examined, adjudged 3 Sep 1897]

1328. George M. Kingsley and family,[204] Fitzwilliam. Came to this town with his wife and several children about 1882 from the state of NY, where I think he was born. Have been helped by Fitzwilliam ever since his wife died on 29 Nov 1893. Minor children as follows: Etha Kingsley, age 19, idiotic; Ida, age 17, has fits; Ella, age 15, now at Providence, RI with her aunt; Mabel, 14; and Herber, 12 years old. [Filed 17 Apr; examined and adjudged 6 Nov 1897]

1329. Bessie Deming, Chesterfield, wife of Beecher Deming of Jay, NY. I was born in Swanzey, am the daughter of Rufus and Susan Field. Married 12 Apr last and lived with him about 2 months. I am 17 years of age and have no means of support. My father has been helped by Cheshire County. [Filed 6 Nov; examined and adjudged 6 Nov 1897]

[447] 1330. Abigail Nash, Alstead by Marry A. Smith. Was born in Winchester Mar 1810. Was married; her husband died in 1867. They moved to Alstead previous to 1850 where they have always lived. Has not owned any property of any amount since 1887. [Filed 30 Jun; examined and adjudged 1 Jul 1897]

1331. Joseph Duplicy, Richmond, French, age 21, b. Canada. Came from Canada in 1871. Have since lived Hinsdale, Winchester and other places. Came to Richmond in Aug 1896. My father Joseph Duplicy came to Richmond 1895. Married;

---

[204] See also #222, page 75.

Cheshire County Paupers
1885-1900

wife's name was Lula D. Webster; was married Jan 1896. [Filed 14 Jun; examined and adjudged 17 Sep 1897]

1332. Andrew J. Curtis, Winchester, born in Winchester, 52 years old. Have always lived in Winchester. Married 17 years ago to Clara Wilson, daughter of George W. Scott. Have 5 children as follows: Harry, age 16; Rhuel A., 13; George W., 10; Leon, 8; girl baby, about 3 months old. Was a soldier of the late war from MA. Am poor and on account of health. [Filed 16 Apr; examined and adjudged 3 Sep 1897]

[448] 1333[205].

1334. Otis Safford, Chesterfield, born in Chesterfield, 75 years old. Never paid a tax in any other town. I have no property. My wife owns a small place. I have been sick for the past 8 years and unable to perform any labor. Have been helped more or less each year by said town of Chesterfield. I was a soldier in the late war, 2d NH Infantry and 1st NH Cavalry, in all 4 years. I receive a pension of $12 a month. [Filed 20 Aug; examined and adjudged 3 Sep 1897]

1335. William Powers, Winchester, born in MA, 38 years old. I never paid a poll tax in NH 7 years in succession on any property to gain a settlement. I was never married. [Filed 22 Oct; examined and adjudged 22 Oct 1897]

1336. Ellen Doody, Keene, 55 years old. Was married to Michael Doody in 1861. We were both born in Ireland. We have one child living; he is 26 years old. Since my husband died, have made my home in Keene. Have not received any aid for the last 20 years until now. [Filed 15 Oct; examined and adjudged 29 Oct 1897]

---

[205] This entry appears after #1339 on original page 450.

Cheshire County Paupers
1885-1900

[449] 1337. Hazel Gates by her grandmother Sarah J. Huntley. Am the grandmother of Hazel Gates. Said Hazel's mother Mira L. Huntley is dead and left no property or anyone to care for her child. Sidney C. Gates is the father of said Hazel; refused to provide for his wife and child, therefore I have to care for it. I am 72 years old and can hardly care for myself and ask for aid to care for the child. [Filed and examined 25 Oct 1897]

1338. Andrew Nash, Keene, 61 years old. I was married in Jul 1863 and my wife procured a divorce from me in 1896. I have 2 children, not of age that live with her, given to her custody by the courts. Since 1897 I have lived in Keene and for 2 years owned a house lot in Keene for which I paid $150. I now ask for aid on account of a broken arm. [Filed 1 Oct; examined and adjudged 1 Oct 1897]

1339. Henry Mansell, Winchester, born in England, 50 years old. Came to the States about 20 years ago. I first came to NH to live Oct 1897. Married 6 years ago; my wife came from Sharon, NH. Her father and mother are both dead. Have never been taxed in NH. [Filed, examined and adjudged 18 Oct 1897]

[450] 1333. Thomas Dame, Richmond, 35 years old, born in Boston. Have been in Richmond about 3 months. Married to Almira Gibbs of Belchertown, MA in 1883. Always lived in MA until I came to Richmond. Have 4 children: Marry L., age 10; Charles A., 6; Viola M., 2 ½ ; and George R., 6 months old. Never received aid from any town before now. [Filed 16 Apr; examined and adjudged 3 Sep 1897]

1340. Mary Flynn, Walpole, Irish, wife of John Flynn of Walpole. Have no knowledge of the John Flynn abode at the present time. Was born in Warner, NH, 37 years old. Have resided in Walpole since 1893. Before that date, have always lived in VT. Have 5 children: John, age 12; Agnes, 9; Jerry, 5; Lizzie, 3; and Hugh, 10 months old. Have no means of support. [Filed 1 Oct; examined and adjudged 1 Oct 1897]

1341. Ellen Sullivan, Walpole, wife of Joseph Sullivan, Walpole. My husband has left home and his present abode is unknown to me. I was born in Ireland, about 31 years old. Lived in Walpole since 1892, lived there until May 1896; moved to Boston, stayed until Jun 1896; removed to North Walpole. I have 4 children, as follows: Kate, age 6; Marry, 4; John, 3; and Nellie, age 9 months. [Filed, examined and adjudged 1 Oct 1897]

[451] 1342. Henry Johnson, Keene, 62 years old. My wife has been dead 30 years. I was born in Denmark; came to this country in 1867. Came to Keene about 11 years ago; made my home ever since. Never owned any real estate in this country. At one time, I had $300 in the savings bank for a few months, less than a year. [Filed 16 Jul; examined and adjudged 3 Sep 1897]

1343. Thomas Nonehan, Keene for Margaret Mendam; died 15 Mar 1897. My father's name was William Mendam; he died in Stoddard about 6 years ago. My father came to Keene about 1884, where they have since lived. My father owned a small place on Easton Avenue, about 3 years. He never owned any other real estate to my knowledge. [Filed 14 Apr 1897; examined and adjudged 3 Sep 1897]

1344. Ezra D. Howard, Winchester, born in Canada East, 66 years old. I was married in 1865 to Sarah Jane Plummer of Winchester. I have 2 children, both are married. Have been aided by the town of Winchester. Have lived in Winchester for the past 30 years. Have not paid a poll tax 7 years in succession. My wife owns the place where we live. [Filed 15 Apr 1897; examined and adjudged 3 Sep 1897]

[452] 1345. Ruth Craig for Florence G. Page. The father of Florence G. Page is about 40 years old and the mother about 38. The father left the family in Oct 1889 and has not been heard from since. The mother Ida L. Page, is in Hartford, CT. She left about the time the father did, leaving the said Florence with me. I have taken care of her all the time since. The mother furnishes some clothes for her. [Filed 15 Apr; examined and adjudged 3 Sep 1897]

1346. Charles E. Pratt, Harrisville, born in Alstead, 34 years old. Lived in Alstead and Walpole about 20 years, after which I lived in various places. Have lived in Harrisville 3 years; Marlborough 2 years; back to Harrisville, lived 2 years; to Keene, lived there until the spring of 1897. His father died in Alstead 20 years ago and left no property. His mother died at the hospital in Keene in 1894. He has no wife. [Filed 13 Jul; examined and adjudged 3 Sep 1897]

1347. Harrison M. Kendall, Jaffrey, born in Jaffrey, 35 years old. Lived in Sharon and paid poll tax there from 1882 to 1891; moved to Jaffrey, where I have since lived. Have never owned any real estate or other taxable property. In 1889 I married Mary L. Flagg, age 24. Have 2 children, names and ages: Herbert M., 5 years, and Edgar F., 2 years old. Wife's father's name was William Flagg, now living in Jaffrey. [Filed, examined and adjudged 17 Sep 1897]

[453] 1350. George A. Kingman, Westmoreland, born in Claremont, NH, 63 years old. Since 1880 lived in Walpole; 1886 to 1889 in Keene; 1 ½ years in Surry; in Walpole until spring of 1896; since then in Westmoreland. Have never

*Cheshire County Paupers
1885-1900*

applied for aid before. [Filed 7 Apr; examined and adjudged 17 Sep 1897]

1354. Charles Sheridan, Walpole, born in Ireland, 60 years old. Lived in the States 30 years; in Walpole for 3 months. Married; his wife Mary is 34 years old. Have one child Charles, age 3. [Filed 13 Jun; examined and adjudged 30 Jun 1897]

1352. Gardiner Fisher, Keene, by S. S. Wyman. Gardiner L. Fisher, son of Lucius Fisher is living at my house and has lived there for about 5 years. He is 9 years old. His father is dead, leaving 7 children. They are all supported by relatives, except this one. [Filed 20 May; examined and adjudged 3 Sep 1897]

[454] 1353. Celia Nash, Marlborough, born in Alstead, 30 years old. Married George L. Nash, 1890; lived 4 years in Alstead; at Richmond about 1 year; and in Marlow about 2 years. Have 4 children: Mary E., age 11; Flossy, 9; Merty C., 6; and George H., 3 years old. My husband is in parts to me unknown. [Filed 7 Sep; examined and adjudged 17 Sep 1897]

1354. Nellie S. Stebbins, Jaffrey, 33 years old, born in Jaffrey. Never lived in any other town. I never owned any real estate. My mother died in 1883; my father died in 1894, and was aided by Cheshire County. His name was Josiah Stebbins.[206] [Filed 18 Dec; examined and adjudged 17 Dec 1897]

1355. Joseph H. Blanchard, Winchester, born in VT, 66 years old. {Died in Winchester 1898.} [Filed 10 Dec; examined and adjudged 10 Dec 1897]

[455] 1356. Mary Lapoint, Fitzwilliam. I, William H. Stone, say that Mary Lapoint, my wife's mother, was born in Canada,

---

[206] See also #729, #872, and #900.

is 81 years old, is at my house sick and poor, and unable to care for herself or to be moved from here. [Filed 6 Nov 1897; examined and adjudged 1 Apr 1898]

1357. Ed W. Spaulding, Marlow, born in Maine, 38 years old. Continued to live in Maine until 1896, when we moved to Marlow. Married; my wife's name was Ida B. Chipman of Lewiston, ME. Have no children. [Filed 25 Dec 1897; examined and adjudged 1 Apr 1898]

1358. George and Hattie M. Bennett, Westmoreland. Charles J. Albee now at our home is of unsound mind and incapable of making affidavit. Was born in Keene, is now 46 years old. To our certain knowledge, he has never resided in this state and he is without means of support. [Filed 6 Nov 1897; examined and adjudged 4 Mar 1898]

[456] 1359. Mrs. Estey, Keene, born in Mount Holly, VT, age 67. I do not possess any real estate to the value of $150, nor personal to the value of $250. My husband never owned any real estate. [Filed 17 Dec 1897; examined and adjudged 21 Jan 1898]

1360. William Bennett, Swanzey, 38 years old, born in CT. Never lived in this state until 1892. Married Hattie Larabee in Keene in '92 or '93. Have no settlement in this state. I have 5 children: William, age 13; Hattie, 11; Henry, 7; Freddie, 5; and Minnie Etta, 2 years old. [Filed 21 Jan 1898; examined and adjudged 21 Jan 1898]

1361. E. B. Wood, born in Lynn, MA in 1852. Lived there until 5 Nov 1896, when I came to Keene, where I have lived since. [Filed 21 Jan 1898; examined and adjudged 21 Jan 1898]

Cheshire County Paupers
1885-1900

[457] 1362. Willis Cunningham, Marlow, 36 years old. For the last 12 years have lived in Cheshire County, but in no town long enough to gain a residence. Am sick and unable to support myself and my mother. My mother has been assisted by Cheshire County. [Filed 20 Feb 1898; examined and adjudged 4 Mar 1898]

1363. John F. Martin, Walpole, born in Ireland or Canada, 57 years old. Never lived in NH until Oct 1895. I moved to Langdon, where I lived until Mar 1896; moved to Walpole and have lived there since. Have a wife and 4 children: Charlot H., age 8; George W., 6; Henry V., 4; and Margaret W., 1 year old. Have no property or means of support. [Filed 6 Nov 1897; examined and adjudged 4 Mar 1898]

1364. Lewis M. Allen, Hinsdale, 24 years old, born in VT. Always lived there until Oct 1894; moved to MA; moved to NH, 1895. Have not gained a residence anywhere for the last 10 years. [Filed 26 Feb 1898; examined and adjudged 4 Mar 1898]

[458] 1365. Charles S. Whitcomb, Hinsdale, 46 years old last Mar, born in Swanzey. Ten years ago was living in Swanzey and continued to live there until Apr 1893; went to MA, where I lived until Dec last; came to Hinsdale, where I have since been. Have not owned personal property or real estate to gain a residence. Have 3 children, under age 21: Ada C., 15 years; Minnie R., 11; and Sylvia S. [Filed 10 Feb 1898; examined and adjudged 4 Mar 1898]

1366. Albert Haskell, Jaffrey, 32 years old. Lived in Jaffrey less than 2 years. Have never lived in any town more than 2 years in succession, since I was 21 years old. Married; wife's name is Esther, age 32. 2 children: Earl, age 3, and Isabelle,

Cheshire County Paupers
1885-1900

1 ½ years old. [Filed 28 Feb 1898; examined and adjudged 4 Mar 1898]

1367. George H. Fairbanks, Swanzey, 65 years old, born in MA. Resided in Richmond from 1893 to 1895; from 1895 to the present time, in the town of Swanzey. Never received any aid before. [Filed 31 Dec 1897; examined and adjudged 1 Apr 1898]

[459] 1368. William Cook, Keene, 33 years old. Married to Nettie Chase in 1885. We have children as follows: Charlie C., age 10; Harry, 5; and Ralph, age 3. My wife is 28 years old. My father is dead; my mother is living in East Westmoreland. I was born in Westmoreland, lived until 1885; moved to Bellows Falls, where I lived until 1894; Westmoreland, where I lived a little more than 1 year; came to Keene in 1896. Have never owned any real estate. [Filed 28 Oct 1897; examined and adjudged 1 Apr 1898]

1369. Francis H. Buffum, Winchester, 53 years old, born in Winchester. Married; my wife was from Hartford, CT. Was a soldier in the late war. The names and ages of my children are as follows: Alice M., 19 years old; Bertha S., 19; Francis H., 18; Jessie H., 15; Warren H., 13; Edward H., 8; Margaret E., 6; Richard H., 4; and Marion, 6 months old. [Filed 6 Nov 1897; examined and adjudged 1 Apr 1898]

1370. Delia M. Larrow,[207] born in ___, 7 Dec 1873; lived there until I was 13 years old; came to NH last Apr. Have no property and am sick. [Filed 7 Jan 1989; examined and adjudged 21 Jan 1898]

---

[207] In the 1880 census for Highgate, VT (Franklin Co.), there was a Dilia M. Larrow, age 7, living with her parents, Medor and Lucy.

Cheshire County Paupers
1885-1900

[460] 1371. Charles Bates, born in Keene, 18 years old. My father lives in Merrimac, MA. He has not lived in NH for the last 10 years. I have been sick and am obliged to ask for aid. [Filed 1 Feb 1898; examined and adjudged 1 Apr 1898]

1372. Mary Bourler, Walpole, born in Ireland, about 60 years old. Lived in Ireland until Apr 1892 when she came to this country, town of Walpole. Has no means of support. A grandchild lives with me, named Mary Bourler. [Filed 19 Nov 1897; examined and adjudged 1 Apr 1898]

1373. Alexander Guyou, Westmoreland, born in France, 56 years old. Came to Keene in 1894. Never lived in NH before. Was a veteran of Co. A., 5th NH Vols. [Filed 5 Jan 1898; examined and adjudged 21 Jan 1898]

[461] 1374. Rosa B. Howe, Chesterfield, 16 years old, daughter of Fred Howe, now living in Guilford, VT. My mother is dead. My father has not gained any residence in any town in this state for the last 10 years. [Filed 9 Mar 1898; examined and adjudged 1 Apr 1898]

1375. Harry Iredale. I am a brother of Alice Iredale, who is 18 years old. Her father Joseph Iredale was born in England. Came to Swanzey to live about 14 years ago, where he lived until he died in 1895. My mother died in Swanzey 11 years ago. My father never owned an equitable interest of $150 or $250 worth of personal property. {Died at Almshouse. Alice died at Almshouse, Dec 1902} [Filed 20 Mar 1898; examined and adjudged 1 Apr 1898]

Cheshire County Paupers
1885-1900

1376. Ellen Burroud,[208] Walpole, born in Ireland, 45 years old. Lived in NH since Oct '97. Names and ages of my children are as follows: Mary, age 15; Edward, 14; and Michael, 12 years old. [Filed 15 Feb 1898; examined and adjudged 4 Mar 1898]

[462] 1377. Stella H. Bartlett, Chesterfield, born in Colerain, MA, 25 years old. Married to Julius Bartlett. Have one child Lillian Streeter, by a former husband. My father was a soldier in the late war and draws $8 a month. [Filed 30 Mar 1898; examined and adjudged 1 Apr 1898]

1378. James A. Stockwell, Keene, 67 years old. Came to Keene, 18 Nov 1897. Not able to earn my own support on account of lameness. {Died at Farm} [Filed 1 Feb 1898; examined and adjudged 1 Apr 1898]

1379. James Martin, Jaffrey, English, born in England, 82 years old. About 1882, he married Mary A. Howard. Married the second time in 1895 to Ellen Gerlin, whereabouts unknown. [Filed 17 Dec 1897; examined and adjudged 7 Apr 1898]

[463] 1380. Nettie L. Crown, Keene, wife of Orman Crown. Was married in 1889; my husband is 42 years old; I am 30. Children: Andrew, age 4, and Adaline, 2 years old. My father is now living in East Swanzey. Has no property; my mother is dead. Since our marriage we have lived in Keene most of the time. Never received aid from any city or town before. Am obliged to call for help on account of my husband serving sentence of court. [Filed 1 Oct 1897; examined and adjudged 6 Apr 1898]

---

[208] In the 1910 census for Walpole, there is a Michael Brummond, age 25 living with Edward Brummond, age 62. Also living there are Edward, age 21 and Mary, age 27, all born in VT. Their last name may be "Beaumond."

Cheshire County Paupers
1885-1900

1381. Eli W. Slack, Marlow, born in VT, about 62 years old. Lived there until I was 18. Soldier in the late war, 17th VT Vols. Came to NH about 1882; to Marlow in 1883, where I have since lived. Have never married. Pension of $12 a month. [Filed 25 Dec 1897; examined and adjudged 1 Apr 1898]

1382. William F. Norcross, Swanzcy, born in Hinsdalc, 8 Jan 1878. Father died about 15 years ago. No permanent home since. Mother has been dead about 5 years. Married in 1896. Have a young child, about 1 week old. Have been sick myself and not able to work, and am obliged to ask for help. [Filed 20 Feb 1898; examined and adjudged 1 Apr 1898]

[464] 1383. Josephine Myah, Marlborough, born in Canada, 75 years old. My first husband John Tellia died about 10 years ago. Then I married Peter Myah of Westboro, MA; lived with him about 2 years until he died. After my late husband died in 1892, I returned to Marlborough, where I have since lived. Have been aided for the past 2 years by the town of M. [Filed 28 Feb 1898; examined and adjudged 8 Apr 1898]

1384. Nelson B. Norcross,[209] Harrisville, born in Dummerston, VT, 25 Mar 1829. Came to Harrisville in 1887. Have lived here ever since. Never received aid from this or any other town before. [Filed 8 Apr 1898; examined and adjudged 8 Apr 1898]

1385. Nancy A. Rice, Keene, 66 years old. Unmarried. Have lived for the last 26 years (*sic*). Am poor and unable to care for myself. Am obliged to call on city of Keene for aid. [Filed 14 Apr 1898; examined and adjudged 14 Apr 1898]

[465] 1386. Louis Tremley, Marlborough, French, born in Canada, 27 years old. Have lived in Marlborough for the last

---

[209] See also #968, page 325.

Cheshire County Paupers
1885-1900

10 years, except 1 year. Married; my wife's name is Julia. Have 4 children: Eunice, age 8; Clinnie, 6; Fred, 4; and Dora, age 2. Have never at any one time owned $150 worth of real estate or $250 of personal property. Have never paid poll tax 7 years in succession. My father and mother have lived in Marlborough the past 10 years, but never owned any property. [Filed 3 Jun 1898; examined and adjudged 3 Jun 1898]

1387. Jennie C. Davis, Harrisville, 30 years old. Never lived in NH until Sep 1897. Married 6 years ago to Charles Davis, who was killed in NY state last Sep. He never lived in NH. My parents are both dead. [Filed 6 May 1898; examined and adjudged 6 May 1898]

1388. Fannie Fish, Keene, 37 years old, unmarried. I moved to Keene from Harrisville in 1890. Have ever since lived in said Keene. My father died in Harrisville about 10 years ago; my mother is living in Keene. We have no property. [Filed 6 Apr 1898; examined and adjudged 7 Apr 1898]

[466] 1389. Jewett J. Hill, Swanzey, born in Swanzey, 64 years old. My home has always been in Swanzey. Was never married. I own no real estate, have not paid any taxes since 1888, only as follows.[210] [Filed 8 Apr 1898; examined and adjudged 15 Apr 1898]

1390. Eugene Pratt, Winchester, born in MA, 27 years old. Came to Winchester about 13 years ago. My father's name is Seth Pratt.[211] I have been married about 2 years. My wife was born in CT, never lived in NH previous to her marriage. [Filed 17 Jun 1898; examined and adjudged 17 Jun 1898]

---

[210] No additional information given after this.
[211] See also #1295, page 435.

Cheshire County Paupers
1885-1900

1391. Louis Pallady, Marlborough, born in Canada, 69 years old, a widow.[212] My husband Joseph Pallady died in Burlington, VT 10 years ago. Have lived in said Marlborough for 17 years. Never owned any real estate. [Filed 17 Jun 1898; examined and adjudged 17 Jun 1898]

[467] 1392. Louis Trombley, Marlborough, 24 years old, born in Canada. Came to Marlborough in 1887. Married; my wife's name Dora Bushey. Have 2 children: Willie, age 2,[213] and Mary Elsie, 5 weeks old. My wife's parents live in Marlborough, but possess no property. [Filed 1 Dec 1897; examined and adjudged 17 Jun 1898]

1393. Fred Lincoln, born in Chesterfield, about 55 years old. Have not lived in NH for the last 24 years, until about 6 weeks ago. Have been married but have lived with my wife for 6 or 7 years and do not know where she is at the present time. Have paid no taxes in any place for the last 10 years. [Filed 23 Jun; examined and adjudged 30 Jun 1898]

1394. Ervin Wesley, Winchester, born in Northampton, MA, 24 years old. I came from VT about 2 months ago. Have a wife and one child, 2 years old. Neither my or my wife's parents ever lived in NH. [Filed 8 Dec 1898; examined and adjudged 30 Dec 1898]

[468] 1395. Nellie F. Freeman, Winchester, niece of Martin D. Bryant. Married and has 2 children, is 32 years old. Her husband is in Greenfield, or was, the last she knew of him. Her husband has never lived in NH nor Mrs. Freeman until this fall. [Filed 23 Dec 1898; examined and adjudged 30 Dec 1898]

---

[212] Transcribed as written in original. Probably this is Louise Palladay.
[213] His birth shown in 1895 *Marlboro Town Report*, on 23 Sep 1895.

Cheshire County Paupers
1885-1900

1396. Carrie E. Towle, Walpole, born in Walpole, 23 years old. Married in 1892 at New Haven, CT. My parents moved from Walpole when I was an infant. Have one child, Nettie F. Towle, age 5. [Filed 15 Dec 1898; examined and adjudged 30 Dec 1898]

1397. Julia Young, Fitzwilliam, 35 years old, born in MA. My husband is Harry Young, present residence is unknown to me. I have 5 children, as follows: Hattie M., age 9; Nellie M., 6; Carrie A., 4; Allice F., 3; and Willie F., age 1 ½. [Filed 16 Sep 1898; examined and adjudged 1 Oct 1898]

[469] 1398. Alonza Marteno, Hinsdale, French, born in Canada, 24 years old. Came to the States in 1891 at said Hinsdale. Have never lived anywhere beside Hinsdale. Have 3 children: Flora, age 3; Annie, 2; and Arthur, 1 year old. Was helped when we lived in Ashuelot by the county. [Filed 29 Sep 1898; examined and adjudged 1 Oct 1898]

1399. Linnie Scribner, born in Marlow in 1882. Lived there until I was 2 years old. Call for help on account of an injury to one of my legs. [Filed 7 Oct 1898; examined and adjudged 1 Oct 1898]

1400. Charles E. Keyes, Troy, born in Keene, 49 years old. My wife Louisa A., was born in England, 38 years old. Have lived in Troy about 4 years. Have 2 minor children: Charles Edward, age 15, and George Harvey, age 9. [Filed 5 Sep 1898; examined and adjudged 1 Oct 1898]

[470] 1401. Thomas Ryan, Keene, born in Keene, 31 years old. Was at County Farm when a boy for a few months. Came to Keene 7 years ago. Never asked for aid before. [Filed 31 Dec 1898; examined and adjudged 24 Mar 1899]

Cheshire County Paupers
1885-1900

1402. Merritt H. Shaw,[214] Winchester, born in Hebron, NY. Came to Winchester last Jul. Never lived in NH before. Married; have 2 children: ages 3 years and 8 months. [Filed 15 Nov 1898; examined and adjudged 15 Nov 1898]

1403. Germaine Martineau, Hinsdale, 31 years old, born in Canada. For the last 10 years have lived in Ashuelot and Swanzey. Came to Hinsdale in 1897. Neither myself or any member of my family have ever been aided before. Have 2 children: Lydia, age 2, and Philip, 1 year old. [Filed 10 Nov 1898; examined and adjudged 24 Mar 1899]

[471] 1404. George F. Cummings, Keene, born in Jamaica, VT, 35 years old. Continued to live in VT and MA until Apr 1897. Have lived in Keene since. [Filed 20 Dec 1898; examined and adjudged 24 Mar 1899]

1405. Mary E. Scribner, Winchester by Julia E. Thompson. Mrs. Scribner died 2 years ago, leaving a baby 2 hours old. I have taken care of the baby since it was 6 months old. The father Gilman T. Scribner agreed to pay me but has failed to do so, and says he's not able to pay. I must apply to the town of Winchester for help. I have known Scribner for some time. He has never lived in any one town more than 2 years at one time. [Filed 21 Oct 1898; examined and adjudged 27 Feb 1899]

1406. Julius Lawrien, Marlborough, born in Finland, age 33, single. I first came to M in 1894. Not owned any property in US. [Filed 4 Nov 1898; examined and adjudged 21 Feb 1899]

[472] 1407. Parker Hart, Nelson, 73 years old, born in Antrim, this state. Have always lived in Nelson. I served in late war 3 years, in the 9th NH Vols., Co. I. My wife's name is Elizabeth.

---

[214] See also #957, page 322.

Cheshire County Paupers
1885-1900

We are in destitute circumstances and am obliged to ask for aid. {Dead} [Filed 1 Oct 1898; examined and adjudged 1 Oct 1898]

1408. Caroline Jane Brown, Keene, wife of William Brown, 57 years old. Have 2 children, ages 7 and 12. Moved from Alstead to Keene in 1898. My husband was injured in the woods and is now at the Elliott City Hospital. We are obliged to call for assistance. [Filed 30 May 1898; examined and adjudged 1 Oct 1898]

1409. Victor Johnson, Keene, 27 years old. Married Amanda Johnson of Keene. Have lived in said Keene 8 years, having both come from Sweden, 9 and 10 years ago. We have 4 children. [Filed 30 May 1898; examined and adjudged 1 Oct 1898]

[473] 1410. Bell Sweeney, Nelson, born in MA, 17 years old. I came to NH, town of Stoddard in 1884, with my father; lived there until Jul 1896; came to Nelson. My father has no residence in NH. I expect to be confined in Apr and obliged to ask for aid. [Filed 20 Jan 1899; examined and adjudged 27 Feb 1899]

1411. William Morris, Keene, born in Poland, 33 years old. Lived in Poland until I came to this country last Apr, where I have since lived. [Filed 3 Jun 1898; examined and adjudged 1 Oct 1898]

1412. John Monehan, Keene, 35 years old. Always lived in Keene. Do not possess enough property to gain a residence. Tax certificate required. [Filed 3 Jan 1898; examined and adjudged 25 Mar 1899]

[474] 1413. Ernest Willett, Harrisville, born in Canada, 22 years old. Have never paid taxes in any place. Have no family,

except a wife. Have called for aid before. [Filed 3 Jun 1898; examined and adjudged 1 Oct 1898]

1414. Nelson Cataract, French, Marlborough, born in Canada, 90 years old. My wife is dead. Have lived in the States about 25 years. {Died at Almshouse} [Filed 20 May 1898; examined and adjudged 1 Oct 1898]

1415. Moses Bushier, Troy, French, born in Canada, 43 years old. Married; my Sophia is 35. Came to Troy in 1891. [Filed 18 Oct 1898; examined and adjudged 1 Oct 1898[215]]

[475] 1416. Marshall W. Bartlett, Swanzey, born in Chesterfield, 36 years old. Married; my wife's name Florence. She came from NY. Have 2 children: Libbie May, age 7, and Raymond A., 5 years old. I have never before applied for aid. [Filed 1 Sep 1898; examined and adjudged 1 Oct 1898]

1417. Francis Taft,[216] Swanzey, born in Swanzey. Married to Lester Taft in 1875; was divorced in 1876. I have 2 minor children: Maude, age 14, and David, 12 years old. [Filed 3 Jun 1898; examined and adjudged 1 Oct 1898]

1418. Bradley Hill, Swanzey, born in Swanzey, 77 years old. Have lived in Swanzey the last 30 years. Have no family; my wife is dead. [Filed 1 Aug 1898; examined and adjudged 1 Oct 1898]

[476] 1419. Annie M. Howard, Marlow, 56 years old. Always lived in Marlow. Said Howard, my husband, is dead. [Filed 1 Sep 1898; examined and adjudged 1 Oct 1898]

---

[215] Date transcribed as written, but it is unlikely that it was filed after it was adjudged.
[216] The divorce of Etta Frances Taft and Newell Lester Taft is noted in *'Til Divorce Do Us Part* by the author, page 234.

Cheshire County Paupers
1885-1900

1420. Arthur Seguin, Hinsdale, French, born in Canada, 23 years old. Ten years ago was living in Canada; continued to live there until 1890; came to Hinsdale, a few months ago. Neither of my parents ever lived in this state. Never was aided before. [Filed 1 Sep 1898; examined and adjudged 1 Oct 1898]

1421. Oliver Boyea,[217] Keene, 36 years old. Have been married; my wife died in Mar 1898, leaving 5 small children and one infant, now being cared for by relatives of my wife. Came to live about 4 years ago. [Filed 2 May 1898; examined and adjudged 27 Feb 1899]

[477] 1422. Ruben Heath, Gilsum, born in Marlow, 40 years old. Have lived in said Gilsum since 1889. [Filed 6 May 1898; examined and adjudged 29 Feb 1899]

1423. Rosella Young, French, by Rosella Jolly. My daughter Rosella married Andrew Young in Keene 22 years ago. They went to MA to live and came back to Keene to live 2 years ago. Mr. Young has no property and is unable to bear the expense of last sickness, who died recently.[218] [Filed 19 Feb 1899; examined and adjudged 27 Feb 1899]

1424. Fannie Kennedy, Winchester, born in Lebanon, NH, 36 years old. Married Chas. E. Richards, when I was 14 years old; was divorced 1890. Was again married to Frank Ball of Marlborough, 1885; lived with ___ 4 years; was divorced from him. Last June was married to Daniel Kennedy of Winchester. [Filed 2 Dec 1898; examined and adjudged 27 Feb 1899]

---

[217] From *Keene Vital Records*, Oliver Boyea, born Malone, NY, age 45, and Nora Zetta, born Ellenburg, NY, age 35, were parents of their 5th child born 15 Feb 1898.
[218] Transcribed as written in original. It is unclear who died recently.

Cheshire County Paupers
1885-1900

[478] 1425. Thomas Rumrill, Winchester, born in Springfield, VT, 75 years old. Came to Winchester in 1863. Have paid no taxes for 5 years. [Filed 18 Jan 1899; examined and adjudged 27 Feb 1899]

1426. Everett Therren by Cyprien Filiault. Said Therren was born in Canada. Came from about 6 years ago to MA; came to said Winchester about 2 years ago. He has a wife and 6 small children: oldest, 11 years old, and the youngest, 1 year old. [Filed 13 Jan 1899; examined and adjudged 27 Feb 1899]

1427. Alfred Bayer,[219] Keene, born in Canada, 25 years old. Came about 3 months ago; a single man. Have one sister in Keene. Ask for aid on account of sickness. {Went to the farm and died there in Jan 189___.} [Filed 16 Dec 1898; examined and adjudged 27 Feb 1899]

[479] 1428. Joseph Boston, Keene, born CT, 26 years old. Lived in CT until 18 years of age with my parents. Both my parents died. I served in the US regular army 2 ½ years. Have lived in Keene about 1 year. Have a wife and two small children. Have never before been helped. [Filed 16 Dec 1898; examined and adjudged 27 Feb 1899]

1429. Charles E. Colley, Troy, born in England, 26 years old. My wife Mary Ann was born in England, 29 years old. Lived in England until 1898. Have no children. [Filed 8 Dec 1898; examined and adjudged 27 Feb 1899]

1430. John Crotty, born in Ireland, now Walpole, 33 years old. Resided in Walpole 5 years. His wife Bridget, age 36, also born

---

[219] The original appeared to be "Payer," but according to the 1899 *Westmoreland Town Report*, Alfred Bayer, age 25, died 23 Jan 1899, a county charge.

Cheshire County Paupers
1885-1900

in Ireland. Has 3 children: Mary, age 4; Catherine, 3; and John, age 1 year. [Filed and adjudged 18 Nov 1898]

[480] 1431. Louis[220] Euber, Keene. Came to Keene to live 1 year ago last Nov. Previous to that, lived in Drewsville, 1 year; before that in Bellows Falls, VT. Husband is dead. [Filed 6 May 1898; examined and adjudged 1 Oct 1898]

1432. Charles E. Shelley, Winchester, born in Swanzey, 25 years old. My mother died in Chesterfield. I have lived in VT until 5 years ago. Two years ago I married Ella F. Parkhurst in CT. She never lived in NH before her marriage, nor her parents. [Filed 13 Jan 1899; examined and adjudged 27 Feb 1899]

1433. Ada Streeter, Winchester, born in Chesterfield, 36 years old. Married to Willis Streeter, 12 years ago. Have one child, 9 years old.[221] My husband has lived in Winchester 6 years. [Filed 13 Jan 1899; examined and adjudged 27 Feb 1899]

[481] 1434. Lucy Frazier, Marlborough, born in Canada, 75 years old, a widow. He died about 4 years ago. Have no children. [Filed 16 Dec 1898; examined and adjudged 25 Mar 1899]

1435. James Murray, Keene, born in Keene, 44 years old. Unmarried; has no property. [Filed 20 Jan 1899; examined and adjudged 25 Mar 1899]

1436. Harriet Hewitt, Keene, born in MA, 77 years old. Married in 1847; husband died 11 years ago. Came to Keene to

---

[220] Though transcribed as it appears in the original, this name is probably Louise.
[221] More on this family at #1484, page 497.

Cheshire County Paupers
1885-1900

live 10 years ago. [Filed 17 Mar 1899; examined and adjudged 25 Mar 1899]

[482] 1437. Newell Pair,[222] Keene, born VT, 51 years old. Was married in 1871 to Martha Grenier. Have 6 children between ages 8 and 27. [Filed 17 Mar 1899; examined and adjudgcd 25 Mar 1899]

1438. A. W. Needham, Winchester, born in Brattleboro, VT, 63 years old. Have a wife and 3 children: eldest 12 years, youngest is 3. Came to Winchester in 1898. [Filed 3 Feb 1899; examined and adjudged 25 Mar 1899]

1439. Edmon Laundry, Marlborough, born in Canada, 34 years old. Lived in Marlborough the last 10 years, with the exception of the year 1895, when he was in MA. His wife died 8 years ago. Has 2 boys: Eddie, age 13, and Joseph, 12 years old. Joseph is now serving a sentence in Industrial School at Manchester. [Filed 30 Jun 1898; examined and adjudged 27 Feb 1899]

[483] 1440. Morris Trey, Keene, born in Boston, MA, 62 years old. Never married. [Filed 31 Dec 1898; examined and adjudged 28 Mar 1899]

1441. J. Putnam, Keene, born in Springfield, 55 years old. [Filed 17 Feb 1899; examined and adjudged 17 Mar 1899]

1442. Ernest R. Mack, born in Marlow, 37 years old. Came to Keene about 1897. [Filed 31 Dec 1899;[223] examined and adjudged 28 Mar 1899]

---

[222] The name appeared to be "Pain," but in the 1890 *Keene Annual Report*, Newll Paire and his wife Martha, both of Canada, had a son born 9 Nov 1890, their 7th child.
[223] Date transcribed as written in original. Probably filed in 1898.

Cheshire County Paupers
1885-1900

[484] 1443. Harry H. Young, born in Petersham, MA, 36 years old. My wife Annie is 31 years old, born in Boston. The names and ages of my minor children are as follows: Hattie, age 10; Nellie, 6; Carrie, 5; Alice, 4; Willie, 2; and Herbert, 4 months old.[224] [Filed 28 Mar 1899; examined and adjudged 28 Mar 1899]

1444. Jennie Cansieno, Winchester, wife of Louis Cansieno, born in NY state, 39 years old. My age is 32, born in MA. Have 6 children as follows: Jennie, age 15; Laura, 12; Earnest, 8; Louis, 6; Ella, 3; and Viola, 1 year old. [Filed 28 Mar 1899; examined and adjudged 28 Mar 1899]

1445. Lewis Bardo, Fitzwilliam, 40 years old, born in Claremont. My wife's name is Marry E. We have 4 children as follows: Lewis A., age 18; Amory, 16; Ester, 12; and Arthur W., 1 year old. Have never been helped before. [Filed 25 Feb; examined and adjudged 3 Mar 1899]

[485] 1446. James Anderson, Richmond, 86 years old, born in Scotland. Came to Richmond in 1880 and lived there since. [Filed 11 Nov 1898; examined and adjudged 28 Mar 1899]

1447. Timothy Curran, Keene, born in Ireland, about 60 years old. Married; my wife and one son live in Keene. I came to America about 5 years ago. [Filed 6 Jan 1899; examined and adjudged 28 Mar 1899]

1448. Burton E. Town, Keene, 35 years old. Married; we have 3 small children, one being 5 weeks old. My wife has been to Elliott City Hospital for treatment. I was born in Marlborough. [Filed 17 Jun 1898; examined and adjudged 28 Mar 1899]

---

[224] These children are listed in an affidavit with their mother Julia as #1397, page 468.

Cheshire County Paupers
1885-1900

[486] 1449. Francis LaClair, Rindge, 56 years old, born in Canada. Came to R when I was 7 or 8 years of age. Married and have 2 children: Arthur, age 4, and Effie, 2 years old. [Filed 25 Dec 1898; examined and adjudged 28 Mar 1899]

1450. Stillman Boutelle,[225] born in Lyndeborough, 37 years old. [Filed 3 Feb 1899; examined and adjudged 28 Mar 1899]

1451. Joseph L. Whipple, Fitzwilliam, born in Richmond, 4 Jul 1843, 56 years old, a widower, with no children. Insane and at the present time is at Concord Asylum. [Filed 22 Feb; examined and adjudged 3 Mar 1899]

[487] 1452. Lena A. Ward, Fitzwilliam, 14 years old, daughter of Albert G. Ward of Fitzwilliam. Said Lena's mother is dead. Said Lena is of weak mind and should be cared for at some institution for that purpose. [Filed 7 May 1898; examined and adjudged 1 Oct 1898]

1453. Clara S. Cole, Swanzey, 58 years old. Have been twice married; first, John A. Rand; second, J. W. Cole of Richmond. [Filed 3 Jul 1896; examined and adjudged 1 Oct 1898]

1454. William Sharkey, Keene, born in Highgate, VT, 29 years old. Married; wife's name Lena Harper of Swanzey. [Filed 15 Mar 1899; examined and adjudged 30 Mar 1899]

[488] 1455. Eddie F. Daigle, born in Canada, 36 years old. Married; wife's name Phebe Parent Daigle, born in Canada, 36 years old. Have lived in Troy since 1889. Have one child, Henry, 5 years old. [Filed 23 Mar 1899; examined and adjudged 23 Mar 1899]

---

[225] The original appeared to be "Bowtell." In the 1900 census for Harrisville, his name is given as Stillman Boutelle.

Cheshire County Paupers
1885-1900

1456. Joseph A. Demarche,[226] Hinsdale, 27 years old, born in Canada. Lived in said Hinsdale about 2 years. Wife's name Amanda Jacobs, daughter of Joseph Jacobs of Keene. Have Ora, age 2, and blind baby, just born. [Filed 23 Mar 1899; examined and adjudged 29 Mar 1899]

1457. Caroline Wilder, Keene, born in Stoddard, 88 years old. My husband died in the west, 9 years ago and left no property. [Filed 3 Mar 1899; examined and adjudged 17 Mar 1899]

[489] 1458. James E. White, single, now of Fitzwilliam. Am an old soldier, Co. C, 29th MA Vols. Born in MA, 63 years old. [Filed 13 Feb 1899; examined and adjudged 3 Mar 1899]

1459. Mrs. Caroline Gibson, Keene. Married in VT; lived there until 5 years ago; came to Keene. Son, Arthur Gibson, 13 years old last May. [Filed 4 Apr 1899; adjudged 5 Apr 1899]

1460. Joseph Gerkie, Rindge, born in Canada, 23 years old. Came to Rindge 5 months ago. Wife, age 22. Four children: one, 3; one, 2; one, 11 months; and a baby, 4 weeks old. [Filed 7 Apr 1899; adjudged 11 Apr 1899]

[490] 1461. William H. Codding, Marlboro, 24 years old last Jul. Never lived in the state until 16 Nov 1899. Wife, Gertrude Codding. No children. Parents never lived in NH. [Filed 14 Apr 1899; adjudged 21 Apr 1899]

1462. Flora B. Howard, daughter of George M. Howard of Keene. At the State Reform School. [Filed 21 Apr 1899; adjudged 5 May 1899]

---

[226] *Keene Vital Records* shows the marriage of Joseph A. Demenche, son of Nicholas Demenche and Judith Clark of Canada, on 17 Jun 1896 to Amanda Jacob, daughter of Joseph Jacob and Herenea Hood, of Canada.

Cheshire County Paupers
1885-1900

1463. Henry Cook, Winchester, 75 years old. One daughter, 33 years old. Ordered to the County Farm. {Died at Farm} [Filed 2 Jun 1899; adjudged 16 Jun 1899]

[491] Robert H. Crofford, Swanzey, 65 years old. A member of the 6th Reg't, NH Vols. {Died at Soldiers Home, Tilton, NH} [Filed 16 Jun 1899; adjudged 16 Jun 1899]

1465. Maude A. Brewer, Winchester, born in MA. Married 21 Jan 1899, Frank Brewer, who has gone to parts unknown. {30 Jul 1902: This woman takes care of herself, but her child was cared for by the county until the fall of 1901 when she or he was bound out to Silas O. Martin of Richmond until of age. The county paying Martin $100. This child is neither a boy or girl.[227] Signed "Wilcox"} [Filed 2 Jun 1899; adjudged 30 Jun 1899]

1466. Charles A. Cooligan, Winchester, 38 years old. Wife and 3 children, named: Minnie, age 15; Ollie, 6; and Cristian, 3 years old. [Filed 2 Jun 1899; adjudged 2 Jun 1899]

[492] 1467. Ethel Marion Carkins, Swanzey, 5 month old. Father and mother left for parts unknown.[228] {This child was bound out until of age to parties who live in Westmore-land. Signed "W"} [Filed 23 Jun 1899; adjudged 30 Jun 1899]

1468. Lottie E. Naramore, Winchester, wife of Will E. Naramore, born in Richmond. Three children: Bessie, 14 years

---

[227] This transcribed as written. Author has no idea what this means.
[228] The 1899 *Swanzey Town Report*, identifies her parents as Isaac Carkins, age 24, born Fitzwilliam, and Alberta L. Desbrisay, age 20, born Nova Scotia.

Cheshire County Paupers
1885-1900

old; Chester, 12; and Willie, 6 years old.[229] [Filed 2 Jun; adjudged 30 Jun 1899]

1469. Nettie M. Cram, Winchester, wife of Martin Cram, born in Washington, VT. Five children: Arthur, age 13; Walter, 10; Horace, 9; Alice, 6; and Daphins, 11 months old. [Filed 22 May 1899; adjudged 30 Jun 1899]

[493] 1470. Lewis Wells, Winchester, 63 years old. Soldier in a NY regiment. [Filed 1 Sep 1899; adjudged 15 Sep 1899]

1471. Bella A. Phillips, Richmond, 18 years old. Sent to the Farm. [Filed 25 Jun 1899; adjudged 9 Jul 1899]

1472. Sarah E. Aldrich, Swanzey, 45 years old. Husband in jail. {Sarah died Jan 1903} [Filed 21 Jul 1899; adjudged 15 Sep 1899]

[494] 1473. Eliza Davis, Winchester. NH soldier's widow. No pension. Three children, all poor. [Filed 1 Sep 1899; adjudged 15 Sep 1899]

1474. Emma Stebbins, Gilsum. Married first William B. Howard, who died 11 Apr 1896. He having a settlement in Gilsum at his death. Married Robert L. Stebbins 24 Jan 1898. Three children by first marriage: Lester W., age 12; Agnes A., 7; one by second marriage, Naomi H., 4 months. {She has become self-supporting. New affidavit should be taken} [Filed 13 May 1899; adjudged 17 Oct 1899]

1475. Lucy Starkey, Troy, 68 years old, widow. [Filed 22 May 1899; adjudged 20 Oct 1899]

---

[229] The divorce of Lottie and Will Naramore is profiled in *'Til Divorce Do Us Part* by author, page 302.

Cheshire County Paupers
1885-1900

[495] 1476. Louis Frechett, Troy, born in Canada, 47 years old. Wife's name Amelia. One child, Homer, age 17. [Filed 20 Oct 1899; adjudged 20 Oct 1899]

1477. Frank Stone, widower, Fitzwilliam, 84 years old. Sent to County Farm. [Filed 20 Oct 1899; adjudged 20 Oct 1899]

1478. Mary Sharkey, born in VT. Lived in Keene, age 16. An infant child.[230] [Filed 21 Apr 1899; adjudged 20 Oct 1899]

[496] 1479. Margaret Southwick, Keene, born in Canada. Married in St. Albans, VT. Husband dead. Lived in Keene 2 years. [Filed 30 Sep 1899; adjudged 20 Oct 1899]

1480. Kate Kennedy, Keene. Married; deserted. Born in Nova Scotia. First marriage in 1884; second, 1898. Came to Boston; in Jun to Dublin and Keene. At hospital, infant child and mother. [Filed 30 Sep 1899; adjudged 24 Oct 1899]

1481. Michael White, Keene, 24 years old. Called for aid on account of sickness. [Filed 19 Oct 1899; adjudged 24 Oct 1899]

[497] 1482. Lena Walforitz, Keene, born in Russia. Came to Keene last Jun. Sick and no one to care for her. [Filed 19 Oct 1899; adjudged 24 Oct 1899]

1483. Walter S. Fairbanks, Winchester, 41 years old. No real or personal estate. Taxes abated in 1892. Single. [Filed 20 Oct 1899; adjudged 3 Jan 1900]

1484. Lottie Streeter, Winchester, daughter of Willis and Ada Streeter, who have lived in Westmoreland, Keene, Jaffrey and

---

[230] The 1899 *Keene Annual Report* shows a son born 19 Mar 1899 to Mary Sharkey, born Highgate, VT, and Ray Dill, also of Highgate.

Cheshire County Paupers
1885-1900

Winchester, but have no settlement in any town. The parents have separated and their whereabouts unknown. [Filed 28 Dec 1899; adjudged 3 Jan 1900]

[498] 1485. Annie Fellows Corey, Keene. Husband's name George W. Corey, gone to parts unknown. Three children, under ten: Carl F., Gladys I., and Bernice J. [Filed 17 Nov 1899; adjudged 3 Jan 1900]

1486. Maria and Caroline Harris, Chesterfield. Maria, 97 next May; Caroline M., about 65 years old. Feeble-minded. [Filed 15 Dec 1899; adjudged 3 Jan 1900]

1487. George Preston and wife Lilla. Lilla is 29 years old. Lived in MA until about 3 years ago when we came to Harrisville; then to Stoddard; then to Nelson. [Filed 15 Dec 1899; adjudged 3 Jan 1900]

[499] 1488. John Holmes, a Finn, 27 years old. Single, poor, Marlborough. {Died at Asylum in Concord] [Filed 23 May 1898; adjudged 2 Jun 1899]

1489. Celina Freeman, Troy, French, 43 years old. Husband left her with the following children: Willie, age 12; Abbie, 10; Alfred, 8; Louis, 6; and Clara, age 4. [Filed 15 Sep 1899; adjudged 5 Oct 1899]

1490. Elsie M. Hill, Troy, age 14. Husband's name Bertman F. Hill. His father has a settlement in Fitzwilliam. [Filed 15 Sep 1899; adjudged 25 Sep 1899]

[500] 1491. William Dument, Troy, French, 44 years old. Came to Troy from MA in spring 1899. Children: Rosa M., age 11; Louis W., 9; and George W., 6 years old. Wife's name Delia, age 36. [Filed 27 Sep 1899; adjudged 5 Oct 1899]

Cheshire County Paupers
1885-1900

1492. Amos A. Blanchard, Keene, 56 years old. [Filed 5 Jan 1900; adjudged 17 Jan 1900]

1493. William Carr, Keene, French, 52 years old. Sick. [Filed 15 Dec 1899; adjudged 17 Jan 1900]

[501] 1494. Alvin W. Houghton, Swanzey, 57 years old. Single. [Filed 28 Nov 1899; adjudged 17 Jan 1900]

1495. Daniel McKittrick, Keene, 25 years old. [Filed 15 Dec 1899; adjudged 17 Jan 1900]

1496. Charles Talbot, Swanzey, 88 years old. His wife Clarrissa is 90 years old. {Charles Talbot dead} [Filed 17 Jan 1900; adjudged 17 Jan 1900]

[502] 1497. Mary Breman, Walpole, 22 years old. Unmarried. Sent to County Farm. Discharged. [Filed 16 Oct 1899; adjudged 17 Jan 1900]

1498. Mary Burke Bigelow, Keene, 66 years old. Don't know where her husband is. Unable to support herself. [Filed 18 Apr 1899; adjudged 17 Jan 1900]

1499. Annie L. Howard, Keene, 25 years old. Single. [Filed 5 Jan 1900; adjudged 17 Jan 1900]

[503] 1500. Emma C. M. Sprague, Keene, 35 years old. Married; husband left for parts unknown 8 years ago. Three children: 15, 11 and 8 years old. Their names not given. [Filed 2 Feb 1900; adjudged 2 Feb 1900]

1501. Mrs. Jennie A. Hadley, Keene, 38 years old. Husband dead. Lived in Keene 18 years. Sick. [Filed 2 Feb 1900; adjudged 2 Feb 1900]

Cheshire County Paupers
1885-1900

1502. Charles A. Britton, Keene, 77 years old. Married. Have been helped by the city of Keene. [Filed 2 Feb 1900; adjudged 2 Feb 1900]

[504] 1503. Samuel C. Richardson, Keene, 76 years old. Married; wife is 77 years old. Both in poor health. A US soldier from NH. {Dead} [Filed Feb 1900; adjudged 2 Feb 1900]

1504. Hattie Cota Towne, Keene, 30 years old, widow. Two children: boy, age 9, and girl, 4 years old. Should have given names of children. [Filed 1 Feb 1900; adjudged 2 Feb 1900]

1505. Mary Lovejoy, Keene, age 60. Lived in Keene since she was age 17. Sick. [Filed 2 Feb 1900; adjudged 2 Feb 1900]

[505] 1506. Charles L. Blood, Fitzwilliam, 58 years old. Married; wife's name Abbie E., age 43.[231] One child, stepson William Reed. Wife has since died. {Gone to MA} [Filed 31 Jan 1900; adjudged 2 Feb 1900]

1507. Charles N. Sebastian, Troy, age 56. Wife: Harriet A., age 46. Four children: Grover C., age 14; Meda, 10; Clifton, 8; and Ellen, age 5. [Filed 2 Jan 1900; adjudged 19 Jan 1900]

1508. Lucy Brett, Winchester, 17 years old, wife of W. H. Brett, a minor son of James Brett, daughter of Charles A. Seward. All poor. [Filed 6 Jul 1899; adjudged 2 Feb 1900]

[506] 1509. Hormedas Sharon, Jaffrey, 51 years old. Wife Zaneide, age 41. Six children as follows: Louis, age 18; Mary, 17; Angelina, 14; Annie, 12; Lannasclas, 11; and Marie, age 3. [Filed 27 Jan 1900; adjudged 2 Feb 1900]

---

[231] This may be the same woman as #1163, page 391.

Cheshire County Paupers
1885-1900

1510. Mary M. Crouch, Keene, born in Troy. Lived all over New England. Poor health. [Filed 5 Jan 1900; adjudged 19 Jan 1900]

1511. Charles Henderson, Winchester, age 34. Married; 4 children, names: Jennie, age 7; Frank, 3; Annie Marion, 10 months; and John, age 6. [Filed 29 Jan 1900; adjudged 2 Feb 1900]

[507] 1512. Mary Looney, Walpole. Husband been dead 33 years. [Filed 2 Feb 1900; adjudged 2 Feb 1900]

1513. Catherine F. Reed Aiken, Keene. No means and no one able or willing to support her. [Filed 2 Feb 1900; adjudged 2 Mar 1900]

1514. Mary Meany or Meanry, 65 years old, Walpole. Husband been dead 24 years. Had 6 children, none of them contribute to her support. [Filed 2 Feb 1900; adjudged 2 Feb 1900]

[508] Mary Armstrong Kelleher, Keene, 36 years old. Married 12 years ago to David Francis Kelleher. Have 6 children: Mary A., age 10; David F., 9; Catherine Y., 7; Timothy, 5; Rachel, 2; and Beatrice, 1 year old. Husband dead, left no property. [Filed 4 May 1900; adjudged 18 May 1900]

1516. John F. Sourrier, Dublin, 41 years old. Children: Mary, age 9; Eva, 6; Charles, 2; and Lewis, age 7 months. Poor and sick. [Filed 21 Apr 1900; adjudged 18 May 1900]

1517. Denis Kearny, Keene, for Cornelus Kearny of Keene, who is out of work and no relatives able or willing to aid him. [Filed 4 May 1900; adjudged 18 May 1900]

Cheshire County Paupers
1885-1900

[509] 1518. Edna Trombley, Keene, 17 years old. At the Hospital. [Filed 4 May 1900; adjudged 18 May 1900]

1519. Julia E. Thompson, Winchester, 59 years old, widow with no property. [Filed 4 May 1900; adjudged 18 May 1900]

1520. Leonard E. Robbins, Roxbury, 69 years old. A soldier in the war of the rebellion, with a pension of $8 a month. [Filed 5 May 1900; adjudged 18 May 1900]

[510] 1521. Margie A. White, Jaffrey, 21 years old. Married to Charles F. White, 14 Jun 1899, who has abandoned her. Is being assisted to the amount of $1.50 per week at her sister's in Franklin, MA at the present. [Filed 17 Feb 1900; adjudged 1 Apr 1900]

1522. Orlando Marston,[232] Troy, 39 years old. Married, born in England. Five children: Emily, 2 years old; John E., 7; Sarah Ann, 12; Hattie, 16; and Jane, age 18. [Filed 16 Mar 1900; adjudged 10 Apr 1900]

1523. Thomas Nelson Woodward, Keene. Married. Soldier in a MA regiment. Two children. Poor and sick. Also served in the 16th NH Vols, Co. I. {Dead} [Filed 16 Mar 1900; adjudged 16 Mar 1900]

[511] 1524. Mrs. George Thurber, Keene, 22 years old. Married; her husband has no property. [Filed 15 Mar 1900; adjudged 10 Apr 1900]

1525. Mrs. Nancy J. Palmer, Keene, 53 years old. Married 26 years ago. Have been helped by the city of Keene. [Filed 4 Apr; adjudged 5 Apr 1900]

---

[232] See also #1138, page 382.

Cheshire County Paupers
1885-1900

1526. Medelpe Carey, Keene, 20 years old. Single, French. [Filed 2 Mar 1900; adjudged 10 Apr 1900]

[512] 1527. Mrs. Nora Shea, 32 years old. Married. Three children: Margaret, 8 years old; Nellie, 3; John Joseph, 6 months old. David Shea is at the County Farm. Keene. [Filed 2 Mar 1900; adjudged 10 Apr 1900]

1528. Andrew Doker, 22 years old, a Finn. Unmarried. Sick. Rindge. [Filed 3 Apr 1900; adjudged 3 Apr 1900]

1529. Emma B. Fortier, Keene, 29 years old. Married 12 years ago. Four children: Louisa, age 10; Georgianna, 8; Arthur, 7; and Cora, age 4. Her husband has left her. [Filed 2 Mar 1900; adjudged 10 Apr 1900]

[513] 1530. Francis Phillips, Alstead, 28 years old. Feeble-minded. {Age here given is not correct, he being a very old man, signed "W"} {Mr. Phillips died Mar 1903. Signed "W"} [Filed 3 Apr 1900; 10 Apr 1900]

1531. Samuel Simms, Keene, 45 years old, born in England. At the hospital with bad foot. [Filed 2 Mar 1900; 18 May 1900]

1532. Dora Phelps, Marlborough, 18 years old, born VT. Unmarried; gave birth to a still born child. [Filed 19 Jan 1900; adjudged 10 Apr 1900]

[514] 1533. Nellie Stebbins, Swanzey, 27 years old. Married, one child: Nellie Marion, 2 years old. Unable to support self and child. [Filed 16___ 1900; adjudged 10 Apr 1900]

1534. John Mead, Alstead, 80 years old. Poor. At the Farm. {Died at the Farm 10 Sep 1903. Signed "W"} [Filed 3 Apr 1900; adjudged 10 Apr 1900]

Cheshire County Paupers
1885-1900

1535. Julia A. Metcalf, Keene, 70 years old. Single. [Filed 4 Apr 1900; adjudged 5 Apr 1900]

[515] 1539. Charles A. Alamo, Walpole, 54 years old. Three or 4 others of the same family. A bad lot. [Filed 2 Feb 1900; adjudged 15 Jun 1900]

1540. Justice R. Rogers, Keene, age 29, born in MA. Married. Poor and sick. [Filed 14 Feb 1900; adjudged 10 Apr 1900]

1541. Carrie D. Hall, Marlow, 23 years old. Married; husband in State Prison. Four children: George, age 6; Clayton, 4; Josie, 2; and Fred, 10 months old, and more to follow. {George and Clayton at Manchester in Notre Dame School. Jessie, dead} [Filed 2 Feb 1900; adjudged 16 Jun 1900]

[516] 1536. Eva Armstrong, Rindge, 36 years old, widow. Is a cripple. {Dead} [Filed 3 Apr 1900; adjudged 10 Apr 1900]

1537. Harry M. Young,[233] Rindge, born in MA. Have a sick wife and 6 children: Hattie M., age 10; Nellie M., 7; Carrie A., 5; Alice F., 4; Millie F., 2; and Herbert E., 1 year old. [Filed 3 Apr 1900; adjudged 10 Apr 1900]

1538. Carpenter family, Fitzwilliam, father, mother, and 8 children. Father's name, Eugene, age 43; Villie, age 47. Children: Villie J., age 18; Peter J., 16; Elsie M., 14; Samuel E., 13; Grover C., 10; Paul S., 8; Anna C., 6; and Charles E., 3 years old. [Filed Nov 1899; adjudged 3 Apr 1900]

[517] 1539. Fred Birgholm, Hinsdale, Finlander, 25 years old. Very sick. [Filed 6 Jul 1900; adjudged 2 Jul 1900]

---

[233] See also #1397, page 468.

Cheshire County Paupers
1885-1900

1540. Annie M. Doyle Malaney, Keene, for May Clarke Doyle, 75 years old. At the farm. [Filed 2 Feb 1900; adjudged 1 Apr 1900]

1541. John Turner, Keene, 38 years old. Sick. Comes pretty near a tramp. [Filed 2 Jun 1900; adjudged 12 Jul 1900]

[518] 1542. Minnie Ella Brewer, Keene, 21 years old. 2 children; husband has deserted her. [Filed 3 Nov 1900; adjudged 10 Apr 1900[234]]

1543. Ann Sweetland, Winchester, 85 years old. [no other information]

1544. Bessie May Mosher, Fitzwilliam, 26 years old. [Filed 9 Jul 1900; adjudged 20 Jul 1900]

[519] 1545. Mary Bragg, Winchester, wife of George Bragg. Five children: Ida M. Maddock, age 17; Leon, age 15; Milan, 13; Ralph, 11; and Charles, age 7. Bad lot. [Filed 9 Apr 1900; adjudged 20 Jul 1900]

1546. Nelson children, Hinsdale.[235] Left by their parents. Two boys, one about 5 years old; parties in Hinsdale have taken him. The baby at the farm. [Filed 14 Feb 1900; adjudged 10 Apr 1900]

1547. Peter Vernoski, Winchester, Russian, 27 years old. Two children: Frances, age 5, and Annie, 3 years old. {Words "wife's name" crossed out. Jennie Jeseph, baby by second wife.} [Filed 5 Jun 1900; adjudged 20 Jul 1900]

---

[234] Date transcribed as written, but it is unlikely it was filed 7 months after it was adjudged.
[235] The Hinsdale town reports show nothing for this family.

Cheshire County Paupers
1885-1900

[520] 1548. C. W. C. Hill, Winchester, 48 years old. Has not lived with his wife for some time. Five children, all in MA. [Filed 3 Apr 1900; adjudged 20 Jul 1900]

1549. Samuel Bentote, Stoddard, English, 81 years old. [Filed 9 Apr 1900; adjudged 2 Jul 1900]

1500.[236] George Norwood, Fitzwilliam, 56 years old. Single. Sick. [Filed 6 Jul 1900; adjudged 20 Jul 1900]

---

[236] Though written as #1500, it was actually record #1550.

Cheshire County Paupers
1885-1900
Appendix A

At the Cheshire County Commissioner's office, there is a book called *Deaths 1894-1944, Cheshire County Farm*. I have copied out the entries that cover 1894-1900 in an effort to further fill in information on some of the paupers covered in this book. I am told that the individual burial sites are no longer able to be located because the markers are missing. I have included the grave numbers, if they were provided in the original text.

Name	age	death date	grave #	where the body was removed to
Nancy Willard	75	15 May 1894	1	
Alpheus Hand	63	12 Sep 1894		Fitzwilliam
Josiah Wilson	74	1 Jul 1894	2	
Nancy Ballou	68	10 Oct 1894		Surry
Eunice Heath	63	24 Sep 1894		
Clara Webber		12 Feb 1895		Walpole
R. E. Guillow	33	12 Dec 1895		Gilsum
L. C. Taft	40	5 Dec 1895		Swanzey
Parmelia Coulliard	32	22 Oct 1895	3	
Clara Parmenter		29 Jan 1896		Worcester, MA
Betsey E. Hendrix	69	22 Apr 1895		
Lucy B. Robbins		10 Jul 1896		
John Buxton	84	23 Aug 1895		Chesterfield
J. D. Lewis	40	12 Apr 1896		
William Perry	71	30 Mar 1896	4	
Asa Robbins	81	20 Dec 1896		Alstead
Alvira Allen	79	6 Jul 1896		Surry
Caroline Poster	54	8 Sep 1896	7	
Loisa W. Nims	74	17 Mar 1896		Keene
Reconsile White	61	1 Jun 1896		Fitzwilliam
Henry J. Pratt	81	15 May 1896	5	
Louisa Hubbard	57	15 Jun 1896	6	
Mary White	77	12 Nov 1897		Troy
Chas. Ballou	25	14 Jun 1897		Keene
James Estey	74	4 Apr 1897 "cancer"		Keene
J. B. Fitzgerald	41	7 Feb 1897		Winchendon

Cheshire County Paupers
1885-1900

Name	Age	Date	#	Place
Fred W. May	19	22 Aug 1897		Leominster, MA
Sylvanus Robbins	80	29 Mar 1897	8	
Julius Vetter	65	25 Jul 1897		
Hannah Morse	70	28 Jun 1897		Dublin
Marriah Wyman	85	11 May 1897		Troy
Edwin Davis	60	20 May 1898		Gilsum
Levi F. Pierce	63	3 Mar 1898		
J. P. Wellman	76	27 Apr 1898		
Caroline Turner	44	20 Sep 1898		
J. A. Stockwell	67	19 Feb 1898		
C. J. Albee		22 Apr 1898		
Wilmer G. Ellis	24	31 Oct 1898		
Bradley Briggs	76	26 Jan 1899		
Chas. Baldwin	75	24 Jan 1899		
Anson S. Briant	3	19 Feb 1899	corner	
Chas. Burns	74	27 Jan 1899		Keene
Michael Clune	65	25 Mar 1899		Loell, MA (sic)
Nelson Catrao	98	14 May 1899	11	
Samuel Kempton	77	21 Oct 1899	12	
Alfred Payer	25	23 Jan 1899		
William Ruffle	71	18 Jan 1899		Keene
J. E. Randall	73	1 Feb 1899		Hinsdale
Nathan Thomas	86	16 Mar 1899		Keene
S. J. Crossfield		18 Mar 1899		Keene
Sarah H. Pratt	83	26 Jan 1899	9	
Susan E. Smith	46	18 May 1899		
Mary Whitcomb		17 Apr 1899	10	
Julius Laurine	32	24 May 1899		
Robbert Butler		12 Apr 1900	14	
Henry Cook	75	7 Nov 1900		
Gilbert Field	76	8 May 1900	15	
H. McManus	54	26 Nov 1900	16	
J. A. Stockwell	68	4 Aug 1900		
Lizzie J. Pierce	42	10 Mar 1900		Keene
John Colburn	50	5 Apr 1900	13	
Eddie Barrett	37	13 Sep 1900		

Subject Index

Abuse 28, 37, 40, 42, 80, 117, 119, 147, 167, 185
Accident 1, 3, 25, 69, 81, 102, 123, 131, 137, 146, 147, 161, 165, 187, 196, 199, 204, 208, 231, 262, 277, 315
Actor 276
Actress 276
Adoption 39, 72, 169, 212, 213, 234, 258
Alimony 139
Amputation 69, 81, 82, 107, 171, 204, 221
Arm problems 117, 119, 145, 165, 171, 200, 201, 204, 205, 208, 249, 301
Army 3, 10, 14, 16, 17, 19, 40, 42, 43, 73, 84, 88, 89, 99, 111, 120, 122, 123, 124, 132, 133, 136, 141, 151, 157, 169, 176, 181, 182, 184, 187, 191, 196, 213, 218, 223, 226, 236, 263, 284, 291, 292, 293, 296, 300, 307, 308, 309, 310, 318, 323, 325, 329, 331
1st NH Calvary 141, 300
1 Prol. Regt NY 40
1st VT Cav 229
2d MA Vols 185
2d ME Calvary 151
2d NH Vols 94, 144, 167, 222, 300
2d NH Regt Brass Band 297
3rd MA Cav 223
3rd VT Vols 121
4th NH Vols 123, 180
4th VT Vols 181
5th NH Vols 91, 130, 308
5th NY Vols 207
5th VT Regt 184, 189
6th NH Vols 120, 141, 170, 210, 324
6th VT Vols 162
7th ME Regt 205
9th ME Vol 151
9th NH Vols 199, 314
11th VT Vols 142, 156
13th OH Regt 200
14th Regt CT 90
14th NH Vols 84, 94, 118, 152, 184, 187, 196, 198, 246, 293
14th NY Artillery 159
16th Nh Vols 331
17th Vt Vols 310
18th NH Vols 10, 158
20th Indiana 141
21st MA Regt 226
22d NY Vols 177
27th MA Vols 291
29th MA Vols 323
35th NY Vols 159
36th MA Regt 210
57th MA Regt 123
96th NY Cav 291
112th NY Vols 269
MA Regt 331
NY Regt 236
Arson 95, 107
Ashuelot Mills 54, 185
Assault 130
Asylum(NY) 26
Asylum for the Insane (Brattleboro, VT) 268
Auction 297
Avon Place Orphan's Home (Cambridge, MA) 114
Axe 21, 146
Bad reputation 33, 49, 52, 191, 201, 333, 334
Baldwin Place House (Boston) 39, 96
Banking 206, 284, 302
Barber 185, 221
Bedridden 64, 147, 151
Begging 8, 104
Bigamy 33, 77, 122, 169, 204, 212
Billiard saloon 44
Blasting rocks 89
Blindness 24, 40, 67, 70, 83, 89, 92, 104, 108, 292, 295, 323
Boarding 37, 38, 88, 90, 94, 107, 114, 121, 137, 160, 169, 173, 178, 193, 222, 242, 281, 287, 314
Boots 95
Bound out 2, 165, 209, 324
Bounty payment 94, 191
Box shop 115
Brain injury 1
Brattleboro Asylum 57
Burdett's shop 184
Burial 16, 23, 45, 48, 53, 54, 55, 59, 62, 67, 73, 76, 79, 82, 112, 118, 134, 156, 162, 163, 165, 184, 187, 203, 215, 236, 238
Burns 125, 129, 134, 213, 214
Butcher 32
Buying horses 137
Cancer 136, 202, 337
Cane 24
Canvassing 112, 261
Chairs 1, 46
Cheshire Provident Institution 166
Cheshire Railroad 116
Children (over six in family) 2, 12, 14, 19, 20, 26, 30, 33, 38, 46, 55, 66, 72, 116, 118, 121, 124, 125, 127, 131, 132, 134, 141, 144, 145, 152, 156, 161, 162, 164, 176, 178, 181, 182, 186, 193, 210, 217, 218, 226, 228, 231, 235, 235, 237, 238, 240, 242, 248, 254, 255, 257, 263, 277, 279, 282, 291, 294, 307, 333
Christmas 87
Circus 77
City Hospital 221

City Hotel 81
City Marshal 52
Civil War 55, 61, 69, 84, 88, 89, 90, 91, 92, 99, 107, 118, 129, 141, 146, 151, 162, 176, 181, 182, 189, 191, 200, 205, 210, 213, 223, 244, 261, 263, 269, 275, 291, 292, 293, 297, 300, 307, 309, 310, 314, 331
Clothes provided 1, 38, 47, 98, 303
Coasting (Sledding) 273
Concerts 62
Confinement (birth) 47, 56, 61, 65, 82, 100, 112, 115, 117, 148, 178, 188, 237, 315
Connecticut River 54, 66
Consumption 3, 7, 12, 18, 37, 43, 49, 58, 92, 95, 189, 208
County Almshouse 2, 4, 5, 6, 7, 9, 10, 15, 16, 17, 18, 20, 21, 22, 24, 25, 28, 31, 33, 36, 37, 38, 39, 42, 43, 44, 47, 48, 50, 52, 53, 56, 57, 58, 61, 62, 63, 70, 73, 75, 76, 78, 79, 80, 81, 82, 83, 86, 88, 93, 95, 96, 97, 99, 102, 103, 104, 105, 107, 108, 109, 120, 132, 137, 141, 144, 145, 146, 148, 156, 158, 160, 166, 172, 175, 178, 182, 183, 187, 188, 190, 194, 200, 202, 204, 205, 207, 209, 210, 213, 215, 228, 246, 266, 268, 285, 308
County Cemetery 76, 107, 145
County Commissioners 105, 111, 164
County Courthouse 105
County Farm 17, 21, 27, 59, 62, 97, 105, 106, 108, 109, 113, 127, 129, 130, 131, 133, 138, 140, 142, 148, 161, 162, 167, 177, 182, 187, 193, 194, 201, 202, 204, 214, 217, 219, 223, 224, 244, 288, 293, 295, 309, 313, 318, 324, 325, 326, 328, 332, 334, 337, 338
Criminal behavior 185
Crippled 60, 333
Crutch 60
Custody granted 301
Cuts 21, 28, 35, 145, 219, 292
Deadbeat 111
Deafness 108
Death 4, 5, 6, 7, 12, 13, 16, 18, 21, 31, 32, 35, 36, 37, 41, 42, 43, 54, 55, 57, 59, 60, 62, 63, 65, 70, 73, 77, 79, 82, 84, 86, 89, 93, 95, 96, 98, 101, 108, 115, 122, 129, 132, 134, 135, 136, 140, 141, 142, 143, 145, 147, 148, 149, 150, 151, 152, 153, 155, 156, 157, 158, 159, 162, 163, 164, 167, 168, 169, 174, 178, 180, 181, 184, 186, 187, 189, 190, 194, 197, 198, 199, 202, 205, 206, 211, 212, 213, 216, 217, 218, 219, 220, 221, 224, 226, 227, 228, 229, 230, 231, 234, 235, 238, 239, 241, 247, 263, 265, 266, 267, 271, 281, 282, 287, 288, 290, 291, 293, 295, 298, 303, 308, 309, 311, 315, 316, 317, 322, 323, 325, 327, 331, 332, 333, 337, 338

Defective contract 79
Deformed 18, 42
Degenerative disease 46
Dementia 83, 99
Deserting from army 94
Desertion by family members 1, 11, 17, 19, 27, 29, 31, 38, 44, 45, 48, 50, 53, 54, 56, 58, 61, 62, 63, 66, 71, 78, 80, 84, 85, 87, 90, 95, 115, 116, 117, 133, 134, 135, 138, 139, 140, 142, 147, 156, 157, 160, 166, 171, 174, 175, 176, 178, 179, 180, 181, 182, 183, 184, 186, 190, 192, 193, 194, 198, 200, 213, 216, 217, 219, 222, 229, 239, 243, 244, 245, 251, 253, 255, 276, 277, 278, 280, 282, 284, 294, 298, 301, 302, 303, 304, 312, 313, 324, 326, 327, 328, 331, 332, 334
Diphtheria 164, 169, 190
Disability 141, 153
Disease 33
Dishonorable discharge 94
Disreputable life 32
Divorce 4, 8, 11, 29, 33, 46, 51, 58, 63, 69, 78, 92, 95, 120, 128, 133, 139, 141, 144, 150, 151, 154, 157, 175, 178, 191, 196, 204, 208, 212, 224, 225, 230, 235, 246, 261, 265, 268, 277, 279, 290, 301, 316, 317
Doctor 137, 272
Dogs 32
Drowning 54, 66, 87, 165, 230
Drug abuse 1
Drunkenness 9, 36, 94, 95, 97, 134, 165, 220
Eagle Hotel 112134
Elderly (age 70+) 5, 9, 12, 13, 15, 16, 18, 23, 24, 31, 35, 37, 39, 41, 42, 45, 49, 50, 52, 55, 57, 60, 62, 64, 68, 69, 70, 71, 72, 73, 78, 79, 80, 84, 86, 89, 91, 93, 94, 97, 100, 102, 104, 105, 107, 108, 112, 117, 119, 123, 126, 129, 132, 134, 136, 138, 139, 140, 141, 143, 144, 146, 149, 158, 159, 163, 168, 169, 171, 174, 177, 179, 182, 187, 188, 200, 202, 207, 205, 209, 214, 221, 223, 224, 227, 228, 230, 244, 245, 247, 257, 260, 263, 266, 267, 268, 269, 270, 280, 284, 288, 290, 292, 294, 297, 299, 300, 301, 305, 314, 316, 318, 319, 321, 323, 324, 326, 327, 328, 329, 332, 333, 334, 335, 337, 338
Elliott City Hospital 315, 321
Emancipation 39
Emigration 101
Engines 99
English 28, 35, 64, 75, 93, 110, 126, 174, 188, 200, 207, 208, 257, 309, 335
Estate 104
Explosion 19, 89, 204
Factory 88, 206
Fall Mountain Paper Mill 88

Faulkner & Colony 105, 149
Feeble 31, 64, 73, 100, 147, 173, 180, 182, 186, 202
Female disease 8
Fever 17, 48, 71, 185, 206, 235
Fever sores 81
Finnish 204, 327, 332, 333
Fire 63, 95, 97, 105, 114, 214, 294
Fireman's muster 69
Fitchburg Railroad Co. 197
Fits 41, 58, 78, 140, 157, 173, 299
Foot problems 24, 35, 86, 123, 128, 137, 221, 293, 332
Fraud 111, 177
French 2, 5, 6, 7, 9, 11, 13, 18, 20, 21, 24, 25, 26, 27, 28, 30, 31, 32, 34, 37, 38, 40, 42, 44, 46, 47, 48, 49, 51, 52, 54, 55, 56, 58, 64, 65, 67, 68, 69, 70, 72, 75, 76, 77, 78, 80, 82, 83, 84, 85, 86, 89, 93, 97, 98, 101, 104, 105, 107, 109, 110, 111, 117, 118, 119, 147, 148, 149, 156, 163, 164, 167, 174, 176, 178, 182, 183, 184, 185, 186, 188, 192, 193, 195, 196, 211, 212, 213, 214, 215, 216, 217, 218, 219, 220, 232, 235, 237, 238, 239, 240, 246, 252, 254, 256, 257, 258, 261, 264, 265, 266, 267, 274, 278, 283, 296, 299, 310, 313, 316, 317, 327, 328, 332
Frequent moves 11, 127, 129, 184, 190, 229, 237, 243, 244, 247, 249, 250, 251, 254, 255, 256, 259, 260, 264, 265, 276, 278, 284, 287, 290, 292, 296, 303, 304, 327
Frostbite 70, 128
Funeral 66
G & GA Robertson's paper mill 19
Gas fixtures 81
German 35, 70, 72, 76, 184, 208, 216, 250, 259
Governor 12, 112
Guardian 82, 99, 107, 179, 180, 207, 297
Gun 131
Hand injury 3, 69, 219, 223, 256, 264, 267
Harness Factory 174
Head ailment 279
Hemorrhage 130
Hillsboro County Farm 167
Home for Little Wanders (Boston) 56, 61, 95, 226
Horses 137
Hospital 118, 129, 135, 278, 279, 281, 326, 331, 332
Hospital affidavit 236
Hotel Marlborough 135
House of Corrections 10, 12, 37, 94, 96, 98, 118, 133, 138, 185, 198, 202, 204, 220
Housekeeper 14, 42, 96, 105, 117, 118
Ice business 104

Idiot 35, 106, 194, 299
Illegal marriage 89
Illegitimate children 5, 14, 20, 43, 52, 61, 65, 73, 75, 81, 96, 109, 115, 148, 158, 170, 188, 189, 216, 217, 230, 232, 237, 253, 315, 326, 332
Illiterate 194
Imbecile 2, 4, 119, 157
Immigrant 2, 3, 4, 5, 7, 8, 9, 10, 11, 12, 13, 15, 17, 18, 19, 20, 21, 23, 24, 25, 26, 27, 28, 35, 36, 46, 47, 48, 49, 51, 53, 54, 55, 60, 67, 68, 69, 70, 73, 74, 75, 79, 81, 82, 83, 84, 86, 87, 89, 90, 92, 93, 94, 97, 98, 99, 100, 102, 105, 110, 111, 112, 113, 115, 117, 118, 119, 120, 121, 122, 124, 125, 126, 128, 131, 132, 134, 135, 136, 137, 139, 140, 141, 143, 145, 146, 147, 148, 149, 152, 153, 156, 160, 164, 166, 168, 177, 178, 185, 186, 187, 188, 190, 192, 197, 198, 199, 200, 201, 203, 204, 206, 210, 214, 215, 216, 217, 218, 219, 220, 221, 222, 223, 224, 225, 226, 228, 229, 231, 232, 235, 237, 238, 239, 240, 241, 243, 244, 246, 247, 249, 250, 251, 252, 253, 255, 256, 257, 258, 259, 260, 261, 262, 265, 266, 267, 269, 270, 271, 272, 273, 274, 275, 278, 280, 285, 286, 287, 288, 289, 290, 292, 296, 297, 300, 301, 302, 304, 306, 308, 310, 312, 313, 314, 315, 316, 317, 318, 321, 322, 326, 331, 332
Impulsive 141
Incest 96
Indigence 31, 156
Industrious worker 55, 90, 105, 111
Inheritance 4, 6, 16, 215
Insanity 15, 17, 18, 26, 33, 36, 38, 54, 57, 71, 83, 88, 98, 99, 105, 107, 108, 115, 121, 140, 160, 165, 175, 180, 182, 191, 215, 219, 221, 274, 292, 294, 322
Intelligent child 39, 95, 97, 110
Intemperate 12, 28, 31, 43, 47, 70, 94, 98, 103, 117, 138, 163, 185, 203
Invalid 6, 19, 41, 104, 136, 153
Invalid's Home 41, 112
Irish 3, 8, 10, 12, 18, 19, 20, 24, 26, 28, 30, 36, 37, 38, 39, 40, 43, 44, 45, 49, 52, 54, 55, 59, 63, 67, 68, 69, 74, 79, 80, 81, 86, 87, 89, 92, 94, 95, 97, 98, 100, 103, 104, 105, 106, 107, 108, 109, 112, 117, 119, 127, 128, 135, 136, 145, 153, 160, 164, 166, 177, 178, 182, 186, 187, 194, 198, 203, 209, 210, 214, 217, 220, 273, 290
Isolation 35
Italian 24
Jail 43, 95, 119, 129, 130, 135, 138, 183, 254, 259, 272, 309, 325
John Sedgewick Post 210
Jordan & Marsh 203

Keene & Manchester Railroad 22, 70, 105
Kidney disease 32
Laborer 114
Lack of medical care 2, 8
Lamp 125
Lazy 77, 103, 104, 105
Left pauper system 32, 97, 104, 114, 142, 146, 183, 187, 201, 219
Leg problems 29, 45, 63, 64, 67, 102, 116, 156, 176, 189, 203, 204, 209, 217, 240, 249, 273, 313
Liar 51
Liquor sales 44
Lost money 10
Lumber industry 176, 292
Machine shop 98
Madoc Indian 177
Malaria 65
Marlborough quarry 99
Marriages (more than 3) 169
Mason 73
MA General Hospital 153, 200, 208
Memory problems 123
Medicine man 177
Mentally impaired 42, 47, 50, 53, 64, 73, 76, 78, 128, 129, 146, 152, 153, 174, 179, 199, 203, 206, 207, 209, 230, 305, 322, 327, 332
Mill 3, 17, 19, 29, 46, 54, 66, 76, 88, 116, 117, 129
Minister 221, 224
Miserable person 44, 173
Morphine 1
Murder 75, 92
Musician 297
Negro 233, 282
Nervous condition 155
NH Asylum for Insane 15, 16, 17, 33, 35, 38, 54, 55, 58, 59, 71, 88, 94, 99, 107, 108, 119, 127, 140, 150, 160, 161, 165, 168, 175, 179, 180, 184, 191, 199, 203, 205, 206, 209, 211, 215, 216, 219, 221, 240, 248, 267, 268, 274, 275, 280, 292, 295, 297, 322, 327
NH Orphans Home. See also Orphans Home (Franklin, NH) 158
Non compos mentis 22, 25, 149, 194, 230
Non-support of dependents 19, 58, 76, 78, 80, 82, 98, 100, 135, 139, 144, 151, 183, 190, 201, 203, 301
Nose problems 46
Notre Dame Hospital 285, 333
Nurse 26, 137
Operation 202, 204, 205
Opium 1
Orphan 3, 24, 37, 57, 67, 74, 75, 94, 96, 108, 117, 118, 121, 124, 125, 127, 144, 150, 156, 166, 167, 172, 179, 184, 189, 193, 194, 195, 206, 211, 218, 219, 223, 225, 231, 232, 236, 244, 253, 258, 262, 272, 276, 278, 282, 289, 290, 295, 298, 301, 304, 310, 311, 318
Orphan's Home (Franklin, NH) 109, 139, 158
Orphan's Home (MA) 75
Ovarian tumor 202
Overseer of the Poor (NH) 1, 4, 5, 10, 19, 23, 46, 68, 84, 102, 103, 117, 154, 167, 176, 196, 202, 263
Painter 12
Paper mill 66, 88
Paralysis 88, 103, 118, 182, 184, 213, 222
Pardon 92, 130
Parental abuse 6
Parental care 7, 139
Paris Green 133
Patents 1
Paternity suit 56
Pauper laws 6, 9, 16, 18, 20, 22, 33, 36, 46, 53, 58, 80, 150, 151, 152, 154, 155, 168, 173, 179, 190, 199, 230, 264
Pauper settlement. See also Settlement Terms 24, 25, 30, 60, 79, 84, 85, 86, 88, 89, 92, 101, 103, 105, 117, 150, 154, 159, 164, 167, 169, 170, 172, 173, 176, 177, 179, 183, 186, 190, 191, 192, 194, 196, 197, 200, 209, 234 280
Pension 5, 10, 42, 49, 55, 73, 84, 88, 89, 107, 136, 169, 180, 181, 185, 222, 244, 261, 280, 291, 297, 309, 310, 331
Personal estate 2, 5, 125, 126, 127, 166, 207
Physical disability 120
Planing 3
Pneumonia 35, 37
Poison 133
Police Court 14, 22, 98, 195, 205
Police Station 52
Polish 215
Poor Farm (VT) 68, 73
Poor House (Ashburnham, MA) 118
Poor House (Natick, MA) 84
Pottery (Keene) 178
Pregnancy 5, 15, 20, 43, 47, 50, 56, 61, 75, 81, 100, 112
Probate 106
Property 12
Publisher 207
Query 181
Railroad 22, 69, 81, 98, 104, 116, 137, 161, 165, 204, 208, 231, 262
Real estate 2, 5, 33, 47, 65, 82, 85, 114, 121, 123, 124, 125, 126, 127, 150, 152, 153, 154, 155, 162, 168, 176, 180, 181, 184, 198, 204, 207, 212, 215, 220, 227, 241, 271, 289, 294, 297, 300, 301, 302, 303, 304
Red Row 105
Reform School 26, 253

Refuse to aid 104
Refuses to leave 105
Remedial treatment 219
Rent-free housing 104, 163
Rheumatic fever 48
Rheumatism 42, 113, 202
Roving life 12
Russian 334
Russian Polander 201
Sawyer 41
Scarlet fever 130
Scottish 153
Scrofula 16
Seduced 117
Selectmen 1, 25, 29, 57, 60, 113, 135, 148, 183, 200, 273
Self-abuse 77
Self-supporting 45, 298
Separation 45, 91, 96, 99, 121, 122, 150, 156, 173, 194, 196, 203, 210, 214, 216, 218, 220, 245, 247, 253, 260, 263, 294, 327, 335
Settlement terms 30, 31, 32, 33, 35, 37
Shiftless behavior 36, 41, 42, 59, 83, 105, 168
Shock (stroke) 68, 103, 182, 213
Shoe Shop 203
Shoes 95
Shooting 10, 119, 135
Shop work 219
Sickness 2, 4, 5, 6, 7, 10, 13, 15, 18, 19, 21, 23, 26, 27, 28, 30, 32, 37, 39, 43, 44, 46, 47, 52, 58, 59, 64, 65, 70, 72, 74, 75, 76, 77, 87, 88, 89, 90, 92, 96, 100, 101, 110, 111, 114, 118, 123, 124, 127, 130, 133, 135, 136, 140, 142, 143, 144, 146, 151, 153, 159, 168, 174, 178, 179, 192, 196, 199, 200, 201, 206, 208, 212, 215, 216, 218, 223, 224, 226, 227, 235, 237, 243, 248, 252, 253, 260, 262, 270, 271, 278, 280, 281, 286, 291, 305, 306, 307, 308, 310, 317, 318, 326, 328, 329, 330, 331, 332, 333, 334, 335
Skate factory 116
Skeete factory 110
Soldier. See Army
Soldier benefit 118
Soldier's Home 198, 324
Sores 12, 33, 46, 209
Spendthrift 208
Spinal difficulty 153
State Industrial School 14, 22, 24, 26, 29, 30, 195, 205, 221, 239, 320
State Overseer of Poor (MA) 145
State Primary School (Monson, MA) 59
State Prison 9, 42, 92, 154, 333
State Reform School 80, 254, 266, 323
Stealing 42
Steam radiator 21

Stepchildren 82, 92, 93, 113, 130, 137, 139, 142, 144, 152, 159, 160, 171, 173, 176, 181, 182, 183, 192, 193, 197, 202, 213, 216, 222, 223, 226, 227, 230, 233, 235, 260, 262, 263, 265, 268, 282, 291, 309, 329, 334
Stillborn child 332
Stipend 155
Stone's Hospital (deserters) 94
Stonecutter 95
Stubborn/disobedient child 22, 26, 30, 195
Substitute money 191
Suicide 9, 21
Supreme Court 29
Surgical operation 101
Swedish 51, 105, 188, 209, 253, 262
Tailor 220
Tanner 34
Tax abatement 32, 294, 326
Tax certificate 315
Taxes paid 32, 33, 34, 127, 241, 264, 303
Tewksbury Almshouse 145
Thanksgiving Day 131
Time given 91
Tobacco 133
Town overseers 3
Tramp 202, 279, 334
Transient 8, 9, 114, 165, 167, 183, 271
Transportation requested 1, 4, 31, 34, 35, 40, 46, 60, 65, 67, 68, 81, 84, 102, 111, 112, 114, 115, 116, 136, 139, 146, 154, 160, 174, 183, 191, 206, 207, 252
Traveled beyond the Northeast 6,7, 15, 26, 28, 57, 63, 67, 70, 71, 78, 80, 82, 95, 133, 136, 142, 156, 180, 202, 206, 221, 225, 229, 233, 236, 241, 245, 250, 253, 257, 259, 260, 268, 273, 280, 282, 288, 290, 323
Twins 3, 19, 31, 52, 127, 183, 238, 264
Typhoid fever 7, 28, 39, 58, 65, 101, 118, 199
Umbrella repair 75
Unable to walk 24
Unemployed 2, 3, 7, 8, 18, 20, 21, 24, 27, 28, 34, 59, 67, 75, 77, 86, 94, 99, 100, 113, 115, 116, 117, 126, 143, 148, 151, 153, 154, 172, 173, 186, 189, 199, 202, 203, 209, 217, 221, 237, 240, 244, 271, 277, 280, 285, 295, 297, 299, 300, 305, 308, 309, 310, 328, 330, 332
Vermont Almshouse 56
Vermont Valley & Sullivan Co. RR 208
Violence 107, 108, 141, 165, 194
Wagon 1, 64, 67
Warner File Works 67
West Keene Cemetery 156
Widow/widower 3, 4, 7, 10, 18, 19, 26, 30, 36, 39, 42, 53, 59, 63, 65, 66, 68, 69, 71, 72, 73, 74, 77, 82, 84, 86, 88, 97, 98, 100, 104, 105, 112, 116, 119, 120, 121, 123, 124, 125, 128,

130, 133, 135, 138, 139, 140, 141, 142, 143,
145, 146, 148, 149, 150, 152, 153, 154, 155,
158, 159, 160, 161, 162, 163, 164, 165, 166,
167, 170, 174, 177, 179, 183, 186, 187, 188,
190, 197, 198, 199, 202, 205, 206, 209, 210,
212, 215, 216, 217, 218, 219, 220, 222, 223,
224, 226, 227, 228, 229, 230, 232, 233, 234,
235, 238, 242, 245, 246, 257, 263, 265, 266,
267, 269, 270, 272, 273, 274, 275, 285, 288,
289, 290, 292, 295, 297, 298, 299, 300, 302,
308, 309, 310, 312, 316, 317, 319, 320, 322,
323, 325, 326, 328, 329, 330, 331, 333
Windham County jail 166
Woodbury's Mill 129
Worcester Insane Asylum 165
Working outside home 39
Wounded 176
Wrist problems 33
Young bride 111

Place Name Index

California 78, 82, 95, 156, 171, 218, 241
Los Angeles 202
Pacific Coast 202

Canada 4, 5, 7, 11, 13, 15, 17, 18, 20, 21, 25, 26, 27, 28, 29, 30, 31, 32, 34, 38, 40, 42, 43, 46, 47, 48, 49, 55, 64, 68, 69, 70, 73, 75, 80, 82, 84, 86, 90, 96, 101, 102, 110, 111, 113, 115, 118, 120, 121, 122, 124, 125, 126, 127, 128, 129, 131, 133, 134, 136, 137, 139, 140, 143, 144, 145, 146, 148, 149, 164, 167, 171, 174, 175, 176, 178, 182, 183, 185, 188, 190, 192, 195, 196, 197, 200, 201, 202, 204, 205, 208, 210, 211, 213, 215, 216, 217, 218, 219, 220, 224, 225, 228, 229, 231, 232, 236, 237, 238, 239, 240, 242, 243, 244, 246, 247, 248, 249, 250, 251, 252, 253, 254, 256, 257, 258, 259, 260, 261, 264, 265, 266, 267, 269, 270, 271, 272, 273, 274, 275, 276, 278, 280, 283, 285, 286, 287, 288, 289, 291, 292, 296, 298, 299, 302, 304, 306, 310, 312, 313, 314, 315, 316, 317, 318, 319, 320, 322, 323, 326
Annapolis County 162
Barnston 122
Corvensville 53
Culberth 58
Cutbert 83
Granby 65, 252
Halifax 42, 90, 148, 210
Lower Canada 18, 99
Montreal 21, 48, 51, 110, 117
New Brunswick 249
Nicolet 84
Nova Scotia 28, 42, 72, 94, 112, 123, 129, 136, 140, 142, 162, 183, 190, 199, 203, 210, 287, 326
Ottawa 192
Quebec 67, 121, 179, 214, 243
St. Amey 20
St. Anne 186
St. Barnaby 243
St. Celestine 127
St. David 9
St. Elule 44   St. Greger 143
St. Gregory 127
St. Hison 59
St. John 100, 113, 176
St. Mary 117
St. Morris 161
Sherbrooke 97
Terrebonne 21
Three Rivers 24, 49, 156, 159
Toronto 146
Veryfield 183

West Farnum 46, 90, 110

Colorado 80, 290

CT 24, 55, 76, 129, 167, 178, 186, 220, 283, 305, 311, 318, 319
Bridgeport 296
Colchester 180
Hartford 172, 187, 191, 303, 307
Middletown 191
Milford 174
New Britain 31
New Haven 51, 173, 313
New London 97, 171, 205
Stafford 5
Stafford Springs 276
Stirlin Village 154
Watertown 112
West Townsend 140

Dakota Territory 250

Denmark 206, 222, 235, 302
Copenhagen 206

England 23, 28, 53, 75, 92, 93, 100, 131, 138, 140, 143, 147, 184, 186, 207, 224, 235, 243, 251, 257, 267, 270, 271, 274, 275, 278, 286, 297, 301, 308, 309, 313, 318, 331, 332
Bolton 182
Bristol 136
Cornwall 174
Huddersfield 51
Island of Guernsey 124
Liverpool 200
London 35, 64, 126
Manchester 188, 241
Taverstock 186

Europe 26

Finland 204, 221, 287, 314

Florida
Jacksonville 193

France 26, 44, 89, 188, 238, 240, 265, 308

Germany 35, 70, 72, 120, 141, 184, 216, 223, 250, 259, 289
Berlin 208

Illinois 142, 206
Belvidere 100
Greenwood 206
Mt. Sterling 95

Iowa
  Dubuque 6

Ireland 3, 8, 10, 12, 14, 18, 19, 20, 24, 26, 28, 30, 36, 40, 43, 45, 49, 54, 55, 57, 59, 60, 63, 66, 67, 68, 69, 74, 79, 80, 81, 86, 87, 89, 92, 93, 95, 98, 100, 112, 115, 117, 119, 120, 127, 128, 131, 132, 135, 136, 140, 143, 145, 147, 149, 150, 152, 153, 155, 160, 164, 166, 168, 177, 178, 187, 188, 198, 203, 209, 210, 211, 214, 220, 223, 226, 239, 246, 255, 273, 274, 275, 278, 279, 287, 290, 300, 302, 304, 306, 308, 309, 318, 321
  Belfast 3
  Carrigan Shore 210
  Cork 24, 152
  Dublin 281

Italy 226

Kansas 245, 250

Kentucky 233

Maine 77, 129, 151, 190, 288, 305
  Augusta 272
  Bangor 63
  Biddeford 258
  Denmark 258
  Fryeburg 212
  Kennebunk 128
  Lewiston 305
  Lincoln 172
  Livermore 154
  Lowell 236
  Pittsfield 100
  Portland 81, 83, 90
  Scarboro 261
  South Freedom 162
  South Windham 83
  Standish 91
  Stuben 261
  Wayne 160

Maryland
  Baltimore 262

MA 10, 13, 40, 49, 59, 71, 72, 81, 86, 92, 93, 96, 114, 122, 131, 133, 134, 137, 146, 150, 155, 160, 161, 186, 190, 201, 225, 228, 229, 232, 239, 243, 244, 247, 258, 259, 260, 264, 278, 284, 288, 290, 294, 295, 296, 300, 305, 307, 311, 313, 314, 315, 317, 318, 319, 320, 321, 323, 324, 327, 329, 333
  Acton 146

Adams 276
Amherst 218
Ashburnham 40, 43, 49, 66, 72, 118, 125, 155, 187, 196, 296
Ashby 7
Athol 50, 75, 126, 207, 210, 271, 279, 284
Attleboro 207
Auburndale 212
Baldwinville 172
Ballardvale 182
Barnardston 125, 187
Belchertown 159, 301
Beverly 223
Bolton 197
Boston 39, 40, 44, 47, 56, 61, 74, 75, 95, 100, 101, 102, 118, 119, 122, 123, 125, 130, 132, 133, 136, 151, 153, 167, 185, 187, 198, 203, 211, 215, 222, 226, 233, 247, 254, 262, 265, 267, 286, 290, 301, 302, 320, 321, 326
Brighwood 292
Brookfield 147, 182
Buckland 126
Cambridge 114, 235, 254
Charlemont 136
Charlestown 95
Chelsea 35, 180
Clerksbury 135
Clinton 8
Colerain 195, 309
Dedham 263
Deerfield 60
Dracut 202
East Bridgewater 230
East Hampton 188
East Randolph 278
Enfield 8
Erving 8, 192
Everett 223
Fall River 286
Fitchburg 1, 8, 13, 39, 72, 110, 130, 180, 203, 234, 270, 285
Foxboro 215
Framingham 99, 112, 159
Franklin 330
Gardner 115, 179, 290, 296
Gill 27
Greenfield 196, 241, 274
Groton 9, 145
Hardwick 74
Haverhill 75
Haydonville 277
Hinsdale 194
Holden 90, 226, 255
Holland 171, 205
Holyoke 67
Hopkinton 11, 291

Hubbardstown 97
Hudson 40
Hyde Park 92
Jeffersonville 150
Lancaster 152, 158
Lawrence 99, 117, 119, 280, 289
Leominster 122, 180, 278, 294, 338
Lowell 28, 45, 68, 113, 134, 182, 185, 194,
  198, 239, 264, 272, 279, 338
Lunenburg 148
Lyden 76
Lynn 139, 305
Malden 104
Marlborough 146
Melrose 254
Merrimac 308
Middlefield 71
Milbury 124, 140
Milford 59
Monson 59, 264
Montague 8, 32
Mt. Washington 195
Naticke 33, 84
New Bedford 210, 273
New Salem 32, 192
Newton 203
North Adams 238, 251
North Braintree 95
North Brookfield 148
North Dana 170
Northampton 27, 87, 145, 312
Northfield 33, 34, 93, 118, 166, 175, 210, 214,
  225, 264, 266, 276, 283, 293
Oakland, 48
Orange 49, 61, 64, 114, 158, 210
Otter River 200, 210, 214, 232, 246, 282
Oxford 74
Palmer 171
Peabody 147
Petersham 16, 190, 321
Phillipston 89, 279
Pittsfield 19
Quincy 114, 162, 172, 252
Randolph 8
Reading 52
Royalston 22, 30, 33, 94, 148, 191
Salem 33, 119, 276
Sandersfield 271
Shelburn Falls 126
Shirley 1, 27
Shutesbury 244, 291
Somerville 73
South Boston 231
South Brookline 8
Southbridge 28
Southampton 243

Springfield 118, 158, 244, 273, 276
Sturbridge 15
Sutton 74, 123
Taunton 30, 59, 195
Templeton 86, 267
Townshend 23, 133
Tyngsboro 235
Uxbridge 289
Warwick 62, 90, 133, 279, 282, 284
Watertown 200
Wayland 179
Webster 96
Wendall 155, 279
West Boston 168
West Chesterfield 64
West Somerville 16
West Springfield 180, 296
West Stockbridge 218
West Townsend 96
West Upton 90
Westboro 310
Westfield 93
Westminster 89, 212, 257
Williamstown 145, 226
Winchendon 7, 25, 60, 111, 120, 133, 179,
  184, 185, 255, 267, 285, 290, 337
Woburn 174
Worcester 12, 23, 46, 88, 119, 122, 144, 145,
  158, 190, 194, 253, 269, 337

Michigan 71, 225, 259, 260, 290
Aurilens 70
Detroit 288
Lansing 70

Minnesota 15, 133

Missouri
St. Louis 67

Montana 253

Nebraska 250
Flat Brook 177

NH
Acworth 6, 23, 152, 163, 199, 219, 223, 268
Albany 151
Alstead 1, 3, 9, 10, 24, 35, 36, 50, 62, 63, 64,
  79, 80, 83, 85, 86, 127, 151, 179, 187, 190,
  194, 196, 200, 210, 223, 228, 234, 243, 263,
  264, 265, 268, 272, 273, 280, 281, 292, 293,
  299, 303, 304, 315, 332, 337
Alton 5
Amherst 283
Andover 100

Antrim 274, 314
Ashuelot 17, 24, 93, 111, 148, 166, 237, 238, 254, 269, 279, 296, 313, 314
Auburn 192
Bath 73, 163
Bennington 27
Bethlehem 112
Bow 191
Bradford 17
Canaan 116, 134, 171, 237
Charlestown 60, 130, 163, 198, 223, 245, 256
Chesterfield 5, 11, 22, 23, 34, 41, 45, 52, 56, 57, 69, 74, 79, 85, 88, 102, 116, 117, 122, 140, 144, 151, 157, 158, 164, 170, 171, 173, 176, 177, 184, 189, 191, 196, 200, 205, 206, 207, 229, 232, 234, 240, 242, 245, 248, 256, 261, 262, 263, 265, 270, 272, 280, 292, 299, 300, 308, 309, 312, 316, 319, 327, 337
Chesterfield Factory 272
Claremont 60, 65, 98, 122, 135, 160, 199, 207, 237, 256, 271, 303, 321
Colebrook 51
Concord 10, 71, 88, 91, 99, 111, 112, 116, 119, 206, 209, 217, 240, 248, 275, 280, 292, 297, 327
Conway 151
Cornish 65, 179, 194
Deering 99
Derry 246
Dover 154, 170, 202
Drewsville 319
Dublin 12, 33, 36, 52, 78, 90, 106, 144, 145, 150, 159, 167, 169, 181, 186, 198, 215, 234, 240, 251, 258, 271, 282, 326, 330, 338
East Jaffrey 48, 164, 255
East Swanzey 108, 161, 309
East Unity 83
East Weare 118
East Westmoreland 61, 307
Farmington 111
Fitzwilliam 3, 4, 18, 20, 25, 33, 46, 47, 48, 52, 58, 60, 80, 86, 90, 91, 93, 107, 111, 113, 119, 129, 132, 133, 134, 142, 146, 148, 159, 160, 162, 165, 169, 170, 182, 190, 193, 197, 202, 204, 209, 212, 214, 242, 243, 251, 252, 253, 255, 258, 259, 262, 269, 271, 285, 286, 287, 290, 294, 296, 299, 304, 313, 321, 322, 323, 326, 327, 329, 334, 335, 337
Franklin 139, 158
Gilsum 6, 7, 8, 14, 15, 30, 31, 32, 38, 47, 48, 54, 63, 64, 66, 89, 101, 102, 103, 106, 111, 113, 127, 129, 130, 138, 159, 163, 165, 167, 172, 173, 192, 196, 206, 213, 256, 265, 267, 268, 274, 275, 279, 280, 289, 293, 317, 325, 337, 338
Gilmanton 223

Goffstown 167, 191
Goshen 144
Grantham 114
Great Falls 217, 272
Greenfield 11, 14, 230, 312
Greenville 283
Hancock 30, 121, 169, 170, 177, 181, 201, 214
Harrisville 1, 2, 6, 11, 27, 35, 48, 52, 55, 70, 74, 78, 84, 96, 103, 105, 115, 149, 161, 167, 175, 182, 185, 186, 191, 202, 205, 214, 220, 225, 234, 237, 242, 249, 303, 310, 311, 315, 327
Hebron 11, 78
Henniker 99
Hill 111
Hillsboro 111, 142
Hillsboro County 78, 99
Hinsdale 6, 10, 19, 25, 27, 28, 30, 31, 32, 34, 44, 45, 49, 51, 56, 60, 61, 62, 63, 65, 66, 67, 68, 72, 73, 74, 76, 82, 84, 87, 88, 93, 96, 100, 105, 106, 108, 117, 119, 120, 121, 123, 125, 127, 131, 133, 134, 143, 146, 150, 156, 157, 163, 164, 166, 172, 176, 177, 181, 183, 186, 187, 191, 194, 195, 196, 200, 209, 211, 215, 217, 220, 225, 226, 229, 237, 239, 240, 241, 242, 244, 248, 250, 251, 252, 254, 255, 256, 259, 261, 262, 264, 270, 275, 276, 283, 291, 298, 299, 306, 310, 313, 314, 317, 323, 334, 338
Holderness 112
Jaffrey 2, 3, 12, 13, 15, 18, 20, 27, 33, 43, 44, 46, 47, 49, 51, 52, 54, 55, 57, 60, 62, 70, 71, 86, 91, 92, 101, 103, 110, 111, 113, 121, 126, 129, 130, 131, 132, 138, 140, 164, 167, 183, 188, 200, 206, 213, 216, 223, 228, 238, 240, 255, 257, 259, 264, 267, 279, 280, 283, 287, 294, 295, 303, 304, 306, 309, 326, 329, 331
Kingston 175
Laconia 5
Langdon 11, 152, 187, 236, 283, 306
Lebanon 37, 122, 279, 295, 317
Lempster 163, 179, 223, 293
Lisbon 111
Littleton 83, 111, 139, 213, 299
Lyme 14, 169, 186
Lyndeborough 33, 94, 234, 322
Manchester 24, 26, 27, 40, 77, 81, 90, 116, 125, 145, 193, 195, 205, 221, 232, 237, 250, 282, 285, 320, 333
Marlborough 6, 9, 11, 12, 17, 18, 21, 22, 23, 24, 27, 28, 32, 34, 46, 48, 53, 55, 58, 59, 63, 65, 68, 75, 76, 78, 79, 81, 83, 84, 85, 89, 91, 92, 94, 97, 99, 101, 113, 118, 119, 120, 122, 124, 125, 129, 131, 135, 136, 137, 139, 140, 141, 147, 148, 149, 151, 155, 162, 164,

167, 168, 169, 175, 176, 177, 178, 182, 183, 187, 188, 190, 197, 202, 203, 204, 208, 211, 212, 215, 217, 222, 229, 230, 232, 234, 235, 236, 241, 248, 249, 252, 257, 261, 263, 266, 268, 270, 272, 273, 279, 281, 283, 285, 293, 296, 304, 310, 312, 314, 316, 317, 319, 320, 321, 323, 327, 332
Marlborough Depot 100, 204
Marlow 9, 13, 16, 34, 52, 53, 91, 127, 138, 141, 179, 194, 197, 199, 205, 213, 220, 265, 268, 275, 293, 297, 304, 305, 306, 310, 313, 316, 320, 333
Mason 3, 48, 263
Meredith 143
Merrimack County 111
Milford 11, 78, 260
Nashua 11, 38, 51, 78, 79, 91, 116, 149, 212, 231, 251, 257, 274, 275
Nelson 4, 11, 14, 15, 20, 21, 27, 78, 80, 94, 101, 114, 123, 126, 137, 151, 154, 164, 177, 185, 203, 221, 239, 314, 315, 327
New Durham 5, 222
New Ipswich 11, 43, 62, 85
Newbury 91
Newmarket 127
Newport 98, 111, 273, 275, 276
North Hinsdale 231
North Richmond 13
North Walpole 12, 120, 166, 171, 184, 208, 302
Park Hill 78
Pembroke 62, 188, 234
Peterborough 12, 18, 41, 66, 101, 153, 161, 214, 215, 249, 255
Pittsfield 100
Plymouth 202, 278
Portsmouth 175
Raymond 192
Richmond 13, 15, 19, 20, 22, 33, 42, 43, 45, 58, 76, 78, 82, 84, 89, 94, 99, 107, 110, 115, 125, 129, 131, 135, 138, 141, 148, 155, 157, 175, 181, 182, 191, 199, 207, 209, 212, 216, 218, 225, 233, 243, 247, 256, 259, 264, 268, 279, 282, 287, 291, 295, 299, 301, 304, 307, 321, 322, 324, 325
Rindge 3, 6, 7, 18, 20, 21, 22, 41, 49, 50, 54, 55, 59, 66, 89, 96, 100, 113, 129, 132, 141, 161, 162, 179, 180, 190, 193, 199, 212, 219, 235, 239, 247, 252, 255, 261, 264, 267, 270, 287, 292, 322, 323, 332, 333
Rochester 170
Rockingham 209
Roxbury 11, 15, 38, 39, 40, 41, 48, 95, 96, 138, 150, 161, 168, 182, 190, 236, 258, 273, 286, 331
Sharon 255, 257, 301, 303

South Acworth 275
South Keene 41
Spragueville 184
Springfield 98, 320
Stoddard 7, 13, 16, 17, 22, 23, 27, 29, 30, 47, 51, 66, 87, 103, 111, 123, 139, 142, 163, 165, 188, 197, 201, 213, 229, 234, 263, 265, 267, 268, 270, 274, 280, 285, 298, 302, 315, 323, 327, 335
Stratham 138
Sullivan 7, 16, 34, 61, 72, 79, 82, 123, 128, 141, 152, 154, 159, 165, 173, 189
Sullivan County 42, 60
Sunapee 138
Suncook 7, 131
Surry 35, 47, 48, 69, 88, 89, 108, 119, 129, 154, 156, 160, 171, 192, 205, 219, 230, 234, 245, 255, 256, 280, 281, 289, 303, 337
Sutton 168
Swanzey 3, 9, 13, 26, 28, 30, 31, 32, 34, 47, 64, 68, 71, 74, 75, 76, 81, 82, 83, 84, 86, 92, 93, 99, 108, 115, 118, 119, 122, 127, 130, 134, 135, 137, 142, 143, 146, 150, 151, 158, 163, 165, 170, 174, 175, 179, 180, 181, 185, 198, 200, 204, 207, 213, 218, 220, 222, 226, 227, 229, 237, 240, 241, 244, 245, 249, 257, 260, 269, 270, 271, 286, 290, 293, 294, 296, 299, 305, 306, 307, 308, 310, 311, 314, 316, 319, 322, 324, 325, 328, 332, 337
Tilton 131, 324
Troy 3, 5, 7, 28, 48, 52, 55, 57, 59, 60, 64, 82, 83, 84, 100, 114, 126, 130, 140, 145, 165, 167, 170, 174, 179, 187, 190, 192, 196, 197, 199, 200, 201, 204, 205, 210, 213, 218, 219, 221, 223, 224, 232, 239, 240, 246, 251, 271, 274, 275, 282, 286, 291, 295, 296, 298, 313, 316, 318, 322, 325, 327, 329, 331, 337, 338
Unity 98, 250, 271, 273
Wakefield 258
Walpole 10, 12, 15, 16, 17, 19, 23, 24, 29, 35, 50, 54, 61, 62, 63, 66, 67, 73, 79, 80, 87, 88, 93, 94, 95, 97, 98, 99, 101, 104, 116, 120, 121, 122, 127, 132, 133, 134, 135, 149, 152, 157, 166, 168, 170, 171, 180, 184, 193, 194, 197, 200, 201, 206, 208, 211, 226, 230, 233, 234, 245, 250, 256, 259, 273, 276, 278, 282, 283, 289, 290, 292, 301, 303, 304, 306, 308, 309, 313, 318, 328, 330, 333, 337
Warner 91, 301
Warren 53
Washington 125
Weare 125
Wendall 212
West Peterborough 214
West Stewartstown 236
West Swanzey 177, 184, 187, 269, 284

Westmoreland 1, 4, 11, 22, 23, 35, 38, 42, 43, 44, 51, 55, 57, 61, 64, 65, 69, 70, 73, 74, 78, 80, 88, 91, 93, 94, 96, 97, 102, 108, 113, 128, 132, 137, 142, 146, 147, 148, 151, 156, 157, 171, 175, 180, 187, 205, 206, 207, 208, 209, 213, 217, 223, 229, 230, 247, 248, 258, 259, 267, 284, 303, 305, 307, 308, 326
Westport 59, 64, 118, 123
Whitefield 10
Wilton 167, 186
Winchester 3, 5, 8, 13, 15, 17, 18, 21, 24, 26, 28, 29, 34, 39, 49, 50, 53, 54, 56, 58, 59, 60, 61, 62, 65, 68, 70, 71, 72, 75, 77, 78, 79, 80, 81, 82, 83, 84, 85, 86, 87, 93, 96, 106, 111, 118, 120, 121, 123, 124, 130, 131, 133, 136, 143, 146, 147, 148, 153, 155, 157, 158, 159, 160, 164, 166, 168, 169, 170, 174, 176, 177, 178, 185, 189, 195, 196, 197, 198, 200, 205, 206, 207, 210, 211, 212, 213, 214, 215, 216, 218, 220, 222, 229, 230, 233, 236, 237, 240, 243, 244, 245, 246, 247, 248, 250, 252, 255, 256, 258, 260, 261, 262, 264, 266, 269, 270, 271, 273, 278, 279, 280, 284, 286, 288, 290, 291, 292, 293, 295, 297, 299, 300, 301, 302, 304, 307, 311, 312, 314, 317, 319, 320, 321, 324, 325, 326, 327, 329, 330, 331, 334
Windham 145

NJ 87, 156, 177
Trenton 257
Vineland 215

NY 5, 11, 13, 26, 41, 52, 58, 60, 70, 71, 76, 77, 85, 88, 93, 113, 122, 131, 137, 139, 169, 184, 189, 211, 225, 227, 229, 238, 239, 244, 246, 250, 252, 260, 264, 276, 277, 281, 291, 299, 311, 316, 321, 325
Albany 31, 62, 76, 176
Allenburg 253
Amsterdam 174
Brandon 19
Brockport 201
Brooklyn 59, 76
Camden 29
Champlain 43, 231
Colton 58
Demorana 124
Essex 225
Essex Co. 214
Fort Ann 217, 235
Glenn Falls 201
Greenwich 165
Hartford 113
Hebron 314
Hoosac Falls 81, 219
Irona 76, 135

Jay 63, 299
Keysville 72, 88, 98
Lewiston 212
Lomton Springs 217
Malone 178
Montgomery 153
NYC 47, 254
Nunda 24
Ogdensburg 116
Parrisville 162
Plattsburg 20, 51, 72, 178, 249
Readfield 29
Rexford 143
St. Johnsville 87
Saratoga 62, 172, 215
Schrom Rivers 63
Stoneybrook 172
Syracuse 19
Ticonderoga 101, 189, 207
Troy 19, 77
Watertown 187
Westville, NY 1, 27
Whitehall 127, 138, 149, 184, 230

Ohio 136, 180
Akron 57
Cleveland 251

PA 111, 221, 253
Bradford 83
Philadelphia 115, 186, 259
Pine Grove 39
Shenandoah 254

Poland 201, 215, 315

Rhode Island 74, 215, 226, 255
Bristol 45
Fall River 48
Newport 215
Providence 47, 49, 78, 115, 166, 177, 190, 203, 255, 289, 299
Westerly 174
Woonsocket 177

Russia 201, 204, 215, 247, 292, 326

Scotland 127, 141, 253, 286, 321
Glasgow 182

Spain 236

Sweden 51, 105, 188, 222, 229, 231, 253, 270, 315
Gottenburg 262
Stockholm 51

Texas 290

VT 1, 4, 14, 21, 30, 41, 46, 63, 68, 71, 113,
   135, 138, 139, 141, 142, 144, 147, 151, 157,
   164, 184, 186, 221, 226, 228, 229, 236, 243,
   245, 247, 250, 253, 264, 266, 268, 285, 287,
   293, 302, 306, 310, 312, 314, 319, 320, 323,
   326, 332
Alburgh 240
Andover 233
Atkins 166
Barnet 116
Barre 135
Bellows Falls 12, 16, 44, 121, 127, 184, 193,
   208, 223, 228, 234, 245, 250, 251, 256, 275,
   281, 282, 307, 319
Bennington 219, 260
Berkshire 126
Bethel 181
Bradford 73
Brandon 16, 173, 189
Brattleboro 4, 5, 10, 11, 27, 56, 57, 68, 76, 85,
   88, 144, 157, 160, 166, 171, 208, 217, 228,
   229, 234, 243, 260, 268, 284, 292, 320
Bridgwater 163, 194
Bristol 65, 260, 261
Burlington 7, 69, 70, 126, 134, 188, 211, 226,
   278, 312
Castleton 68
Chelsea 35, 179
Chester 31, 115
Clarendon 151, 176
Colchester 188
Derby 111
Dover 250, 266
Dummerston 88, 151, 310
East Bethel 179
East Middlebury 270
Ely 19, 120
Ely Mines 184
Fairlee 163
Georgia 179, 193
Goshen 17
Grafton 206, 209
Granby 224
Grand Isle 65
Granville 8
Guilford 25, 181, 308
Hartford 138, 293
Hartland 224, 245
Highgate 117, 211, 255, 256, 322
Highgate Falls 201
Jacksonville 189
Jamaica 96, 176, 314
Jericho 1, 27

Landsgrove 34, 197, 198
Londonderry 116, 216, 224
Ludlow 285
Marlboro 25, 76
Middleborough 204
Middlebury 76, 204, 245, 261, 272
Milton 178
Montgomery 57
Montpelier 7, 253
Moretown 185
Mount Holly 305
Newfane 39, 96, 217, 250
North Hartford 138
North Rupert 217
Northfield 180, 191
Perkinsville 130, 154
Pittsford 114
Plymouth 286
Poultney 268
Putney 69, 184, 262
Readsboro 159
Richford 57
Rochester 173
Rockingham 12, 19, 23, 49, 283
Royalston 284
Rutland 12, 67, 87, 102, 153, 198
St. Albans 266, 326
St. Johnsbury 68
Saxon's River 17
Scranton 259
Searsburg 31, 189
Sharon 131
Sheldon 9, 285
Somerset 39
South Dorset 219
South Londonderry 39
South Royalton 75
South Vernon 63, 284
Springfield 6, 23, 152, 318
Stockbridge 130
Stratton 39
Sunderland 195
Sutton 10, 265
Swanton 119
Townsend 272
Underhill 101
Vergennes 6, 158, 203
Vernon 87, 94, 125, 264
Wallingford 172
Wardsboro 25, 42, 196
Washington 179, 190, 325
Waterville 132
Weathersfield 79, 127, 191
West Dorset 158
West Salisbury 252
West Wardsboro 96

Westfield 233, 290
Westminster 17, 91, 171, 183, 188, 281
Whitingham 142, 200, 229, 265
Whitington 220
Windhall 165
Windsor 229
Woodstock 183

Virginia 28, 268, 282

Wales 276

Washington, DC 94

West Indies Islands 236

Wisconsin 63
　Lodi 172
　Ripon 201

All Name Index

Abar, Louisa 217
Abbott, B. B. 37
Abbott, Comr. 1, 179
Abbott, Freeman 282
Abbott, J. B. 39, 51, 114, 180
Abbott, John P. 144
Abbott, Maria 282
Abbott, Sarah E. [Griffith] 144
Abbott, Sylvia 116
Adams, George 93
Adams, Austin O. 113
Adams, Austin O., Mrs. 113
Adams, C. E. 270
Adams, Harry 27
Ahern, John 66, 67
Aikens. See also Aiken
Aikens, Enoch 163, 196
Aikens, Frank C. 163, 196
Aikens, Joanna (Valentine) 163
Aiken. See also Aikens
Aiken, Catherine F. Reed 330
Alamo, Charles A. 333
Albee, Charles J. 305, 338
Aldrich, Barton 51
Aldrich, Betsey 86
Aldrich, Betsey, Jr. 86
Aldrich, Daniel W., Mrs. 88
Aldrich, David S. 86
Aldrich, Mary Ann 141
Aldrich, Robert T. 230
Aldrich, Sarah E. 325
Aldrich, Sarah O. 110
Alex. See also Alix
Alex, Joseph 103
Alix. See also Alex
Alix, Emma (Whitcomb) 90
Alix, Joseph 90
Allard, Amy B. 114
Allard, Bruce 114
Allard, Emily C. 114
Allard, Frank D. 114
Allard, Grace B. 114
Allard, Ralph C. 114
Allen, Alice 221
Allen, Alvira 337
Allen, David 70
Allen, David, Jr. 70
Allen, Elvira 69
Allen, Elvira (Whipple) 182
Allen, Henry Clay 52
Allen, Isabella C. 52
Allen, John A. 52
Allen, Lewis M. 306

Allen, Lucy T. 101
Allen, Mary J. 172
Allen, Noah 70
Allen, William L. 172
Allridge, Catharine 21
Amidon, Annie K. 294
Amidon, Fred P. 294
Amidon, Henry H. 294
Amidon, James C. 294
Amidon, James G. 294
Amidon, Mary J. 208
Amidon, Nathaniel 209
Amidon, Susan 294
Anderson, Charles 105
Anderson, James 321
Andrew, Adolphus 231
Andrew, Mary 231
Andrew, Minerva (Scrow) 231
Andrew, Minnie 231
Andrew, Nelson H. 231
Antoiniotti, Amelia 249
Antoiniotti, Frank A. 249
Antoiniotti, Josephine A. 249
Antoiniotti, Mitchell 249
Applin, Perrin 52
Arington, Sophia 38
Arlen. See Arling
Arling, Ethel H. (Sawtelle) 93
Arling, Florence E. 93
Arling, Frank W. 93
Arling, James W. 93
Arling, Lucy E. 93
Arling, William N. 34
Armstrong, Alpheus H. 84
Armstrong, Amanda C. 220
Armstrong, Estalle 220
Armstrong, Eva 333
Armstrong, Henry A. 220
Armstrong, Jerome 220
Armstrong, Joseph M. 220
Armstrong, Lilly 145
Armstrong, Louisa 84
Armstrong, Maggie 63
Armstrong, Nellie 220
Asher, Harry S. 240
Asher, Lena (Collins) 240
Austin, Celia 272
Austin, Hannah 290
Austin, Julia A. 9, 85
Austin, Kendall 9
Avord, Albina 259
Avord, Anthony 259

Bailey, Colton C. 229
Bailey, Mrs. 110
Baker, Arthur 245

Baker, Charles S. 53
Baker, Edgar 245
Baker, Edward 245
Baker, George D. 252
Baker, Ida May 245
Baker, Lula M. 252
Baker, Mary M. 53
Baker, Nellie 252
Balch, Mary E. 260
Baldwin, Charles 267, 338
Baldwin, Mr. 41
Ball, Charles 136
Ball, Fannie (Percival) [Richards] 317
Ball, Frank 317
Ball, Gerdice F. 136
Ball, Hatte L. 136
Ball, Isabelle 136
Ball, Martha 136
Ball, Martha Elizabeth 136
Ball, Sarah Ann 136
Ballane, Solomon 121
Ballou, Albert 276
Ballou, Charles A. 277, 337
Ballou, Clara 156
Ballou, Edward 153
Ballou, Filetus 212
Ballou, Frank M. 277
Ballou, George H. 156
Ballou, Harvey 156
Ballou, Ira F. 212
Ballou, Joseph 230
Ballou, Laura S. 212
Ballou, Mary (Paro) 276
Ballou, Mary E. (Califf) 156
Ballou, Nancy 108, 337
Ballou, Nellie O. 230
Ballou, Polly H. 245
Ballou, Sarah 295
Bancroft, C. P. 16, 199
Bandeen, Agnes 182
Bendeen, Alice 182
Bandeen, Christina 182
Bandeen, David 182
Banshaw, Elizabeth 266
Baraby, Josephine 110
Barcomb, Rosina 269
Bardo, Amory 321
Bardo, Arthur W. 321
Bardo, Ester 321
Bardo, Lewis 321
Bardo, Lewis A. 321
Bardo, Marry E. 321
Barlow, Arthur J. 207
Barlow, LeRoy 207
Barlow, Mary J. 207, 208
Barlow, Nathaniel A. 207

Barnard, Alvin 34
Barnard, Clara 34
Barnard, Emma 34
Barnard, Henrietta 34
Barnard, Henry 34
Barnard, Mary 34
Barney, Harvey 179
Barns, Albert 213
Barns, Etta (Howard) 213
Barrett, Charles 65, 66
Barrett, Eddie L. 105, 338
Barrett, Eugene H. 250
Barrett, Whitney 65
Barrus, Mrs. 65
Barry, Hannah 19
Barry, J. M. 276
Barry, James 19, 268
Barry, James M., Mrs. 276
Barry, John 19
Barry, Nellie 19
Barry, Norman T. 276
Barry, Sarah H. 268
Barry, Sylvia (Sargent) 91
Barry, William J. 19
Bartlett, Charles C. 65
Bartlett, Clarance C. 25
Bartlett, David N. 65
Bartlett, Edgar C. 65
Bartlett, Florence 316
Bartlett, Frederick 250
Bartlett, Harriet L. 65
Bartlett, John R. 142
Bartlett, Julius 309
Bartlett, Libbie May 316
Bartlett, Lizzie 142
Bartlett, Marshall W. 316
Bartlett, Mrs. 83
Bartlett, Nelson G. 139
Bartlett, Raymond A. 316
Bartlett, Sarah O. 25
Bartlett, Stella H. 309
Barton, Anna 203
Barton, Thomas E. 203
Bastarache, Alivine 243
Bastarache, Joseph 243
Batchelder, Stephen 134
Bates, Archie B. 64
Bates, Bertha L. 198
Bates, Charles 308
Bates, Charles A. 64
Bates, Daisy M. 34, 197, 198
Bates, Eddy 106
Bates, Edward H. 34
Bates, Edwin J. 64
Bates, Eliza (Perry) 104
Bates, Forest E. 279

Bates, Francis 29, 30, 279
Bates, Francis A. 111
Bates, Ida M. 279
Bates, James M. 34, 197, 198, 229
Bates, Jennie (Nash) 29, 30
Bates, Julia A. (Crown) 64
Bates, Lillie 34
Bates, Lucius 64
Bates, Lucy (Whittimore) 34, 197, 198
Bates, Maria L. 5
Bates, Marion G. (Holbrook) 111
Bates, Mary L. 34
Bates, Minnie F. 34
Bates, Rosa E. 34, 197, 198
Bates, Rose E. 229
Batty, Bridget [Waskins] 28
Batty, Joseph 28
Baufor, John 185
Bayer. See also Payer
Bayer, Alfred 318
Baylis, Edward 224
Baylis, Effie 224
Baylis, Etta 224
Bayou, Alfred 227
Bayou, Delia 227
Bayou, Joseph 227
Bayou, Leander 227
Bayou, May 227
Bayou, Octavia Antiene 226
Bayou, Orgius 227
Bayou, Theodore 227
Beach, Fanny A. 177
Beach, Mary E. 177
Beach, Mary E., Jr. 177
Beach, William B. 177
Beach, Willie E. 177
Beal, Clara A. (Jones) 35
Beal, Lyman T. 35
Bean, Adelia 53
Bean, Charles 53
Bean, Frank 53
Bean, John 102
Bean, John, Mrs. 102
Bean, Peter 53
Bean, Pheba 53
Bean, Pheba, Jr. 53
Beaufor, Joseph 28
Beaufor, Rosa 29
Beaumond. See Burroud
Beckwith, Oliver Chapin 64
Begai, Ignacas 201
Belduke, Napoleon 288
Belknap, Elizabeth 13
Bell, Abraham 176, 193
Bell, Ada 183
Bell, Anna 183

Bell, Ellen 183
Bell, Elvira E. 193
Bell, Frank 176
Bell, Fred 183
Bell, Jane 183
Bell, John 182
Bell, Laura P. [Kent] 176, 193
Bell, Lillie 183
Bell, Lizzie 183
Bell, Louisa 183
Bell, Melvina (Young) 182
Bell, Minnie 183
Bell, Phoeba 183
Bell, Zoa 183
Belletete, John 238
Bemis, Edmund 179
Bemis, S. D. 191
Benjamin, Joseph 1
Bennett, Alvena [Croshea] 233
Bennett, Alvena, Jr. 234
Bennett, Freddie 305
Bennett, George 305
Bennett, George H. 233
Bennett, Hattie 305
Bennett, Hattie (Larabee) 305
Bennett, Hattie M. 305
Bennett, Henry 305
Bennett, Julia 237
Bennett, Lizzie 234
Bennett, Lottie B. 265
Bennett, Minnie Etta 305
Bennett, Nettie 264
Bennett, William 305
Bennett, William, Jr. 305
Bennett, William D. 264
Bentote, Samuel 335
Bergeron, Annie 270
Bergeron, Clemen 270
Bergeron, Florence 270
Bergeron, Florence, Jr. 270
Bergeron, Henry 270
Bergeron, Ida 270
Bergeron, Michael 270
Bergnon, John 238
Berman, Sadie 221
Berthiame,, Maime 131
Bertram, Agnes 212
Bertram, Alba 212
Bertram, Charles 211
Bertram, Clara 212
Bertram, Cordelia 211
Bertram, Ellen 211
Bertram, Emma 211
Bertram, Rosa 211
Beshaw, Nelson 239
Bevens, Henry 28

Bigelow, George 200, 208
Bigelow, Mary 103, 200
Bigelow, Mary Burke 328
Bigelow, Mary J. 208
Bigelow, Mary J. (Amidon) 208
Biggie, Bertie H. 246
Biggie, Charles 246
Biggie, Christopher 246
Biggie, Edmond 246
Biggie, Jessie A. 246
Bigwood, Amber G. 243
Bigwood, George A. 243
Bigwood, Hattie E. 243
Bigwood, William 243
Bigwood, Willie 243
Bill, Willard, Jr. 102
Billings, Henry C. 155
Billings, Keziah E. 35
Bingham, Alanson 1
Bingham, Charles W. 66
Bingham, George A. 66
Bingham, Gracie M. 66
Bingham, Joseph C. 66
Bingham, Lilla J. (Brown) 66
Bingham, Miles J. 66
Bingham, Osmon A. 1
Birch, Charles 1
Birch, Josephine 1
Birch, Lenora 1, 2, 27
Birch, Nelson 1, 27
Birgholm, Fred 333
Bishop, Abbie Belle 112
Bishop, Arthur P. 112
Bishop, Charles M. 136
Bishop, Eddie 136
Bishop, Edgar Truman 112
Bishop, Esther E. 294
Bishop, Fred C. 294
Bishop, Hannah (Day) 294
Bishop, Louisa 136
Bishop, Luella Maud 112
Bishop, Marsden 112
Bishop, Olive A. 112
Bishop, Pearl 294
Bishop, Samuel M. 139
Bixby, Edward 29
Bixby, Thankful P. (Felch) 29
Black, Alalander 286
Black, Bessie 286
Black, Edith 286
Black, Edward 286
Black, Elbridge H. 26
Black, Nettie 286
Black, Nettie (Osborn) 286
Black, Orrin 26
Black, William 286

Black, Winfield M. 26
Blair, Richard 214
Blais, Alfred 82
Blais, Alice [St. Peter] 82
Blais, Faretense 82
Blais, Lewis 82
Blake, Charles A. 205
Blake, Clifford 205
Blake, Henry 205
Blake, Levi 257
Blake, Nellie (Miller) 205
Blake, Richard C. 64
Blanchard, Amanda (Stockwell) 125
Blanchard, Amelia 174
Blanchard, Amos 130
Blanchard, Amos A. 328
Blanchard, Annie M. 298
Blanchard, Arzelia 174
Blanchard, Bertha 27
Blanchard, Clerance 130
Blanchard, Daniel 27
Blanchard, Edward C. 125
Blanchard, Eva 174
Blanchard, Flora 174
Blanchard, Flora I. 130
Blanchard, Frances 27
Blanchard, Fred 27
Blanchard, Hannah B. 162
Blanchard, J. Henry 130
Blanchard, James A. 298
Blanchard, Joseph 164, 174
Blanchard, Joseph H. 304
Blanchard, Mary 27
Blanchard, Mary L. 164
Blanchard, Minnie 164
Blanchard, Nancy R. 130
Blanchard, William H. 162
Blanchard, Willie 27
Blanchard, Willie A. 130
Blanchet, Amelia 174
Blanchet, Arzelia 174
Blanchet, Eva 174
Blanchet, Flora 174
Blanchet, Joseph 174
Blodgett, Joseph 264
Blood, Abbie E. [Reed] 329
Blood, Charles L. 329
Blood, Fanny A. (Beach) 177
Blood, Lucy A. 17
Boardman. See also Bordman
Boardman, Charles 202
[Boestr], Mary 218
Boles, Joseph 144
Bolster, William L. 106
Boman, Hilma 270
Boovier. See also Bouvier

Boovier, Charles 71
Boovier, Charles, Mrs. 71
Bordwin, Albert 222
Bordwin, Anna 222
Bordwin, Carrie 222
Bordwin, Eliza (Markes) 222
Bordwin, Lela (Cole) 222
Bordwin, Oscar J. 222
Borgan, Shisia 143
Borron, Peter 134
Borron, Peter T. 134
Bosley, Angeline 2
Bosley, Emma 2
Bosley, Exennce 2
Bosley, Fred 2
Boslcy, Mary 2
Bosley, Raymond 2
Boston, Joseph 318
Bosworth, Ada (Davis) 284
Bosworth, Orrin K. 284
Bosworth, William H. 2
Bouchard. See also Bourchard
Bouchard, Estancelaer 275
Bouchard, Rose 275
Boufor, Adele (Gonyou) 121
Boufor, Anne 121
Boufor, Cyrelo 121
Boufor, Emma 121
Boufor, Florence 121
Boufor, George 121
Boufor, Georgianna 121
Boufor, Joseph 121
Boufor, Leon 121
Boufor, Mary 121
Boufor, Richard 121
Bourchard, Estanestace 274
Bourler, Mary 308
Bourler, Mary, 2d 308
Bourn, John C. 134
Bourrett, Albert 196
Bourrett, Gracie 196
Bourrett, Harvey 196
Bourrett, Laura E. 196
Bourrett, Louis 196
Bourrett, Louis D. 196
Bourrett, Mamie 196
Boutelle, Stillman 322
Bouter, Alexander 205
Bouter, Mary 205
Bouvier. See also Boovier, Bouvir
Bouvier, Lewis 80
Bouvier, Rose 80
Bouvir. See also Bouvier
Bouvir, Ellen B. 135
Bouvis, Cora 278
Bouvis, Delia 278

Bouvis, Emma 278
Bouvis, Flora 278
Bouvis, Joseph 278
Bouvis, Malvina 278
Bouvis, Willie 278
Bowen, Clarence S. 285
Bowen, Ellen F. Tyrell 261
Bowen, Freddie 285
Bowen, George 261
Bowen, George M., Mrs. 209
Bowen, Guy 285
Bowen, Ida 285, 286
Bowen, Jennie (Gamill) 285
Bowers. See Bowiss
Bowers, William 64
Bowiss, Julia 257
Boyea, Oliver 317
Bradbury, Arthur L. 254
Bradbury, Edward 254
Bradbury, Ernest 254
Bradbury, Florence R. 254
Bradbury, Frank H. 254
Bradbury, Frank H., Jr. 254
Bradbury, Harry 254
Bradbury, John J. 254
Bradbury, Mary S. (Low) 254
Bradbury, William R. 254
Bragg, Charles 334
Bragg, George 334
Bragg, Ida M. Maddock 334
Bragg, Leon 334
Bragg, Maria L. 195
Bragg, Mary 262, 334
Bragg, Milan 334
Bragg, Ralph 334
Bragg, Randall N. 195
Brala, Mat 287
Breasseur, Ada 257
Breasseur, Fred 257
Breasseur, Joseph 257
Breasseur, Joseph, Jr. 257
Breasseur, Mary 257
Beasseur, Rosa 257
Breau, Angeline [O'Neil] 183
Breau, Charles 183
Breau, Joseph, Jr. 183
Breau, Joseph, III 183
Breed, Annie 271
Breed, Fanny 271
Breed, Frank 271
Breed, Fred 271
Breed, Ina 271
Breed, Lucius 271
Breed, Lucius F. 123
Breen, Sarah E. 129
Breman, Mary 328

Brett, James 329
Brett, Lucy (Seward) 329
Brett, W. H. 329
Brewer, Frank 324
Brewer, Maude A. 324
Brewer, Minnie Ella 334
Brian, James C. 280
Brian, James P. 280
Briant. See also Bryant
Briant, Anson S. 338
Brickley, Thomas 273
Bridges, Maria L. 230
Brien, Malachy 132
Briggs, Bradley 2, 4, 338
Briggs, Philana D. 4
Bristol, Mr. 62
Britton, Azubah 192
Britton, Benjamin 192
Britton, Benjamin H. 192
Britton, Charles A. 260, 329
Britton, Jennie C. 261
Britton, John L. 261
Britton, Lewis G. 261
Britton, Mary E. (Balch) 260
Britton, Sabra M. (Tufts) 261
Brooks, Addie D. (Perham) 191
Brooks, Arthur J. 191
Brooks, Bertie 191
Brooks, Eva 191
Brooks, Mabel 191
Brooks, Walter 191
Brooks, Winfield 191
Brown, Caroline Jane 315
Brown, Charles 64
Brown, Edmund 103
Brown, Ellen M. (McCoy) 66
Brown, Frank E. 144
Brown, George F. 83
Brown, George S. 258
Brown, Joseph H. 64
Brown, Julia M. 82
Brown, Lilla J. 66
Brown, Mr. 61
Brown, Rodney J. 66
Brown, Rosa A. 64
Brown, Stella M. 191
Brown, William 315
Brummond. See Burroud
Brunell, Clara 239
Brunell, Eddie 239
Brunell, Emma 239
Brunell, Henry 239
Brunell, Moses 239
Bryant. See also Briant
Bryant, Avery 180, 296
Bryant, Emeline/Emily C. 111, 140

Bryant, Ermina C. 110
Bryant, Ernest G. 233
Bryant, Frank A. 233
Bryant, Hattie M. [Button] 233
Bryant, Josephine 216
Bryant, Kendall B. 130, 216
Bryant, Leonard 90
Bryant, Louisa [Moultney] 130, 216
Bryant, Luke 111, 140
Bryant, Martin D. 312
Bryant, Peter G. 140
Bryant, Sarah A. (Morey) 181, 296
Bryant, Viola E. 233
Bryant, William 216
Buck, Mary 257
Buckley, John 103
Buel, John 22
Buffum, Alice M. 307
Buffum, Bertha S. 307
Buffum, C. F. 145
Buffum, Edward H. 307
Buffum, Francis H. 307
Buffum, Francis H., Jr. 307
Buffum, Jessie H. 307
Buffum, Margaret E. 307
Buffum, Marion 307
Buffum, Richard H. 307
Buffum, Warren H. 307
Bugbee, Charles N. 121
Bugbee, Francis C. 121, 132
Bugbee, William A. 132
Bunker, Arthur E. 265
Bunker, Daniel 265
Bunker, Ella (Wilder) 265
Burcham, Huldah W. 180
Burcham, Joseph 180
Burchstead, ___ 165
Burdett, Luke H. 93
Burdett, Mary A. [Stevens] 93
Burgess, Eliza 148, 149
Burgess, Minnie Agnes 149
Burgess, Myric 148
Burgess, Walton Eaton 148
Burgess, Warren J. 148
Burn. See also Burns
Burn, Mary 79
Burn, Nancy A. 79
Burn, Owen 79
Burnham, Roswell 80
Burnham, William 80
Burnell, Angeline 7
Burnell, John 7
Burnell, John Henry 7
Burns. See also Burn
Burns, ___ 165
Burns, Agnes D. 79, 184

Burns, Barney 53
Burns, Charles 36, 106, 338
Burns, Mary (Hickey) 36
Burns, Nancy A. 184
Burns, Timothy C. 36
Burpee, Asaph E. 36, 106
Burpee, Jennie L. 139
Burpee, John L. 139
Burrell, Bell 189
Burroud, Edward 309
Burroud, Ellen 309
Burroud, Mary 309
Burroud, Michael 309
Burroughs, Eliza M. 156
Burt, Mr. 16
Bushier, Moses 316
Bushier, Sophia 316
Bushey, Barney 269
Bushey, Bertie 219
Bushey, Delia 269
Bushey, Dora 269, 312
Bushey, Earnest 219
Bushey, Elenor 269
Bushey, Ellen 65
Bushey, Henry 219
Bushey, Jennie 219
Bushey, Joseph 219
Bushey, Mary 269
Bushey, Rosina (Barcomb) 269
Butler, Mrs. 214
Butler, Robert 283, 338
Butler, W. H 226
Butterfield, William H. 66
Button, Albert C. 233
Button, Hattie M. 233
Buxton, John 337
Buzzell, Arthur E. 35
Buzzell, Ellen Mabel 35
Buzzell, Nellie M. 35
Buzzell, Olive V. M. 35
Byam, John 143
Byron, Frank 124
Byron, Louisa 124

Cadigan, James 26
Cahill, John 66, 67
Cahill, Mary 66
Califf, Mary E. 156
Calkins, Charles 181
Calkins, Christie 181
Calkins, Edward 181
Calkins, Forest 181
Calkins, Edward F. 284
Calkins, Ellen A. (Pratt) 181
Calkins, George E. 284
Calkins, Horace 181

Calkins, Irus 181
Calkins, Nahun 181
Calkins, Sarah (Nickerson) 284
Calkins, W. H. 181
Calkins, William 284
Calkins, Willie 284
Callahan, Mary 108
Cameron, Alexander 2
Cameron, Annie M. 2
Cameron, Carrie 2
Cameron, Donald 2
Cameron, Donald, Jr. 2
Cameron, Edith 2
Cameron, Elizabeth 2
Cameron, Frank 2
Cameron, Gertie 2
Cameron, Minnie 2
Camfill, Margaret 128
Campbell, George P. 261
Campfield, George 214
Canfield, Johnnie 156
Cansieno, Earnest 321
Cansieno, Ella 321
Cansieno, Jennie 321
Cansieno, Julie, Jr. 321
Cansieno, Laura 321
Cansieno, Louis 321
Cansieno, Louis, Jr. 321
Cansieno, Viola 321
Capren. See also Capron
Capren, Delia 261
Capron. See also Capren
Capron, Benjamin F. 3, 293
Capron, Ellen M. (Wheeler) 3, 293
Capron, Emma J. 3
Capron, Mary Edith 3, 293
Carey, Bridget 53
Carey, Calista R. 40
Carey, Medelpe 332
Carey, Michael 53
Carkin, Ada J. 235
Carkin. See also Carkins
Carkin, Isaac A. 235
Carkin, William O. 235
Carkins. See also Carkin
Carkins, Ethel Marion 324
Carlton, Elvira (Poland) 80, 158
Carlton, Frank P. 80
Carlton, Judge 80
Carlton, Sidney 80, 158
Carlton, Widow 290
Carney, Isabella 225
Carney, Isabella (Connelly) 225
Carney, James 225
Carney, John D. 225
Carney, Mary 225

Carpenter, Anna C. 333
Carpenter, Charles E. 333
Carpenter, Daisy C. 127
Carpenter, Elmer V. 127
Carpenter, Elsie M. 333
Carpenter, Eugene 333
Carpenter, Grover C. 333
Carpenter, Ida V. 127
Carpenter, James 127
Carpenter, Mabel 153, 154
Carpenter, Paul S. 333
Carpenter, Peter J. 333
Carpenter, Samuel E. 333
Carpenter, Susan A. 127
Carpenter, Villie 333
Carpenter, Villie J. 333
Carr, Bridget (Leary) 95
Carr, Frank 53
Carr, Frank David 275
Carr, Henry D. 275
Carr, Mary 68
Carr, Rosie Ann (Daniels) 275
Carr, William 328
Carran, Cyprian 25
Carroll, Nettie C. 278
Carroll, Wilson 278
Carson, H. L., Mrs. 112
Carter, Ellen 66
Carter, Ezra 66
Carter, Jennie 66
Carter, John 66
Carter, Joseph 66
Carter, Mary 66
Carter, Norris C. 142
Carter, Olive 66
Carter, Willie 66
Casey, Edward 186
Casey, Ellen 186
Casey, George 186
Casey, John 186
Casey, Margaret 186
Casey, William 186
Cass, Abigail 110
Cass, Lydia 110
Cass, Nahum, Mrs. 141
Castor, Addie 256
Castor, Arthur 255
Castor, Charles 256
Castor, Eddie 255
Castor, Eva 256
Castor, Freddie 255
Castor, John 256
Castor, Lewis 255
Castor, Lewis, Jr. 256
Castor, Lizzie May 255
Castor, Matilda 255

Castor, Phillip 255
Castor, Sophry 255
Castro, Joseph 117
Castro, Joseph, Jr. 117
Castro, Margaret 117
Caswell, Alton Earl 160
Caswell, Mattie A. [Phelps] 160
Caswell, William A. 160
Cataract. See Catrao
Cataract, Nelson 316
Catrao. See Cataract
Catrao, Nelson 338
Caverly, Betsey M. 146
Caverly, Hiram L. 146
Caverly, Hiram M. 146
Centre, Ann H. 165
Centre, Charles H. 165
Centre, Emmaette 165
Centre, John H. 165
Centre, Lilla B. 165
Centre, Markey 165
Chabot, Louis 26
Chace, Sarah Ann 132
Chamberlain, Darius 216
Chamberlain, Mrs. 13
Chambers, John 172
Champagne. See also Champaign, Champaigne, Champane
Champagne, Alfred J. 205
Champagne, Clara 236
Champaign. See also Champaigne, Champane, Champagne
Champaign, Albina 250
Champaign, Collis 277
Champaign, Edith 277
Champaign, Eliza B. (Morris) 204
Champaign, Emma (Prigson) 250
Champaign, Frank 277
Champaign, George 204
Champaign, George, Jr. 204
Champaign, Henry 250
Champaign, Isaac 250, 276
Champaign, Maud 250
Champaign, Olive 250
Champaign, Oliver 277
Champaign, Oliver, Jr. 277
Champaign, Permelia 277
Champaign, Vina 277
Champaign, Vina, Jr. 277
Champaigne. See also Champane, Champaign, Champagne
Champaigne, Charles 32
Champaigne, David 32
Champaigne, Franklin 32
Champaigne, Joseph 32
Champaigne, Myrta 32

Champane. See also Champaigne, Champagne,
  Champaign, Champany
Champane, Elizabeth 115
Champane, George 115
Champane, George, Jr. 115
Champany. See also Champaigne, Champagne,
  Champaign, Champane, Champney
Champany, Celine 283
Champney. See also Champany
Champney, Charles E. 119
Champney, Lewis 25
Champney, Louisa 119
Chandler, Albert 148
Chapin, Alba 213
Chapin, Joseph M. 64
Chapman, Charles H. 167
Chapman, James C. 32
Chapman, King 104
Charton, Albina (Alvord) 259
Charton, Archie 259
Charton, Edmond 259
Charton, Edward 259
Chase, Nettie 307
Chausse, Adelia 99
Chausse, Emile 99
Chausse, Eugene 99
Chausse, Josephine 99
Chausse, Louis 99
Chausse, Minnie 99
Chausse, William 99
Chebois, L. 137
Cheney, Clara 288
Chicoine, Emma 296
Chipman, Bertie 67
Chipman, Daisy 67
Chipman, Edward S. 67
Chipman, Grant E. 67
Chipman, Ida B. 305
Chipman, Josannah H. 67
Chipman, Lulu May 67
Cilley, Alice 142
Cilley, Eliza M. 142
Cilley, Elliott C. 142
Cilley, Ezra 142
Cilley, William F. 142
Clark, Alexander 226
Clark, Alice M. 171
Clark, Amanda C. [Armstrong] [Foster] 220
Clark, Arthur F. 197
Clark, Benjamin 129
Clark, Bessie V. 197
Clark, Bridget 166
Clark, C. H. 193
Clark, C. Prentiss 166
Clark, Caroline 187
Clark, Carrie 197

Clark, Edgar E. 193
Clark, Edith Jane 166
Clark, Edward A. 166
Clark, Eidith 226
Clark, Erford A. 171
Clark, Esther A. (Shaw) 218
Clark, Everett 197
Clark, Fred Leslie 166
Clark, Lelia 193
Clark, Maria 60
Clark, Mike 254
Clark, Nettie 197
Clark, Preston 197
Clark, Sarah M. 197
Clark, Walter 197
Clark, Warren I. 220
Clasby, George 104
Clegg, Ellen M. 292
Clegg, Victor K. 292
Clegg, William L. 292
Clegg, William N. 292
Clement, Fidelia (Witherel) 290
Clement, Rodolphus 290
Cleywod, Alma 224
Cleywod, Jennie (Fish) 225
Cleywod, Joseph 224
Cleywod, Lora 224
Clough, Charles E. 250
Clough, Edith E. 251
Clough, Edna G. 251
Clough, Winnie 251
Clune, Michael 272, 338
Clune, Nellie 272
Cobb, Martha 103
Cobb, Walter 232
Cobleigh, Edward O. 227
Codding, Gertrude 323
Codding, William H. 323
Coffe. See also Coffey, Coffee
Coffe, Daniel, Mrs. 214
Coffee. See also Coffe, Coffey
Coffee, May 220
Coffey. See also Coffe, Coffee
Coffey, Daniel 128
Coffey, Daniel, Jr. 128
Coffey, Julia 128
Coffey, Julia, Jr. 128
Coffey, Timothy 128
Coffin, Cynthia T. 112
Colburn, John 338
Cole, Anna 222
Cole, Clara S.[Rand] 322
Cole, Hattie S. 155
Cole, J. W. 322
Cole, John 106
Cole, Lela 222

Cole, Mrs. 160
Coleman, Lena C. 216
Coleman, William 216
Colley, Charles E. 318
Colley, Mary Ann 318
Collins, Ellen 80, 203
Collins, Eunice A. 81
Collins, Ezekiel B. 25
Collins, Lawrence 203
Collins, Lena 240
Colomy, Ella J. (Harvey) 222
Colomy, George D. 222
Colomy, George W. 222, 223
Columbia, Harriet 14
Columbia, Irving 14
Columbia, Sophia 14
Columbia, Vangybelle 14
Comer, Edward 67
Comstock, Abigail 175
Comstock, George F. 266
Comstock, Otis D. 175
Condon. See also Congdon
Condon, Margaret 152
Condon, William 152
Congdon. See also Condon
Congdon, John H. 114
Connelly, Isabella 225
Conroy, Ellen 147
Conway, Andrew 186
Conway, Eddie 186
Conway, Frank 186
Conway, James 195
Conway, John 186
Conway, Joseph 186
Conway, Joseph, Jr. 186
Conway, Mary 186
Conway, Mary Ann 221
Conway, May 186
Conway, Nellie (Fowler) 195, 196
Conway, Rosa 186
Cook, Annette 230
Cook, Charlie C. 307
Cook, George 147
Cook, Harry 307
Cook, Henry 147, 178, 195, 324, 338
Cook, Henry, Mrs. 195
Cook, John 178
Cook, John H. 178
Cook, Joseph 178
Cook, Mary 147, 178
Cook, Nettie (Chase) 307
Cook, Ralph 307
Cook, William 307
Cooligan, Charles A. 324
Cooligan, Cristian 324
Cooligan, Minnie 324

Cooligan, Ollie 324
Cooper, Lula 31
Cope, Robert 3
Corey, Albert R. 54
Corey, Amos L. 92
Corey, Annie Fellows 327
Corey, Bernice J. 327
Corey, Carl F. 327
Corey, Carrie E. [Sperry] 92
Corey, Delor 26
Corey, Ellen 26
Corey, George W. 327
Corey, Gladys I. 327
Corey, Henry 26
Corey, Herbert 26
Corey, Herman 26
Corey, James 26
Corey, Mary Jane 26
Corey, Medon 26
Corey, Nestor 26
Corey, Sarah Jane (McCoy) 54
Coriveau, Alace 137
Coriveau, Eliza 137
Coriveau, Joseph 137
Coriveau, Willie 137
Cornell, Ellen 241
Cornet, Jeremie 89
Cornfield, Johnnie 120
Cornfield, Margaret 120
Costello. See also Custello
Costello, John 24
Coster, Lucy 238
Costine, Ellen 67
Cota, Carrie (Trudo) 260
Cota, Charlie 260
Cota, Dick 96
Cotas, Henry 260
Cota, Joseph 260
Cota, Rose (Perry) 260
Cotto, Daniel 202
Cotto, John 202
Cotto, William 202
Coughlin, Mary A. 225
Coulliard, Parmelia 337
Coy, Margaret 119
Coy, Mary 117, 119
Crabb, Ann 54
Crabb, George 54
Crabb, Michael 54
Crabb, William 54
Crabb, Willie 54
Cragen. See also Cragin
Cragen, Mary 135
Cragin. See also Cragen
Cragin, Fred O. 3
Cragin, George W. 3

Cragin, Lucy J. 3
Craig, Allen Aaron 92, 277
Craig, Dr. 205
Craig, Ida 277, 303
Craig, Ruth 277, 303
Crain, Mercy 24
Cram, Alice 325
Cram, Arthur 325
Cram, Daphins 325
Cram, Horace 325
Cram, Martin 325
Cram, Nettie M. 325
Cram, Walter 325
Crato, Delia (Pluff) 48
Crato, Delia 48
Crato, George 48
Crato, John 48
Crato, John, Jr. 48
Crechon, Annie M. (Blanchard) 298
Crechon, Clara 298
Crechon, Pauline 298
Crechon, William 298
Crofford, Robert H. 324
Crosby, Benjamin 106
Crosby, Benjamin J. 160
Croshea, Alvena 233
Croshea, Joseph 234
Croshea, Joseph, Jr. 233
Croshea, Richard 233
Crossfield, Abbie C. 161, 228
Crossfield, Caroline M. 228
Crossfield, Charles H. 161, 228
Crossfield, Kendall 228
Crossfield, Mary Jane 267
Crossfield, S. J. 338
Crossfield, Sadie C. 161
Croteau. See Crotto, Croto
Croto, Ellen 252
Croto, Ephraim 273
Croto, Judson 273
Crotto. See also Croto
Crotto, Alfred 65
Crotto, Ellen 65
Crotto, Josephine 65
Crotty, Bridget 318
Crotty, Catherine 319
Crotty, John 318
Crotty, John, Jr. 319
Crotty, Mary 319
Crouch, Hannah 102, 116
Crouch, Mary M. 330
Crown, Adaline 309
Crown, Andrew 309
Crown, Andrew J. 64
Crown, Julia A. 64
Crown, Nettie L. 309

Crown, Orman 309
Crown, Rosina A. 64
Cumings. See also Cummings
Cumings, Ann 36
Cummings. Se also Cumings
Cummings, Adelene N. 36
Cummings, Arthur W. 152
Cummings, Benjamin F. 133
Cummings, Fannie B. 252
Cummings, Frank W. 152
Cummings, George F. 314
Cummings, George Frank J. 36
Cummings, Harrison A. 152
Cummings, Hattie E. [Raymond] 133
Cummings, Isabelle Jane 36
Cummings, Jasher R. 36
Cummings, Lena A. 152, 271
Cummings, Lucretia 152, 271
Cummings, Mamie 36
Cummings, Mary Jane 36
Cummings, Ora A. 152
Cummings, Oscar E. 252
Cummings, Russell W. 36
Cummings, Sadie E. 281
Cummings, William 271
Cummins, Ebenezer 273
Cummins, Hannah 273
Cunningham, Eddie 255
Cunningham, Hannah 255
Cunningham, Hannah [Cummins] 273
Cunningham, Isabel 255
Cunningham, James 255
Cunningham, John 255
Cunningham, Lizzie 255
Cunningham, Mary 255
Cunningham, Maurice 255
Cunningham, Nellie 255
Cunningham, Robert 273
Cunningham, Terance 204
Cunningham, Willie 255
Cunningham, Willis 306
Curran, Timothy 321
Currier, Lawrence 67
Curtin, Thomas 24
Curtis, Andrew J. 300
Curtis, Clara (Scott) [Wilson] 300
Curtis, George W. 300
Curtis, Harry 300
Curtis, Leon 300
Curtis, Rhuel A. 300
Custare, Joseph 186
Custare, Joseph, Jr. 186
Custare, Margaret [Casey] 186
Custello. See also Costello
Custello, Morris 167
Cutler, Fred P. 84

Cutting, Charles F. 118
Cutting, George W. 211
Cutting, Lydia K. 210
Cutting, Samuel 210

Daggett, James H. 132
Daginon, John 37
Daigle, Angelena 40
Daigle, Eddie F. 322
Daigle, Henry 322
Daigle, John 40
Daigle, John W. 40
Daigle, Nathlie D. 40
Daigle, Phebe Parent 322
Dame, Almira (Gibbs) 301
Dame, Charles A. 301
Dame, George R. 301
Dame, Marry L. 301
Dame, Thomas 301
Dame, Viola 301
Dament, Alfred 283
Dament, Arthur 283
Dament, Celine (Champany) 283
Dament, Dora 283
Dament, Flora 283
Dament, Fred 283
Danforth, Benjamin F., Jr. 50
Daniels, J. G. 277
Daniels, Rosie Ann 275
Dargant, Louisa 239
Darren, Addia E. 276
Darren, Charles C. V. 276
Darren, Gertrude L. 276
Darren, Grover C. 276
Darren, Hyland L. 276
Davis, Ada 145, 284
Davis, Alice 231
Davis, Allen W. 20
Davis, Amasa 94
Davis, Amasa B. 215
Davis, Amos 94
Davis, Annie A. (Waters) 271
Davis, Bessie L. 271
Davis, Charles 94, 311
Davis, Chauncey, Jr. 160
Davis, Chauncey, Sr. 160
Davis, Clerice E. (Plummer) 130
Davis, Edna B. 271
Davis, Edwin 159, 338
Davis, Edwin F. 281
Davis, Eliza 325
Davis, Eliza E. 122
Davis, Ella A. 19
Davis, Elliott 154
Davis, Everett A. 209
Davis, Frank B. 145

Davis, Frank E. 223
Davis, Fred W. 130, 270
Davis, George 6, 96
Davis, George W. 279
Davis, Ida M. [Bates] 279
Davis, James L. 122
Davis, James L., Mrs. 102
Davis, Jane 94
Davis, Jennie C. 311
Davis, John W. 145
Davis, Lelela M. 281
Davis, Lilly (Armstrong) 145
Davis, Lucius 47, 48
Davis, Maria 239
Davis, Marvin A. 145
Davis, Mary 129
Davis, Mr. 10
Davis, Nettie E. 145
Davis, Orrin J. 169
Davis, Pheba J. (Shaw) 218
Davis, Sarah 154
Davis, Sarah E. (Dingman)[Rumrill] 169
Davis, Sarah J. 296
Davis, Susan 145
Davis, Tama 160
Davis, Wallace 94
Davis, William A. 145
Dawson, Jane 104
Day, Hannah 294
Debell, Arthur N. 195, 248
Debell, Calista 195, 248
Debell, Cora 195, 248
Debell, Della E. 195, 248
DeBell, Eva M. 248
Debell, Florence A.(Worder) 195
DeBell, Fred 169
Debell, George A. 195, 248
DeBell, Henry L. 196
DeBell, Herman J. 248
Debell, Homer 195
Debell, Maud L. 195, 248
DeBell, Mr. 42
DeBell, Sarah E.(Dingman)[Rumrill][Davis]
  [Stone] 169
Decamp, Charles 54
Decamp, Edgar E. 54
Deering, Bertie 179
Deering, Earnest 179
Deering, Lonnie 179
Deering, Monroe 179
Deeth, Elvira 161, 162
Deeth, Moses S. 161
DeLane, Rosa 219
Delphy, Margarette 68
Delphy, Joseph 68
Demarche, Amanda (Jacobs) 323

Demarche, Joseph A. 323
Demarche, Ora 323
Demarco, Joseph 226
Demery, Bert P. 271
Demery, James L. 271
Demery, Lena (Cummings) 271
Demery, Viola 271
Deming, Beecher 299
Deming, Bessie (Field) 299
Demuris family 188
Denno, Floyd 272
Denno, Gracie 272
Denno, John 272
Denno, Josie 272
Denno, Mabel 272
Derby, Charles 61, 79
Derby, Susan R. [Spauldin] 61
Desalires, Emma (Chicoine) 296
Desalires, Joseph 296
Desalires, Paul 296
Devilaire, Henrietta 214
Dexter, Harry A. 288
Dexter, Howard 287
Dexter, Mary 288
Dexter, Minnie L. 287
Dexter, Sarah (Fancy) 287
Deyo, Ellen 135
Deyo, John 135
Dickinson, Sarah 108
Dillion, Daniel 89
Dillion, Margery 89
Dingman, Alvena 258
Dingman, George S. 258, 258
Dingman, John G. 169
Dingman, Mary 258
Dingman, Sarah E. 169
Dodge, Anna R. 158
Dodge, Frank 95
Dodge, Frederick 158
Dodge, Helen S. 158
Dodge, Henry 95
Dodge, Mary A. (Galbin) [Powers] 95
Dodge, Phoeba 23
Dodge, Rufus 297
Doherty. See also Dougherty
Doherty, James 100
Doker, Andrew 332
Dolan, Bridget (Marsy) 87
Dolan, Eliza 87
Dolan, Jerry 87
Dolan, Jerry, Jr. 87
Dolan, Katie 87
Dolan, Thomas 87
Donnally, John 106
Donovan, Cornelius 150, 297
Donovan, Daniel 150, 155

Donovan, Dennis 3
Donovan, Hannah 155
Donovan, James 3, 150, 297
Donovan, Jeremiah 150, 297
Donovan, Jerry 150
Donovan, Jerry, Mrs. 150
Donovan, John 68, 150, 155
Donovan, Kate 68
Donovan, Margaret 3
Donovan, Mary 297
Donovan, Mary Ellen 155
Donovan, Michael 3
Donovan, Timothy 3, 150, 297
Donovan, Timothy, Jr. 3
Doody, Ellen 300
Doody, Michael 300
Doolittle, Cyrina M. 6
Doolittle, Edwin 68
Doolittle, Joseph, Mrs. 180
Doolittle, Landers 37
Doolittle, Philana D. 4
Doolittle, Titus 4, 6
Door. See also Dorr, Dore
Door, Jane 37
Door, Jennie S. 37
Door, Joseph 37
Door, Joseph Chester 37
Dore. See also Door, Dorr
Dore, Jane 37
Dorr. See also Door, Dore
Dorr, George 4
Doucette, George 24
Doucette, John 24
Dougan, Charles H. 113
Dougherty. See also Doherty
Dougherty, John 94
Dougherty, Susan (McLear) 94
Douglas. See also Douglass
Douglas, Mrs. 94
Douglass. See also Douglas
Douglass, Elvira 55
Dow, Agnes Jane 189
Dow, Eldridge N. 189
Dow, Emma G. 189
Dow, Eva 189
Dow, George O. 189
Dow, Myrtle M. 189
Doyle, Edward J. 240
Doyle, Fred 38
Doyle, Lizzie 87
Doyle, Mary 88, 209
Doyle, May Clarke 334
Doyle, Michael 87
Doyle, Sylvester, Jr. 37, 38
Drake, Charles 68
Drake, Joseph 68

Driscoll, Cornelius 164
Driscoll, Daniel 164
Driscoll, Dennis 164
Driscoll, Eliza 149
Driscoll, Hannah L. 164
Driscoll, James 164
Driscoll, Jeremiah 164
Driscoll, John 38, 164
Driscoll, Margaret 164
Driscoll, Mary 164
Driscoll, Michael 164
Driscoll, Morris 149
Drollette, Frank 227
Drollette, Rosella 227
Drollette, Victoria (Durant) 227
Drummer, John 104
Dube, Eugenia 283
Dubois, Henry 69
Duclow, Donelda 137
Duclow, Joseph 137
Duclow, Lydia 137
Duclow, Phoebe 137
Duclow, Sarah 137
Duclow, William 137
Ducy, Louisa 133
Duffee, Ann 187
Duffee, John 187
Duffee, John, Jr. 187
Duffee, Rachel 187
Dugan. See also Dougan
Dugan, David, Mrs. 160
Dument, Delia 327
Dument, George W. 327
Dument, Louis W. 327
Dument, Rosa M. 327
Dument, William 327
Dunbar, George 14
Dunbar, Sophia [Columbia] 14
Dunbary, James 160
Duplesy, Candace 118
Duplesy, Johnny 118
Duplesy, Joseph 118
Duplesy, Joseph, Jr. 118
Duplesy, Mary 118
Duplesy, Phillip 118
Duplesy, Simon 118
Duplesy, Victoria 118
Duplex, Emma 6
Duplex, Frank 6
Duplex, Freddie 54
Duplex, Mary 6
Duplex, Mary Jane 54
Duplex, Selina (LaClair) 54
Duplex, Sophia 54
Duplex, William 54
Duplex, William, Jr. 54

Duplicy, Joseph 299
Duplicy, Lula D. (Webster) 300
Dupree. See also Duprey, Duprei
Dupree, Arthur T. 239
Dupree, Maria (Davis) 239
Duprei. See also Duprey, Dupree
Duprei, Carrie 4
Duprei, Dolly 4
Duprei, Effie 4
Duprei, Eva 4
Duprei, Joseph 4
Duprei, Joseph, Jr. 4
Duprei, Laura 4
Duprei, Marion 4
Duprei, Robert 4
Duprei, Reuben 4
Duprei, Rubert 4
Duprey. See also Duprei, Dupree
Duprey, Delia 55
Duprey, Ella 55
Duprey, Emery 55
Duprey, Fredie 38
Duprey, George 55
Duprey, John 55
Duprey, Joseph Elder 38
Duprey, Julia Ann 38
Duprey, Louis 38
Duprey, Meddie 55
Duprey, Peter 55
Duprey, William 55
Duprias, Eva B. 293
Duprias, Joseph 293
Durant, Cloe 148
Durant, Eddie 38
Durant, Ella 38
Durant, Frank 38, 227
Durant, Fred 149, 249
Durant, Hellen 249
Durant, Ida 249
Durant, James 38
Durant, John 38
Durant, John, Jr. 38
Durant, Joseph 149, 249
Durant, Joseph, Jr. 149
Durant, Josephine 249
Durant, Lillia 249
Durant, Louis 149
Durant, Louisa 241, 242
Durant, Malvina 149
Durant, Malvina (LaBounty) 149
Durant, Mary 38
Durant, Moses 38
Durant, Rosetta 149
Durant, Sophia (Arington) 38
Durant, Theodore 249
Durant, Victoria 227

Durant, Willie 38
Durues, Agnes 288
Dyer, Augdni 134
Dyer, Delia 134
Dyer, Eben 134
Dyer, Elizabeth 134
Dyer, Frank 134
Dyer, John 134
Dyer, Josephine 134
Dyer, Julia 134
Dyer, Melvin 134
Dyer, Simon 134
Dyton, James A. 159

Eames, F. H. 5
Eames, Harry 68
Eastman, Edward W. 13, 175
Eastman, Elizabeth (Belknap) 13
Eastman, Frances P. 154
Eastman, Frank P. 175
Eastman, George W. 31
Eastman, Harry 175
Eastmna, Herbert A. 175
Eastman, Hiram 154
Eastman, Hiram W. 13, 175
Eastman, Jane (Tufts) 31
Eastman, Lizzie N. 175
Eastman, William 106
Eddy, Alvaretta M. 39, 96
Eddy, David 39
Eddy, Idella M. 39, 96
Eddy, Flora 224
Eddy, Flora L. 39, 96
Eddy, Henry 96
Eddy, Louisa L. 39
Eddy, Lydia L. (Roberts) 39, 96
Eddy, Mr. 19
Eddy, Rosa A. 96
Eddy, Sidney H. 39
Eddy, Willie H. 39, 96
Edwards, George W. 297
Elgar, Adderet (Elmore) 266
Elgar, Charles L. 266
Ella, Fred, 2d 146
Ellenwood, Catherine S. R. 199
Ellis, Aaron, Mrs. 152
Ellis, Bertie S. 161
Ellis, Birdie C. 38
Ellis, Charity M. 161
Ellis, Clara M. 161
Ellis, Cyrus K. 161
Ellis, Daniel 247
Ellis, Daniel K. 161
Ellis, Edwin W. 38
Ellis, Elmira L. 161
Ellis, Eunice A. 38

Ellis, Eva B. (Duprias) 293
Ellis, George H. 161
Ellis, Henry 38, 293
Ellis, Ida M. 161
Ellis, John 39
Ellis, John H. M. 38
Ellis, Louisa A. 38
Ellis, Louisa E. 38
Ellis, Marrion L. 161
Ellis, Moses 43
Ellis, Olive M. 161
Ellis, Perley W. 161
Ellis, Rosa E. 38
Ellis, Wilmer G. 161, 338
Elmon, Emily A. 172
Elmon, Fred 172
Elmon, George A. 172
Elmore, Adderet 266
Elmore, Florence 133
Elmore, Frank 133
Elmore, Lizzie (Whitney) 133
Elmore, Neal 133
Elmore, Oscar 133
Emerson, Chauncey W. 62
Emerson, Julia A. 62
Emerson, Mrs. 180
Emery, Eugene R. 11
Emery, Fanny (Percival) [Richards] 11, 78
Enwright, Dennis 55
Enwright, Ellen (Hill) 55
Enwright, Even 298
Enwright, Kate 298
Enwright, Lizzie 298
Enwright, Marion 298
Enwright, Nellie 298
Enwright, Thomas 298
Erikson, Annie 222
Erikson, Annie, Jr. 222
Erikson, Carrie 222
Erikson, Eddie 204
Erikson, Elisa 222
Erikson, Eric 222
Estey. See also Esty
Estey, James 337
Estey, Mrs. 305
Esty. See also Estey
Esty, George 153
Euber, Louis 319
Evans, R. R. 164
Evans, William G. 23

Fairbank. See also Fairbanks
Fairbank, Adeline H. 168
Fairbank, Franklin 168
Fairbanks. See also Fairbank
Fairbanks, George H. 307

Fairbanks, Maria D. [Wheeler] 290
Fairbanks, Mr. 290
Fairbanks, Mrs. 30
Fairbanks, Walter S. 326
Fallaize, John P. 124
Fancy, Sarah 287
Fannigan, Daniel 223
Farnham. See Farnum
Farnsworth, John, Mrs. 16
Farnum, Frank G. 126
Farnum, John M. 70
Faro, Clarence 252
Faro, Cora 252
Faro, Ellen (Croto) 252
Faro, Felia 252
Farr, Asa F. 184
Farr, Laura S.[Ballou] 212
Farr, Mr. 78
Farr, William 212
Farrar, Elizabeth 162
Farrington, Lottie 212
Farrington, Ripley 212
Farwell, Julia 126
Fassett, J. W. 167
Felch, Thankful P. 29
Feloe, Albert 237
Feloe, Alden 237
Feloe, Alexander 237
Feloe, Alexander, Jr. 237
Feloe, Arthur 237
Feloe, Clara 237
Feloe, Delina 237
Feloe, Eveline 237
Feloe, Henry 237
Feloe, Leoneda 237
Felt, Irene W. 123
Felt, Leander 123
Fenton, Benny 221
Fenton, Charles S. 221
Fenton, Sadie (Berman) 221
Field, Bessy 262
Field, Charles E. 56, 106, 262
Field, Frank H. 56, 262
Field, Frederick R. 56, 262
Field, Gilbert 174, 338
Field, Mary (Bragg) 262
Field, Rufus D. 56, 106, 262, 299
Field, Susan E. (Robbins) 56, 262, 299
Filiault, Aldea 236
Filiault, Alexander 236
Filiault, Cyprien 236, 318
Filiault, Dena 236
Filiault, Edmond 236
Filiault, Elvina 236
Filiault, Henry 236
Filiault, Ida 236

Filiault, Phoebe 236
Fish, Deborah A. 108
Fish, Deborah (Perham) 108
Fish, Fannie 311
Fish, James 108
Fish, Jennie 225
Fisher, Archie E. 268
Fisher, Burton E. 268
Fisher, Gardner 304
Fisher, Gardner L. 304
Fisher, Lucius 304
Fisher, Lyman H. 62
Fisher, Mary 56
Fisher, Mary E. 268
Fisk, Abner 171, 205
Fisk, Harry A. 95
Fisk, Mary L. 171, 205
Fisk, Sarah M. 205
Fisk, William A. 205
Fitzgerald, Edward 220
Fitzgerald, Elizabeth 14
Fitzgerald, Hattie B. 285
Fitzgerald, John 106, 285, 337
Fitzgerald, Maggie 220
Fitzgerald, May (Coffee) 220
Fitzgerald, Shemas 220
Fitzgerald, Thomas, Mrs. 18
Fitzsimmons, Edward 198
Fitzsimmons, Helen (Sullivan) 198
Flag. See also Flagg
Flag, Rosa 211, 242
Flagg. See also Flag
Flagg, Ada J. 111
Flagg, Almon M. 111
Flagg, Ermina C. (Bryant) 110
Flagg, Lizzie M. 111
Flagg, Mary L. 303
Flagg, Robert F. 111
Flagg, William 303
Flagg, William A. 110
Flannery, Ellen (Mahoney) 168
Flemming, Charles 106
Fletcher, Earnest Mann 40
Fletcher, Effie Rose 40
Fletcher, Elizabeth A. 182
Fletcher, Gertrude E. 182
Fletcher, H. D. 40
Fletcher, H. M. 1
Fletcher, Jannette 40
Fletcher, May Bell 41
Fletcher, Thomas W. 182
Fletcher, William E. 182
Flood, Joseph 91
Flynn, Agnes 302
Flynn, Hugh 302
Flynn, Jerry 302

Flynn, John 301
Flynn, John, Jr. 302
Flynn, Lizzie 302
Flynn, Mary 301
Foley, Edna R. 173
Foley, Ellen 39
Foley, Hannah 136
Foley, James 39
Foley, John 69
Foley, Mary 39
Foley, Putnam H. 173
Foley, Thomas 136
Foley, Thomas E. 142
Foley, William 39
Forches, Alfonce 143
Fortier, Arthur 332
Fortier, Cora 332
Fortier, Emma B. 332
Fortier, Georgianna 332
Fortier, Louis 296
Fortier, Louisa 332
Foster, Alice 238, 265
Foster, Amanda C. [Armstrong] 220
Foster, Annie 237
Foster, Clarisa 88
Foster, George W. 220
Foster, Gideon 101
Foster, John 237, 265
Foster, Johnnie 238, 265
Foster, Josephine 265
Foster, Julia (Bennett) 237, 265
Foster, Malvina 238
Foster, Rose 238, 265
Foster, Rozella Tolman 148
Foster, Rufus J. 82
Fountain, Delina/Delia 134, 171
Fountain, Peter 134, 171
Fowler, Nellie 195, 196
Frame, Chavin 40
Frame, Grover C. 167
Frame, James K. 167
Frame, Jane 40
Frame, John 40
Frame, Lewis J. 167
Frame, Millor 40
Frame, Mora Ain 40
Frame, Nora 40
Frame, Rindia A. 167
Frame, Walter L. 167
Frances, James 154
Frances, Lilly 154
Frances, Rose 154
Frary, Charles 27
Frazier, Lucy 319
Frechett, Amelia 326
Frechett, Homer 326

Frechett, Louis 326
Frederick, G. H., Mrs. 76
Frederickson, John Paul 262
Frederickson, Lizzie 262
Freeman, Abbie 327
Freeman, Alfred 327
Freeman, Celina 327
Freeman, Clara 327
Freeman, Julia 126
Freeman, Louis 327
Freeman, Menirva 245
Freeman, Nellie F. 312
Freeman, Willie 327
French, Flora (Eddy) 224
French, Lura Bell 224
French, Mr. 86
French, Watson S. 224
French, Wilford H. 224
French, Winforn H. 224
Frezier, Mary 275
Frink, Eddie O. 69
Frink, Oscar T. 69, 140
Frink, Westley L. 69
Frost, Rufus S. 155
Fullam, George L. 41, 56, 106
Fuller, Elisha L. 132
Fuller, Ellen M. 132
Fuller, George F. 132
Fuller, Hattie B. 132
Fuller, Levi A. 100
Fuller, Nellie M. 217
Fuller, Sarah Ann (Chace) 132
Fuller, William H. 132
Fuller, William H., Jr. 132

Gabarees, Louis 144
Gabarees, May 144
Gabounes, Louis 133
Gains, Maria 113
Gakey, Julia 238
Galager. See Gallagher, Galliger
Galager, William 142
Galbin, Mary A. 95
Galbin, Mr. 95
Gallagher. See also Galager, Galliger
Gallagher, E. M. 109
Galliger, Bessie 278
Galliger, Catherine 278
Galliger, James 278
Galliger, Jennie 278
Galliger, John 278
Galliger, Katie 278
Galliger, Margaret 278
Galliger, Mary 278
Gamill, Jennie 285
Gamlin, Frances 188

Gannette, Adaline 143
Gannette, Agnes 143
Gannette, Delia 143
Gannette, Olive 143
Gannette, Peter 143
Gannette, Virginia 143
Gardner, Sarah 289
Garfield, Sarah M. (Fisk) 205
Garfield, William A. 205
Garrett, George 176
Garrett, Paul 176
Gassett, George H. 88
Gassett, Reuben 23, 133
Gates, Hazel 301
Gates, Ira D. 185
Gates, Joseph 210
Gates, Mary (Kelley) 210
Gates, Sidney C. 301
Gauthier, John 146
Gay, Proctor R. 111
Geisick, George 70
Genyer, Eliza 244
Gerard, Clarinda L. 236
Gerard, Louis 236
Gerkie, Joseph 323
Gerlin, Ellen 309
Gero, Frank 56, 105
Gero, Mahala 56
Getty, William 208
Gibbs, Almira 301
Gibbs, Barry 145
Gibson, Arthur 323
Gibson, Caroline 323
Gibson, Frank 11
Gibson, Reuben 48
Gilbo, Daniel 100
Gilbo, John Luke 100
Gilbo, Mary 100
Gilbo, Mary, Jr. 100
Gilbo, Willie 100
Gillett, George 41
Gilman, Eddie 282
Gilman, Ellen 258
Gilman, Lucy 282
Gilmore, Carrie G. 30
Gilmore, Charles G. 30
Gilmore, Fannie M. 30
Gilmore, Joseph A. 112
Girard. See also Girouard
Girard, Charles 56
Girard, Frank Joseph 56
Girard, George Albert 56
Girard, Mahala (Gero) 56
Girouard. See also Girard
Girouard, Marie 249
Glass, Isabella 215

Glidden, Clarrisa 5
Glidden, Maria B. 5
Gobiel, Charles 267
Gobiel, Clara 267
Gobiel, Henriette L. 267
Gobiel, John 267
Gobiel, Rosida 267
Gongan, Archer 5
Gongan, Joseph 5
Gongan, Louis 5
Gongan, Luke E. 5
Gongan, Rose 5
Gonyon, Archie 192
Gonyon, Clough 192
Gonyon, Ella 192
Gonyon, Johnie 192
Gonyon, Lena 192
Gonyon, Mary 192
Gonyon, Mary, Jr. 192
Gonyou, Adele 121
Good, Caroline 136
Goodenough. See also Goodnough
Goodenough, Jennie 285
Goodhue, Asenath 199
Goodhue, Augustine 199
Goodnough. See also Goodenough
Goodnough, Mary 157
Goodrow, Dolfise 183
Goodrow, George 183
Goodrow, George, Jr. 183
Goodrow, Mary 183
Gookey, Emma 225
Gookey, Fred 225
Gookey, Joseph 225
Gookey, Willie 225
Gordon, Charles P. 192
Gordon, Edna 192
Gordon, Malvina E. 192
Gordon, Mary Jane 192
Gordon, Mary Jane, Jr. 192
Gorman, Joseph 128
Gorman, Mary 128
Gould, Frank 166
Gould, Hannah P. 138
Gould, May E. 166
Gould, Oliver K. 138
Gould, Rowland 83
Goulet, Anna 258
Goulet, Delina 248
Goulet, Edmond 258
Goulet, Emma 258
Goulet, Joseph 258
Goulet, Mary 258
Goulet, Peter J. 258
Goulet, Victoria 258
Gowdy, Edward M. 98

Gowdy, James 98
Gowdy, James Clarence 98
Gowdy, John Henry 98
Gowdy, Margaret Ella 98
Gowdy, Margy Ella 98
Goyette, Frank E. 110
Goyette, George 110, 117
Goyette, Josephine (Baraby) 110
Goyette, Lena 117
Goyette, Louis A. 110
Grando, Addie 140
Grando, Albert 140
Grando, Deru 141
Grando, Joseph 140
Grando, Mary 140
Granger, Fred E. 129
Granger, Sarah A. (Rivet) 129
Granier, Aleck 121
Granier, Alice 121
Granier, Annie 121
Granier, Annie (Nellitt) 121
Granier, Demorest 121
Granier, Leander 121
Granier, Philemon 121
Granier, Velcemer 121
Grasier, Nellie O. 230, 265
Graves, Alice E. 150
Graves, Arthur J. 230
Graves, Emma G. 150
Graves, Emma J. 57
Graves, Florence E. 150
Graves, James D. 229, 265
Graves, Joseph 189
Graves, Nellie 189
Graves, Nellie O. (Grasier)[Ballou] 230, 265
Graves, Oliver C. 150
Graves, Willard R. 181
Greeley, Bertie G. 171
Greeley, George W. 171
Greeley, Harriet 171
Greeley, James G. 57
Greeley, James M. 171
Greeley, Mary (Witham) 171
Green, Barbara E. 287
Green, Mr. 97
Green, Rosetta W. 29
Greenough, Jennie 285
Greenough, Leon 285
Greenway, George 174
Greenway, Grace 174
Greenway, John 174
Greenway, Richard 174
Greenwood, E. S. 41
Greenwood, James W. 150
Greenwood, Mary (Laws) 41
Greenwood, Mary C. 150

Greenwood, Sarah L. 150
Gregwon, Clara 161
Gregwon, Frances 161
Gregwon, George 161
Gregwon, Lodie 161
Gregwon, Mary 161
Gregwon, Mary, Jr. 161
Gregwon, Palmer 161
Gregwon, Vangie 161
Grenier, George 70
Grenier, Martha 320
Griffin, Henry 101
Griffin, Polly 101
Griffith, Charles G. 260
Griffith, Della A. 154
Griffith, Edward V. 144
Griffith, Frank E. 144
Griffith, Freddie I. 154
Griffith, Harriet J. 225
Griffith, Irving 154
Griffith, Jane E. 144
Griffith, John Gilman 260
Griffith, Mabel (Carpenter) 154, 155
Griffith, Martha A. M. 260
Griffith, Mertie M. 154
Griffith, Nettie C. (Carroll)[Griffin] 278
Griffith, Sarah E. 144
Griffin, Nettie C. (Carroll) 278
Griffin, Wilfred 278
Grigs, Helen E. 287
Grimes, Hosea 106
Grimes, Mary 106
Grogan, Annie 167
Grogan, John 167
Grout, Charles F. 100
Grout, Charles F., Mrs. 100
Grout, Cora A. 6
Grout, Emily (Putnam) 6
Grout, John 6
Grout, Milan 6
Grover, A. M. 144
Grovner, Benjamin 202
Guier, Victor 258
Guillmette, Dolphia 238
Guillmette, Henry 238
Guillmette, Orvila 238
Guillmette, Rosa 238
Guillow, Blanchie L. 165
Guillow, Chester K. 165
Guillow, Jehial B. 165
Guillow, Lione P. 165
Guillow, Luther H. 165
Guillow, Rosie E. 165, 337
Guillow, Rufus E. 15, 106
Guinap, Charles 291
Guinap, John 291

Guinap, Kate 291
Guinap, Lydia 291
Gunn, Andrew A. 290
Gunn, Fidelia 290
Gunn, Hannah (Austin) 290
Gunn, Harriet E. 290
Gunn, Marrilla A. 290
Gunn, Mr. 58
Gunn, Mrs. 58
Gunn, William 290
Guyou, Alexander 308
Gwinn. See also Gwinne
Gwinn, Clement 237
Gwinne. See also Gwinn
Gwinne, Jane 282
Gyle, Abby M. 219

Hackett, Ebenezer 148
Hackett, Electa D. 148
Hadley, Ada M. (Medcalf) 212
Hadley, Edwin W. 185
Hadley, Isaac C. 185
Hadley, Jennie A. 328
Hadley, Rebecca J. 185
Hale, Abigail [Comstock] 175
Hale, Asenath (Swan) 22, 204
Hale, Ellen 292
Hale, Emma (Stevens) 235
Hale, Gertie Mable 22
Hale, Grace 109
Hale, Grace O. 175
Hale, Grace O., Jr. 175
Hale, James 23
Hale, Jane (Davis) 94
Hale, John 50
Hale, Jonas S. 22, 204
Hale, Mary Ann 50
Hale, May Bell 204
Hale, Perley LaForest 175
Hale, Sarah M. 41
Hale, Shurburn P. 235
Hall, Carrie D. 333
Hall, Clayton 333
Hall, Eunice 41
Hall, Eva B. 41
Hall, Fred 333
Hall, George 286, 333
Hall, Gracia M. 42, 196
Hall, Henry 41, 57
Hall, Henry B. 70
Hall, Henry H. 196
Hall, Herbert A. 264
Hall, Hermon H. 41, 196
Hall, Horace H. 201
Hall, Josie 333
Hall, Laura A. 264

Hall, Lizzie S. 41, 196
Hall, Jonathan 42
Hall, Sophia 286
Halstat, Emma 192
Hamblet, Mary E. (Hammond) 125
Hammond, Frank 71
Hammond, Joseph 93
Hammond, Mary (Oliver) 71
Hammond, Mary E. 125
Hammond, Oren 125
Hammond, Oren, Mrs. 125
Hand, Alpheus 337
Handy, Alpheus 107
Handy, Elizabeth 97
Handy, Paul 107
Haradon, Lucinda 55, 68, 94, 147, 156
Hardy, Charles 230
Harley, Frank 47
Harley, Hannah 239
Harper, Lena 322
Harrigan, Delia 184
Harrigan, Michael 184
Harrington, Anson S. 214
Harrington, Bertha L. 174
Harrington, Edgar N. 174
Harrington, Isis E. (Nash) 174
Harris, Caroline M. 327
Harris, Maria 327
Harris, Warner 99
Harrison, John 286
Harrison, J. C. 109
Hart, Ann E. 188
Hart, Charles 188
Hart, Elizabeth 314
Hart, Parker 314
Hartley, Adolphus 143
Hartley, Emma 143
Hartley, Joseph 143
Hartley, Mindrell Alice 143
Hartwel, Asa J. 213
Hartwell, Charles H. 212, 213
Hartwell, Ella L. (Ray) 212, 213
Harvey, A. J. 270
Harvey, Ada L. 157
Harvey, Ann S. 176
Harvey, Charles L. 85, 173
Harvey, Clara E. 176
Harvey, Ella J. 222
Harvey, George O. 176, 222
Harvey, Ida 85, 173
Haskell, Albert 306
Haskell, Earl 306
Haskell, Esther 306
Haskell, Isabelle 306
Haskell, Joseph 96
Haskell, William F. 123

Hastings, Abbie E. [Reed] 263
Hastings, Allie 227
Hastings, Bertha 227
Hastings, Carl 227
Hastings, Catharine B. 152
Hastings, Charles 263
Hastings, Everett 227
Hastings, Fred E. 227
Hastings, Hattie P.(Sawyer) 227
Hastings, Lizzie 227
Hastings, Nellie I. 100
Hathaway, John B. 255
Hathorn, Alice A. 194
Hathorn, Eliza A. 194
Hathorn, Henry S. 194
Hathorn, Mary J. 194
Hatt, Almira 199
Hatt, Joseph 199
Hatt, Sadee 199
Hatt, Walter 199
Hatt, Warren 199
Hawley, Frank 7
Heald, Mr. 104
Healy, Elizabeth 115
Healy, Mary 115
Heath, Abby J. 197
Heath, Amanda 13
Heath, Eunice 337
Heath, Hannah 12
Heath, Nathaniel 13
Heath, Ruben 317
Hebert. See also Heberts
Hebert, Eddie 224
Hebert, Freddie 224
Hebert, Freeman 224
Hebert, Josephine 224
Hebert, Julia 224
Hebert, Napolean 224
Hebert, Tommy 224
Heberts. See also Hebert
Heberts, Freeman 232
Heberts, Maria 232
Hemmingway, Luther 57
Hemmingway, Sally 57
Henderson, Annie Marion 330
Henderson, Charles 330
Henderson, Frank 330
Henderson, George 123
Henderson, James 253
Henderson, Jennie 330
Henderson, John 330
Henderson, Margaret 123
Hendrix, Benjamin 259
Hendrix, Betsey 259, 337
Herbert, Leopold 250
Hernois, Annie 251

Hernois, Bertha 251
Hernois, Dora 251
Hernois, Emma 251
Hernois, Eva 251
Hernois, John 251
Hernois, John, Jr. 251
Hernois, Rosa 251
Herrick, Henry A. 234
Herrick, Lisia (Wilson) 234
Herse, S. M. 130
Hewins, Alfred 271
Hewins, Elsie 271
Hewins, Harold 271
Hewins, Harry 271
Hewins, Jane 271
Hewitt, Harriet 319
Hilie, Eliza (Genyer) 244
Hilie, Gideon 244
Hill, Abner 47
Hill, Ankust 249
Hill, Arthur 65
Hill, Arthur, Jr. 65
Hill, Bertman F. 327
Hill, Bradley 316
Hill, C. W. C. 335
Hill, Charles F. 15
Hill, Ellen 55
Hill, Elsie M. 327
Hill, Flora 270
Hill, Fred E. 42, 107
Hill, Gardiner C., Mrs. 206
Hill, Gardner T. 245
Hill, George 189
Hill, George W. 232
Hill, Helen L. 189
Hill, Henry 189, 270
Hill, Jewett J. 311
Hill, Lawson 163
Hill, Mary A. 15
Hill, Minnie M. 232
Hill, Naomi (White) 232
Hill, Nellie (Webster) 15
Hill, Orman 269
Hill, Orman, Jr. 270
Hill, Pheba (Stone) 269
Hill, Romniso 135
Hill, Taylor E. 245
Hinds, Elizabeth (Handy) 97
Hinds, Carrie E. 120
Hinds, Charles Frederick 120
Hinds, Charles J. 97, 120
Hinds, Charles W. 97
Hinds, Jarvis H. 97
Hinds, William Leonard 120
Hodge, Amasa 86
Hodge, Edward L. 86

Hodge, John 86
Hodge, Polly 86
Hodskins, Harriet 168
Holbrook, Erastus 23
Holbrook, Francilla 23
Holbrook, Fred 23
Holbrook, I. S. 109
Holbrook, Marion G. 111
Holbrook, Mathew 111
Holbrook, Mr. 23
Holbrook, Susan S. 141
Holden, Arthur J. 298
Holden, Ellen S. 95
Holman, Louisa B. [Smith] 137
Holman, Rebecca J. (Hadley) 185
Holman, William H. 137
Holmes, Alvin 71
Holmes, John 327
Holmes, Justice 266
Holmes, Matilda J. 71
Holmes, Roxanna 71
Holt, Bathsheba 179
Holton, Mary 295
Hopkins, George F. 191
Horton, Aaron H. 221
Horton, Persis 86
Horton, William 86
Hosley, Samuel 220
Houghton, Alvin W. 328
Houghton, Charles E. 281, 289
Houghton, Charles H. 281
Hould, Caroline 298
Hould, George 264
Houle, Albert 239
Houle, Frank 239
Houle, Gena 239
Houle, Julia 239
Houle, Louisa 239
Houle, Louisa (Dargant) 239
Houle, Robetin 239
Howard, Agnes A. 325
Howard, Ambrose 289
Howard, Ann M. 141, 316
Howard, Annie L. 328
Howard, Charles 230
Howard, Emma 325
Howard, Etta 213
Howard, Eunice 289
Howard, Ezra 103, 141, 213
Howard, Ezra D. 302
Howard, Fanny 31
Howard, Flora B. 323
Howard, Frances A. 129
Howard, George M. 323
Howard, Hattie M. 103
Howard, Letser W. 325

Howard, Perley E. 103
Howard, Martha E. 163
Howard, Mary A. 309
Howard, Mrs. 102
Howard, Sarah A. 155
Howard, Sarah J. 155
Howard, Sarah Jane (Plummer) 302
Howard, William B. 325
Howe, Angelia E. (Jefts) 163
Howe, Eliakim 71
Howe, Emily T. 70
Howe, Enoch F. 70
Howe, Fred 308
Howe, Johnie A. 163
Howe, Lottie 71
Howe, Lucetta (Piper) 268
Howe, Mary (Whittemore) 163
Howe, Mary F. 70
Howe, Reuben G. 163
Howe, Rosa B. 308
Howe, Thadie 71
Howe, Willie W. 163
Howard, Risby 130
Howland, P. 102, 103, 112, 114, 115, 146
Hoyt, David Frederic 207
Hoyt, Elliot Dix 207
Hoyt, Fred S. 207
Hoyt, Helen E. 207
Hoyt, Helen May 207
Hoyt, Ruby Emma 207
Hoyt, Vina Faith 207
Hubbard, Alice 30
Hubbard, Carrie G. (Gilmore) 30
Hubbard, Idella 142
Hubbard, Leonard L. 142
Hubbard, Lester L. 30
Hubbard, Louisa M. 141, 337
Hubbard, Mr. 22
Hubert, John 11
Hudson, Samuel C. 113
Hughes, Eddie 135
Hughes, James 135
Hughes, Kate 135
Hughes, Lizzie 135
Hughes, Mary J. 135
Hughes, Michael 135
Hughes, Stephen 135
Huntley, Mira L. 301
Huntley, Sarah J. 301
Hurd, Cuthbert H. 90, 91
Hurd, Ella G. 90
Hurd, Horace E. 90
Hurd, Nettie E. (Prouty) 90
Hussey, John 178
Hustis, Catherine 42
Hutchins, Otis 171

Ingram, Cordelia 46
Iredale, Alice 308
Iredale, Harry 308
Iredale, Joseph 308

Jackson, Edwin 57
Jacobs, Ada 289
Jacobs, Amanda 323
Jacobs, Dillon 289
Jacobs, Ida 289
Jacobs, Joseph 289, 323
Jameson, Daniel 167
Jefts, Angelia E. 163
Jefts, Carl E. 293
Jefts, Emma (Whittemore) 293
Jefts, Frank 293
Jefts, Mabel E. 293
Jefts, Rosa M. 293
Jennings, Edna 98
Jetts, Eddie 279
Jetts, Joseph H. 279
Jetts, Mary 279
Jewell, Elbridge E. 168
Jewell, Emma M. (Thomas) 168
Jewell, Susie E. 168
Jillson, Ella A. 42
Jock, Frank 266
Jock, Frank, Jr. 266
Jock, John 266
Jock, Mary 266
Jodrey, Stephen E. 28
Johansen, Wilhelmina 188
Johnson, Agatha 183
Johnson, Amanda 315
Johnson, Arthur W. 121
Johnson, Axel N. 209
Johnson, Cranswick H. 183
Johnson, Emily S. 270
Johnson, Etta May 155
Johnson, H. C. 222
Johnson, Hattie S.(Cole) 155
Johnson, Hazel C. 270
Johnson, Henry 302
Johnson, Hilma (Boman) 270
Johnson, Jessie 183
Johnson, John 270
Johnson, John H. 270
Johnson, Mack 285
Johnson, Mary E. 183
Johnson, Nathan H. 155
Johnson, Nellie E. 121
Johnson, Peter 253
Johnson, Royal W. 270
Johnson, Thomas 146
Johnson, Victor 315

Johnson, William 137
Johnson, Willie W. 270
Joiyle, Julia 20
Jolley. See also Jolly
Jolley, Caroline 251
Jolley, Delbert H. 251
Jolley, Delia 251
Jolley, John 251
Jolly. See also Jolley
Jolly, Adelia 47
Jolly, Arthur Russell 47
Jolly, Delia 48
Jolly, Ellen (Sharkee) 98
Jolly, Isaac 72
Jolly, John 98
Jolly, John, Jr. 98
Jolly, Joseph 85, 98
Jolly, Lewis 47, 48
Jolly, Lois 47
Jolly, Lucy 85
Jolly, Rosella 85, 317
Jolly, Saloma 48
Jones, Clara A. 35
Jones, Edward 57
Jones, Ella 58
Jones, Herbert 251
Jones, Lizzie 58
Jones, Mary 57
Jones, Mary, Jr. 58
Jones, Willie 58
Jordon, Katie 97
Jordon, Maggie (O'Brien) 97
Jordon, Marnie 97
Julian, Christine 42
Julian, Freddie 42
Julian, Jule 42
Julian, Lavinia 42
Jutrus, Annie 259
Jutrus, Ellen L. 259
Jutrus, Joseph 259

Kearny, Cornelus 330
Kearny, Denis 330
Keats, Alfred 235
Keats, Clara 235
Keats, Edward 235
Keats, Ernest 235
Keats, Fred 235
Keats, Harold 235
Keats, Lawrence 235
Keats, Teddy 235
Keats, Thomas 235
Keats, Willie 235
Keep, Elizabeth 284
Keizer, Charles 22
Keizer, Daniel 22

Keizer, George E. 72
Kelleher, Beatrice 330
Kelleher, Catherine Y. 330
Kelleher, David F. 330
Kelleher, David Francis 330
Kelleher, Mary A. 330
Kelleher, Mary Armstrong 330
Kelleher, Rachel 330
Kelleher, Timothy 330
Kelley. See also Kelly
Kelley, Charlotte A. (Turnstall) 147, 177
Kelley, Ellen 22
Kelley, Mary 210
Kelley, Richard 22
Kelley, Rose 43
Kelley, Samuel, Mrs. 147
Kelly. See also Kelley
Kelly, Charlotte A. 177
Kelly, Maru 127
Kelly, Michael 127, 177
Kelly, Robert 177
Kelly, Samuel 177
Kelton, Mary Ann 72
Kelton, Sarah A. 72
Kelton, Wheaton 72
Kempton, Asa 115
Kempton, Elnora E. 256
Kempton, Eunice E. (York) 256
Kempton, Henry 256
Kempton, John 256
Kempton, Leland S. 256
Kempton, Mary 256
Kempton, Samuel 282, 338
Kempton, Sarah (Pertred) 282
Kempton, Simon 115
Kempton, Viola V. 256
Kendall, Asa A. 119
Kendall, Edgar F. 303
Kendall, Harrison M. 303
Kendall, Herbert M. 303
Kendall, Mary L. (Flagg) 303
Kennedy, Daniel 317
Kennedy, Fannie (Percival)[Richards][Ball] 317
Kennedy, Kate 326
Kennedy, Mary 130
Kenney. See also Kenny
Kenney, Alice M. (Nash) 170
Kenney, Annie (Grogan) 167
Kenney, George Avery 170
Kenney, George H. 170
Kenney, Grace E. 167
Kenney, Hattie M. 219
Kenney, I. Mabel 170
Kenney, James 118, 167
Kenny. See also Kenney
Kenny, Charles 89

Kenny, Ella 89
Kenny, George 89
Kenny, Hattie M. 89
Kenny, Ida 89
Kenny, Jennie 89
Kenny, W. R. 89
Kent, Alfred J. 193
Kent, Jessie M. 193
Kent, John 137
Kent, L. 193
Kent, Laura P. 176, 193
Kenyon, Thomas 131
Keyes, Amasiah 107
Keyes, Charles E. 313
Keyes, Charles Edward 313
Keyes, George Harvey 313
Keyes, Louisa A. 313
Keyes, Roselthia 83
Kidder, Harriet L. 206
Kilburn, Lyman G. 218
Kimball, Addia E. [Darren] 276
Kimball, George H. 188
Kimball, William 276
King, Barney 179
King, Barney, Jr. 180
King, Caroline 72
King, Emma E. 43
King, Florence D. 43
King, Hattie E. 43
King, Henry P. 43
King, Josephine C. 43
King, Lenora [Birch] 27
King, Mary A. 43
King, Mabel 180
King, Melvin 180
King, Mr. 27
King, Octavia (LaClair) 179
King, Philip 43
King, Rosa C. 43
King, T. 72
Kingman, George A. 303
Kingsbury, S. L. 13
Kingsley, Berton 58
Kingsley, Ella 58, 299
Kingsley, Eltha E. 58, 299
Kingsley, George M. 58, 299
Kingsley, Heber 299
Kingsley, Ida 58, 299
Kingsley, Mabel 58, 299
Kinney, Edna 281
Kinney, George H. 280
Kinney, George L. 281
Kinney, Thomas 281
Kinnirey, Henry 226
Kinnirey, John 226
Kinnirey, John, Jr. 226

Kinnirey, Joseph 226
Kinnirey, William 226
Kinson, Addie 118
Kinson, Alfred Decatur 125
Kinson, Annie E. (Murdo) 125
Kinson, Captola Mary 125
Kinson, Clarence Austin 125
Kinson, Claud 125
Kinson, Edgar 125
Kinson, Henry 125
Kinson, Ionia Estella 125
Kinson, Ira A. 125
Kinson, Jessie F. 118
Kinson, John Q. 118
Kinson, Willie D. 118
Knapp, Agness Ella 217
Knapp, George W. 217
Knapp, Richard 23
Knight, Charles 128
Knight, Emma 234
Knotts. See Notts
Knowles, Rose 128, 129
Knowlton, Charles L. 138
Knowlton, Dexter B. 15
Knowlton, Emma E. (Wood) 138
Knowlton, Harry 27
Knowlton, Henry 159
Knowlton, Howard 27
Knowlton, Mary A. [Hill] 15
Knowlton, Walter G. 138
Kober, Ellen 216
Kober, Joseph 216

LaBounty, Agnes 72
LaBounty, Antoine 149
LaBounty, Denie 72
LaBounty, Georgianna 72
LaBounty, John 72
LaBounty, Joseph 116
LaBounty, Mary F. (Wood) 116
LaBounty, Mary Louisa 72
LaBounty, Matilda 72
LaBounty, Peter 73
LaBounty, Rosana 72
LaBounty, Wilford 72
LaCharity, Albert 291
LaCharity, Alfred 291
LaCharity, Annie 291
LaCharity, Ascula 291
LaCharity, Clara 291
LaCharity, Elmer 291
LaCharity, Nancy 299
LaCharity, Oclure 291
LaCharity, Rus 291
Lachint, Paul 208
LaClair. See also LeClair, LeClaire

LaClair, Arthur 322
LaClair, Effire 322
LaClair, Eugene 179
LaClair, Francis 322
LaClair, Louisa 179
LaClair, Octavia 179
LaClair, Selina 54
LaClose, Annie L. 267
LaClose, Eugene 267
Laflame, Adelin 131
Laflame, Arche 131
Laflame, Bertie 131
Laflame, Frank 131
Laflame, Josephine 131
Laflame, Laura 131
Laflame, Matilda 131
Laflame, Nelson 131
Laflamine, Fred 259
Lahiff, John 294
Lahiff, John, Mrs. 294
Lakin, Annie 294
Lakin, Samuel C. 294
Lally, John 166
Lally, Michael J. 166
Lally, Winnie 166
Lamiraude, Harry 111
Lamiraude, Laura 111
Lamiraude, Mary Jane 111
Lamiraude, Onesime 111
Lamonanda, Alzevine 120
Lamonanda, Caroline 120
Lamont, Alfred 217
Lamont, Almon 217
Lamont, Eli 217
Lamont, Eugene 217
Lamont, Louisa (Abar) 217
LaMore, Nora 43
LaMountain, John 252
Lamphere, Olive 169
Lane, Delia 186
Lane, Horace G. 187
Lane, Joseph 170
Lane, Mabel M. 187
Lane, Munroe H. 187
Lane, William 187
Lane, William J. 170
Lanfair, Alice 32
Lanfair, Lyman 32
Lang, Alfred 221
Lang, Ambrose B. 141
Lang, Anna F. 223
Lang, Anna G. 141
Lang, Earnest C. 141
Lang, Edward B. 141
Lang, Emma E. (Shaw) 218
Lang, Fannie M. 141

Lang, Frederick C. 141
Lang, Hattie I. 141
Lang, Oscar W. 141
Lang, Susan S. (Holbrook) 141
Lanigan, Andrew T. 194
Lanigan, James 194
Lanigan, Lilla 194
Lanigan, Mathew 194
Lanigan, May 194
Lanigan, Nellie 194
LaPlant, H. A. 116
LaPlant, Harvey I. 116
LaPlant, John 116
LaPlant, Lewis A. 116
LaPlant, Mary 116
LaPlant, Richard 116
LaPoint, Delia (Harrigan) 184
Lapoint, Julia (Freeman) 126
Lapoint, Lewis 126
Lapoint, Mary 304
LaPoint, Willie 184
LaPoint, Willie, Jr. 185
Laporte, George 4
Laporte, Jane 37
Laporte, Jennie S. 37
Laporte, Joseph Chester 37
Larabee, Carrie M. 162
Larabee, Hattie 305
Larkin. See also Larkins
Larkin, Annie 281
Larkins. See also Larkin
Larkins, Parker 9
Larrabee, Alta M. 234
Larrow, Delia M. 307
Larson, Elizebeth 222
Lascomb, Georgianna 175
Laseaker, John 215
Lasick, Andrew 215
Latellier, Archie 259
Latellier, Catherine 259
Latellier, Cyrel 259
Latellier, Edmond 259
Latellier, Kate 259
Laundry, Eddie 320
Laundry, Edmon 320
Laundry, Joseph 320
Laurine. See Lawrien
Laurine, Julius 338
Lauyen, A. L. 251
Lavine, Adelia 97
Lavine, Anna 97
Lavine, Benjamin 97
Lavine, Delemore 97
Lavine, Georgianna 97
Lavine, Joseph 97
Lavine, Mary 97

Lavine, Phillip 97
Lavine, Walter 97
Lawan, Charles H. 179
Lawan, Delia 178
Lawan, Ephraim 179
Lawan, Gertie Ellen 179
Lawan, Josephine M. 179
Lawan, Nelson 179
Lawan, Raymond 178
Lawan, Rosa Bell 179
Lawrence, Amos 58
Lawrence, J., Mrs. 277
Lawrence, Luther 58, 59
Lawrence, Thomas 236
Lawrien. See Laurine
Lawricn, Julius 314
Laws, Mary 41
Lawton, Mary (Healy) 115
Leakey, Honora 26
Leakey, John 26
[Leakey], Scott 26
Leary, Bridget 95
Leary, Florance 95
Leary, Mary 95
LeClair. See also LeClaire, LaClair
LeClair, Fred 21
LeClaire. See also LeClair, LaClair
LeClaire, Eugene 21
LeClaire, Louisa (Morsett) 21
Lee, Kate 150
Lemire, Adelbert 228
Lemire, Arliam 228
Lemire, Cadies 228
Lemire, Clodia 228
Lemire, Clophret 228
Lemire, Denis 228
Lemire, Evangeline 228
Lemire, Joseph 228
Lemire, Joseph, Jr. 228
Lemire, Manda 228
Lemorand, Cloe (Durant) 148
Lemorand, Joel 148
[Leon] 138
Leon, Joseph 21
LeRose, Hattie 242
Leshure, Samuel 44
Levine, Joseph 30
Levine, Phillip 30
Leware, Delia [Smith] 265
Leware, Ephraim 265
Leware, Gertrude E. 265
Leware, Josephine 265
Leware, Kayman 265
Leware, Nelson 265
Leware, Rose Bell 265
Lewis, Albert A. 229

Lewis, Edna (Jennings) 98
Lewis, Harrison 15
Lewis, James D. 98, 99, 337
Lewis, Marvin 98
Lewis, Mary A. 15
Lewis, Mary A. (Spooner) 8
Lewis, Mary G. 98
Lewis, Matilda J. (Holmes) 71
Lewis, Minnie 15
Lewis, Rosa 15
Lewis, Rose E. (Bates) 229
Lewis, Zenas 8
Lincoln, Fred 312
Lincoln, Tyler 73
Linde, Rose 276
Lindergan, Bryan 81
Liscord, Caroline (Hould) 298
Liscord, Flossy 267
Liscord, Henry 267, 298
Liscord, John 298
Liscord, Minnie 298
Liscord, Peter 298
Little, Achsah 113
Little, Emma 86
Little, J. H. 113
Little, Joseph 86
Little, Joseph, Jr. 86
Little, Lora 86
Little, Willie 86
Livingston, Mary 15, 73
Loisell, Eva 113
Loisell, Gloria 113
Loisell, Ida 113
Loisell, John 113
Loiselle, Lena 113
Loisell, Sophia (Selline) 113
Long, Maria 7
Longever, Ella D. 169
Looney, Mary 330
Lourien, Julius 287
Louzen, Agnes (Wilcox) 58
Louzen, Albert 58
Louzen, Mary 58
Louzen, Peter 58
Lovejoy, Mary 329
Low, Mary S. 254
Low, Tice 146
Lowell, Harry E. 91
Lowell, Mary R. 91
Lower, Antoine 211, 242
Lower, Ellen 211, 242
Lower, Freddie M. 211, 242
Lower, Jerry 211, 242
Lower, Mary L. 211, 242
Lower, Rosa (Flag) 211, 242
Lower, Rosa 211, 242

Lunderville, George 209
Lunderville, Margaret 209
Lynch, Daniel 81
Lynch, John 117
Lynch, Margaret 117
Lynch, Mary (Coy) 117
Lynch, Michael K. 209
Lynch, Richard 117, 119
Lyons, Julius 44

M. 292
MacClaine. See also McLane
MacClaine, Charles 127
Mack, Ernest R. 320
Mackie, T. 96
Madden, Nora Ann 81
Madison, Addie (Rock) 263
Madison, Harry 263
Mahar, Ann 152
Mahar, Ellen 152
Mahoney, Bridget 168
Mahoney, Ellen 168
Mahoney, Hanora 168
Mahoney, Mary 168
Mahoney, Mary, Jr. 168
Mahoney, Michael 168
Malaney, Annie M. Doyle 334
Mallry, Frank 45
Mallry, James 45
Mallry, Lizzie 45
Mallry, Lizzie, Jr. 48
Manigan, Mary 214
Mann, James 20
Mansell, Henry 301
Mansfield, Edward 44
Mansfield, John 44
Mansfield, John, Jr. 44
Mansfield, Larry 12, 44
Mansfield, Mary 44
Mansfield, Mary A. 44
Mansfield, Mr. 12
Mansfield, Mrs. 12
Marble, Lucy 247
Marcaux, Benjamin 231
March, Achsah 194
March, Luther 194, 207
Marcott, Mary 104
Markes, Eliza 222
Marrion, Alice (Allen) 221
Marrion, Annie 221
Marrion, George 221
Marrion, Harold 221
Marrion, May 221
Marrion, Peter T. 221
Marrones, Josephine 129
Marsh, Catharine (Allridge) 21

Marsh, David 21
Marsh, Frances 21
Marston, Emily 331
Marston, Hattie 331
Marston, Jane 331
Marston, John E. 331
Marston, Nancy 100
Marston, Orlando 257, 331
Marston, Sarah Ann 331
Marsy, Bridget 87
Martell, Clarence J. 242
Martell, Ernest G. 242
Martell, Florence H. 242
Martell, Hattie (LeRose) 242
Martell, Joseph 242
Martell, Zephire 208
Marteno. See also Martineau
Marteno, Alonzo 313
Marteno, Annie 313
Marteno, Arthur 313
Marteno, Flora 313
Martenraux, Joseph 280
Martin, Alvin 107
Martin, Ansel 107
Martin, Charlot H. 306
Martin, Converse 84
Martin, Eliza A. (Hathorn) 194
Martin, Ellen (Gerlin) 309
Martin, Ephraim 89
Martin, George W. 306
Martin, Henry V. 306
Martin, James 309
Martin, John F. 306
Martin, Lucy 84
Martin, Margaret W. 306
Martin, Mary A. (Howard) 309
Martin, Nellie A. 74
Martin, Roxana 13
Martin, Sarah T. 73, 163
Martin, Silas O. 324
Martin, Truman C. 73
Martin, Willard 13
Martineau. See also Marteno
Martineau, Germaine 314
Martineau, Lydia 314
Martineau, Philip 314
Marvin, Byron O. 210
Mason, Elijah 47
Mason, Eliza 12
Mason, Ellen L. 206
Mason, Fred, Mrs. 146
Mason, Georgianna (Lascomb) 175
Mason, Harry 175
Mason, Hartley D. 12
Mason, John 175
Mason, Lowell C. 119, 255

Mason, Simeon 206
Mason, Simon 255
Mason, Willie 175
Mason, Willie H. 12
Mason, Zua A. 206
Masse, Charles 197
Masse, Charles, Jr. 197
Masse, Henry 197
Masse, Severine 197
Massier. See also Messiah
Massier, Eli 124
Massier, Elicha 124
Massier, Emily 124
Massier, Esther 124
Massier, Fred 124
Mathews, Emma V. 144
May, Albert B. 282
May, Charles P. 282
May, Erwin C. 282
May, Flossie May 287
May, Fred W. 278, 338
May, George 287
May, Herbert H. 282
May, Joseph 282
May, Joseph S. 282
May, Josephine L. 282
May, LeForest I. 282
May, Mary E. 287
May, Orin O. 282
May, Peter 145
McAllister. See McCallester, McCollister
McBride, Michael 247
McCallester, Martin 10
McCarney, William 107
McCarty, Alice M. 135
McCarty, James 135
McCarty, John 135
McCarty, Mary (Cragen) 135
McCarty, Michael 135
McCarty, Michael, Jr. 135
McClearn, James C. 203
McClure, Christina 274
McClure, David 274
McClure, John 274
McColley, John 286
McCollister, George O. 202, 203
McCollister, Harry E. 203
McCollister, Sarah C. 203
McCollister, Willie G. 203
McColumbia, Hattie 14, 32
McColumbia, Irving 14
McColumbia, Vangybelle 14
McCoy, Ellen M. 66
McCoy, Osman 66
McCoy, Sarah Jane 54
McCurdy, Chester Arthur 198

McCurdy, George 198
McCurdy, Millie L. 198
McCurdy, Robert H. 198
McDonald, Agnes 242
McDonald, Alburt 242
McDonald, Christie 242
McDonald, Clifford 242
McDonald, Dora 242
McDonald, Ernest 242
McDonald, Esther 202
[McDonald], Exelia 202
McDonald, Florence 242
[McDonald], Henry 202
McDonald, Jennie 242
[McDonald], Josephine 202
McDonald, Octave 202
McDonald, William 278
McDonald, Willie 242
McGinnis, Matilda 178
McGinnis, Rosa 178
McGinnis, Roselbeau 178
McGinnis, William 178
McGovern, Mary 231
McGravey, Edward F. 59
McGravey, Peter 59
McGravey, Peter, Mrs. 59
McGregger, Ellen (Cornell) 241
McGregger, John, Jr. 241
McGregger, John, III 241
McKittrick, Daniel 328
McLane. See also MacClaine
McLaughlin, Hugh 92
McLaughlin, Mary 92
McLaughlin, William A. 92
McLear, Susan 94
McManus, Henry 165, 338
McManus, Patrick 74
McNamara, Ann 12
McNamara, Ann, Jr. 12
McNamara, Bridget 12
McNamara, Hanora 12
McNamara, Margaret 12
McNamara, Mary 12
McNamara, Michael 12
McNamara, Patrick 12
McNamara, Peter 12
McNamara, Thomas 12
Mead, John H. 151, 228, 332
Mead, Julia A. 151, 228
Mead, Myra J. 151
Mean/Meanry, Mary 330
Medcalf, Ada M. 212
Medcalf, Emily S. (Peirce) 212
Medcalf, George 212
Medcalf, Lawrence 212
Melo, Charles 85

Melo, Charles A. 85
Melo, Gilbert 85
Melo, Lucy (Jolly) 85
Melo, William H. 85
Mendam, Margaret 302
Mendam, William 302
Menning, Joseph 145
Merrifield, Ann 48
Merrifield, Maria 48
Merrifield, Simeon 48
Messiah. See also Massier
Messiah, Samuel 135
Metcalf, Augusta 246
Metcalf, Julia A. 333
Metcalf, Lucius 246
Metcalf, Orinda Beckwith 63
Metcalf, Richard Kimball 63
Meyett, Emily 20
Meyett, Mary (Sharkee) 20
Meyett, Peter 20
Meyett, Peter, Jr. 20
Miles, Jonas 107
Miller, Charles 85
Miller, Charles A. 85
Miller, Gilbert 85
Miller, Lucy (Jolly) 85
Miller, William A. 85
Millet, Caroline (Good) 136
Millet, Carrie 136
Millet, Clord 136
Millet, Della 136
Millet, Emma 136
Millet, George 136
Millet, Mary 136
Millet, Rosie 136
Milo, John 292
Milo, Mary 292
Mitchell, John 100
Mitchell, Mary 105
Mitchell, Mr. 24
Mitchell, Nellie I. (Hastings) 100
Mitchell, Robert 114
Monahan. See also Monehan
Monahan, ___ 165
Monahan, Lawrence 145
Monehan. See also Monahan
Monehan, John 315
Monroe, Ella F. 233
Monroe, Fred 233
Montegney, Joseph 20, 216
Montegney, Louisa (Shaker) 20, 130, 216
Montegney, Mary 20, 130, 216
Montery. See Montegney
Montpleiseur, Agnes (Durues) 288
Montpleiseur, Alexander 288
Montpleiseur, Clara (Cheney) 288

Montpleiseur, Dillium 288
Montpleiseur, Emma 288
Montpleiseur, Josephine 288
Montpleiseur, Julinmory 288
Montpleiseur, Zuinany 288
Monty, Arthur 201
Monty, Carl Alvin 201
Monty, Fredy 201
Monty, Hannah 204
Monty, Henry 201
Monty, Julia E. 201
Monty, Louisa 201
Monty, Oscar 204
Monty, William 201
Moor. See also Moore
Moor, Edward 122
Moor, Ellen 122
Moor, Jerry 122
Moor, Lizabeth 122
Moor, Selina 122
Moore. See also Moor
Moore, Ada M. 87
Moore, Alice E. 87
Moore, Catherine 113
Moore, Charles 113
Moore, Clarence E. 87
Moore, Eva G. (Stanford) 87
Moore, Fred W. 87
Moore, John Andrew 113
Moore, Lottie E. 87
Moore, Martha L. 113
Moore, Mary Ann 113
Moran, Eliza (Shorty) 220
Moran, Joseph 220
Moreney, James 112
Moreney, Lizzie 112
Morey, Sarah A. 181
Morrin, Edmond 213
Morrin, Eugene 213
Morrin, Josephine 213
Morrin, Josephine, Jr. 213
Morrin, Pierse 213
Morris, Arla 159
Morris, Eliza B. 204
Morris, Ella A. 159
Morris, Freddie 159
Morris, John 159
Morris, Lucinda 159
Morris, William 315
Morrison, Elizabeth (Healy) 115
Morrison, John 115
Morse, Alfred 119
Morse, Eliza 45
Morse, Hannah 338
Morse, Hatty (Rivers) 119
Morse, James 44

Morse, John 44
Morse, Joseph 45
Morse, Mary 44
Morsett, Louisa 21
Mosher, Arthur 162
Mosher, Bessie May 334
Mosher, Eliza E. 162
Mosher, Henry 162
Mosher, Josee 162
Mosher, Kenneth 162
Mosher, Maud 162
Mosher, Nellie 162
Mosher, Uriah 162
Mosher, Uriah, Jr. 162
Moultney. See Montegney
Moulton, Charles 49
Moultroup, Addie May 10
Moultroup, Charles 10
Moultroup, Elisha C. 10
Moultroup, Harley E. 10
Moultroup, Myrtie A. 10
Mountainor, Joseph 73
Mudgett, C., Mrs. 1
Mulgreen, Peter 177
Mulgrew. See Mulgreen
Mulqueny, Thomas 92
Mulvie, Elizabeth (Fitzgerald) 14
Mulvie, Thomas 14
Murdo, Annie E. 125
Murphy, Anna M. 140
Murphy, Annie 140
Murphy, Daniel 140
Murphy, Daniel J. 140
Murphy, Elizabeth 140
Murphy, John 37, 140
Murphy, Mary 119
Murphy, May E. 140
Murphy, Patrick H. 140
Murray. See also Murry
Murray, James 319
Murry. See also Murray
Murry, James 45
Murry, James, Jr. 45
Murry, Lizzie 45
Murry, Mary 45
Murry, Michael 45
Myah, Josephine [Tellia] 310
Myah, Peter 310

Nailer. See also Naylor
Nailer, Carrie 20
Nailer, Charles 20
Nailer, Felix 20
Nailer, Jennie 20
Nailer, Jessie M. 20
Nailer, Julia (Joiyle) 20

Nailer, Maggie 20
Nailer, Mary F. 20
Nailer, William 20
Nailer, William 20
Nallette, Adelia 148
Nallette, Annie 148
Nallette, Clora 148
Nallette, Emma 148
Nallette, George 148
Nallette, Mary 148
Nallette, Rosa 148
Naramore, Bessie 324
Naramore, Chester 324
Naramore, Lottie E. 324
Naramore, Will E. 324
Naramore, Willie 324
Nash, Abigail 299
Nash, Alexander 29
Nash, Alice A. 61
Nash, Alice M. 170
Nash, Andrew 301
Nash, Calvin A. 170
Nash, Celia (Austin) 272, 304
Nash, Eliza Jane 29
Nash, Eliza E. [Davis] 122
Nash, Eliza T. 45
Nash, Elizabeth 29
Nash, Ephraim 267
Nash, Florence M. (Perkins) 75, 170
Nash, Flossy 304
Nash, George 272
Nash, George H. 304
Nash, George L. 5, 29, 304
Nash, Harry J. 170
Nash, Henry H. 61
Nash, Isis E. 174
Nash, Jennie 29
Nash, John 122
Nash, Lizzie Ellen (Nevers) 5
Nash, Mary E. 304
Nash, Mary Jane (Crossfield) 267
Nash, Merty C. 304
Nash, Oliver L. 75, 170
Nash, Orrisa L. 170
Nash, Oscar W. 61, 62
Nash, Reuben 45
Nash, Stillman D. 29
Nash, Susan A. (Spauldin) 61
Nash, Warren A. 170
Nash, William H. 29
Naylor. See also Nailer
Naylor, Charles 96
Naylor, Joseph 96
Naylor, Mary S. 96
Naylor, Peter 96
Naylor, Rosa 96

Needham, A. W. 320
Needham, Thomas 43, 44
Nellitt, Annie 121
Nelson family 334
Nelson, John 235
Nevers, Bertha 130
Nevers, Charles Albert 5
Nevers, Daniel J. 130
Nevers, Enos 130
Nevers, Flossie 130
Nevers, Franklin G. 5
Nevers, Gertie 130
Nevers, Jerome 130
Nevers, Lizzie Ellen 5
Nevers, Maria L. (Bates) 5
Nevers, Risby (Howard) 130
Newell, Darius 182
Newell, Everett W. 182
Newell, Italie A. 182
Newell, Kate D. 182
Newell, Lee M. 182
Newell, Mary Ann 182
Newton, Annie 122
Newton, Fannie M. 245
Newton, Frank 122
Newton, Harry 245
Newton, Hubbard H. 245
Newton, M. F. 107
Newton, Marshall F. 133
Newton, Mary E. 245
Nickerson, Ella L. (Ray) 74, 212, 213
Nickerson, Horace M. 74, 213
Nickerson, Sarah 284
Nickerson, Sarah W. 74, 213
Nickerson, Willie F. 74, 213
Nims, Ann [Howard] 141
Nims, Archie Wallace 173
Nims, Blanche A. 173
Nims, Charles F. 141
Nims, Charlie 228
Nims, Edith V. 173
Nims, Edna A. 173
Nims, George H. 173
Nims, Georgie 228
Nims, Harrington D. 173
Nims, Lois (Wright) 228, 337
Nims, Woodbury J. 228
Noel, Gideon 229
Noel, Regina 229
Noel, Rosa 229
Noice, Fanny W. 138
Noice, George P. 138
Nolen, Catherine (Sullivan) 241
Nolen, William 241
Nonehan, Thomas 302
Noonan, Orpha C. 235

Noonan, Thomas 235
Norcross, Josephine M. 220
Norcross, Nelson B. 220, 310
Norcross, William F. 310
Norwood, George 335
Notts, George W., Mrs. 174

O'Brien, Annie A. 153
O'Brien, Ellen 149, 153
O'Brien, James 8
O'Brien, Kate 97
O'Brien, Katie E. 149, 153
O'Brien, Lawrence J. 149, 153
O'Brien, Margaret "Maggie" 149, 153
O'Connor, Patrick 153
O'Keefe, James 93
O'Keefe, Margaret (Sullivan) 93
O'Keefe, Patrick 72
O'Neil, Angeline (Breau) 183
O'Neil, John 183
O'Neil, William 183
Oliver, Mary 71
Orne, Frank 9
Orne, Julia A. (Austin) 9, 85
Osborn, Nettie 286

Packard, Charles 192
Packard, Clarence 192
Packard, Emma 192
Packard, Estella 192
Packard, James A. 39
Packard, Sidney H. 39
Page. See also Paige
Page, Beloa May 122
Page, Florence G. 303
Page, Frank E. 122
Page, George B. 122
Page, George H. 122
Page, Horace 99
Page, Ida L. 303
Page, Jane A. 33, 46
Page, Jonathan 46
Page, Mary E. (Smith) 122
Paige. See also Page
Paige, Florence G. 277
Paige, Ida (Craig) 277
Paige, William E. 277
Paine, Persis 102
Pair, Martha (Grenier) 320
Pair, Newell 320
Palladee. See also Pallidee, Pallady
Palladee, Joseph 59, 312
Palladee, Louisa 59, 312
Pallady. See also Palladee, Pallidee
Pallady, Louis 312
Pallidee. See also Palladee, Pallady

Pallidee, Joseph 28
Pallidee, Mary 28
Palmer, Joseph 105
Palmer, Nancy J. 331
Paridis, Devry 240
Paridis, Eava 240
Paridis, Fred 240
Paridis, Mary 240
Paridis, Ned 240
Paridis, Peter 240
Parker, Carrie E. 140
Parker, Charles 74
Parker, Frank H. 193
Parker, Harry 172
Parker, John 2d, Mrs. 45
Parker, Phocba (Wilder) 79
Parker, William 79
Parkhurst, Charles 285
Parkhurst, Ella F. 319
Parkhurst, Flora V. 287
Parkhurst, Helen E. (Grigs) 287
Parkhurst, Henry M. 287
Parkhurst, Lizzie G. 284
Parks, Elmira L. 76
Parks, James L. 76
Parmenter, Clara 337
Parmenter, Clara E. 232
Parmenter, Clara E., Jr. 232
Parmenter, John W. 232
Parmerleau, Annie 274
Parmerlaeu, Clara 274
Parmerleau, Frank 274
Parmerleau, Fred 274
Parmerleau, John 274
Paro. See also Perrault, Perrault
Paro, Mary 276
Paro, Thomas 282
Parrault. See also Perrault, Paro
Parrault, Adeline 200
Parrault, Felix 200
Parrault, Henry 200
Parrault, Joseph 200, 232
Parrault, Julia 200
Parrault, Maria (Heberts) 232
Parrault, Mary 200
Parrault, Nettie 200
Parrault, Thomas 232
Parrent, Alberteen 218
Parrent, Eva 218
Parrent, Joseph 218
Parrent, Matilda 218
Parrent, Sam 218
Parrent, Wilder 218
Passano, Alta M. 212
Passano, Cora 212
Passano, Edward N. 212

Passano, Freddie 212
Passano, Israel 212
Passano, Walter L. 212
Patch, Florence 251
Patnode, Annie 124
Patnode, John 124
Patnode, Mary 76
Patnode, Mike 76
Patterson, Bessie 240
Patterson, Birdie 240
Patterson, Eddie 240
Patterson, George 76
Patterson, Henry 240
Patterson, John 240
Patterson, Lucy J. 240
Patterson, Tuffield 240
Patterson, Willie 240
"Pattie" 109
Paul, Hellen J. 211
Paul, Joseph 211
Paul, Mary A. 211
Paul, Mary A., Jr. 211
Paul, William Pratt 211
Payer, Alfred 318, 338
Peal, Spenser 208
Pearson, George 100
Pearson, Nancy (Marston) 100
Peckins, Fred H. 296
Peckins, Sarah J. (Davis) 296
Peirce. See also Pierce
Peirce, Emily S. 212
Pelkey, Anthony 184
Pelkey, Charles A. 184
Pelkey, Ida May 184
Pelkey, John E. 184
Pelkey, Julius Hiram 109
Pelkey, Mabel 184
Pelkey, Mary S. 184
Pelto, David 244
Pelto, David, Jr. 244
Pelto, Eddie 244
Pelto, Florence 244
Pelto, Florence (Bascomb) 244
Pelto, Nancy 244
Pelto, Wilmer 244
Percival, Fanny 11, 78
Percival, James 11
Percival, Josephine 11, 78
Perham, Addie D. 191
Perham, Deborah 108
Perkins, Florence M. 75, 170
Perkins, Horatio M. 75
Perkins, Mary Ann 75
Perkins, Nellie M. (Sargent) 91
Perkins, Waldo H. 297
Perreault. See Parrault, Paro

Perrault, Bertha 282
Perrault, Maria (Abbott) 282
Perrault, Sammy 282
Perrault, Thomas 282
Perrault, Thomas, Jr. 282
Perry, Albert 224
Perry, Anna 140
Perry, Charles 215
Perry, Eliza 104
Perry, Ernest R. 215
Perry, Francis A. 185
Perry, Fred M. 90
Perry, Fred R. 185
Perry, George B. 288
Perry, George W. 104
Perry, Georgie 224
Perry, Isabella (Glass) 215
Perry, Jennie 224
Perry, Mary 224
Perry, Mary A. 224
Perry, Melinda 224
Perry, Nahum, Mrs. 13
Perry, Peter 140
Perry, Rose 260
Perry, Victoria 185
Perry, William 215, 337
Pertred, Sarah 282
Perusse, Ellen 217
Perusse, Mary Ellen 211, 217
Peterson, Amanda 19
Peterson, Emma 226
Peterson, Jens Sofus 206
Peterson, John 226
Phelps, Dennis A. 116
Phelps, Dora 332
Phelps, Julia E. 158
Phelps, Luella Bell 160
Phelps, Mattie A. 160
Phelps, Sylvia (Abbott) 116
Philbrick, Caleb 168
Phillips, Albert M. 175
Phillips, Almira M. 175
Phillips, Bella A. 325
Phillips, Francis 332
Phillips, Jennie Belle 96
Phillips, John 46
Phillips, Mary E. 46
Phillips, Mary W. 175
Pibbs, James E. 131
Piche, Edward 128
Piche, Rosie 128, 129
Pickering, Almira/Elmira 82
Pickering, Loring 82
Pickering, Lucy P. 82
Pickett, Alice 19
Pickett, Anna 19

Pickett, Augusta [Metcalf] 246
Pickett, Catharine 19
Pickett, Horatio G. 246
Pickett, Hosea G. 297
Pickett, James 19
Pickett, John 19
Pickett, Julia 19
Pickett, Mary 19
Pickett, Stephen 19
Pickett, Thomas 19
Picole, Dennis 85
Picole, Frank 85
Picole, Isabel 85
Picole, Joseph 85
Picole, Julius 84
Picole, Julius, Jr. 85
Pierce. See also Peirce
Pierce, Charles 46
Pierce, Cordelia (Ingram) 46
Pierce, Ellen (Whitcomb) 90
Pierce, Fred E. 46
Pierce, Fred J. 191
Pierce, George 295
Pierce, Hattie W. 46
Pierce, Herbert C. 46
Pierce, Ida 295
Pierce, J. W. 46
Pierce, Jabez 157
Pierce, Laura A. 74, 157
Pierce, Levi F. 338
Pierce, Lizzie J. 295, 338
Pierce, Lone E. 46
Pierce, Sarah E. 46
Pike, Annie 292
Pike, Bessie 292
Pike, Joel 292
Pike, Louis 292
Pike, Morris 292
Pike, Sarah 292
Pike, Willie 292
Piper, Ambrose H. 268
Piper, Bertie E. 191
Piper, Eddie C. 191
Piper, Herbert E. 191
Piper, Lucetta 268
Piper, Mattie M. 191
Piper, Stella M. (Brown) 191
Pippin, Joseph 46
Pippin, Mary 46
Plasteridge, Amasa 180
Plasteridge, Charles 180
Plasteridge, Etta 180
Plasteridge, Jennie E. 180
Plasteridge, Mary A. 180
Pluff, Daniel 249
Pluff, Delia 48

Pluff, Delia (Woods) 248
Pluff, Frank 48, 76
Pluff, Henry 249
Pluff, Joseph 248
Pluff, Joseph, Jr. 249
Pluff, Mary J. 249
Pluff, Napoleon 249
Pluff, Nellie M. 249
Plummer, Clerice E. 130
Plummer, J. C. 107
Plummer, Sarah Jane 302
Poland, Elvira 158
Pollard, Annie L. 163
Pollard, Charles 213
Pollard, Etta (Howard) [Barns] 213
Pollard, Martha E. (Howard) 163
Pollard, Nora 244
Pollard, Peter 244
Pollard, Salina Brooks 244
Pollard, Silvia 244
Pollard, Walter S. 163
Pollard, Willie 244
Pollard, Willie H. 163
Pollard, Winnee May 163
Pond, Mr. 62
Poole, Bessie 234
Poole, Elmer 234
Poole, Emma (Knight) 234
Poole, Frank A. 234
Poole, George E. 295
Poole, Samuel 234
Poole, Vernie M. 234
Pooler, Charles 47
Pooler, Fred 47
Porey, Annie 143
Porey, Emma 143
Porey, Flora 143
Porey, Fred 143
Porey, Joseph 143
Porey, Rosie 143
Porey, Shisia (Borgan) 143
Porter, Charles 76
Porter, Mr. 80
Porter, Walter E. 76, 107
Posey, Arthur 156
Posey, David 156
Posey, Dona 156
Posey, Eddie 156
Posey, Edmund 156
Posey, Joseph 156
Posey, Peter 156
Posey, Regina 156
Posey, Rose 156
Post, Minnie 288
Poster, Caroline 337
Potter, Polly 159, 162

Powers, Joseph 75
Powers, Mary A. 95
Powers, Mary A. (Galbin) 95
Powers, Mary Florence 95
Powers, Reuben C. 95
Powers, Reuben R. 95
Powers, William 300
Pratt, Albert 170
Pratt, Alice (Lanfair) 32
Pratt, Archie F. 291
Pratt, Calvin S. 33, 84
Pratt, Charles 293
Pratt, Charles E. 303
Pratt, Ellen A. 181
Pratt, Eugene 311
Pratt, Fanny M. 170
Pratt, George 211
Pratt, Henry J. 244, 337
Pratt, Horace 32
Pratt, Laura 291
Pratt, Lucy (Martin) 33, 84
Pratt, Sarah H. 244, 338
Pratt, Seth 291, 311
Pratt, Thomas 211
Pratt, William W. 289
Pray, Carrie E.(Parker) 140
Pray, Eva May 140
Pray, Joseph Parker 140
Pray, Willie 140
Predum, Aurilla 157
Predum, Eliza 157
Predum, Ella 157
Predum, Mary 157
Predum, Thomas 157
Pregent, Edward 253
Pregent, Flanie 253
Pregent, Frank 253
Pregent, Hattie 253
Pregent, Joseph 253
Prentice, Ira 90
Prescott, Mabel M. 145
Prescott, Nellie H. (Towne) 199
Pressey, E. E., Mrs. 119
Preston, Ellsworth E. 31
Preston, Esther 31
Preston, George 327
Preston, Lilla 327
Preston, Lula (Cooper) 31
Price, John 212
Priest, Balinda 30
Priest, George 103
Priest, Samuel 105
Prigson, Emma 250
Prouty, Dr. 202, 205
Prouty, J. S. 273
Prouty, Mr. 90

Prouty, Nettie E. 90
Proux. See also Prux
Proux, Arselia 167
Proux, Arthur 75
Proux, Ascelia A. 167
Proux, Ashley 167
Proux, Clara 168
Proux, Frank 167
Proux, Merrit 167
Proux, Samuel 167
Prux. See also Proux
Prux, Florence 125
Prux, Lewis 125
Prux, Lucy 125
Pullisior, Louis 271
Punts, Mr. 16
Putnam, Albert 60
Putnam, Charles F. 264
Putnam, Emily 6
Putnam, Flosa 264
Putnam, George R. 114
Putnam, J. 320
Putnam, Mary 114
Putney, Ella A. (Davis) 19
Putney, Emma M. 19
Putney, Etta M. 19
Putney, George A. 19
Putney, Henry E. 19

Quinlan, Patrick 38

Rafferty, Margaret 59, 156
Ramir, Adolph, Mrs. 279
Rand, Clara S. 322
Rand, John A. 322
Rand, Josiah Kendall 253
Randall, J. E. 338
Randall, Joseph E. 56
Randall, Stephen L., Mrs. 70
Rasmundson, Alek 262
Raulaugh. See also Rollet
Raulaugh, Charles 240
Raulaugh, Eugena 240
Raulaugh, Eugene 240
Raulaugh, Louis 240
Raulaugh, Mary 240
Raulaugh, Paul 240
Raulaugh, Rose 240
Ray, Asa M. 123, 213
Ray, Eliza 123
Ray, Ella L. 74, 212, 213
Raymond, Alsead 232
Raymond, Anna E. 139
Raymond, Arthur W. 139
Raymond, Carroll 133, 134
Raymond, Charles M. 139

Raymond, Charles W. 103
Raymond, Christopher F. 133
Raymond, Curtis 275
Raymond, Demars 232
Raymond, Edward W. 275
Raymond, Eliza A. 139
Raymond, Gilman J. 139
Raymond, Hattie E. 133
Raymond, Jennie L.[Burpee] 139
Raymond, Joseph W. 275
Raymond, Mary 232
Raymond, Olivan 232
Read. See also Reed
Read, Walter 126
Reardon, Catherine 166
Reardon, Michael 166
Reed. See also Read
Reed, Abbie E. 263, 329
Reed, Annie 77
Reed, Annie T. 77
Reed, Arthur 263
Reed, Clara E. 263
Reed, Edward 233
Reed, Emma 233
Reed, Ernest 233
Reed, Frank R. 218
Reed, Grace 263
Reed, Ida 233
Reed, James E. 263
Reed, John 77
Reed, John M. 77
Reed, Joseph 233
Reed, Lillie 263
Reed, Lucy 263
Reed, Mary 77
Reed, Mary [Boestr] 218
Reed, Nellie 218
Reed, Olive K. 218
Reed, Susan A. 233
Reed, Vicar 233
Reed, Walter W. 263
Reed, William 77, 329
Reed, William F. 218
Reed, William H. 233
Reed, Willie I. 263
Reil, Heber 269
Reux, Corliss 253
Reyneau, Emma 131
Reyneau, John 131
Reyneau, Johny 131
Reyneau, Mary C. 131
Reyneau, Willie 131
Reynolds, Lucius D. 49
Reynolds, Miss 181
Reynolds, Mr. 78
Rice, Abigail 177

Rice, Charles B. 235
Rice, Nancy A. 310
Richard, Victoria 127
Richards, Charles E. 11, 78, 317
Richards, Charles W. 11, 78
Richards, Fanny (Percival) 11, 78, 317
Richardson, Abbie 243
Richardson, Abby (Tufts) 31
Richardson, Charles W. 219
Richardson, Eli 47
Richardson, Flossie L. 219
Richardson, Fred E. 219
Richardson, Hattie M. (Kenney) 219
Richardson, Samuel 31, 219
Richardson, Samuel C. 329
Richart, Frank 256
Richart, Freddie 256
Richart, Lewis 256
Richart, Lizzie 256
Richart, Rosa 256
Riel, Cordelia 77
Riel, Emma Phoeba 78
Riel, Heber 13, 77
Riel, Heber, Jr. 77
Riel, Mary C. 77
Riel, Peter 77
Riel, Peter, Jr. 77
Riel, Wilfred 77
Riley, Bridget 109
Riley, Joseph E. 40
Rineau, Eustin 78
Rineau, Eustin, Jr. 78
Rineau, Mary 78
Rines, Lizzie A. 18
Rines, Nancy 18
Rivers, Hatty 119
Rivers, Jane (Sampson) 285
Rivers, Joseph 285
Rivers, Joseph C. 285
Rivers, Mary A. 285
Rives, Charles 9
Rives, Mary 9
Rivet, Peter 128
Rivet, Rose 128
Rivet, Rosie 128, 129
Rivet, Sarah 128, 129
Rivet, Theodore 128
Robbins, Anna 134
Robbins, Asa 221, 337
Robbins, Daniel 263
Robbins, Daniel E. 56
Robbins, Edgar 263
Robbins, Eliza 134
Robbins, Emmah 134
Robbins, Ervin 263
Robbins, Frank 263

Robbins, George 263
Robbins, Hannah 263
Robbins, Henry 134
Robbins, Ida May 263
Robbins, John 49
Robbins, Leonard E. 331
Robbins, Lucy B. 199, 337
Robbins, Mary A. 263
Robbins, May 134
Robbins, Sarah E. 263
Robbins, Silas 134
Robbins, Susan 263
Robbins, Susan E. 56
Robbins, Sylvanus 224, 338
Robbins, Victory 134
Roberts, Lydia 96
Robinson, Aaron L. 9
Robinson, Arabella 9
Robinson, Louisa A. 8
Roby, Leonard T. 78
Roche, Katie 281
Rocheleau, Allice 246
Rocheleau, Charles 246
Rocheleau, Frankie 246
Rocheleau, George 246
Rocheleau, Napoleon 246
Rocheleau, Noel 246
Rock, Addie 263
Rock, Gabriel 104
Rock, Gabriel, Mrs. 104
Rock, Lewis 263
Rockwood, Edward C. 212
Rockwood, Florence E. 212
Rockwood, H. P. 212
Rockwood, Lottie (Farrington) 212
Rogan, May 288
Rogers, Calvin R. 77
Rogers, Henry E. 77
Rogers, Isaac W. 77
Rogers, John H. 129
Rogers, Justice R. 333
Rogers, Mary E. (Beach) 177
Rollet. See Raulaugh
Rorke, James 90
Rorke, Mary 90
Rourke. See Rorke
Rowan, James H. 288
Rowan, Mary Elizabeth 288
Rowan, Minnie (Post) 288
Rowe, Nathan B. 71
Rowland, Emma 291
Rowland, George 291
Royce. See also Royse
Royce, Harriet 79
Royse. See also Royce
Royse, Sarah S. 142

Ruderham, William F. 100
Ruffle, Carl William 172
Ruffle, Hattie L. 172
Ruffle, Margaret 48, 209
Ruffle, Samuel 48
Ruffle, William 108, 338
Ruffle, William J. 108, 172
Rugg, Mary (McGovern) 231
Rugg, Mary Margaret 231
Rugg, Susan Clara 231
Rugg, William P. 231
Rumrill, Charles F. 271
Rumrill, Emily M. 174
Rumrill, Florence A. 127
Rumrill, John W. 169
Rumrill, Sarah E. (Dingman) 169
Rumrill, Thomas 318
Rumrill, Thomas, Mrs. 174
Rumrill, Willard H. 127
Russell, Alfred 134, 135
Russell, Alfred, Mrs. 135
Russell, Delia (Jolly) 48
Russell, Ira W. 245
Russell, Joseph 48
Russell, Lucy P. 109
Russell, Mary E. 109
Russett, Adaline [Tissier] 143
Russett, Elijah 143
Ryan, Bridget 18
Ryan, Catherine 30
Ryan, John 18, 105, 210
Ryan, Kate 58
Ryan, Mary 105
Ryan, Mary A. 72
Ryan, Thomas 313
Ryan, Timothy 30

Saben, Levi 205
Safford, Otis 300
St. Cyr. See also Sansea
St. Cyr, Alfred 251
St. Cyr, Miss 280
St. John, Charles 193
St. John, Eva Bell 193
St. John, Frank 193
St. John, George 193
St. John, Jane 193
St. John, Jane, Jr. 193
St. John, Joseph Peter 193
St. John, Louisa 193
St. John, Lovina 193
St. Peter, Alice 82
St. Peter, Rosa 82
St. York, Frank 266
St. York, Frank, Jr. 266
St. York, John 266

St. York, Mary 266
Sampson, Jane 285
Sansea. See also St. Cyr
Sansea, Eviline 252
Sansea, Fred 251
Sansea, Henry 252
Sargent, Alfred G. 91
Sargent, Charles B. 91
Sargent, Charles C. 91
Sargent, Hannah M. 91
Sargent, Nellie M. 91
Sargent, Sylvia 91
Satave, L. 207
Sawin, Isabelle 103
Sawtell. See also Sawtelle
Sawtell, Lucy D. 71
Sawtelle. See also Sawtell
Sawtelle, E. H. 87
Sawtelle, Edward H. 93
Sawtelle, Ethel H. 83
Sawyer, Alfred 294
Sawyer, D. W. 16
Sawyer, Hattie 227
Schilling, Augusta 254
Schilling, Bertha 254
Schilling, Charles 254
Schilling, Fred 254
Schilling, Gustave 254
Schilling, Pauling 254
Scott, Adolphus 79
Scott, Agnes D. (Burns) 79, 184
Scott, Alice B. 63
Scott, Bertie G. 79
Scott, Clara 300
Scott, Diantha (Stearns) 79
Scott, Francis A. 63
Scott, George D. 79, 184
Scott, George W. 300
Scott, Ida D. 79
Scott, Martha B. 223
Scott, Nancy A. (Burns) 79
Scott, Rose 63
Scott, Samuel T. 223
Scovell, C. M. 1, 207
Scovell, Mrs. 207
Scribner, Gilman T. 314
Scribner, Linnie 313
Scribner, Mary E. 314
Scripture, G. I., Mrs. 4
Scrow, Minerva 231
Searle, Fred A. 186
Searle, Fred L. 186
Searle, Jennie 186
Searle, Salome C. 186
Seaver, Emma F. (Whitney) 216
Seaver, Luman, Mrs. 177

Seaver, Samuel H. 216
Sebastian, Charles N. 329
Sebastian, Clifton 329
Sebastian, Ellen 329
Sebastian, Grover C. 329
Sebastian, Harriet A. 329
Sebastian, Meda 329
Seguin, Arthur 317
Selline, Sophia 113
Sentre. See Centre
Seveyer, Dolphus 201
Seveyer, Virginia 201
Seward, Charles A. 83, 329
Seward, David 16
Seward, George W. 34
Seward, Josiah 16
Seward, Lucy 329
Seward, Ruth C. 34
Seward, Sally 16
Seward, Sarah V. 16
Seward, Thomas 16
Shackett, John 299
Shackett, Nancy (LaCharity) 299
Shaker, Louisa 20, 130, 216
Shallum, John 139
Shambs, Antoine 101
Shambs, clara 101
Shambs, Felix 101
Shambs, Fred 101
Shambs, George 101
Shambs, Henry 101
Shambs, Rosanna 101
Shanessey, Edward E. J. 241
Shanessey, Katie 241
Shanessey, Lillie May 241
Shanessey, Mary (Sheeny) 241
Shanessey, Ruby Etta 241
Shanessey, William Edward 241
Shantley, Ezra 176
Shantley, Gusta 176
Sharkee. See also Sharkey
Sharkee, Ellen 98
Sharkee, Mary 20
Sharker, John 49
Sharker, Julia 49
Sharker, Peter 49
Sharkey. See also Sharkee
Sharkey, Albert 289
Sharkey, Arthur 238
Sharkey, Delia 238
Sharkey, Frank 238
Sharkey, Fred 238
Sharkey, George 243
Sharkey, Jerry 289
Sharkey, Jessie 238
Sharkey, Laura 238

Sharkey, Lena (Harper) 322
Sharkey, Lucy 289
Sharkey, Lucy (Coster) 238
Sharkey, Mary 238, 326
Sharkey, Matoon 238
Sharkey, May (Rogan) 288
Sharkey, Patsey 289
Sharkey, Peter 288, 295
Sharkey, Rosa 289
Sharkey, Sarah 295
Sharkey, Sarah (Gardner) 289
Sharkey, Susie (Wall) 243
Sharkey, William 238, 322
Sharkley, Eliza 137
Sharkley, John 137
Sharon, Angelina 329
Sharon, Annie 329
Sharon, Hormedas 329
Sharon, Lannasclas 329
Sharon, Louis 329
Sharon, Marie 329
Sharon, Mary 329
Sharon, Zaneide 329
Shattuck, Albert G. 176
Shattuck, George W. 176
Shattuck, Perley E. 176
Shattuck, Sarah A. (White) 176
Shaver, Charlie 161
Shaver, Emma 161
Shaver, John 241
Shaver, John Herbert 241
Shaver, Lena 161
Shaver, Louisa (Durant) 241, 242
Shaver, Lovisa May 241
Shaver, Martha 161
Shaver, Peter Alfred 241
Shaw, Emeline 218
Shaw, Emma E. 218
Shaw, Ernest M. 218
Shaw, Esther A. 218
Shaw, Ida M. 218
Shaw, John O. 218
Shaw, Kate B. 218
Shaw, Merritt H. 218, 314
Shaw, Pheba J. 218
Shaw, Reuben 218
Shaw, Tom 51
Shea, David 332
Shea, John Joseph 332
Shea, Margaret 332
Shea, Nellie 332
Shea, Nora 332
Shedd, George 8
Shedd, Mrs. 180
Sheehan, Bessy 60
Sheehan, Johannah 60

Sheehan, Maggie 60
Sheehan, Nellie 60
Sheehan, Patrick 60
Sheehan, Timothy 60
Sheehy, John 86
Sheeny, Mary 241
Sheldan, Ella B. 129
Sheldan, Eva E. 129
Sheldan, George W. 128
Sheldan, Grace G. 129
Sheldan, Herbert E. 129
Sheldan, Phoeba 128
Shelley, Charles E. 319
Shelley, Ella F. (Parkhurst) 319
Shepardson, Bert E. 279
Shepardson, Eliza (Stacy) 279
Shepardson, Elliott A. 279
Shepardson, Gertrude S. 279
Sheaprdson, Justice F. 279
Shepardson, Lorenzo P. 279
Shepardson, Patrick G. 279
Shepardson, William J. 279
Sheridan, Charles 304
Sheridan, Charles, Jr. 304
Sheridan, Mary 304
Shockley, A. G. 128
Shockley, Anna G. 128
Shockley, Mary E. 128
Shockley, Matilda 128
Shockley, Walter W. 128
Short, Fred 272
Short, John C. 219
Shorty, Eliza 220
Shortell, Mary 49
Shortell, Mary (Vincent) 217
Shortell, Thomas C. 217
Shortell, William 49
Shove, Elmira L. (Parks) 76
Shullon, Joseph 43
Shullon, Nora (LaMore) 43
Shupple, Mary 197
Sidella, Louis 149
Siefert, Charles A. 115
Siefert, Ida 115
Siefert, Katie 115
Siefert, Mary K. 115
Simms, Samuel 332
Simons, Clafse 195
Simons, Delima 195
Simons, Rosanna 195
Simpson, Charles S. 229
Simpson, Pauline C. 229
Skivington, Mary 101
Skivington, William 101
Slack, Eli W. 310
Slate, Mr. 196

Smith, Alice 263
Smith, Anna 109
Smith, Bridget D. 109
Smith, Charles 169, 247
Smith, Delia 265
Smith, Edward 137
Smith, Ellen 274
Smith, Elmira 152
Smith, Erastus 152
Smith, Frank 137
Smith, Fred A. 282
Smith, George 274
Smith, George, Jr. 274
Smith, Harriet 169
Smith, Harry M. 265
Smith, J. M. 274
Smith, Jacob 247
Smith, Jennie 247
Smith, Jestin P. 298
Smith, Julia 247
Smith, Lottie 51
Smith, Louisa B. 137
Smith, Lucy [Gilman] 282
Smith, Mark 51
Smith, Marry A. 299
Smith, Mary Ann 274
Smith, Mary E. 274
Smith, Mr. 10
Smith, Noble T. 190
Smith, Patrick 279
Smith, Sarah P. R. 50
Smith, Sophie 139
Smith, Susan E. 338
Smith, Thomas 263
Smith, Toba 247
Snow, Silvia 104
Son, David 269
Son, Emma B. 269
Son, Joseph Alexander 190
Son, Levi 190
Son, Levi, Jr. 190
Son, Mamie 190
Son, Mary Jane 190
Son, Mary Jane, Jr. 190
Son, Mary Louisa 190
Son, Phebe 269
Souls, Darwin 253
Souls, Eliza 253
Souls, Mabel 253
Sourrier, Charles 330
Sourrier, Eva 330
Sourrier, John F. 330
Sourrier, Lewis 330
Sourrier, Mary 330
Southwell, Charles Arthur 138
Southwell, Frank Orrel 138

Southwell, John 137
Southwell, John Faniel 138
Southwell, Mary J. 137, 216
Southwick, Edmund M. 158
Southwick, Jessie Pearl 158
Southwick, Margaret 326
Sparke, Luther B. 32
Sparks, Mr. 137
Spauldin. See also Spaulding
Spauldin, Dauphin, 2d 61
Spauldin, Susan A. 61
Spauldin, Susan R. 61
Spaulding. See also Spauldin
Spaulding, Ada L. 164
Spaulding, Ed W. 305
Spaulding, Ida B. (Chipman) 305
Spaulding, Sarah L. (Greenwood) 150
Spear, Lucius 114
Sperry, Carrie E. 92
Sperry, Charles 92
Sperry, Charles H. 92
Sperry, Sadie E. 92
Spitzenberger, Frank 120, 184
Spitzenberger, Theresa 120, 184
Spofford, Mary Jane 298
Spofford, William 298
Spooner, Alonzo A. 8
Spooner, Mary A. 8
Sprague, Emma C. M. 328
Spring, Herbert 128
Squire, George G. 5
Stack, Bernard 50
Stack, Edward 50
Stack, James A. 50
Stack, John F. 50
Stack, Kate 49
Stacy, Agnes 231
Stacy, Alace M. 217
Stacy, Alice 231
Stacy, Alice (Davis) 231
Stacy, Earnest 231
Stacy, Eben 201
Stacy, Edward 217
Stacy, Edward, Jr. 217
Stacy, Eliza 279
Stacy, Esther 231
Stacy, Esther E. 217
Stacy, George 217, 231
Stacy, James 217, 231
Stacy, Josephine 217, 231
Stacy, Julie 217
Stacy, Lottie 217
Stacy, Mary A. 217
Stacy, Pearl 231
Stanford, Eva G. 87
Stanford, George W. 87

Stanley, Abner 60
Starkey, Lucy 325
Starkey, Miss 193
Stearns, Diantha 79
Stebbins, Emma [Howard] 325
Stebbins, Josiah 164, 200, 206, 304
Stebbins, Josiah Clark 164, 200, 206
Stebbins, Naomi H. 325
Stebbins, Nellie 332
Stebbins, Nellie Marion 332
Stebbins, Nellie S. 304
Stebbins, Robert L. 325
Stenpoise, Charles 287
Stephens. See Stevens
Stevens, Abbie (Richardson) 243
Stevens, Arthur F. 93
Stevens, Burin C. 143
Stevens, Carrie 93
Stevens, Charles G. 93, 243
Stevens, Clark D. 91
Stevens, Emma 235
Stevens, G. S. 93
Stevens, George S. 93
Stevens, Gilbert T. 230
Stevens, Hattie M. 93
Stevens, John 8
Stevens, Joseph 79, 143, 247
Stevens, Martha C. 143
Stevens, Mary A. 93
Stevens, Mr. 91
Stevens, Mrs. 98
Stevens, Phoeba (Wilder) [Parker] [Wheeler] 79, 109
Stevens, Ruth A. 143
Stevens, Sarah 143
Stevens, Sarah L. 143
Stevens, Willie A. 243
Stevenson, Julia 206
Stewart, Electa D. 148
Stockwell, Amanda 125
Stockwell, James A. 309, 338(2)
Stone, Addie 296
Stone, Edmund 213
Stone, Frank 326
Stone, G. S. 158
Stone, Hattie M. 296
Stone, Henry 296
Stone, James M. 158
Stone, Norris C. 158, 169
Stone, Pheba 269
Stone, Rose A. (Lapoint) 296
Stone, Sarah E.(Dingman)[Rumrill][Davis] 158, 169
Stone, William H. 296, 304
Stowell, Hiram 137
Stowell, Mary A. [Powers] 95

Strafford, Fidella 159
Strafford, Samuel 159
Stratton, Martha 109
Street, Ada Bell 216
Street, Alexandria 144
Street, Alma 144
Street, Ansitia 144
Street, Archille 144
Street, Bell (Sumner) 216
Street, Georgeanna 144
Street, Gracie 217
Street, Hortense 144
Street, Ida 144
Street, William 144, 216
Streeter, Ada 319, 326
Streeter, Denzil M. 88
Streeter, Lillian 309
Streeter, Lottie 326
Streeter, Luther 34
Streeter, Stella H. 309
Streeter, Willis 319, 326
Sullivan, Annie L. (LaClose) 267
Sullivan, Bridget 198
Sullivan, Catherine 241
Sullivan, Daniel 289
Sullivan, Dennis 142
Sullivan, Dennis, Mrs. 142
Sullivan, Dennis G. 151
Sullivan, Ellen 302
Sullivan, Ethel 267, 289
Sullivan, Eunice (Howard) 289
Sullivan, Fred 289
Sullivan, Hagen 289
Sullivan, Helen 198
Sullivan, Henry D. 289
Sullivan, James 267
Sullivan, James B. 115
Sullivan, John 8, 302
Sullivan, Joseph 302
Sullivan, Kate 302
Sullivan, Lilla E. 151
Sullivan, Margaret 93
Sullivan, Marry 302
Sullivan, Mary (Leary) 95
Sullivan, Mattie R. (Tobey) 151
Sullivan, Maude 289
Sullivan, Mrs. 19
Sullivan, Nellie 302
Sullivan, Thomas O. 198
Sumner, Bell 216
Surprenout, Albert 31
Surprenout, George 31
Surprenout, Joseph S. 31
Surprenout, Mary 31
Surprenout, Olive 31
Surprise, Alice 225

Surprise, George D. 225
Surprise, George M. 225
Surprise, Julia 225
Surprise, Mary M. 225
Swan, Asenath 22, 204
Swan, Ebenezer 22
Swan, Roxana (Martin) 13
Swartelle, John, Mrs. 16
Sweeney, Bell 315
Sweeney, Joseph 280
Sweeney, Mary 79
Sweetland, Ann 334
Swenson, Carl 231
Swenson, Oscar L. 231
Swinington, Charles 14
Swinington, Ella M. 94
Swinington, Emily L. 14, 94
Swinington, Etta May 14
Swinington, Georgianna 14
Swinington, Ida M. 94
Swinington, Josiah T. 14, 94
Swinington, Leroy A. 94
Swinington, Leroy L. Burter 14
Swinington, Mary Etta 14
Swinington, Walter P. 14, 94

Tacy, Annie 260
Tacy, Lizzie 93, 260
Tacy, Louis/Lewis 93, 260
Tacy, Louis, Jr. 93, 260
Tacy, Maggie G. 93, 260
Taft, David 316
Taft, Francis 316
Taft. Lester 316
Taft, Lovell C. 99, 337
Taft, Maude 316
Taft, Smith B. 200
Talbot, Charles 328
Talbot, Clarrissa 328
Tallia, John 129
Tallia, Josephine (Marrones) 129
Tarbox, Arthur C. 177
Tarbox, Arthur C., Mrs. 177
Tatro, Annie (Foster) 237
Tatro, Clement 141
Tatro, Joe 237
Tatro, Margaret 141
Tellia. See also Tellier
Tellia, Georgeanna 261
Tellia, John 310
Tellia, Josephine 310
Tellier. See also Tellia
Tellier, Fidelia 84
Tellier, Joseph 84
Terrien. See also Therien, Therren
Terrien, Bessie 273

Terrien, Emilie 273
Terrien, Equrn H. 273
Terrien, Katie 273
Terrien, Lidia 273
Terrien, Oral 273
Thayer, Eli 222
Thayer, Josephine M. (Norcross) 220
Thayer, Laura 168
Thayer, Sarah O. (Aldrich) 110
Thayer, Sybel A. 222
Thayer, Warren A. 220
Therien. See also Terrien, Therren
Therien, Cadi Thomas 254
Therien, Emilia 254
Therien, Evenste 254
Therien, Horass 254
Therien, Robin W. 254
Therren. See also Terrien, Therien
Therren, Everett 318
Thomas, Clara A. 280
Thomas, Clarisa (Foster) 88
Thomas, Emma M. 168
Thomas, Joseph 51
Thomas, Lottie [Smith] 51
Thomas, Nathan 338
Thomas, Philip 88
Thompson, Alice M. 171
Thompson, Allen R. 268
Thompson, Bertie W. 171
Thompson, Frank L. 171
Thompson, Joseph 108, 171
Thompson, Julia E. 314, 331
Thornton, David 233
Thornton, Ida M. (White) 233
Thornton, Michael C. 290
Thornton, Ralph S. 193
Thornton, Willis 193
Thurber, George, Mrs. 331
Thurston, Dr. 202
Thurston, Frank L. 87
Thurston, Horace R. 60
Tibbetts, Bessie J. 243
Tibbetts, Emma 243
Tiffany, John D. 221
Tiffany, John J. 221
Tiffany, Mary Ann (Conway) 221
Tilden, George 78
Tilden, George, Mrs. 78
Tillison, Harry H. 223
Tissier, Adaline 143
Tobey, Mattie R. 151
Tobey, Thomas E. 151
Todd, Harry A. 101
Todd, Lizzie J. 101
Todd, Lucy T. (Allen) 101
Todd, Simon W. 101

Tonghey, Patrick 178
Tower, Amy A. 185
Tower, J. H. 185
Tower, J. Wesley 185
Towle, Carrie E. 313
Towle, Nettie F. 313
Town. See also Towne
Town, Burton E. 321
Town, George H. 248
Town, Samuel C. 207
Towne. See also Town
Towne, Catherine S. R. (Ellenwood) 199
Towne, Fanny M. (Pratt) 170
Towne, Francis L. 18, 190
Towne, Hattie Cota 329
Towne, Lizzie A. (Rines) 18
Towne, Mary A. 18, 190
Towne, Nellie H. 199
Towne, Oscar Alfred 170
Towne, Samuel C. 199
Towne, Sarah V. (Seward) 16
Towne, Solomon F. 18, 190
Towne, Willie A. 170
Towns, George 205
Townsend, Edwin J. 200
Townsend, Sabra D. 200
Trainor, James 173
Traxler, Bertrice Pearl 234
Traxler, Frances 234
Traxler, Perly 234
Treax, Clarissa A. 7
Tremley, Clinnie 311
Tremley, Dora 311
Tremley, Eunice 311
Tremley, Fred 311
Tremley, Julia 311
Tremley, Louis 310
Trey, Morris 320
Troller, James A. 63
Troller, James A., Jr. 63
Troller, Maggie 63
Troller, Maggie (Armstrong) 63
Troller, William J. 63
Trombley. See also Trombly
Trombley, Dora (Bushey) 312
Trombley, Edna 331
Trombley, Louis 312
Trombley, Mary Elsie 312
Trombley, Willie 312
Trombly. See also Trombley
Trombly, Dora 261
Trombly, Eugene 261
Trombly, Frank 261
Trombly, George 261
Trombly, Georgeanna (Tellia) 261
Trombly, Lewis 261

Trombly, Lois 261
Truax, Carrie 63
Trudo, Carrie 260
Tufts, Abby 31
Tufts, Catharine 31
Tufts, George 31
Tufts, James 31
Tufts, Jane 31
Tufts, Sabra M. 261
Tufts, Sarah 31
Tufts, William 31
Turner, Alta M. (Larrabee) 234
Turner, Caroline H. 18, 338
Turner, Clement 228
Turner, Frank Draper 235
Turner, Frank E. 228, 234
Turner, Frank H. 228
Turner, John 334
Turner, Lula 228
Turner, Luna J. 235
Turner, Mr. 18
Turner, Susie 228
Turner, Susie Q. 235
Turnquest, John 51
Turnquest, John Algat 51
Turnstall, Charlotte A. 147, 177
Turnstall, Elizabeth 147, 177
Turnstall, Robert 147
Turnstall, Timothy A. 147
Twitchell, Daniel 245
Twitchell, Daniel, Mrs. 161
Twitchell, Dr. 1, 202
Twitchell, Menirva (Freeman) 161, 245
Tyrell. See also Tyrrell
Tyrell, David B. 262
Tyrell, Ellen F. 261
Tyrrell. See also Tyrell
Tyrrel, Ephraim 169
Tyrrel, Miss 170

Urbane, Frank 7
Urbane, Maria (Long) 7

Valede, Alfred 190
Valede, Alfred, Jr. 190
Valede, Delima 190
Valede, Lora 190
Valede, Lydia 190
Valentine, Joanna 163
Valley, Albert 216
Valley, Louisa (Shaker) [Bryant][Montegney] 216
Van Ness, Joseph 188
Van Ness, Julia 188
Vaughan, John 274
Venne, Ellery 219

Vernoski, Annie 334
Vernoski, Frances 334
Vernoski, Jennie Jeseph 334
Vernoski, Peter 334
Verry, Annie C. 248
Verry, Daniel, Mrs. 279
Verry, Frank E. 248
Verry, Maria J. 248
Verry, William H. 248
Vetter, Julius H. 289, 338
Vigar, Charles 51
Vigar, Eliza V. 51
Vigar, Georgia A. 51
Vigar, John 52
Vigar, Lizzie 51
Vigneau. See also Vigneault
Vigneau, Abbott 237
Vigneau, Charles 18
Vigneau, Clara 237
Vigneau, George 237
Vigneau, John 92
Vigneau, Martin 237
Vigneau, Mary 237
Vigneau, Peter 237
Vigneau, Peter, Jr. 237
Vigneau, Sophronia 92
Vigneault. See also Vigneau
Vigneault, Ernest 127
Vigneault, Glory 127
Vigneault, Jennie 127
Vigneault, Joseph 127
Vigneault, Victoria 127
Vigneault, Victoria (Richard) 127
Vigneault, Willis 127
Vincent, Mary 217

Wade, Nicholas 230
Waite, Clarra C. 277
Waite, Henry 277
Wake, Stella 110
Walcott, Ada 226
Walcott, Eidith [Clark] 226
Walcott, Harvey 226
Walcott, Harvey, Jr. 226
Walcott, Marion 226
Waldron, Albert H. 30
Waldron, Alice M. 31
Waldron, Bertin 31
Waldron, Fanny (Howard) 31
Waldron, Harry J. 31
Waldron, Homer J. 31
Waldron, Lena L. 31
Waldron, Otis H. 31
Waldron, Susan R. 31
Walforitz, Lena 326
Wall, Susie 243

Wallback, Arthur 257
Wallback, Fred Giles 257
Wallback, John Vincent 257
Wallback, Joseph 257
Wallback, Mary (Buck) 257
Wallback, Mary Josephene 257
Wallback, Thomas 257
Ward, Albert G. 322
Ward, Asenath (Swan)[Hale] 204
Ward, Eunice H. 232
Ward, George P. 187, 196, 232
Ward, Ithama 108
Ward, Lena A. 322
Ware, Delany 126
Ware, Dexter D. 126, 136
Ware, John 126
Ware, Roxana 126
Ware, Sarah E. 136
Ware, Sylvester M. 126
Warren, Charles, Mrs. 268
Warren, Frank 7
Waskins, Bridget 28
Waskins, Lewis 28
Waterman, H. L., Dr. 242, 262, 272
Waters. See also Watters
Waters, Annie A. 271
Waters, Edward 153
Waters, Ellen 153
Waters, Fanny E. 138
Waters, George E. 138
Waters, George L. 138
Waters, Hattie May 138
Waters, Mary Jane 138
Watters. See also Waters
Watters, Edward A. 87
Watters, Fanny Ellen 87
Webb, Adeline 266
Webb, Charles 88
Webb, Elizabeth 266
Webb, Elizabeth (Banshaw) 266
Webb, Mary 266
Webb, Rosanna 266
Webb, Satina 266
Webb, Joseph 266
Webb, Nathaniel 88
Webber. See also Weber
Webber, Amy F. 151
Webber, Andrew P. 151
Webber, Clara 337
Webber, Fanny 151
Webber, Ivory O. 151
Weber. See also Webber
Weber, Andrew 35
Weber, Carrie L. 35
Webster, Lula D. 300
Webster, Nellie 15

Weeks, William 62
Welch, John J. 283
Welch, William 61
Welch, Willie 283
Weld, Albert 110
Weld, George M. 110
Weld, Jane 110
Weld, Willie W. 110
Wellington, Leonard 207
Wellman, Achsah J. 33
Wellman, Carrie E. 33
Wellman, Jesse P. 33, 338
Wellman, Mary E. 33
Wells, Lewis 325
Wesley, Ervin 312
West, Angie 17
West, Freddie F. 17
West, Leonard 17
West, Mable 17
West, Scott 17
West, William H. 17
West, Willie F. 17
Weston, Edward 35
Wheeler, Abby J. (Heath) 197
Wheeler, Abby M. (Gyle) 219
Wheeler, Alice 197
Wheeler, Barbara E. (Green) 287
Wheeler, Bertha M. 286
Wheeler, Dexter 290
Wheeler, Ellen 197
Wheeler, Ellen M. 3
Wheeler, Eva G. (Stanford) [Moore] 87
Wheeler, Frank 286
Wheeler, Frederick H. 219
Wheeler, Harry B. 286
Wheeler, Jacob 219
Wheeler, Joseph 79
Wheeler, Louisa 197
Wheeler, Maria D. 290
Wheeler, Mary (Shupple) 197
Wheeler, Orlan B. 286
Wheeler, Phoeba (Wilder) [Parker] 79
Wheeler, Rosa (DeLane) 219
Wheeler, Solon 197
Whipple, Elvira 182
Whipple, Joseph L. 322
Whipple, Marshall S. 200
Whipple, Moulton 142
Whipple, Silas 182
Whipple, Stephen M. 157
Whitaker, E. F. 181
Whitaker, Jane E. 181
Whitaker, Jennie B. 181
Whitcomb, Ada C. 306
Whitcomb, Charles S. 306
Whitcomb, Cyrel 81

Whitcomb, Ellen 90
Whitcomb, Emma 90
Whitcomb, Esther 158
Whitcomb, Eunice A. (Collins) 81
Whitcomb, Fred 232
Whitcomb, Gilman 155
Whitcomb, Joseph 110
Whitcomb, Mary 110, 338
Whitcomb, Minnie M. (Hill) 232
Whitcomb, Minnie R. 306
Whitcomb, Mr. 5
Whitcomb, Rebecca 214
Whitcomb, Silas 158
Whitcomb, Sylvia S. 306
Whitcomb, William F. 81
White, A. H. 14
White, Charles F. 331
White, Charles S. 209
White, Charles V. 268
White, Florence M. 268
White, Frank 278
White, Girtie 233
White, Ida M. 233
White, Ida M. (Shaw) 218
White, J. M. 57
White, James E. 323
White, Lucia A. 17
White, Margie A. 331
White, Mary 337
White, Mary E. [Fisher] 268
White, Mattie E. 268
White, Michael 326
White, Naomi 232
White, Nora 233
White, Orren L. 268
White, Reconcile E. 255, 337
White, Sarah A. 176
White, William R. 17
Whitemore, David L. 246
Whitemore, Emma J. 246
Whitemore, Freeman C. 247
Whitemore, Herbert 246
Whitemore, Herman E. 246
Whitemore, Nellie E. 246
Whitemore, Victor S. 247
Whitney, Addison 119
Whitney, Alivia S. 62
Whitney, Charles E. 242
Whitney, Charles R. 119
Whitney, Emma F. 216
Whitney, Gertrude 242
Whitney, Gracie 242
Whitney, Harry 242
Whitney, Hattie 242
Whitney, John S. 62
Whitney, Lizzie 133

Whitney, Milton 242
Whitney, Nellie L. 242
Whitney, Perley E. 119
Whitney, Rufus Foster 119
Whitney, Susie 242
Whittemore. See also Whittimore
Whittemore, David 293
Whittemore, Emma 293
Whittemore, Mary 163
Whittimore. See also Whittemore
Whittimore, Lucy 34, 197, 198
Wight, Jonas 52
Wight, Lucretia A. 52
Wight, Mabel 52
Wight, Mrs. 146
Wilber. See also Wilbur
Wilber, George 181
Wilber, Hannah (Heath) 12
Wilber, Jennie B. (Whitaker) 181
Wilber, LuPrelett 12
Wilber, Mr. 119
Wilber, Seth 132
Wilbur. See also Wilber
Wilbur, Oren 147
Wilcox, A. C. 284, 285, 288, 324, 332
Wilcox, Agnes 58
Wilcox, Andrew 83
Wilcox, Fabian 272
Wilcox, Mary 83, 272
Wilcox, Minnie 272
Wilcox, Simon P. 83
Wilcox, Theodore 272
Wilder, Caroline 323
Wilder, Charles 157
Wilder, Ella 265
Wilder, Emily 157
Wilder, Ivory P. 215
Wilder, Jennie S. 215
Wilder, Julia E. 157
Wilder, Phoeba 79
Willard, Bertie L. 60
Willard, Dennis A. 50
Willard, Ella Phelps 60
Willard, George 60, 269
Willard, Henry 187
Willard, Ida J. 50
Willard, Mrs. 89
Willard, Nancy 337
Willard, Sarah 269
Willett, Ernest 315
Williams, A. R. 81
Williams, George 131
Williams, James 62
Williams, James E. 131
Williams, John 131
Williams, Stephen, Mrs. 110

Willis, Andrew 257
Willis, Ellen (Hale) 292
Willis, Flossie Annie Diantha 292
Willis, George A. 85
Willis, George W. 99, 134
Willis, Julia A. (Austin) [Orne] 85
Willis, Mary Ann (Hale) 50
Willis, Wilber F. 50, 292
Willis, Willard 292
Wiloby, Laura Ann 1
Wilson, Charles H. 129, 269
Wilson, Clara (Scott) 300
Wilson, David, Mrs. 9
Wilson, George 79
Wilson, Josiah 108, 337
Wilson, Lisia 234
Wilson, Mrs. 173
Winham, Ellen J. 297
Winham, Sarah J. 297
Winn, Joseph 275
Winn, Moses 275
Winn, Rose (Bouchard) 275
Winters, Willie 114
Witham, Marston 171
Witham, Mary 171
Withame, Alvin W. 236
Witherel, Fidelia 290
Withington, Seth 52
Wood. See also Woods
Wood, Arthur 291
Wood, Charles 116
Wood, E. B. 305
Wood, Elijah 116
Wood, Elizabeth 116
Wood, Emma E. 138
Wood, Henry 17
Wood, Julia 17
Wood, Leander 17
Wood, Louis 133
Wood, Maria 247
Wood, Mary F. 116
Wood, Peter 91
Wood, Rosa 17
Woodcock, Rhoda 110
Woods. See also Wood
Woods, Clark 210
Woods, Delia 248
Woods, Emma 210
Woods, Frank 210
Woods, Frank, Jr. 210
Woods, Hannah B. 210
Woods, Henry 210
Woods, Joseph 210
Woods, Mabel 210
Woods, Mary 210
Woods, Orman W. 273

Woods, Sadie 210
Woodward, Thomas Nelson 331
Woodward, William H. 128
Worder, Aaron 195
Worder, Florence A. 195
Works, John 102
Worster, Betsey (Aldrich) 86
Wright, Albert, Mrs. 1
Wright, George K. 129
Wright, Hester 267
Wright, J. A. 10
Wright, Lois 228
Wright, Virgil A. 150
Wyman, Maria 48, 338
Wyman, S. S. 304

Yardley, Eleanor W. 139
Yardley, Ethel B. 139
Yardley, Manley R. 139
York, Eunice E. 256
Young, ___ 165
Young, Addeline 215
Young, Alice F. 313, 321, 333
Young, Andrew 317
Young, Annie 321
Young, Carrie A. 313, 321, 333
Young, George W. 16
Young, Harry 313
Young, Harry H. 321
Young, Harry M. 333
Young, Hattie 321
Young, Hattie M. 313, 333
Young, Herbert E. 321, 333
Young, John B. 215
Young, Julia 313
Young, Laura 215
Young, Lucy A. (Blood) 17
Young, Melvina 182
Young, Millie F. 333
Young, Nellie M. 313, 321, 333
Young, Rosella (Jolly) 317
Young, Willie F. 313, 321

www.ingramcontent.com/pod-product-compliance
Lightning Source LLC
Chambersburg PA
CBHW050833230426
43667CB00012B/1979